HOOKED ON
HOLLYWOOD

Hooked on
HOLLYWOOD

Discoveries from a
Lifetime of Film Fandom

Leonard Maltin

GoodKnight Books

Portions of this book originally appeared in *Film Fan Monthly* and *Leonard Maltin's Movie Crazy* newsletter.

Photo credits and acknowledgments: Warner Bros., Columbia Pictures, 20th Century Fox, MGM, United Artists, Universal Pictures, Paramount Pictures, The Walt Disney Company, Hal Roach Studios, RKO Radio Pictures, Republic Pictures, Academy of Motion Picture Arts and Sciences, CBS, ABC Television, NBC, Howard Green, Tracey Goessel, Suzanne Lloyd, John McElwee, Marc Wanamaker, Peggy Webber, Paul Wurtzel, Arthur Gardner.

Published by GoodKnight Books, an imprint of Paladin Communications, Pittsburgh, Pennsylvania.

www.goodknightbooks.com

Printed in the United States of America

Library of Congress Control Number: 2018936920

ISBN 978-0-9983763-9-4

Book and cover design by Sharon Berk.

To the women in my life, who make everything possible: Alice and Jessie.

CONTENTS

Later In-Depth Interviews (cont'd)

The Forgotten Studio

INTRODUCTION

Being your own editor and publisher is a heady experience. Just ask Charles Foster Kane—or if he's not available, ask me. I embarked on my first publishing venture when I was in the fifth grade and kept at it for years to come.

When I was 13 I was an avid reader of Forrest J. Ackerman's *Famous Monsters of Filmland* magazine, like so many baby boomers. (Others include Steven Spielberg and Stephen King.) In one issue he published a survey of fanzines—that is, amateur magazines that dealt with film history, science fiction, and other related topics. I promptly submitted articles to two of them: *The 8mm Collector*, which was published by furniture dealer Samuel K. Rubin in Indiana, Pennsylvania, and *Film Fan Monthly*, which came out of Vancouver, Canada, courtesy of Daryl Davy. They both accepted my submissions; only then did I tell them I was 13. Sam didn't care and Daryl confessed that he was 19! They gave me the thrill of seeing my first bylines in print. There was no money involved, as this was a labor of love for all concerned. (*The 8mm Collector* survives today as *Classic Images*, with Bob King as editor.)

I became a regular contributor to both magazines while publishing my own humble journal called *Profile*, which was literally cranked out on a mimeograph machine. Two years later, in 1966, Daryl Davy told me he no longer had the time to put out a monthly magazine and wondered if I would be interested in taking over *Film Fan Monthly*. Of course I would! He had 400 subscribers, mostly in North America but also in Australia, New Zealand, and even Western Europe. What's more, he was professionally printed, which would liberate me from the ink-stained mimeograph and enable me to illustrate my articles with movie stills. I assumed ownership in May of 1966 with issue #59. My cover was adorned with the face of Robert Benchley, in a portrait still I bought for 50 cents from Manhattan movie memorabilia dealer Henry Kier.

I continued writing, editing, publishing, stamp licking, envelope stuffing, and post office schlepping for the next nine years. Fortunately, I had help along the way. My original grade-school partner in crime was Barry Ahrendt. Barry Gottlieb joined me for *Profile,* integrating articles about his favorite subject, magicians. (I served as Barry's assistant at a handful of children's birthday party gigs.) Warren Dressler then became *Film Fan Monthly's* business manager until he went off to college, whereupon my father gamely assumed those responsibilities. My pal Louis Black asked why he wasn't credited in the magazine, and I responded, "Because you didn't do anything." He was still a bit miffed so in the next issue I added to the masthead "Friend in need: Louis Black." The next month it read "Friend indeed: Louis Black." For the next nine years I concocted a different title for Louis every month.

Once the magazine established itself I didn't have to write every article. I was grateful to receive contributions from a number of talented writers who didn't mind working for free, just to have an outlet for their work.

I was 15 when *FFM* came into my life, at which point schoolwork took a definite back seat. Fortunately, I was able to slide by and continued doing so through four years at New York University—by which time I had sold my first books to New American Library. With each passing year it became more difficult to justify the time and effort I was expending on the magazine, and when I got married at age 24 and started paying rent, it seemed the right moment to retire. Many readers blamed my bride and thought of Alice as my Yoko Ono, which simply wasn't the case. What had begun as a genuine labor of love had become a chore.

Fortune smiled on me and I was able to make a living as a freelance writer and author. Some years after that I stumbled into a television career. But every now and then I longed for the complete freedom of writing whatever pleased me with no one looking over my shoulder and second-guessing my decisions.

The turning point couldn't have been more unpredictable. I sold an article to *Vanity Fair,* for more money than I'd ever been paid for such a gig, in the year 2000. It was based on my discovery of Orson Welles' hitherto-unknown flirtation with Warner Bros. to direct and star in *The Man Who Came to Dinner* in 1941, just before the debut of *Citizen Kane.* I was thrilled that my research coup (courtesy of the Warner Bros. Archives at USC) would reach such a wide, mainstream audience. But it was not to be. The magazine killed the piece several months after I signed a contract with them because they published an article that mentioned *Dinner* playwright George S. Kaufman and thought it would be redundant. At least, that's what they told me. I was paid my full fee, which I appreciated, and recovered the rights to the article. That's what led me to embark on my second self-publishing venture, *Leonard Maltin's Movie Crazy*, in 2001. Contents of the first 18 issues were assembled in a paperback book of the same name, published by Mike Richardson of Dark Horse Comics under his M imprint.

I wrote every word of *Movie Crazy*, not because I didn't have offers from possible contributors but because I wanted to. This was my baby, a place to print interviews I'd never published before and articles I was inspired to write. I even got to draw on my lifelong collection of movie stills. The "heavy lifting" of preparing this material digitally and dealing with the printer and post office was assumed by my computer tutor, Jeanne McCafferty.

Alas, my attempt to maintain a quarterly schedule ran aground after just a few years. While I enjoyed working on every issue I had to admit to myself that it was starting to feel like a chore. I recognized that feeling and ultimately acted on it, 10 years after launching the (very) non-profit venture.

Still, I am proud of what I accomplished and appreciate this opportunity to bring my work to a wider audience than I was able to reach on my own. For this I thank Robert and Mary Matzen, whose enthusiasm and encouragement have spurred me on.

In choosing a title for this volume, we considered a number of possibilities but finally decided to keep it simple. I've been "hooked on Hollywood" since I was a kid, and I've spent more than half a century making discoveries about the period known as the Golden Age. This collection of articles and interviews reflects that lifelong pursuit.

When I was researching and writing *Movie Crazy*, I called on a number of valued friends as sounding boards and sources of information. The Internet is a great resource, but it can't take the place of human memory and experience; I proved that over and over again as I dug into my often-obscure subjects. I am grateful to Robert Bader, Richard W. Bann, Rudy and Stacey Behlmer, Steve Bingham, the late Bob Birchard, Peter Bogdanovich, Kevin Brownlow, Ned Comstock, Grover Crisp, the late Robert Cushman, the late Marvin Eisenman, Ray Faiola, Michael Feinstein, Richard Finegan, Howard Green, Ron Hutchinson, J.B. Kaufman, Miles Kreuger, Sandra Joy Aguilar, Emily Leider, Suzanne Lloyd, Peter Mintun, John Morgan, Patrick Picking, David Pierce, Randy Skretvedt, Phil Spangenberger, Karl Thiede, Frank Thompson, Lou Valentino, Marc Wanamaker, Tom Weaver, Brent Walker, Eddie Brandt's Saturday Matinee, Robert Wall at Four Jays Music, the Warner Bros. Archives at USC Doheny Library Special Collections, Sean Too, Trevor Totaro, Matt Severson, and Jeanie Braun at the Academy of Motion Picture Arts and Sciences, Eddie Richmond, Todd Wiener, and Steven Hill, UCLA Film and Television Archive.

Naturally, I want to thank my interviewees for giving me their time and, in many cases, access to their personal photos and scrapbooks. Many of them have passed on since I published my conversations, which makes me doubly glad I spoke to them when I did.

My warmest thanks go, as always, to my family. My wife, Alice, has been at my side for 43 years, and while she doesn't share my passion for some of these topics, she puts up with my compulsive ways and never loses her sense of humor. She is my lifeline, my soulmate, my best friend. Our daughter, Jessie, has become my ally, partner, and sharpest critic. We love working together and that happiness has only grown with the arrival of her smart, funny husband, Scott.

From the outset of my self-publishing career I have valued feedback from my readers more than I can say. I feel like a performer who can't function without an audience. Thank you, friends, for your support and encouragement all these years.

LEONARD MALTIN
Hollywood, USA

HOLLYWOOD
FEATURETTES

As Songs Go By:
ALL THE MUSIC OF CASABLANCA

Channel-surfing not long ago, I came upon my all-time favorite movie, *Casablanca*. Having seen—or perhaps the better word is absorbed—this film as many times as I have, I didn't think anything about it had escaped my attention. I was wrong.

As Sam (Dooley Wilson) started to play the old standard "Avalon" for Ilsa (Ingrid Bergman) it occurred to me, for the first time, how many different songs were integrated into the picture that's so closely associated with only one, "As Time Goes By." In fact, songs by Cole Porter, Eubie Blake, Ray Noble, Harry Warren, Johnny Mercer, and other stalwarts dot the soundtrack. It's a tribute to the artful way they are used that they don't call attention to themselves but provide perfect, appropriate accompaniment to the action on-screen.

The British sheet music for *Casablanca*'s most famous song.

As I set out to learn more about the score, the only fact I remembered was that "As Time Goes By" wasn't written for the film. It was composed in 1931 by Tin Pan Alley songsmith Herman Hupfeld and introduced by Frances Williams in the Broadway musical *Everybody's Welcome*. Hup-

1

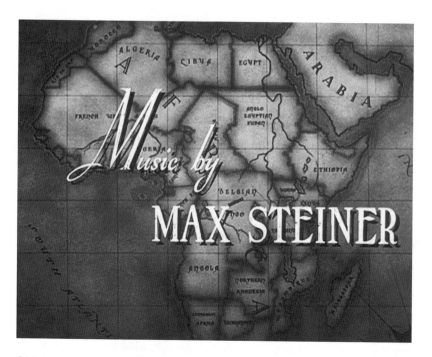

feld, known to his show-business friends as Dodo, was primarily known for novelty songs like "Goopy Gear," which inspired a 1932 Merrie Melodies cartoon, and "When Yuba Plays the Rhumba on the Tuba." Because Warners owned several major music publishers, including Chappell & Co., which published the song, there was no hurdle in acquiring the rights to Hupfeld's most enduring composition.

Examining a music cue sheet for *Casablanca* in the Warner Bros. Archives at USC, I discovered just how many other vintage popular tunes were interpolated into the score. The fact that so much action takes place in an American-style nightclub justifies the presence of such well-known numbers as "Crazy Rhythm," "The Very Thought of You," "Baby Face," "I'm Just Wild About Harry," "Heaven Can Wait," "Perfidia," "If I Could Be with You (One Hour Tonight)," and "You Must Have Been a Beautiful Baby." But how were all these songs, and song cues, chosen? I turned to a battery of film music experts for answers.

Soundtrack producer Ray Faiola explained, "With respect to the source cues [the songs heard in the background], their selection was based as much on their musical character as the idea they may have represented. It's more than likely that [Warner Bros. executive] Hal Wallis and [composer] Max Steiner conferred on which songs would be played at Rick's Café Americain. Steiner, a former Broadway musical director who worked with Ferde Grofé on the orchestration for 'Rhapsody in Blue,' had a very thorough knowledge of American popular music." Film historian Rudy Behlmer points out that the background songs often comment subtly on the action, as when Sam plays "Speak to Me of Love" when Ilsa and Victor Laszlo (Paul Henreid) first walk into Rick's café. After they are approached by an underground agent, followed by Claude Rains' prefect of police, the piano segues to "Love for Sale."

To reinforce the international flavor of the nightclub, Latin-American singer Corinna Mura appears briefly as the *other* entertainer at Rick's, singing "Tango Delle Rose" while strumming a guitar. She later joins in the singing of "La Marseillaise," a major story point that is told musically. When a group of German soldiers sing "Die Wacht Am Rhein," Laszlo orders the orchestra to play "La Marseillaise," and the French anthem ultimately drowns out the Nazis. It is one of the strongest, most memorable scenes in the picture.

Behlmer reveals that the studio was unable to use its first choice, "Horst Vessel," because the song was controlled by a German publisher, but the substitution works like a charm. The clever counterpoint of these two contrasting songs was arranged by Steiner himself.

By this time, Max Steiner had composed original scores for more than 125 feature films, including *King Kong* and *Gone With the Wind* and was capable of doing a first-rate job scoring this movie. But the studio's head of production, Hal Wallis, had very specific ideas about every aspect of important films like this. Rudy Behlmer illustrated how incisive and brilliant Wallis was through his publication of extensive studio memos in the book *Inside Warner Bros. 1935-1951* (Viking, 1985). Here is what the executive wrote in his "cutting notes" for Reel 2 of *Casablanca*:

"Start the piano as Ilsa and Laszlo come in the door. You can stop the piano playing at the table with Ilsa when Renault brings Strasser over to the table. Then don't start the music again until Sam introduces the guitar player. When Ilsa calls Sam over to play, let that go on just as it is until the scene is interrupted by Renault coming back, saying, 'Oh, you have already met Rick.' Now, at that point, when Rick and Ilsa exchange glances, on the first of their close-ups, start an orchestration using 'As Time Goes By.' And *score* the scene. Let Steiner do this. And carry this until right through the Exterior until the lights go out."

Later in the same reel, Wallis noted, "On the Marseillaise, when it is played in the café, don't do it as though it was played by this small orchestra. Do it with a full scoring orchestra and get some body into it. You should score the piece where the Gendarmes break the door in and carry that right through to the dissolve to the Police Station."

Wallis knew what he wanted, but it was up to Steiner to make it all work musically. Faiola assesses the results in Reel 2: "When Ilsa meets Sam and asks him to play 'some of the old ones,' Sam plays 'Avalon.' Next he plays 'As Time Goes By.' Then he sings 'As Time Goes By.' The song is interrupted and followed by an underscore cue beginning with a sustained chord that leads into 'As Time Goes By.' The progression of these multiple music elements has to make musical sense and the selection of the first element—'Avalon'— is critical to the sequence. The wistful nature of the melody, and the key in which it is played, makes the song as much a part of the 'scoring' as the thematic underscore cue that eventually follows.

"Other songs heard in the café do not reflect any particular tempo being played by the orchestra and could easily have been selected and recorded after the film was rough-edited and a desired musical character was required. But in each case, the key assignment of each song has to make some musical sense in relation to what may have followed or preceded it on the soundtrack. It doesn't have to be the same key, but it should at least be in a natural modulation."

Max Steiner poses with an award from *Photoplay* magazine.

"Of course," Faiola continues, "many of the melodies heard as source music—'As Time Goes By,' 'La Marseillaise,' 'Die Wacht Am Rhein,' 'Das Lied der Deutschen'— are also interpolated by Steiner into the fabric of his underscore. Small snatches are played in minor key for dramatic effect or in major key such as 'La Marseillaise,' which serves as the End Title."

Sometimes, however, the context of a scene demanded an original composition. "When Sam plays 'a little somethin' of my own' it's actually a little something by Frank Perkins, one of the Warner orchestrator/composers," Faiola points out. "All of the above was pretty much standard practice by most of the music departments in Hollywood. Songs were never merely 'inserted.' In the same way that a score for a Broadway show has to hang together, so too does a picture score that includes both thematic underscoring and proactive source music."

Musicologist and soundtrack producer John Morgan agrees, and says

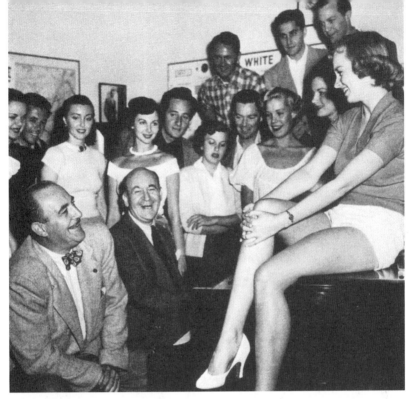

Jack Scholl and M.K. Jerome (at the piano) pose with Warners chorus girls and boys in this publicity photo for *The Hard Way* (1943).

that Steiner's attention to the "big picture," musically speaking, explains why his scores are so listenable when played or programmed on albums. "Even when cues are separated by long musical silence, Steiner was always aware of the key of a previous cue and really thought as scoring as one long piece of music that may or may not be connected."

Says Morgan, "I remember Steiner telling me, although not specifically for *Casablanca*, that he preferred doing the source music himself. His scores, including *Casablanca*, are filled with source cues that are part of the underscore where going from source to underscore or vice versa would be composed as one big complicated piece of music. He always felt all the music should somehow be interrelated and felt the primary composer should at least oversee all the music, if possible."

Steiner wasn't inflexible on this point. Says Morgan, "Of course there were the exceptions like [the Gershwin biopic] *Rhapsody in Blue* or *The Glass Menagerie*, where Ray Heindorf did the period arrangements. Steiner even started the trend at Warner Bros., where the film's composer wrote the original trailer music, rather than having a music editor put stuff together like most of the other studios did.

"It is not surprising to hear one of Steiner's themes from a previous film being played on the radio or in a nightclub setting [in a Warner Bros.

picture]. Of course, this provided more ASCAP income for him as well as promoting his music," adds Morgan with a smile. "So maybe it wasn't only artistic considerations, but always appropriate. [It added a few shekels to the coffers of Warners' music publishing companies, as well.—Ed.] The two most obvious examples of which are 'It Can't Be Wrong' from *Now Voyager* played on a Victrola in *Mildred Pierce* and the theme from *A Summer Place* being played at a youngster's party in *Parrish*."

Above all, Steiner had no hesitation in "borrowing" from himself. The main title cue in *Casablanca*, which is meant to establish the setting of the film, is lifted (and orchestrally enhanced) from his score for the 1934 desert saga *The Lost Patrol*, made at RKO!

"As Time Goes By" was forced on Steiner, who would have preferred to write something original; the song was specifically mentioned in Murray Burnett's play *Everybody Comes to Rick's*. Steiner's longtime orchestrator, Hugo Friedhofer, recalled, in an oral history for the AFI, that "Steiner didn't have the feeling that 'As Time Goes By' would work in the orchestra at all, because he had a concept of it as being kind of a square tune, which requires translation from what's in the printed piano part to a more relaxed version. So, I say this with all modesty, I said, 'Max, think of it this way (singing 'As Time Goes By' but very broadly).' With trip-

Sheet music for Scholl and Jerome's ditty so often heard in Warner Bros. cartoons.

let phrasing. He kind of thought about it, and that's the way it came out. But it's a good tune. Let's face it. And it's a kind of phrasing that jazzmen fall into naturally."

Steiner wasn't the only studio stalwart who was assigned to work on *Casablanca*. Two men who were under contract to Warners for years—and rarely celebrated for their work, to this very day—contributed one of the movie's featured songs, performed start to finish by Dooley Wilson, "Knock on Wood." Their names were Jack Scholl and M.K. Jerome.

Scholl had written short stories, sketches for Broadway shows (like 1934's short-lived *Keep Moving*), and lyrics with such collaborators as Louis

Alter, Victor Schertzinger, and Eubie Blake before signing on at Warners. By the 1940s he was able to convince the powers that be to let him write and direct musical shorts, many of which featured songs he and his new partner, M.K. Jerome, wrote for the occasion. These ranged from band shorts with everyone from Spade Cooley to Desi Arnaz, as well as *Nautical But Nice, Frontier Days*, and a series of sing-along novelties.

M.K. Jerome was apparently born Moe (or Maurice) Kraus, but everyone who knew him called him Moe. Says pianist and popular-music maven Peter Mintun, "He must have been a good pianist, because after he toured in vaudeville he became a staff pianist at the publishing house of Waterson, Berlin & Snyder, which published his 'Jazz Baby' (lyrics by Blanche Merrill) in 1919. George Jessel introduced a song of Jerome's in the 1925 show *The Jazz Singer*. He went to Hollywood in 1929 and was with Warners for 18 years."

Pianist, performer and music historian Michael Feinstein says, "Jerome fascinates me because he did so much work at Warners that it is mind boggling, writing songs, underscore and special material for probably hundreds of projects. He's the Max Steiner of the Warners songwriters. Rarely did he get screen credit for these songs."

Dooley Wilson plays for Bogart and Bergman in the Paris flashback sequence.

Dooley Wilson sings "Knock on Wood."

Most notably, adds Michael, "He wrote those wonderful extra verses and interludes heard in *Yankee Doodle Dandy* in the Little Johnny Jones sequences that people now think were written by Cohan—'Good Luck, Johnny' and 'All Aboard for Old Broadway.' (They were even used without credit in the short-lived Broadway production of *Little Johnny Jones* starring Donny Osmond.) His son, Stuart Jerome, started as a page at Warners and eventually became a contract writer, later penning a book about his career." (The book is called *Those Crazy Wonderful Years When We Ran Warner Bros.*, published by Lyle Stuart in 1983.)

Warner Bros. cartoon aficionados may be most familiar with Scholl and Jerome from repeated use of their song "My Little Buckaroo" over the years, and for the jaunty number "As Easy as Rolling Off a Log," sung by Johnny "Scat" Davis in the 1938 cartoon *Katnip Kollege*.

"Knock on Wood" gave Scholl and Jerome one of their all-time best showcases, although the song never had much life beyond its performance at Rick's Café Americain. Still, their status as house songwriters earned them credit in the main titles of *Casablanca*.

The man who sang that ditty, as well as "As Time Goes By," also reached the apex of his screen career in *Casablanca*. Dooley Wilson was born in 1886 and was 56 years old when he won the role of Sam over Hal Wallis' first choice, actor-musician-playwright-composer Clarence Muse, who was unavailable. (Muse later played Sam in Warners' short-lived *Casablanca* TV series in the 1950s.) A veteran of minstrel shows, vaudeville, and the legitimate stage, Wilson had just been put under contract to Paramount when he was loaned out (at $500 a week, $350 of which he got to keep) to play Humphrey Bogart's piano-playing sidekick. Had he been a Warners player, it's likely the studio would have followed up with other featured parts to capitalize on his success as Sam. Although he did appear in Fox's all-black musical *Stormy Weather* (1943) and RKO's *Higher and Higher* (1943) he never again had a movie role as notable as the one in *Casablanca*. He enjoyed success on Broadway in the 1944 musical *Bloomer Girl*, where he introduced the song "The Eagle and Me," and toward the end of his life had a recurring role on the TV series *Beulah*.

Oddly enough, Wilson never got to sing "As Time Goes By" in one continuous performance in *Casablanca*. He is also heard singing snatches of other familiar songs like "It Had to Be You" and "Shine," but "Knock on Wood" is the only song that receives a complete performance. When *Casablanca* became a smash hit, Warners had no recording of "As Time Goes By" to promote. In fact, because of a musician's union recording ban in 1943, the key beneficiary of the song's revival was Rudy Vallee, whose original 1931 record was reissued to great success. What's more, Vallee included Herman Hupfeld's wistful verse, which was never sung in the film. In October of 1943, months after the movie's release, Decca (the first record company to settle with the American Federation of Musicians) did release a 78 rpm record of Dooley Wilson singing "As Time Goes By" and "Knock On Wood," but it never caught on.

Ironically, the man who played one of movies' most famous pianists couldn't actually play the instrument (although he had been a drummer), so during filming Wilson fingered a dummy keyboard—a miniature one, at that, with only 58 keys—while musician Elliot Carpenter performed just off-camera. Decades later, when the producers of a Warner Bros. 50th Anniversary record album set wanted a complete rendition of "As Time Goes By," they hired jazz pianist Jimmy Rowles to flesh out Wilson and Carpenter's rendition.

The conclusion one reaches after exploring this multifaceted soundtrack is that, like almost every film of this period, *Casablanca* was the result of collaboration and the efficient use of the studio system. If Warners didn't have such a "deep bench" in the music department, or a skilled staff orchestra, or access to the catalogs of several major music publishers, or geniuses like Max Steiner and Hal Wallis orchestrating these elements, it might not have been the great movie it became. Yet nothing was done by rote, or formula: if so, Warners could have turned out a *Casablanca* every year.

In so many ways, from writing to casting to timing in light of world events, this movie caught lightning in a bottle. That is why it remains one of a kind.

Birthing the Blues:

BLUES IN THE NIGHT

When asked which came first, the music or the words, Oscar-winning lyricist Sammy Cahn always answered, "The phone call." Without a specific job to fulfill, he'd explain, there would have been no reason for him and Jule Styne to concoct a song called "Three Coins in the Fountain," or for anyone to devise tunes with titles like "To Each His Own" or "Love is a Many Splendored Thing."

It all began in late 1940, when a reader at Warner Bros. took a shine to an unproduced play by German-born writer and sometime-lyricist Edwin Gilbert. Set in a New Jersey roadhouse and focusing on a dedicated musician searching for a special sound, it went through a series of clever titles: *Soothe the Savage Breast, Opus 802* (referring to the New York local of the Musician's Union), and *Big Boy Blue*. In its final incarnation, *Hot Nocturne*, Gilbert shared a questionable writing credit with Elia Kazan, who hoped to direct it on Broadway.

Warners producer Robert Lord wasn't convinced of the play's qualities, however, writing in a memo, "Some of it is very well done; a lot of it seems bungling, loose and amateurish." He was overruled, and in February of 1941 Kazan, Gilbert, and their producer sold the property to Warner Bros. At this point, Kazan's name mysteriously disappeared from the credits, even though he wound up playing a supporting role in the picture. (He doesn't mention the play or Gilbert in his autobiography.)

Typical of studio-planted news stories, when *The New York Times* reported the sale on February 12, 1941, it said James Cagney was set to star. This made for a juicy item, but it wasn't true. In fact, Warners was looking at a number of people for the leading role, including two stage actors, Richard Whorf and Nick (later Richard) Conte.

Other films made around this time (*Birth of the Blues, Syncopation*) purported to tell the story of jazz and celebrate its beginnings, but they were compromised by clichéd writing as well as their unwillingness to turn the spotlight on black musicians and composers. *Blues in the Night* had a better chance, given its socially conscious screenwriter (Robert Rossen) and the participation of Harold Arlen and Johnny Mercer, who were able to absorb and channel the feeling of black music better than any of their white peers.

But first, there was the matter of a screenplay. The project was assigned to Henry Blanke, one of Warners' smartest producers (and a former assistant to Ernst Lubitsch), who selected Anatole Litvak to direct. Perhaps as a sop to the playwright, Warners accepted Gilbert's treatment, "correcting former weaknesses," on May 10. But as staff writer Rossen's extensive treatment is dated May 12, it would seem the studio hadn't been counting on the original author to craft the finished film. (Gilbert did collaborate on a few Warners pictures in the 1940s, notably *All Through the Night* and *Larceny, Inc.*, but never achieved great success on stage or screen.)

Gilbert's (and, at this point, Kazan's) play *Hot Nocturne*, a story of white musicians set entirely in a second-rate New Jersey roadhouse called The Jungle ("Dining and Dancing in a Real African Jungle...never a cover charge") where a pianist named Jigger plays in a small band led by a slick but untalented fellow named Del Davis, who knows how to please audiences and club owners alike. Jigger's fellow musicians are devoted to him and his pursuit of the blues. At one point a woman he's forced to hire as his band vocalist tells him, "You're got more to offer than anyone within a thousand miles—but you hide your head on the piano, walk around here a collection of hurt feelings. Del stomps all over you, Rudy, too—and they don't come up to your shoelaces. Grow to your own size—meet the world—fight for what's yours." Jigger later tells his colleague Hymie, "There's a girl who makes me feel seven feet tall."

The roadhouse owner becomes involved with gangsters, while bandleader Davis does whatever it takes to keep everybody happy.

Gilbert's "improved" screen treatment, no longer stage-bound, opens in St. Louis, where Jigger and drummer Peppi are thrown in jail after a nightclub altercation. There they meet up with another musician friend, bass player Pete Bossett. According to the treatment, "The three are suddenly attracted by the wailing chant of an old negro in a nearby cell. Jigger is fascinated and yearns for a piano—here is the blues—this is the real American music."

A pesky clarinetist named Hymie cajoles his way into Jigger's band by bailing out the three musicians, who head to New Orleans in search of another old friend, trumpeter Leo Powell and his singer-wife, "a luscious, flip little dame nicknamed Character." They all take to the road, traveling by boxcar, where they encounter Del Davis, a shady character who robs and then befriends them when they don't hold a grudge for his actions. He takes them to his uncle Sam Paryas' place in New Jersey, where Del falls for a sexy chanteuse named Kay and insists that she sing with the band.

Wallace Ford and Betty Field in a dramatic pose.

At this point, the treatment gets bogged down in clutter involving Kay's ex-husband, a murder, and a special song Jigger writes for Kay.

Native New Yorker Robert Rossen, who cut his teeth in the theater, was by now one of Warners' top screenwriters, with such gutsy films as *Marked Woman*, the Southern mob-rule drama *They Won't Forget*, and the cerebral adaptation of Jack London's *The Sea Wolf* to his credit. It wasn't coincidental that these pictures expressed his social awareness; he was an idealist who later revealed a decade-long membership in the Communist party, which he renounced in the years following World War II.

He must have conferred with Gilbert at some point, as his lengthy treatment features many of the ingredients the playwright included in his second studio draft, along with most of his original character's names. (It's also possible that Gilbert took some cues from an early version written by Rossen

12

Elia Kazan, Peter Whitney, Billy Halop, and Richard Whorf in the jail scene; that's former Keystone Kop Hank Mann on the bunk bed.

that no longer exists in the Warner Bros. studio files.) In any case, where Gilbert's writing is self-aware in its colloquialism, Rossen's leaps off the page. Then, as now, a screenwriter's descriptive prose is never heard by the audience, but it can have an impact on the director's and the actors' interpretation of the material.

He introduces pianist Jigger as "a gaunt, fiery young man…in his twenties. As he plays, he seems lost. We get the feeling that he isn't even in this café. He's someplace else. Nothing in this place can ever move or touch him. The only thing that matters to him is his piano."

When he and his drummer pal Peppi land in the clink, they have a life-altering experience. "From the other cell, a negro's voice, deep and low. 'What's the matter with them white boys? Got the miseries?… We all got the miseries in here. All of us.' And then a voice rich in song. The negro singing the blues, a haunting strain with the inherent loneliness and misery that only a negro can express. On the faces of the boys, their admiration…they crowd to the bars, listening." (As in the case of much material written decades ago, the word 'negro' was not capitalized in Rossen's screenplay.)

Jigger says, "That's the blues. That's real, low-down New Orleans blues."

This is a cue to change the setting to the Crescent City, where our heroes go in search of their trumpet-playing pal Leo and his wife, Character. They all go out to dinner.

"Suddenly, over the scene come the strains of a band. They all look around. A negro orchestra has filed in and taken its place on the bandstand. There are four pieces without a piano. Their rhythm is the same pulsating kind of beat that the negro sang in the jail.

"The boys become transfixed, listening. Leo's voice, almost like a prayer. 'To play like that—to be able to get that kind of a beat!'

"Suddenly Jigger gets up. He walks over the piano that is unused. He sits down. In the middle of the song he picks up the beat as though he was part of the band. The negroes look at him, at first resentfully and then as they feel

the beat of his piano, they accept him."

One by one, Jigger's cronies join in.

"Soon," writes Rossen, "they're all in swing. They've all lost themselves and found themselves at the same time. They're as one, playing with the negro orchestra."

This certainly has the makings of a good scene, but one has to wonder: was Rossen naive or deliberately trying to push the envelope? Surely he must have known that in 1941 no Hollywood movie would show black and white musicians playing together.

(The one notable exception was in a 1937 Warner Bros. movie, *Hollywood Hotel*, when the hugely popular Benny Goodman Quartet was permitted to appear on camera. Dressed in stylish but casual clothes, Goodman and Gene Krupa, both white, make beautiful music with Lionel Hampton and Teddy Wilson, both black. Legend has it that the script called for Hampton and Wilson to play kitchen workers who would spontaneously join their colleagues on the bandstand, but Goodman nixed the idea. I have found no confirmation of this in the Warner Bros. files, but the end result speaks for itself. On the other hand, in the famous 1944 Warners short *Jammin' the Blues* the presence of one white musician—guitarist Barney Kessel—in the midst of a black ensemble was camouflaged by high-contrast lighting and the use of shadows. After World War II, integrated all-star jazz groups did appear in such films as *The Fabulous Dorseys* and *A Song Is Born*.)

Unfortunately, Rossen's vibrant screen treatment gets just as bogged down as Gilbert's with unwanted pregnancy, murder, double-crossing, and countless other tangents. One must assume that at some point producer Blanke insisted the story be simplified. Music is supposed to be the picture's driving force, but it's difficult to portray artistic motivation on-screen.

On April 2, before there was a finished script, thoughts about casting were thrashed about. It makes sense that the studio would put John Garfield at the top of its list for the part of Jigger: he was already under contract and had achieved stardom portraying a brooding pianist in *Four Daughters*.

But Warners had its eyes on an up-and-comer named Richard Whorf, who occupied second position on the list. He had recently appeared on stage in Los Angeles with the Lunts in *There Shall Be No Night* alongside another actor the studio was keen on, Sydney Greenstreet. (Just six months later it was announced in a newspaper column that both Garfield and Whorf were being considered to star in Warners' upcoming screen biography of George Gershwin.) It seems likely that whoever filled out this "wish-list" knew that one of those two actors would almost surely land the part, because the other names cited for the role of Jigger make little or no sense: Ronald Reagan, George Raft, and Dennis Morgan.

Garfield and Whorf were also the leading contenders to play the roguish good-bad guy Del Davis, followed by Humphrey Bogart (not yet an A-list star on the lot—*The Maltese Falcon* wouldn't be released till October of that year), the ever-present George Raft, "Tony" Quinn, Cesar Romero, Van Heflin, Lee Bowman, Sheldon Leonard, Lloyd Nolan, and Elia Kazan. (Nolan won out.)

Kazan, who had impressed Warners executives in the 1940 picture *City for Conquest*, was considered for three possible roles in the film, including Hymie (later renamed Nickie), the clarinet player. Others in contention for that role included Leo Gorcey, Elisha Cook, Jr., Leon Belasco, Mischa Auer, Joseph Buloff, John Garfield, Glenn Ford, Shepperd Strudwick, William Holden, Tom Neal, and Billy Halop. (William Holden in a part that might have gone to Leo Gorcey? It's right there on paper.)

For the "good girl" part of Character, Betty Grable occupied first position, but Lucille Ball's name was underlined right below hers. This is strong recognition of Lucy's potential in 1941, but Warners never did hire her for a film. Among the other names on this long list: Frances Farmer, Jane Wyman, Brenda Marshall, Carole Landis, Laraine Day, Betty Field, Eve Arden, Joan

William Gillespie introduces "Blues in the Night" in this jailhouse scene.

Blondell, Glenda Farrell, Uta Hagen, and Ella Logan.

For Kay Graham, society singer, Ginger Rogers' name was underlined, indicating interest that would have to be backed up by serious money, to borrow the services of an A-list star from another studio. The extremely random list that followed included Alice Faye, Ann Sheridan, Dorothy Lamour, Priscilla Lane, Barbara Stanwyck, Rita Hayworth (also underlined—though she was not yet a major star), Margaret Sullavan, Loretta Young, Jean Arthur, Ruth Hussey, Paulette Goddard, and Mary Martin. Again, one must take these roll calls with a snowball-sized grain of salt.

What's most interesting is the studio's awareness of (and interest in) New York stage actors. Uta Hagen made the aforementioned list, while Nick Conte was underlined for the role of Peppi the drummer, along with Eddie Bracken, Myron McCormick, and Ezra Stone, all of whom were still screen fledglings.

For the role of Leo the trumpeter, the casting people thought of Milton Berle, Red Skelton and Ray Bolger, and the bright new light of the New York stage, Jose Ferrer. On May 2, studio honcho Steve Trilling informed Blanke and director Litvak, "The RKO test of Jose Ferrar [sic] and Uta Hagan [sic again] has been placed in projection room number 2." Leo was ultimately played by Jack Carson, at the outset of his decade-long run on the Warner Bros. roster.

A week later, on April 8, Steve Trilling sent an inter-office memo detailing who was unavailable for the proposed summertime production: agent Zeppo Marx had just sealed a deal for Barbara Stanwyck, Rita Hayworth was starting a musical for Columbia with Fred Astaire, etc.

He writes, "Betty Field might be available if she doesn't go into Preston Sturges' *Sullivan's Travels*—we won't know definitely on this for about a week.

Elia Kazan is set to direct a play for the [Theatre] Guild and might not be available till the middle of May, so he would like to have some news

as soon as possible so he can make some arrangements to get out of it or have a definite finishing date. William Holden finishes in Columbia's *Texas* around June 1 which I'm sure will be too late for us. Nick Conte goes into rehearsals for the Guild show which opens April 28 but he can give

Lyricist Johnny Mercer with his protégé, Margaret Whiting, at Capitol Records, the company he co-founded in the 1940s.

his two weeks' notice if we will let him know definitely. He is asking $500 and a four week guarantee. We'll have film on him from *Heaven with a Barbed Wire Fence* for you to see Wednesday."

At the end of May, before other plans were solidified, Warners arranged to borrow Betty Field—who lost the part in *Sullivan's Travels* to Veronica Lake—from Paramount for the role of Kay. Initially this was to be a trade-out in exchange for Priscilla Lane's services, later amended to a cash deal for $1,000 a week. (Field's performance impressed Warners enough for her to earn a plum role in the studio's subsequent feature *Kings Row*.)

On June 4, 1941, a production number was assigned to *Hot Nocturne*, as it was then called, and the various departments got busy preparing to shoot the movie. On June 13, studio production manager T.C. Wright issued a shooting schedule: 44 days total, from June 13 to August 1, Saturdays included but with a day off on July 4. (Two days later, the budget department trimmed the shoot by two days, given the decision to cover some material in the script by way of montages, to be shot by staffer Don Siegel.)

Elia Kazan was hired to play Hymie for $1,000 a week with a four-week guarantee. A rider added to the boilerplate contract noted, "Producer agrees to furnish artist with railroad transportation and lower berth from New York to Los Angeles, and in the event he returns to New York within 30 days, return railroad transportation and lower berth to New York."

Others not under contract to Warners came on board with similar deals: Billy Halop and Wally [Wallace] Ford each got $1,000 a week with a two-week guarantee.

After some talk of hiring Duke Ellington, the studio decided on swing bandleader Jimmie Lunceford for four days' work at $1,000—$4,500 total with his 15-member band. (Trilling added, "He is stopping at the Dunbar

Hotel"—a favorite spot for black jazzmen in Los Angeles—"and is currently playing at the Casa Mañana.") The studio also considered hiring the famous Golden Gate Quartet to play the vocalizing black prisoners, for $2,500 a week plus transportation, but decided to save money by hiring local day players including Ernest "Bubbles" Whitman, Dudley Dickerson, and baritone William Gillespie. (According to Harold Arlen's biographer, Edward Jablonski, the composer knew Gillespie was going to perform his song and felt an obligation to "come up with something worthy of the fine voice, something musically strong.")

Production records reveal that each of the five songs written for the movie was designed to serve a specific function in the screenplay. The songwriters weren't required to come back with something brilliant, but they did. As a result the movie originally titled *Hot Nocturne* and later called *New Orleans Blues* was renamed *Blues in the Night*.

On June 3, Henry Blanke set out the pattern for integrating songs and musical themes into the movie with Harold Arlen, Johnny Mercer, and longtime Warner Bros. musical director Leo Forbstein. In a follow-up memo he spotlighted the key moments, which would change over the next few months: first, an introductory number when we meet Jigger and Peppi in the St. Louis Café. Then the "blues" number in jail, followed by a hot number in New Orleans played by a "colored band" with Leo joining in on trumpet. (Blanke said Arlen was temporarily referring to this as "The Bug.") Following this would be a little bit of "the ballad," sung by Character during the boxcar scene. The ballad would be fleshed out in a sequence beginning when Kay overhears the band rehearsing, continuing in the nightclub, where after a brief jitterbug dance Character resumes her song. (The ballad became one of Arlen and Mercer's loveliest songs, "This Time the Dream's on Me.") Soon afterward, Kay will sing a "corny song" while the boys are eating in the kitchen. A planned montage would feature the ballad, and Jigger would reprise the blues for another scene.

"This is as far as the script goes at present, and we have already mentioned that when Jigger is playing with the commercial band we shall have a tune which shall be a caricature on all commercial bands in general," Blanke concluded. The result, "Says Who? Says You, Says I!," delivered by comedienne Mabel Todd, doesn't seem to have been taken as a parody of anything but a hummable tune that later wound up as background music in the Bugs Bunny cartoon *Wabbit Twouble*.

Three weeks later, Blanke reported to Forbstein that songwriters Arlen and Mercer had played the songs they had finished so far for Hal Wallis and gotten them approved. The magnum opus was, of course, "Blues in the Night."

In her book *It Might As Well Be Spring* (Morrow, 1987, co-written with Will Holt), singer Margaret Whiting, the daughter of composer Richard Whiting, recalls frequent gatherings at their home in Beverly Hills with musical luminaries of the time and talented youngsters like herself. "The night I remember best was when Harold Arlen and Johnny showed up around nine-thirty. They were working on a song for a Priscilla Lane movie and wanted to see how we'd like it. Harold sat down at the piano and played a few blues chords and Johnny began to imitate a train whistle. All his life, Johnny was fascinated by trains. He began to sing:

My mama done tol' me,

When I was in knee pants,

My mama done tol' me, Son!...

"The room grew very still. I looked around. Mel Tormé's mouth was hanging open. Judy [Garland] had her head down and just her eyes were peering up at Arlen. Everyone in the room knew something great was happening. Just to watch Arlen and Mercer perform was a treat. They 'wailed' before the term came into fashion but this night, we were also being introduced to that extraordinary song, 'Blues in the Night.' We had them play it nine times.

"When it was over, we couldn't get Mel Tormé up off the floor and for the first time Martha Raye didn't have anything funny to say. Everyone wanted to sing it. Judy and I rushed to the piano to see who could learn it first. I remember the excitement of that night—and most remarkably, there was not an ounce of envy."

Although there is no specific record of how it was received upon its first performance at Warner Bros., Wallis was sufficiently impressed to announce that *Hot Nocturne*, later rechristened *New Orleans Blues*, would now be titled *Blues in the Night*.

The song certainly warranted that distinction. Arlen had worked especially hard to create a melody with a blues feeling without conforming to a traditional popular-song template: his wide-ranging tune ran 52 bars instead of the conventional 32. This in

Vocalist-turned-composer Harold Arlen sings out.

19

Four images from Don Siegel's delirium montage featuring tormented musician Richard Whorf.

turn challenged Mercer's ingenuity. He intended to open the song with the repeated refrain "I'm heavy in my heart," but Arlen noticed another phrase among Mercer's four pages of notes: "My mama done tol' me." He suggested using this instead—something he rarely did with his then-partner—and the lyricist agreed. As Whiting noted, Mercer needed no prodding to make reference to the wail of a train, which came right from his Southern roots. He later reflected, "Trains are a marvelous symbol. Somebody's always coming in or leaving on one, so it's either sadness or happiness."

In short order, "Blues in the Night" was recorded for use in the jailhouse scene and a subsequent montage of blacks working in cotton fields and along the docks of the Mississippi. "How many people will sing, and how it will be supplemented by orchestra, we can decide when the picture is cut as this is a scoring job." The background score (eventually composed by Heinz Roemheld) would also reprise "Blues in the Night" during a montage depicting Jigger's illness and delirium. "This montage will be a symphonic-jazz arrangement," Blanke explained. All the songs and on-camera musical performances were the province of stalwart studio arranger Ray Heindorf.

Also approved was "Hold onto Your Lids, Kids (Here We Go Again)," which by this time had been slotted into the film as a kind of informal anthem for the band members. Led by Character (Priscilla Lane), they sing and play it for the first time while riding happily in a railroad boxcar, then whistle it as they are crossing the parking lot and entering The Jungle roadhouse for the first time. It is reprised once more as they begin to make themselves at home there, and it will be used as a bookend in the final scene of the picture.

One other song didn't make it to the final cut. Rossen's script included a nightclub scene in which a drunken man reacts to a recording of "On the Road to Mandalay" being played on a jukebox. One of Warners' music department people informed Leo Forbstein, "It is impossible to secure a quotation for a vocal use of 'On the Road to Mandalay' due to the estate of Rudyard Kipling will not at this time permit such a usage. I have, however, secured a quotation for the juke box use, which is $750. You understand, of course, that the rendition on the juke box must be an instrumental use." He added, "It will be perfectly OK for the drunk to request the playing of 'On the Road to Mandalay' just so long as he does not sing it."

By this time the movie was in full swing, and various department heads had indicated their budgetary needs: $2,511 for makeup salaries, $1,180 for hairdressers, $100 for wigs, $4,882 for wardrobe (including labor), a paltry $1,482 for montages, $82,317 for primary cast ($38,733 for contract talent, the rest for freelancers), $19,325 for extras, $28 for animal trainers or handlers, $800 for the shooting of stills, etc. Total direct cost: $48,655, to which $14,420 was added for depreciation and $191,925 for studio overhead, bringing the grand total to $687,000. (Republic Pictures, located just a few miles away from Warner Bros. in the San Fernando Valley, could have made a handful of B Western features for what Warners wrote off to overhead!)

These numbers did not go unquestioned. On June 17, the ever vigilant studio executive Hal Wallis wrote to Henry Blanke, "The attached budget on *New Orleans Blues* speaks for itself. I don't have to tell you that a picture of this type and with this type of casting will have a hell of a time getting its cost back based on these figures." He encouraged his producer to economize on all fronts and take as many short-cuts as possible.

Wallis wasn't the only one concerned about spending. Three days later, Jack L. Warner wrote to Wallis, "In last night's dailies [director Anatole] Litvak shot a whole day on just the one scene at the pool table. It seemed to me he took at least four unnecessary angles of Kazan talking to Jack Carson. It wasn't the amount of takes, it was the unnecessary angles and I am sure he could have done much more work had he just made the shot, panned Kazan in, done one reverse shot of Carson and it would have been over. That is about all we will use when it is cut." He urged Wallis to talk to producer Blanke and if necessary show them what had made Warner so unhappy.

The following day J.L. received a letter from the Production Code Administration warning him that "we regret to report that the title and refrain of this particular lyric 'Hang onto your lids, kids, here we go again' is a paraphrase of an expression which is on the list of words and phrases forbidden by the Association. This, on account of it being a tag line of a dirty joke." I wish I knew what joke the letter refers to, but in any event, this objection was overruled and the song remained intact.

Every week brought its bumps in the road. On July 2, Blanke beseeched Wallis not to eliminate rain effects in the film's final sequence, as production manager T.C. Wright recommended in order to save money.

On July 9, Wright wrote to Wallis, exasperated over Don Siegel being stalled about starting to shoot his three montage sequences by producer Blanke and director Litvak after Wallis had approved them all. "This is quite a routine, and I would suggest that you get Blanke and Siegel in your office and settle it once and for all." He adds, "I have told Siegel not to figure writing any long, involved montages where we use the cast for a week, as per your instructions…"

In the finished film, those montage sequences play a vital role in pushing the narrative forward—and they do involve the principal cast members. While montages are no longer part of a contemporary director's toolkit, at this time they were valued in Hollywood, and specialists like the incomparable Slavko Vorkapich and the much younger Siegel—soon to be promoted to the director's chair—were experts in this specialized field. (Siegel once told me that he ran afoul of Michael Curtiz when he submitted one of his montage scripts to his producer first and then the explosive director, who refused to cooperate. From that point on, Curtiz saw everything first.)

And yet, some things never change. On September 5, as the film was in post-production, Siegel was forced to go directly to Hal Wallis because director Litvak wanted him to remove a shot of Priscilla Lane singing from the "travel" montage, showing the band members hitch-hiking their way across the country. "This is a very short flash which I shot with sound in case you want to hear her voice. I feel we should at least see her singing in order to establish her part in the band. If you want this out of the montage it will necessitate remaking the montage optically—a delay of two days."

And, having negotiated to use the great Jimmie (astoundingly misspelled Jimmy) Lunceford Band in the movie, Warners received a telegram stating that "these men did not like the idea of playing in cheap clothes." Although it is never explained, Lunceford and company—who were well-known as sharp dressers in the music world—are seen in the introductory New Orleans sequence wearing ordinary work clothes. With no ability to alter the completed footage, the best Warners could do to placate Lunceford was to bill him and his group as "a barnstorming band."

However, Anatole Litvak *did* figure out a way to enable Jack Carson's character (not Richard Whorf's, as indicated in the Robert Rossen treatment) to play one hot chorus with the band: by standing at his table amongst the customers and joining in on trumpet. Whorf couldn't very well have

Jimmie Lunceford fronts his swinging band—in work clothes.

contributed a piano chorus without actually joining the black musicians on the bandstand.

(In need of a successful band for Whorf to play with in a later scene, Warners hired Will Osborne and his Orchestra, although the leader and his men were merely visual stand-ins for the studio musicians who actually played on the soundtrack.)

The production file on this film in the Warner Bros. Archives reveals just how much detail work went into making a creditable picture, even if it wasn't one of the company's prestige productions that year. For instance, the studio research department fielded a wide variety of questions. Montage man Siegel wanted to know the diagnosis for a disturbed mental condition. Men's Wardrobe asked what New Orleans and St. Louis police and jail uniforms actually looked like. Screenwriter Rossen solicited suggestions of police precinct names in St. Louis; the research team obliged and suggested fictional variations he might use.

In that regard, it was the department's job to alert production executives of possible legal issues. For instance, they advised producer Blanke, "In Scene One there is a supposed St. Louis Café. There is a real St. Louis Café in St. Louis. We cannot use this name without permission." They suggested changing the name to either the St. Louis Star Café or St. Louis Lark Café.

Another missive went to studio production manager Wright: "Max Parker, art director on *New Orleans Blues*, needs to have pictures of the southwest corner of 48th Street and Broadway in New York from various angles. We have exhausted the possibilities in this department, the public library and several of the other research departments which we have the privilege of calling. We would appreciate your getting pictures of this location and letting us have the negs as well as the prints so that we would be able to make the required number of prints for our purposes." The resources of the studio were summoned to make this happen.

The finished film didn't impress or overwhelm anyone. True to Hal Wallis' fears, it lost money, earning $572,000 domestically and $325,000 overseas. Since its "negative" or production cost was $716,000, a little more than originally budgeted, it showed a loss on the books of $143,250.

Richard Whorf made a decent impression and turned in some good performances in other films of the 1940s, but never achieved stardom. Following World War II he moved behind the camera and enjoyed a long and prolific career as a director, moving from feature films to television where he piloted scores of popular shows.

Priscilla Lane sings "Hang Onto Your Lids, Kids (Here We Go Again)" with Whorf strumming his guitar behind her.

Looking back on the picture in his book *Elia Kazan: A Biography* (HarperCollins, 2005), author and critic Richard Schickel wrote, "The film has a nice, dark atmosphere, and thanks to Rossen, who was a Communist at the time, it has a certain proletarian pungency about it. The band, despite the romantic cross-currents swirling through it, does its best to maintain its musical 'authenticity,' deriving strength from their proletarian values....

"On the other hand, the movie is very much some white guys' idea of what black music is about, and clearly Tola Litvak hasn't the slightest idea of what that meant. He's just doing a studio assignment on a picture that was less important than originally intended."

Schickel adds, "At one time Cagney had been mentioned for the film, and John Garfield, too, but it went forth with essentially a B picture cast, doing, frankly, B picture work. Kazan does his best to play the clarinet, but he's none too persuasive, and his performance is fussy and aggressive; he wants to be noticed, but succeeds largely in being kind of a minor pest at the edge of the fame, which [Kazan] later admitted. 'The only thing about the production that impressed me was the musical side. Jimmie Lunceford and his band were the best artists on the lot. Close at hand were Johnny Mercer, who wrote the lyrics and with him the man who wrote, the music, Harold Arlen, a genius.' Everyone else, including himself, he writes, were 'second raters.' "

Kazan may have been harsh, but he wasn't wrong: *Blues in the Night* is a film that doesn't fulfill its promise. What's more, the magnificent title song never receives one complete or satisfying performance in the course of the picture. Fortunately, the movie's disappointing performance at the box office did nothing to hinder the success of the song.

Artie Shaw was the first to enjoy success with his recording of it in October of 1941, a month before the film's release. But it was fellow bandleader Woody Herman who scored a hit record just weeks later, remaining on the charts for eighteen weeks, four of them in the number one position. He also had an eight-week run with another song from the movie, "This Time the Dream's on Me," which was on the flip side of the disc.

Herman's success on the charts spurred further recordings in 1942. Jimmie Lunceford had been scooped in

A newspaper ad from Kingsport, Tennessee.

getting to it first, but he made up for that by recording the entire song, in two parts, on both sides of a 78 rpm record. Benny Goodman, Dinah Shore, and Cab Calloway (who also featured it in a Soundie short), were among the other artists who covered the song. Following the custom of the day, alternate words were offered for Shore and other female vocalists. "When I was in knee pants" became "When I was in pigtails," "Son" became "Hon'," etc.

Three separate recordings made the Top 10 list on *Billboard* magazine's chart of national record sales for February 14, 1942, and two others ranked high among regional sales. As the movie continued to play out in cities and towns around the country, enterprising theater owners emphasized the hugely popular song, and its opening line, "My mama done tol' me," in their newspaper ads for the feature.

The song so permeated the American scene that Carl Stalling, music

25

director of the Warner Bros. cartoon department, used snatches of it (with parody lyrics) in a number of animated shorts including *Bugs Bunny Gets the Boid* and *Coal Black and the Sebben Dwarfs*.

"Blues in the Night" has remained a standard in what is now known as the Great American Songbook. Rosemary Clooney had a hit in 1952, a decade after it was introduced, and others as varied as Bing Crosby, Frank Sinatra, Doris Day, Ella Fitzgerald, Louis Armstrong, Quincy Jones, Little Milton, Van Morrison, Chicago, and Katie Melua have recorded it over its 70-year lifespan.

In his acclaimed book, *American Popular Song: The Great Innovators 1900-1950* (Oxford University Press, 1972), the erudite composer and sometime-lyricist Alec Wilder wrote, "'Blues in the Night' is certainly a landmark in the evolution of American popular music, lyrically as well as musically.... It is much too earthy to be an aria, but it could be."

But as popular as "Blues in the Night" became, it did not win the Academy Award as Best Song for 1941. That honor went to "The Last Time I Saw Paris," a poignant, topical song by Jerome Kern and Oscar Hammerstein II that MGM interpolated into a movie already in production, *Lady Be Good*. Kern admired "Blues in the Night" and felt he and Hammerstein had won unjustly; he began campaigning for the Academy of Motion Picture Arts and Sciences to change its rules so only songs written specifically for a movie would qualify for the award. What higher compliment could one composer pay another? (Kern actually wrote a letter of apology to Arlen.)

Mercer's longtime friend and collaborator Robert Emmett Dolan told a parallel story about the reaction of a fellow lyricist. As quoted in *The Complete Lyrics of Johnny Mercer* edited by Robert Kimball, Barry Day, Miles Kreuger, and Eric Davis (Knopf, 2009), Dolan recalled, "I was in New York and Kern and Hammerstein's 'The Last Time I Saw Paris' had just won the Academy Award over 'Blues in the Night.' Oscar said to me, 'When you get back to Hollywood, tell Johnny he was robbed.' He was robbed of an Oscar by an Oscar."

Diary of a Disaster...or:
WHERE DID THE MUSIC GO?

How could a 1936 Broadway musical hit become a 1939 movie flop? Why would a studio pay top dollar for the rights to a show with a score by Rodgers and Hart and then jettison all the songs? How did an actor with no terpsichorean skills wind up with the starring role in a story about a dancer?

Those are some of the questions that puzzled me as I set out to explore the story behind Warner Bros.' ill-fated production of *On Your Toes*. After enjoying a revival of the play by Rodgers, Hart, and George Abbott as part of UCLA's *Reprise* series, I was inspired to revisit the film, which had left little impression on me when I first saw it many years ago. Watching it again, I realized why: it is eminently forgettable. Yet I was intrigued enough to want to learn how this misfire came about, so I went to the Warner Bros. Archives at the Doheny Library Special Collections, University of Southern California for answers.

The Musical Miracle!

Heavenly

Zorina

(She's the new Movie Queen-a) in

"ON YOUR TOES"

Gayer! Girlier! Greater than the Play!
(By Rodgers and Hart, and George Abbott)
with EDDIE ALBERT · Alan Hale · Frank McHugh
Directed by RAY ENRIGHT · Screen Play by Jerry Wald and Richard Macaulay · Adaptation by Sig Herzig and Lawrence Riley
A First National Picture

These memoranda, letters, notes and publicity materials form a diary of disaster—a chain-reaction of impulsive decisions and unheeded warnings, resulting in a gung-ho effort to make the best of a bad situation.

On Your Toes opened on Broadway at the Imperial Theatre on April 11, 1936, under the direction of Worthington C. Miner, with a cast headed by Ray Bolger, Tamara Geva, and Monty Woolley.

Original sheet music from the Broadway production of 1936.

The story opens on a family vaudeville act, The Three Dolans. When Phil Dolan, Jr. grows up, he leaves his dancing career behind to teach music appreciation in college, where he bonds with a talented student who has composed a jazz ballet. They try to interest a Russian dance impresario in staging the piece, but while he wavers on the idea, Phil becomes romantically involved with the star ballerina. Later, when the show's wealthy backer blackmails the flamboyant director into staging the jazz ballet, with Phil dancing the male lead, the ballerina's ex-lover—who thinks the idea of a jazz ballet is insulting—hires some gangsters to bump off Dolan at the finale of the piece. Of course, everything is straightened out in the nick of time.

The score includes "There's a Small Hotel," "On Your Toes," "Glad to Be Unhappy," and such clever pieces as "The Three B's," "Quiet Night," and "Too Good for the Average Man," along with the finale, Richard Rodgers' ballet "Slaughter on Tenth Avenue."

Within a week of the play's debut a reader in the Warner Bros. story department read a treatment submitted by the William Morris Agency, but no action was taken. Then, on December 29, 1936, Warner Bros. purchased the film rights to *On Your Toes* for a not-inconsiderable $60,000, including the rights to all eight of its songs. Yet almost immediately the studio seemed uncertain as to how the property could yield an effective movie.

The obvious choice of leading man for this film would have been Warners' contract star James Cagney, but at that moment he was battling with Jack Warner, and left the studio to produce his own movies for the short-lived Grand National Pictures.

A week before the contract was finalized, staff producer Robert Lord (credited at that time as an associate producer) wrote to executive producer Hal Wallis, "We need Bolger or someone like him for the picture; and if we

don't get Bolger, I think it's going to be quite a job to get someone like him."
He was right.

The following month, Warners director Archie Mayo saw the show
during a trip to New York City and conveyed several thoughts to Wallis: first,
that the studio should consider hiring leading lady Tamara Geva. "It seems
to me that this girl, if properly publicized, is another one of those foreign
importations who, if enough glamour is put around her, might be a personality. At any rate she is intelligent, and certainly from what I've seen, a damn
good actress." (Wallis wasn't impressed with her screen test, and despite a
handful of appearances, Geva—the first wife of George Balanchine—never
had a Hollywood career.)

Mayo also passed along an idea that Larry Hart suggested: why not
change the gender of the leading role and cast Ginger Rogers in the Ray
Bolger part? Warners did like this idea and developed a treatment with her in
mind, dated February 13, 1937, but apparently had a devil of a time getting
an answer from the RKO star. Nearly a full year was wasted in this pursuit,
while *On Your Toes* simmered on Warners' back burner.

In May of that year one executive, impressed with Jack Haley's work in
the Fox musical *Wake Up and Live*, suggested him as a possible contender,
but no one took him up on the idea. One might call that a missed opportunity. Later, in November, Warners executive Jacob Wilk talked to MGM
about taking over the rights "because they have the right man to do it, Ray
Bolger." But Mervyn LeRoy, who had just moved from his longtime home
at the Burbank studio to Metro, read the script and returned it without
comment.

Finally, on January 17, 1938, Hal Wallis was obliged to implore his
boss, Jack Warner, "Don't you want to try to get Ginger Rogers' mother on
the phone and get some answer on *On Your Toes*? We have to go to work on
this if she is going to do it, and I don't understand why they are stalling so
much." One can only conclude, from the lack of further correspondence,
that this idea either died a quiet death, or that Miss Rogers finally said no.

In July of that year, the studio sent out two other feelers to see if they
could recover their investment in the property: one was to British producer
Alexander Korda, who might have seen it as a vehicle for his musical-comedy
star Jack Hulbert, and the other was to Samuel Goldwyn, who had signed
Norwegian-born ballerina Vera Zorina after her great success on Broadway
in another Rodgers and Hart show, *I Married an Angel*. (Prior to that, she
played the lead in the London production of *On Your Toes*.) As it happens,
there were no takers. In one of his letters, Jack Warner later referred to a
$75,000 offer for the rights from agent Mike Levee (on behalf of an un-
named client), but there is no confirmation of this anywhere else in the

studio files.

On September 24, 1938, producer Lord, having developed the first screenplay for the property, became proactive, and wrote to Wallis, "Here's a wild idea for you: What would you think of the possibility of putting Eddie Albert in *On Your Toes*? The part fits him to a tee, except for the dancing." The studio was high on its production of the Broadway comedy *Brother Rat*, and had signed New York transplant Albert to a term contract. Lord goes on to explain that Albert is now working with George Balanchine on a new musical show [Rodgers and Hart's *The Boys from Syracuse*, which became a smash hit—Ed.] and that the choreographer guarantees to make him an effective dancer. He concludes, "I don't believe you ever read our script for *On Your Toes*, did you?... I think it is a very funny script despite the nausea it induced in Miss Ginger Rogers."

It wasn't until early 1939 that Warner Bros. decided to put *On Your Toes* on its production schedule, one way or another. In February Jack Warner expressed interest in Zorina. Wallis realized that if they hired her they would have to rewrite the script that was tailored for Rogers—who was to play an American *impersonating* a Russian dancer.

No director was yet assigned. William Keighley read the current script and reported that "some of the spirit has been lost in the screen version." There was discussion of using contract man Lloyd Bacon, who worked well with Busby Berkeley on such hits as *42nd St.* and *Footlight Parade*, while agents pitched various clients to the studio, including Fred Astaire and Ginger Rogers' director Mark Sandrich. Eventually Wallis handed the film to Ray Enright, a studio stalwart whose credits included *Dames, Ready, Willing and Able,* and *Gold Diggers in Paris.*

Early that year studio exec Walter MacEwen sent a memo to Hal Wallis saying that agent Phil Berg had offered the services of Rodgers and Hart should Warners want any new material written for the film. Wallis' response is written emphatically in pencil on the memo itself: "NO."

On March 2, 1939, *The New York Times* reported that Warner Bros. was going to borrow Ray Bolger from MGM to star in their film version of *On Your Toes*. This proved to be untrue. During a trip to New York, Jack Warner met with Eddie Albert, who must have charmed the mogul. On March 12 he wrote on Waldorf-Astoria letterhead to Hal Wallis back on the West Coast, "Am highly enthused with the possibilities of Albert and Zorina in this picture... I feel we are doing the right thing to advance our own personality, as Eddie Albert is, rather than worry about the possibility of Cagney, who may not be with us or Ray Bolger who definitely means nothing. Feel sure that Albert can dance sufficiently well, and with good direction we can get a good comedy picture." Zorina was officially borrowed from Samuel

Vera Zorina is attended to by a hairdresser on the set of *On Your Toes*.

Goldwyn, who had placed her under contract when she made *The Goldwyn Follies* for him in 1938.

But reality started setting in just two days later, when producer Robert Lord reported to Wallis, "I've just finished an interview with Mr. Balanchine who informs me that Eddie Albert cannot dance at all. Furthermore, he informs me that it would take years before Mr. Albert knew enough about dancing even to fake the part in *On Your Toes.*"

The choreographer also told Lord that he didn't like the new direction the story had taken and hoped to have a chance to work on the script. He added that his now-wife, Vera Zorina, would want him to stage the dances as she is "a very timid creature and finds herself frightened of other dance directors."

Lord concluded, "Unless we do some calm, clear and collected thinking now, we're going to find ourselves in the middle of a real clambake about six weeks from now."

Wallis agreed, and responded immediately that there was only one conclusion to draw from this: "We do not want Mr. Balanchine anywhere in or near the studio during the making of the picture."

Later that same day, March 14, Lord had reason to send a follow-up memo to his boss, having overheard a rumor that if they didn't sign Balanchine, Zorina would refuse to make the movie. In that case, he reasoned, it might make more sense to hire Balanchine and slot Ray Bolger or James Cagney in the lead. "You know," he wrote, "that there is a certain degree of sense in Balanchine's objection to Eddie Albert. It is not easy to make a picture about a dancer played by an actor who can't dance at all."

While trying to solve this dilemma Jack L. Warner's casting director, Steve Trilling, sent a memo to Hal Wallis in April noting that their timing was inopportune. Suddenly, it seemed, a great many musicals were going into production around town and dance directors were at a premium, with the services of Bobby Connolly, Dave Gould, Albertina Rasch, and LeRoy Prinz already spoken for. He checked with a production supervisor at the Goldwyn studio who worked with Balanchine on *The Goldwyn Follies* and found him reasonable to work with, "no more temperamental than a [Busby] Berkeley or Bob Alton." (The memo misspelled his name as Altmon.)

At the bottom of this fateful report Robert Lord wrote in ink, "Hal: Under the circumstances, I think we'd better take Balanchine."

So it was that on May 19, 1939, Warner Bros. signed George Balanchine, who was represented by the William Morris Agency, to supervise the dance numbers in *On Your Toes*, which was set to go before the cameras

A madcap moment with Eddie Albert, Leonid Kinskey, and players.

in June. His salary was $1,500 a week, with a six-week guarantee, and in those days of train travel, Warners agreed to furnish "round trip transportation, including compartment, if available, from New York City." (A special rider to the contract provided that if Balanchine so wished, and served notice within three weeks after the commencement of photography, his name would not be publicized in connection with the film. He chose not to invoke that clause, but his agent should have protected him in one other way: his name was misspelled Ballanchine in the movie's opening credits.)

Now everyone at the studio was paying attention. Legal executive S. H. Aarons, noticing pre-production hubbub surrounding the two key dance numbers in the film, "The Princess Zenobia" and "Slaughter on Tenth Avenue," wrote that Warners' contract wasn't clear whether they had acquired the rights to those set-pieces. "Ballets not specifically mentioned in contract and this raises serious doubt in my mind."

Hal Wallis' executive assistant, Walter MacEwen, with all good intentions, queried the film's producer, "Are the original lyrics of 'Slaughter on Tenth Avenue' to be used in the picture? As you probably know all lyrics used in pictures have to go to the Breen Office in the same way as scripts do." He didn't know that 'Slaughter' was an orchestral piece, not a song.

There is no indication in any of this correspondence as to when the studio decided not to use Rodgers and Hart's songs.

The mystery of why no Rodgers and Hart songs were performed in the movie version of their Broadway musical hit *On Your Toes* remains unsolved to this day.

On May 5, 1939, publicity chief Charles Einfeld suggested to studio production chief Hal Wallis that they commission a title song, "like '42nd Street,' to build up the picture." Wallis then wrote to Herman Starr at Music Publishers Holding Corporation in New York asking if he had any staff tunesmiths who could turn out such a song, not to be performed in the film itself but for tie-in and promotional use upon its release. (In this letter he specifically states Warners' intention to use only the two Richard Rodgers ballets in the film.) Apparently Starr did provide a song which producer Robert Lord later deemed "ghastly. If the picture is good, it will do business without a song; if it's bad, I don't believe a song will help it."

For some reason no one ever referred to the delightful Rodgers and Hart song "On Your Toes." Was it considered too difficult, too sophisticated, too different from the hummable hits turned out by Warner Bros.' staff songwriters? We'll never know.

This much is certain: Rodgers and Hart got a bum rap from Hollywood. In 1939, the same year that *On Your Toes* was released, MGM made its screen version of another R&H Broadway success, *Babes in Arms*, with only its title number and "Where or When" intact, leaving behind such great songs as "I Wish I Were in Love Again," "My Funny Valentine," "Johnny One-Note," and "The Lady Is a Tramp," although one can detect snatches of the latter melody in the movie's underscore. (Likewise, Warners used bits of "There's a Small Hotel" and "Quiet Night" as background music throughout *On Your Toes*. Why not? They paid good money for them back in 1936.)

Interestingly enough, the studio anticipated this kind of wholesale revision. MGM's contract with Rodgers and Hart for *Babes in Arms* specifically states—in what may have been boilerplate language—"we shall have the exclusive right to adapt, change, translate...and to substitute an entirely new story, dialogue and/or characters and/or entirely new music and/or lyrics."

Thus ended an especially unhappy decade in Hollywood for the gifted collaborators, even while they were enjoying their greatest successes on Broadway. As far back as 1932 Rodgers and Hart labored for MGM on a screenplay for *I Married an Angel*, which they adapted (in collaboration with Moss Hart) from a Hungarian play. After a year's worth of revisions they gave up, but had the last laugh when producer Dwight Deere Wiman licensed the stage rights, and helped them turn it into a Broadway hit in 1938.

In point of fact, most of Rodgers and Hart's Broadway musicals weren't filmed at all. Those that were endured varying degrees of compromise, including the eventual MGM version of *I Married an Angel* (1942). *On Your Toes* wasn't an anomaly but just one more blow in a succession of frustrating experiences.

And here's the kicker: After the show was successful on Broadway, Richard Rodgers wrote a byline article for *The New York Times* in which he revealed that he and Lorenz Hart had originally conceived the idea—in Hollywood!

Young Donald O'Connor, James Gleason, and Queenie Smith take a bow in the opening vaudeville sequence of *On Your Toes*.

"I had heard that Pandro Berman, the head of RKO, was looking for a story for a new Fred Astaire picture," he revealed in the article, which appeared on June 14, 1936. "Hart and I sat down and worked for a couple of hours one afternoon, finishing up with a two-page synopsis telling the tale of a hoofer mixed up with the Russian Ballet. We took it around to Ber-

Rodgers and Hart in their element—far from Hollywood—launching the Broadway musical *I'd Rather Be Right* in 1937. Clockwise from left: producer Sam Harris, Hart, book writers Moss Hart and George S. Kaufman, star George M. Cohan, and Rodgers at the piano.

man, who liked it. He took it around to his associates, who rejected it. It was as simple as that. It didn't matter much, we figured, since we had invested so little time.

"A few weeks later in New York we ran into Lee Shubert and Harry Kaufman. The thing that had been keeping them up nights was the unhappy business of finding a vehicle for Ray Bolger.... Standing on the corner of Forty-fifth Street and Broadway we told Mr. Shubert and Mr. Kaufman the story of the hoofer and the Russian Ballet. They liked it, and this time were no associates to be consulted. We concluded the deal standing there on the corner."

What a shame the subsequent road from stage to screen was so bumpy.

As production finally geared up at Warner Bros., one element still had to be resolved: the casting of co-starring and supporting roles, first and foremost the Russian dance director. Hal Wallis' first choice was the flamboyant Mischa Auer, who would have been ideal except for a prior commitment at his home studio, Universal. Akim Tamiroff was then sought, but he was about to begin work on *Untamed*, which had been written especially for him at Paramount. Wallis wrote to casting director Steve Trilling, "I saw the test of George Tobias and I'm afraid he isn't good enough for *On Your Toes*. He doesn't seem very funny. He seems to be laboring all the time." After another disappointment he wrote, "What about Lionel Stander?"

Wallis ordered studio contract player Alan Hale to make a test, in special makeup, which didn't satisfy him. He also rejected tests of Leon Belasco and Erik Rhodes. "Rhodes is very phoney [sic] to me," he wrote. "He is obviously faking an accent, and somehow or other, the thing doesn't come off at all. I still think we would be much better off with Curt Bois or Fritz Feld...."

With filming less than a month off, another possibility arose, and the studio went for it in a big way even though it would cost them a lot of money. On May 2, Adolphe Menjou said he liked the script, although he asked for "a little better ending for himself." His fee: $50,000 for six weeks' work. But Menjou would be finishing *Golden Boy* for Columbia on June 5 and starting *The Housekeeper's Daughter* for Hal Roach on July 1, so on May 8 Wallis was, once again, forced to ask Jack L. Warner to intervene in order to get a definitive answer. "Just a reminder to please call Hal Roach as soon as you come in and see if you can get him to postpone his starting date on Menjou, so that we can use Menjou beginning June 5." He added, with a condescending air befitting a major studio boss referring to an independent producer, "I'm sure he can postpone his picture three or four weeks without any serious problem."

Apparently, Roach did have a problem, and Menjou was taken out of the running. With no apparent alternatives, on May 9 Wallis asked producer Lord to test Alan Hale again for the role of Sergei and spend a bit more time on it. "If Hale is working, he can come back at night at six or seven o'clock and put in a couple of hours, and let Brick [Ray Enright] arrange to come back too and handle this thing." No effort was too great for an employee of Warner Bros., in Wallis' eyes, even if it meant returning to the studio after dinner.

Freelancers were hired to fill out the ensemble: James Gleason to play Phil Dolan, Sr. at $1,500 a week, with featured billing and a two-week guarantee. Queenie Smith would get $500 a week as his wife. Screen veteran Berton Churchill commanded $1,000 a week for the role of Henderson, with Paul Hurst earning $750, Erik Rhodes $750, Leonid Kinskey $650, and movie newcomer Donald O'Connor signed for $600 a week and a two-week guarantee as the young Phil Dolan, Jr. Sergei Temoff earned just $66 in total for his performance as a eunuch in the "Princess Zenobia" ballet.

As for the screenplay, Lord sent a memo to Wallis in March of 1939 in which he said, with great candor, "I am really afraid to start another musical picture with the same old refrain: 'Of course, the story is terrible but...' " The lengthy treatment which Lord co-authored two years earlier with Lawrence Riley and Sig Herzig was reasonably faithful to the outline of the play, but hardly inspired. Accordingly, a new screenplay was commissioned from Jerry Wald and Richard Macaulay. This version, which was finalized on April 7, 1939, had a strange finale involving the gangsters, with Junior stuck in a steam cabinet at a Turkish bath. But even with rewrites, the filmmakers finally opted to close the picture with a sight gag and a rather weak punchline. (The play ends as a musical comedy should, with the leading characters reprising "There's a Small Hotel," joined by the entire company for a rousing chorus of "On Your Toes.")

Meanwhile, Riley and Herzig, the writers of the first draft screenplay got wind of the fact that they weren't going to be credited for their two-year-old work, and registered a protest. Warners was willing to credit them for Adaptation and Wald and Macaulay for the screenplay, but the legal eagles remembered that Rodgers and Hart and George Abbott had a clause in their contract stating that their names had to be in larger type than the screenwriters. Eventually the situation was handled to everyone's satisfaction; all four screenwriters' names appeared on-screen, just slightly smaller than Rodgers, Hart, and Abbott.

Because there were no songs, the final screenplay placed a much greater emphasis on comedy and expanded the roles of Sergei (Alan Hale) and Ivan (Leonid Kinskey), whose bombastic performances bordered on the obnoxious. What remained held little if any of the charm that had made the show

Alan Hale strikes a pose on the piano top, while Eddie Albert, Zorina, Frank McHugh, and Leonid Kinskey react.

a success.

The best part of the picture, in many ways, was the opening vaudeville sequence, which was shot by a separate unit headed by dance director Robert Vreeland. Thirteen-year-old Donald O'Connor is delightful to watch, doing a song-and-dance act with James Gleason and Queenie Smith. (Warners had to clear the usage of such old songs as "Sidewalks of New York" and "Happy Days Are Here Again" for use in the background of these early sequences, for fees ranging from $100 to $150. Leo Forbstein fared much better when he assimilated familiar Russian music into the score. As Warners' New York office noted, "'A Life for the Tsar' by Glinka is OK, no cost, as composer died in 1857 in Berlin.")

Ray Enright, his cast and crew were sent over to the long-unused Vitagraph Studios in Hollywood—purchased but virtually abandoned by Warner Bros. years earlier—to film many of the backstage scenes on a standing theater set. "Everybody had a slight case of horrors," reported journalist Thornton Delehanty in *The New York Herald-Tribune*. "There was a bygone smell to the place, a chill of dead memories in the air. They wanted to get the scene over and shake the mildew from their hair. In the afternoon they would be returning to their home studio, and the afternoon couldn't come too soon."

Delehanty also got a sense of the movie's tone from his set visit and conversation with the participants. He predicted, correctly, "Those of us who saw and relished 'On Your Toes' on the stage will find little that is recognizable in the screen version. The plot has been hacked, revamped, excised, revised and amended, partly in the interests of cinema technique.... The satirical content has been modified considerably. The familiar Rodgers and Hart numbers have been omitted and the holes thus left will be plugged with bits of a new plot."

Ray Enright would wrap up all his scenes by July 21, but there was still the matter of preparing and filming two elaborate ballet sequences. The first stumbling block arose when no one could provide clean, readable copies of the orchestral scores. Even a piano copy for rehearsal purposes proved elusive, as Victor Blau in Warners' New York office explained to studio conductor Leo Forbstein in a June 15 Air Mail letter: "It seems that Dick Rodgers turned over his copy to Chappell, the publisher of the music, and it has gone astray."

On June 30, unit manager Bob Ross wrote in his daily production report, "Balanchine unit is rehearsing the Zenobia number and Slaughter number on Stage 22, starting today. Production is 3 days behind schedule."

On July 3, he wrote, "Mr. Enright didn't have a very good day SATURDAY. We started out Saturday morning with a RETAKE involving a change

The Warner Theater in Memphis developed an elaborate theater-front display—including spinning cut-out dancing girls and lighting effects to throw the spotlights on a glitter globe—all to promote this turkey.

of dialogue that Mr. Lord wanted done right away. Later on in the afternoon we had some added scenes to make in a previous sequence; then about 4:00 we started on the MORRISINE sequence, which starts with a dance, so it was necessary to have Balanchine come over to frame the dance with ERIC [sic] RHODES and ZORINA, leaving his rehearsal. We rehearsed from 4:25 to 5:45 p.m. and will start on it first thing this morning."

By July 6 the production was five days behind schedule. On July 24, Ross wrote, "Saturday morning, Balanchine unit began shooting Zenobia number on Stage 7."

Three days later he could report that rehearsal had begun in earnest on "Slaughter on Tenth Avenue." Hal Wallis urged Robert Lord to keep a sharp eye on Balanchine and suggested having the "cutter" on the set to make sure all of his shots matched up. Lord had already assigned editor Clarence Kolster to be there for most of the shooting. "I think that everything shot will match," he reassured Wallis, "because it has been very carefully planned."

Production was interrupted briefly on July 28 when Edward Selzer (who would later be assigned to run the Warner Bros. cartoon department) shot a special preview trailer featuring "Zorina and the girls." For this brief coming-attractions piece cinematographer Sol Polita made fourteen setups.

With so much pressure to complete the film, work continued on the weekends, and on August 5, the company rehearsed on Sunday. Finally, on August 12, Ross could write of the previous day's work, "This finishes the number and the picture."

But it wasn't quite that simple.

On July 31, Ross reported that even with cuts from director Ray Enright, the big "Zenobia" production number was running 13½ minutes in length. Producer Robert Lord was notified and came to the stage, where he worked with the director to shave 3½ minutes from that total.

Problems remained with the finale, as well. On August 21, Lord wrote to Wallis, "I would like to run the 'Slaughter on 10th Avenue' number with you before or after you run your dailies. We have been cutting and recutting the end of this number for three days and I think I've got it in a fairly effective fashion. Your objective critical faculties would be most valuable in this problem—and it seems to have become quite a problem."

The next night Jack Warner ran the film at his home, where apparently it didn't wow the invited audience, but Warner wrote to Lord, "I am not at all worried about the picture.... In front of an audience it must have a million laughs that we could not get at the house." Apparently Warner never lost his enthusiasm for the piece, in spite of all the evidence around him.

Promotional pitchman Charles Einfeld was similarly optimistic. In mid-August he

hatched an idea to have Zorina stand on her toes on top of the Perisphere at the New York World's Fair, "as I'm sure this will be good for picture and newsreel breaks. I can guarantee that Universal Newsreel will cover it if you arrange stunt. [There is no evidence that this actually came to pass.—Ed.]

This picture wants and deserves the same treatment as we gave *42ⁿᵈ St.* and the *Gold Digger* shows."

The exhibitor's pressbook was full of other grand ideas, like *Throwaways Spell Zorina*. "Distribute throwaways containing one letter of Z-O-R-I-N-A. Award free tickets to your showing to person submitting complete set of six letters spelling out her name. You can control the number of Annie Oakley's by limiting the letter 'Z' to twenty-five." (An Annie Oakley, for the uninitiated, is carnival-speak for a free ticket—with a hole punched through the middle.)

In addition, Warners arranged product tie-ins for the ballerina with Capezio dance footwear, Westmore cosmetics, and Vanity Fair stockings. There was a separate contest for best theater-front display.

Final cost of *On Your Toes* was reckoned at $421,459; to that was added 45% for studio overhead, or $189,468, plus $21,073 for depreciation, making a grand total cost of $632,000. Among the line items: "Wigs purchased and rented, $450. Animal handlers, teachers, $72." The picture netted $238,000 in U.S. rentals, and another $125,000 from overseas, for a disappointing total of $414,000.

Did Warner Bros. spend its money wisely? It seems foolish to have purchased a musical only to throw out all of its songs. Then again, *On Your Toes* took an unusually long time to make its way from stage to screen under the normally fast-paced studio system. By 1939 the studio may have been concerned that the Rodgers and Hart score would seem overly familiar to moviegoers, at a time when songs could wear out their welcome on the radio in a matter of weeks. (In the decades to follow, studios changed their attitude toward this situation in bringing major Broadway shows to the screen.)

Were any lessons learned from the experience? Probably not by the studio, but it helped the creators of the show develop a whole new outlook on dealing with Hollywood. It's telling that when Richard Rodgers teamed up with Oscar Hammerstein II in the 1940s, he insisted on retaining complete control of movie rights to their musical plays and having final say about every aspect of their production. He wasn't about to repeat his sorry experience with movie studios in the 1930s.

Hollywood Faces the Great Depression:
REMEMBERING
FORGOTTEN MEN

Most generalizations about film history don't hold up to scrutiny. We're told that moviegoers of the 1930s paid their money to escape from the drudgery of the Depression. That's largely true, but there were some notable exceptions.

Time and again, the scrappy, street-smart films made by Warner Bros. defied that trend and delivered pungent social commentary, wrapped in entertainment. This was never truer than in the unforgettable musical finale to *Gold Diggers of 1933*. Joan Blondell appears as a streetwalker who recites "Remember My Forgotten Man"—a plaintive hymn to American men who fought for freedom in World War I, only to find themselves 15 years later in the army of the unemployed. (Those real-life men—the so-called Bonus Army—marched on Washington, D.C., in 1932 to collect the bonuses they were promised but never received. On order of President Hoover, they were dispersed in a violent confrontation with the actual U.S. Army.)

Busby Berkeley's spectacular visualization of the song encapsulates the lives of these men—marching off to war, returning as heroes, then winding up in breadlines. The number reaches a dramatic climax as Blondell and a chorus bring the song to a close against a backdrop of silhouetted soldiers marching, not as individuals but as a never-ending parade of disenfranchised men.

The movie ends with this haunting production number, sounding a somber note as "The End" flashes on-screen. It may well be the only movie musical in history to end that way. (The contrast is even more striking because the movie opens so memorably with the optimistically defiant anti-Depression anthem, "The Gold Diggers Song [We're in the Money].")

As Richard Corliss wrote in a *Time* magazine website article about composer Harry Warren, "What did audiences take home with them? Not that the 25% of unemployed men were forgotten, but that someone, far away in

Hollywood, remembered them."

And *Variety* opined, "That rousing, rah-rah finish which, while Cohanesque, is timely and patriotic..., a bing-bang build-up that'll have the American Legion proclaiming paeans of endorsement for the flicker."

How did such an uncommon idea come to fruition?

The term "forgotten man" entered the vernacular when Franklin D. Roosevelt delivered his first important campaign speech in New York on April 7, 1932, one year before *Gold Diggers of 1933* appeared on theater screens.

According to Amity Schlaes, author of *The Forgotten Man: A New History of the Great Depression* (HarperCollins, 2007), "The forgotten man was the idea of a speechwriter, Raymond Moley...[who] wrote to his sister about how he had come up with that phrase.... Roosevelt, Moley said, 'was trying to reach the underdog. And I scraped from my memory an old phrase, the forgotten man, which has haunted me for years.'"

Schlaes explains that Moley remembered the term because it was popularized in the late 19th century by Yale professor William Graham Sumner, who "wrote prophetically about the voter who was not included in

Joan Blondell sings "Remember My Forgotten Man."

an interest group, the forgotten man 'who is never thought of.... He works, he votes, and he always pays.' "

However, FDR's speech used the resonant term in an entirely different context. "Roosevelt...spoke of the plight of the average American—two in ten of whom were unemployed—and the former soldiers, the economic infantry of the nation. These men, Roosevelt said, deserved more attention. They were 'the forgotten man' at the bottom of the economic pyramid."

That man hadn't been forgotten in Tin Pan Alley. E.Y. Harburg and Jay Gorney wrote their potent Depression ballad "Brother, Can You Spare a Dime?" in 1931, and it was incorporated into a Shubert Broadway revue, *New Americana*, in 1932. But it wasn't until October of that year (a month before Roosevelt's election), when both Bing Crosby and Rudy Vallee recorded the song, that it became a sensation. The lyrics declared it a national

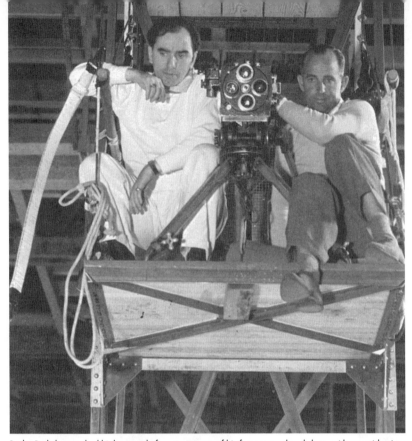

Busby Berkeley perched high on a platform to get one of his famous overhead shots, with an unidentified cameraman.

shame that men who fought for our country ("in khaki suits") and built our railroads should now be begging for handouts. It remains one of the most dramatic popular songs ever written.

But how did such a grimly realistic topic make its way into a lighthearted Hollywood musical? I explored the Warner Bros. Archives at the University of Southern California in search of answers.

Warners, like several other studios, soured on musicals after the glut of all-talking, all-singing, all-dancing films of the early sound era, which had resulted in a public backlash. Samuel Goldwyn's Eddie Cantor vehicles and Paramount's Ernst Lubitsch baubles were among the few tuneful films to pass muster during the relatively fallow period of 1931–32.

But Warners saw in Busby Berkeley's elaborate, eye-popping production numbers for those Cantor films a revitalized approach to the genre, and feeling certain that the public would respond to its topical musical *42ⁿᵈ St.* (which featured three Berkeley showpieces), the studio held that film back from release until early 1933 so it could have a follow-up waiting the wings. They were right: *42ⁿᵈ St.* was a great success. Even so, songwriter Harry Warren later remarked, "None of us thought that it would be *that* big and that it would start a whole cycle of these things."

On November 10, 1932, Warner Bros. production chief Darryl F. Zanuck wrote to his associate Lucien Hubbard about his plans to have a staff writer freshen the screenplay of the 1929 picture *Gold Diggers of Broadway*, retaining as much of the old picture as possible, "especially the great comedy sequences." (We'll never know how great; the soundtrack survives, but except for two musical scenes, the film is considered lost.) He also suggested casting Ruby Keeler as the ingénue, Dick Powell as the juvenile, George Brent as the guardian of the boy, Glenda Farrell or Aline MacMahon in the Winnie Lightner role, and—incredibly—*Roscoe Arbuckle* or Guy Kibbee as the sucker. "We can drop the Nick Lucas character entirely," he concluded.

"On the tenth of December, [Al] Dubin and Warren will be here to write the new songs. Busbee [sic] Berkeley, of course, will do the dances."

(Arbuckle, off screen for a decade following a notorious scandal, had just been given a comeback opportunity in Warners' Vitaphone short subjects; the first one was released in November of 1932. Zanuck's memo implies that he might have worked in feature films as well had he not succumbed to a heart attack in June of 1933. Just before the Vitaphone deal came through, he was directing a series of two-reel comedies for RKO Pathé called—believe it or not—

Berkeley supervises his chorus girls' diet, according to the caption of this 1932 publicity photo. That's Toby Wing (one of his favorites) second from the front on the left, her sister Pat up front on the right, and Dorothy Coonan (later Mrs. William Wellman) sixth from the front on the left. William Wellman, Jr., identified her after this photo first ran in the *Movie Crazy* newsletter.

The Gold Diggers, until someone in the legal department was reminded of Warner Bros.' "hold" on the title. The series was released as *The Gay Girls* instead.)

Erwin Gelsey and James Seymour promptly crafted a story outline which closely followed the narrative of *Gold Diggers of Broadway*, "with slight alterations in the introduction and finish." That finish was described thusly:

"With all three couples happily linked we go into a sensational production number." Changes were made during story conferences in December of 1932, including the decision that the closing number of the show-within-a-show would also be the finale of the movie.

The first hint of what that number might be appears in a draft dated January 6, 1933, where a new character is introduced: "Carol is a Libby Holman type, a blues singer. Her numbers will not conflict with the songs of the leading characters." Indeed. (A celebrated Broadway singer who introduced such standards as "Moanin' Low" and "Body and Soul." Holman was virtually synonymous with the term "torch song.")

That same draft contains this notation: "The concluding number in the picture is not the concluding number of the play—but license can be taken to make this a big number that will top off the picture and yet not seem to indicate that it is the end of the musical comedy on the stage."

Another version of the script dated January 18, 1933, by James Seymour and David Boehm places Carol's big song—yet undetermined—midway through the film, following a call on-screen for "Second act!"

"As auditorium lights dim and curtain rises on Carol's 'blues' number. She stands by lamp post in the rain. As she sings we see panorama in background of Bonus Army marching. Tramp of marching feet comes through music. Man's [sic] voices join Carol's in last chorus. (Tune similar to 'Too Many Tears.') As number ends we FADE OUT."

This solidifies the concept of the song intended to be sung by Joan Blondell, even referencing a minor-key torch song introduced by Dick Powell in the 1932 movie *Blessed Event*—and written by Warren and Dubin. (In fact, it was the first song they wrote together.) But who came up with the idea?

Composer Harry Warren told film—and film music—historian Tony Thomas, "We were called in to preproduction conferences, which was largely a waste of time because it was usually a discussion of costs, and the Warner executives were obsessed with economy. After that we would get a script, but there was seldom anything in it to suggest the songs, other than an indication of where they might go. For this one we knew we needed a song about the Gold Diggers, but there was nothing in the script about a Shadow Waltz or a Forgotten Man. Those were Dubin's ideas, and he deserves the credit for them."

A "revised, final script" dated February 8, 1933 (credited to Seymour, Boehm, and Ben Markson) is pretty much the film as shot, with lyrics of key songs now typed in along with the dialogue. But the film is set to end with "Shadow Waltz," followed by dialogue and a reprise of "The Gold Diggers Song [We're in the Money]."

As late as February 22, 1933, a "cutting script" places Carol's number— now set in stone as "Remember My Forgotten Man"—in the middle of the film, with "Pettin' in the Park" as the closing song.

In fact, "Remember my Forgotten Man" was the last segment of the picture to be filmed, in April of 1933. The Daily Production and Progress Reports, preserved at USC, give us some idea of how much work went into the creation of this sequence, and why Busby Berkeley was known as a taskmaster. (Dubin and Warren called him "the madman.")

The stirring finale of "Remember My Forgotten Man," involving scores of dancers and extras.

On April 6, 277 extras (including "stock girls") were called to Stage 2 at 9 a.m. to rehearse with cameraman Sol Polito. As Berkeley's scenario involved soldiers marching on treadmills—even in the rain!—with women cheering on the sidelines, it's easy to understand why they didn't finish until 9:25 that night.

On April 7, recording was scheduled for the morning, and shooting of the treadmill scenes in the afternoon. The report indicates that 40 singers, 19 orchestra members, 1 piano player, 2 bit singers, 81 men, and 100 girls were called. Recording began shortly after 10 a.m. and finished three hours later. The first camera setup began immediately thereafter, and was shot at 3:45; the final shot was completed at 10:55 that night.

Saturday, April 8, was a marathon for Joan Blondell and the crew. With a full camera staff plus effects specialist Fred Jackman, Jr., Berkeley and company worked on the treadmill and bridge, and set up "glass shots," from 9:00 a.m. until 3:25 the next morning! (As Blondell would tell me years later, "They got their money's worth out of us." Is it any wonder that this same year, 1933, the Screen Actors Guild was formed?)

Still, there was more to do. Many of the same people had to return to Stage 2 on Sunday afternoon, April 9 at 2:00, where they put in another nine hours of work. The production report shows that one stand-in (to spell an exhausted Blondell, perhaps?), one singer (unnamed), 20 orchestra members, one piano player, and 11 extras were employed that day. Principal achievement: "Recorded Miss Blondell singing Forgotten Man." (And was that extra singer her voice double? Good question.)

When the company left Warner Bros. in Burbank at 11:00 Sunday night, the assistant directors were able to declare, "Finished, Picture closed" on their log sheet. (A few minor shots were picked up one afternoon the following week.)

Comparing "the greatest campaign speech of the last century," by FDR, about the forgotten man, with the song it inspired, political blogger Ralph Brauer remarks, "The substitution of the word 'my' for the more generic 'the' personalized the plight of millions of Americans and adding 'remember' to the title reinforced the importance of the message. Their song is uncannily constructed like Roosevelt's speech, beginning with World War I, then moving on to the farmer and the family (tariffs just aren't song worthy)."

Joan Blondell recites the lyrics one time through, then a black woman (Etta Moten) perched on a tenement windowsill actually sings the tune, to a bluesy orchestral accompaniment. At the end of the sequence Blondell reprises the song one last time, pouring her heart into it and revealing a lusty contralto voice.

Brauer, like many others, credits Etta Moten with dubbing Blondell's vocal, but film historian Miles Kreuger once asked her about this and she said no, although she was aware that people thought it was she. He also queried Marian Anderson, who for many years was thought to have been the voice, and she, too, denied having recorded the number.

In fact, Blondell's final chorus was recorded by a Los Angeles-based vocalist named Jean Cowan, known for her bluesy style. Cowan appeared regularly on local L.A. radio shows, and was featured in nightclub revues. Her only other film work was recording two songs for the 1941 Warner Bros. drama *The Sea Wolf*. Rudy Behlmer obtained her name from longtime Warners music director Ray Heindorf in 1973 when Rudy was working on a box set of LPs commemorating Warner Brothers' 50th Anniversary, but her identity has remained obscure for decades, allowing others to be credited for her work.

Busby Berkeley proudly took credit for choosing Blondell to deliver the number on-screen, however, explaining, "Joan Blondell can't sing; but I knew she could act it; I knew she could 'talk it' and put over the drama for me." He was right.

In a lengthy interview with Dave Martin, published in *The Genius of Busby Berkeley* (CFS Books, 1973), Berkeley went on to explain how he wound up appearing on-screen,

Theater owners were invited to feature life-sized standees of the Gold Diggers chorus girls in their lobby. There were six choices at $4.95 apiece. What moviegoer wouldn't have been impressed to encounter one of these?

calling out, "Everybody on stage for the 'Forgotten Man' number!" Warners realized that it needed insert shots of workers backstage, knocking on doors and announcing cues, but they didn't want to pay any actors at that late stage of production. "They said don't hire anyone, use the office help," Berkeley remembered. So he used a couple of male secretaries on the lot and then cast himself as a callboy. "On opening night at the Chinese, the Berkeley girls roared with laughter when they saw me come on the screen.... I was strictly the director."

That he was. Berkeley established early on in his relations with Warners that when it came to rehearsing and filming the musical sequences, he

TAKE SID GRAUMAN'S TIP!
You're giving them more laughs
—more songs—more girls—*more
show* than "42nd Street." ..
So it's worth more money!
RAISE YOUR ADMISSION SCALE
FOR "GOLD DIGGERS OF 1933"

This admonition appeared in advertising aimed at exhibitors.

was solely in charge. If he wanted 150 extras to portray marching men, he got 150 extras. Mervyn LeRoy may have directed the non-musical scenes in *Gold Diggers of 1933*, but when it came to the songs, Busby was the boss.

Berkeley honed his skills—and his take-charge demeanor—in the United States Army. During World War I, he was stationed in France, with the 312th Field Artillery of the 79th Division. Among his other duties, he was assigned to conduct the parade drill. In *The Busby Berkeley Book* (New York Graphic Society, 1973), he told Tony Thomas, "I got tired of the old routine, and to make things more interesting, I had worked out a trick drill for the twelve hundred men. I explained the movements by numbers and gave the section leader instructions for their companies and had them do the whole thing without any audible orders. Since the routines were numbered the men could count out their measures once they had learned them. It was quite something to see a parade square full of squads and companies of men marching in patterns, in total silence."

Berkeley always claimed that he "cut in the camera." He also worked closely with film editor George Amy, so it wasn't long before studio executives could screen "Remember My Forgotten Man." Jack L. Warner and Darryl F. Zanuck apparently thought it was so powerful that a) it might "stop the show" if it appeared midway through the movie, or b) it was an irresistible finale. The change of placement was made with just weeks to go before *Gold Diggers'* release. Being thrifty, the studio decided not to reshoot the moments leading up to it, so in those climactic backstage scenes you still see Ruby Keeler and the chorus girls in costume for "Pettin' in the Park."

Hollywood is accused of being sequel-happy nowadays, but in the heyday of the studio system, producers didn't make actual sequels so much as carbon copies. If the public liked something once, they usually got it over and over again. But even musical buffs may not realize that, thanks to strategic planning, Warners had *Gold Diggers of 1933* in theaters just a few months after *42nd St.* sold audiences on Dick Powell, Ruby Keeler, and Busby Berkeley's kaleidoscopic chorus girls.

The film was an unqualified hit. Warners urged theater owners, "Don't

sell it as 'another *42nd St.*' but get the 'bigger and better' slant into all copy."
A serialized story prepared for newspaper use ran under the headline, "Read
how they beat the Depression!" and readers obviously responded. Grauman's
Chinese Theater raised its top price to $1.50 for the *Gold Diggers* engage-
ment—and got it. Warners responded with an advertising insert in the trade
papers under the headline, *Take Sid Grauman's Tip!* "You're giving them
more laughs—more songs—more girls—more *show* than '42nd Street'...*So
it's worth more money!* Raise your admissions scale for *Gold Diggers of 1933.*"
The hike in admissions didn't seem to deter audiences, however. The studio
reported that the film exceeded the box-office take of its predecessor by 32%
in its first three big-city engagements.

(In the end result, the film cost about the same to make as *42nd St.*,
$433,000. But the new musical took in $2,173,000 at the domestic box
office with an additional $1,029,000 from overseas, topping *42nd St.*, which
made $1,419,000 at home and $843,000 abroad—all of this in spite of the
fact that the Great Depression hit rock bottom in 1932–1933.)

Rival Samuel Goldwyn even got in on the action, reissuing Eddie Cantor's first talkie feature, *Whoopee!* (choreographed by Busby Berkeley), the
same week that *Gold Diggers of 1933* opened. United Artists' trade adver-
tisements for *Whoopee!* encouraged exhibitors to "CASH IN on the "current
craze for musicals with the greatest money-making musical ever made!"

"Remember My Forgotten Man" was a sensation, a feather in the cap of
Busby Berkeley and Joan Blondell. But there wouldn't have been a number
to stage if Al Dubin hadn't written those stirring lyrics. His daughter, Patricia
Dubin McGuire, wrote about her father and this song of "social protest" in
her book *Lullaby of Broadway* (Citadel Press, 1983). McGuire states that a

Harry Warren tries out a song with his writing partner Al Dubin in a 1937 publicity shot.

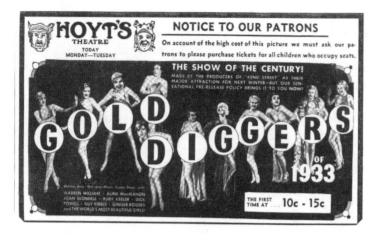

few years after its introduction, it was banned from being performed on the radio, a censor "contending that the lyrics were not in the best interests of the country's morale and were 'subversive.' Al loved that; he took it as a real compliment and it promptly became one of his favorite lyrics.

"For though Al was then living high off the hog, he was painfully aware of the suffering of the vast numbers of unemployed, often explaining that his way of helping out was to write songs that everyone could sing to help them forget about all those things they didn't have—like rent money. Neither did he ever forget that it was the 'little guy' and 'little gal' (financially speaking) who sang his songs, bought his songs, and enabled him to live the elegant lifestyle. He respected his 'customers,' unlike many Hollywood personalities who exploited and laughed at a public so gullible, so hungry for dreams. Al couldn't laugh at them because he was just as dream hungry as they were."

"Al Dubin had a talent for putting his lyrical finger on the moment," his daughter continues. "[He] was able to put into words what the majority felt, so people who sang his songs often had that feeling of recognition—'Ah yes, that's the way it is.' And therein lay the secret, in part, of Al Dubin's success. Certainly there were cleverer, more sophisticated lyrics. But Al...seemed to be able to speak for people's vulnerable feelings."

Dubin perfectly, and poignantly, expressed what many Americans were thinking. Even today, an audience can readily understand the meaning of those lyrics; perhaps that's why we still remember his "forgotten man."

Young and Beautiful:

GRADE B—BUT CHOICE

Quick: what movie offers budding starlets, grade-A character actors, grade-B musical numbers, a pair of vaudevillians, a look behind the scenes of Hollywood, bogus appearances by Charlie Chaplin and Buster Keaton, and a script by Dore Schary?

The answer is an obscure musical called *Young and Beautiful*, produced by Mascot Pictures in 1934, and while it isn't terribly good, it is fascinating in its own way.

Even 75 years ago, the idea of giving moviegoers an insider's view of Hollywood wasn't new; there are films of this sort dating back to the teens. From the very beginning, writers and producers were willing to expose some of Tinseltown's well-known foibles while whitewashing others.

With the birth of talkies, a new spate of Hollywood-on-Hollywood movies emerged. Fly-by-night studios liked them because they offered a whiff of glamour, even if they didn't actually deliver. The major studios didn't shy away from them either. Universal Pictures' founder Carl Laemmle congratulated himself (in an introductory title card) for having the nerve to bring

The WAMPAS Baby Stars strike a pose.

George S. Kaufman and Moss Hart's hilarious play *Once in a Lifetime* to the screen intact in 1932. In that story, three world-weary vaudevillians invade the movie capital in the early days of talking pictures and present themselves as voice experts. A bombastic mogul played by Gregory Ratoff is even convinced that the trio's resident simpleton (perfectly played blank-faced by Jack Oakie) is a genius.

MGM followed suit one year later with *Bombshell*, starring Jean Harlow, an uncharacteristically astringent view of the movie world which was also based on a play (by Caroline Francke and Mack Crane). Lee Tracy plays a publicity hound who'll do anything for a story, and Harlow suffers the consequences, but what she endures at the studio is nothing compared to her home life, where she is victimized by her leech-like family and a morally dubious household staff. Only one person is spared the screenplay's slings and arrows: the studio chief, painted here as a wholly benevolent figure. (No surprise, as Louis B. Mayer wasn't known for his rollicking sense of humor.)

Starlets pose by the pool (above) while the shot below reveals the Mack Sennett (later Mascot) Studio lot.

By the time low-grade Mascot Pictures got around to this topic in 1934 the go-getting publicity man and the dyspeptic Jewish studio boss were archetypes, if not downright clichés. For a leading man, Mascot was able to make a two-picture deal with William Haines, the once-popular leading man who'd been dismissed by MGM. The openly gay actor later claimed that Louis B. Mayer had blackballed him at all the major studios; by the time he landed this deal he was just happy to be working. One can imagine Haines deriving a certain amount of satisfaction out of playing a character who repeatedly confounds and outsmarts studio boss Herman Klein (played in dialect by stage and screen veteran Joseph Cawthorn).

The real-life boss behind this film, Mascot's Nat Levine, must have relished landing a "name" like Haines, but in spite of his MGM pedigree Haines didn't get billed above the title of *Young and Beautiful;* that honor went to The WAMPAS Baby Stars.

The association of publicists known as WAMPAS (Western Association of Motion Picture Advertisers) had begun naming its "stars of tomorrow" in 1922, and over the next decade got considerable ink for such up-and-comers as Colleen Moore, Clara Bow, Mary Astor, Joan Crawford, Mary Brian, Janet Gaynor, Fay Wray, Lupe Velez, Jean Arthur, Joan Blondell, Frances Dee, Karen Morley, Mary Carlisle, Ginger Rogers, and Gloria Stuart, to name just a few. (Their collective clout could do nothing for the likes of Maryon Aye, Kathleen Key, or Derelys Perdue, however.)

WAMPAS broke up in 1934 after naming one last group of promising stars, the weakest lineup in the organization's twelve-year run. Naturally, it was *this* group that wound up in a Mascot Picture. For the record, the starlets were Judith Arlen (sister of Ann Rutherford and not to be confused with *Young and Beautiful*'s leading lady Judith Allen), Betty Bryson, Jean Carmen, Dorothy Drake, Jean Gale, Hazel Hayes, Ann Hovey, Neoma Judge, Lucille Lund, Lu Anne Meredith, and Katherine Williams. Several others from the group did not appear in the film, for whatever reason, including Helen Cohan (George M.'s daughter), Gigi Parrish, and the most talented and successful of the bunch, Jacqueline Wells, who later thrived under the name Julie Bishop.

The WAMPAS girls participate in the highlight of *Young and Beautiful,* one of the strangest musical numbers ever staged, in which actors wearing full-face masks of major stars appear on stage together. At first, you're not sure whether or not to believe your eyes; some of the caricature-masks are quite good. Some of the performers adopt the actors' body language, and appear in costumes from the stars' most recent roles: John Barrymore as he appeared in *Reunion in Vienna,* Wallace Beery as Pancho Villa from *Viva Villa,* George Arliss as *The Iron Duke,* Joe E. Brown in uniform from *Son of a Sailor,* Eddie Cantor in costume from *Roman Scandals,* along with Clark Gable, Maurice Chevalier, Adolphe Menjou, Jimmy Durante, Charlie Chaplin, Buster Keaton, Stan Laurel, and Oliver Hardy. After an introductory sequence, the bogus stars participate in a kind of elaborate parade with the WAMPAS lovelies.

If these young actresses are something of a disappointment, there are plenty of old hands on board who serve up exactly what they're supposed to. Any movie that features a close-up of Franklin Pangborn in its first scene can't be all bad! (He welcomes Herman Klein, "president and guiding genius of Superba Pictures" and other luminaries to his radio microphone, as he covers the WAMPAS banquet. His mike bears the call letters NLMP—which obviously stands for Nat Levine Motion Pictures.) Other familiar faces in the cast include John Miljan as an oily "Pasadena playboy" who has his eyes on the new arrivals in town, the allegedly amusing Vince Barnett as Haines' leg man, the redoubtable dese-dem-and-dose Warren Hymer as a prizefight champ, Syd Saylor as a reporter, Rolfe Sedan as a French maitre d', and perpetual policeman/detective Fred Kelsey as a studio projectionist. (As in seemingly every film of this period, Dennis O'Keefe can be spotted as a dress extra in a nightclub scene.)

Popular 1930s bandleader Ted Fio Rito is also featured briefly in a scene that's supposed to take place at the Cocoanut Grove, with Candy Candido pretending to play the violin in the front line. (That same year Candy had a specialty number with partner Coco in MGM's *Sadie McKee*, but he doesn't get to open his mouth here.) "A Pretty Girl, A Lovely Evening," composed by Fio Rito, Harry Tobias, and Neil Moret, sung by Don Raymond, becomes the main theme of the uncredited score, written by prolific B-movie composer Edward Kay. But it's another song, from Eddie Cantor's 1933 hit musical *Roman Scandals*, that provides this movie's title: Harry Warren and Al Dubin's "Keep Young and Beautiful."

If you've seen the restored late-1920s Vitaphone shorts you might be likely to recognize Ray Mayer (of the song-and-patter duo Mayer and Evans) as a songwriter, and the vaudeville team of Shaw and Lee, who acquired a whole new generation of fans after their 1928 short *The Beau Brummels* was restored by the UCLA Film and Television Archive. Unfortunately, their material here isn't funny, although they do perform a bit of eccentric dancing in a lively if oddly photographed musical number called "Hush Your Fuss," written by Jay Kern Brennan and Ted Snyder. (Bandleader and *Movie Crazy* reader Vince Giordano has added this number to his repertoire, I'm happy to report.)

The setup for the film is lively and fun, but in spite of five people laboring over the script, it runs out of steam about halfway through its 68 minutes. In terminology that might test the mettle of any Writers Guild of America arbitrator, the credits read: Story and Adaptation by Joseph Santley and Milton Krims, Screen Play and Dialogue by Dore Schary, Additional Dialogue and Construction by Al Martin and Colbert Clark.

This was Schary's sixth screen credit since breaking into the business in 1933. He, of course, went on to bigger and (much) better things, as did Krims (who later wrote or co-wrote such films as *Green Light*, *Confessions of a Nazi Spy*, *A Dispatch from Reuters*, and *Prince of Foxes*). Al Martin started out in the silent era, went on to write dozens of B movies in the 1930s and '40s, and remained active in television through the 1960s on such series as *77 Sunset Strip* and *My Favorite Martian*. Harvard-educated Colbert Clark left writing behind to become a prolific producer of B movies, specializing in Westerns, through the 1950s. And writer-director Joseph Santley stayed put, as Mascot was absorbed into Republic Pictures in 1935; he was the studio's main man for musicals and comedies.

The fact that we get to see some of that historic studio lot is another reason *Young and Beautiful* has film-buff appeal. A number of scenes are shot outdoors (to avoid building sets and having to light them, we presume), revealing the handsome Spanish-style stucco buildings and green spaces that had been designed for Mack Sennett when he moved in just four years earlier. During the "Hush Your Fuss" number, as two girls tap-dance on top of a table, one can glimpse a soundstage (at an extreme angle) bearing the name MACK SENNETT STUDIO.

There is a brief chase scene which would require a clearer print than the one that exists to identify street signs, but several scenes take place at Union Air Terminal, later known as Bob Hope Airport in Burbank. [Today it's called Hollywood Burbank Airport.]

It's there that William Haines' protégé and girlfriend June Dale (played by beautiful Judith Allen) welcomes Superba Pictures' newest

Extras in masks portray (from top) Laurel and Hardy, John Barrymore and Clark Gable, Charlie Chaplin, and Buster Keaton.

star, a Frenchman who may be even better than Chevalier, we're told. Later, when posing for an endless round of publicity photos, the actor asks, "When do you find time to *live* in this mad place?" "You don't," says a disheartened Dale, "unless you can find a few minutes between work and publicity gags." Says the exasperated Frenchman, "And someone told me it was an art!"

The foolishness of publicity stunts is central to the story line. PR man Bob Preston (Haines) has a slogan: "You Can Do Anything with a Headline." On the night of the WAMPAS banquet, he approaches the Postal Telegraph clerk in the hotel lobby to make sure she's sending through a group of telegrams to June Dale from Will Rogers, Wallace Beery, Mary Pickford, Jimmy Walker, Paul Muni, and Mussolini. "They sure are a nice bunch of telegrams," says the girl on duty. "They ought to be, precious," Haines replies. "I wrote 'em myself."

Haines goes so far as to have June Dale pretend to be kidnapped on her way to the WAMPAS event. He later tells his boss that she'll be "the biggest thing since Garbo," though Mr. Klein isn't buying, and promises June, "You'll be in the newsreel with the President, Max Baer, and Aimee," referring to the three most celebrated people of the day, the latter being flamboyant preacher Aimee Semple McPherson. He justifies his constant stunts by saying, "It's part of the movie merry-go-round. Stars aren't born; they're made, and it's headlines that make 'em. You can do anything with a headline."

To the newcomers, however, he offers this advice: "Now listen, girls. You're starting up that rickety ladder to success. As WAMPAS stars, you're halfway there already, but how far you'll get is up to nobody but your own sweet selves."

The inimitable Franklin Pangborn.

Ah, that rickety ladder! Hollywood has always portrayed itself as a place where some dreams come true—and others are shattered. This purportedly honest portrayal was old-hat by the 1920s, but it continues to serve novelists and dramatists to this day, as willing audiences continue to find al-

Mascot Pictures sprang for this full-page ad in the *Motion Picture Herald* to entice theater owners to book *Young and Beautiful*.

lure in the drama of show business.

Sure enough, one of the starlets in *Young and Beautiful* (Katherine Williams) is disillusioned after a day of posing for cheesecake photos by a swimming pool. "I dreamed of such different things, like Juliet, Hedda Gabler, Roxanne..." she muses aloud. But when she gets her big break, she becomes so overwrought that she spoils ten takes—the ultimate sin at a B-movie factory—and is fired on the spot by Herman Klein. Moments later, she commits suicide. This causes June Dale to lash out at Klein—little dreaming the camera is still running. When Klein sees that footage the next day he realizes that the girl has talent and signs her up at $500 a week!

If one were to remake this picture today, the dollar amounts would change, and so would some of the topical references, but the essence of the story would remain the same. Nothing has really changed in the land of dreams.

First Silents, Then Talkies, and Then:
ACT THREE: TELEVISION

Television introduced me to silent movies. This was back in the 1950s, before the 200-channel universe made it possible to scan a galaxy of programming and still find nothing to watch. The most popular children's program of the era, *Howdy Doody*, showed silent-comedy shorts on a regular basis, and even the *Little Rascals* television package included a handful of late-1920s silents.

But there were also stars who served as living links to the silent era, none more prominent than Buster Keaton, who worked on TV from its earliest days through the mid-1960s. As I became enamored of Keaton, I learned to scan *TV Guide* and my local newspaper listings so I wouldn't miss any of his appearances with Ed Sullivan, on *Candid Camera* or even on *The Donna Reed Show*. I have an indelible memory of seeing him do a pantomime skit

Buster Keaton and Joe E. Brown in the "Journey to Nineveh" episode of *Route 66* in 1962.

on a weekend program hosted by Paul Winchell. Imagine my shock when I encountered a kinescope of that very broadcast on Laughsmith Entertainment's wonderful DVD collection *Industrial Strength Keaton* and learned that it had aired in 1957, when I was just six years old. Talk about making a lasting impression!

Keaton credited TV with rejuvenating his ca-

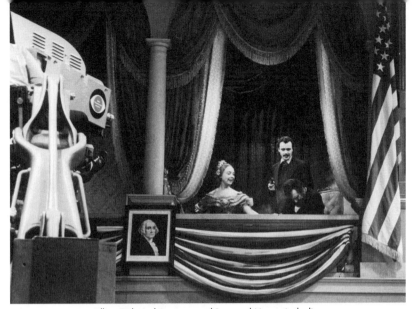

Lillian Gish, Jack Lemmon, and Raymond Massey in the live
TV drama *The Day Lincoln Was Shot* (1956).

reer—and his spirits. In his autobiography *My Wonderful World of Slapstick*
(written with Charles Samuels) he recounted a dressing-room conversation
with Charlie Chaplin when they worked together on *Limelight* in 1951.
Charlie asked Buster how he stayed in such good shape, and before responding, Buster asked if Charlie ever watched TV. At this, Chaplin delivered a
tirade against the new medium, adding that he forbade his children from
watching. Again he complimented Buster on looking so hale and hearty and
asked what was responsible. "Television," Buster replied.

If the Hollywood moguls were afraid of the new upstart medium, many
stars considered television to be "beneath" them, just as stage actors looked
down at silent movies in the nickelodeon days. More practical-minded performers saw TV as a source of employment, especially welcome since the
studios (reeling from the double-whammy of competition from TV and the
government-ordered breakup of movie studios and theater chains) were cur-
tailing production and letting go of contract players at this time.

Many stars were quite young when they launched their careers in the
silent era, so when television came along they were in their 50s, active and
eager to work. Remember, Gloria Swanson had to be aged to play the iconic
role of Norma Desmond in Billy Wilder's *Sunset Boulevard*. (1950). Unlike
her character, Swanson was still sharp and attractive in her early 50s; she
had made her film debut at the age of 17. I recall seeing a still-spry Swanson
performing an amusing silent-movie skit with Ben Blue on *The Hollywood
Palace* in the 1960s. She continued working well into the following decade.
(Celebrated author Harlan Ellison is proud of the fact that he wrote scripts
for both Gloria Swanson and Buster Keaton when they appeared on the
1960s series *Burke's Law*.)

A side view of the Mack Sennett studio, for which Studio City, California, was named. In the early 1930s, it sat in the midst of orange groves.

Ramon Novarro's hair may have gone gray, but he still cut a dashing figure when I saw him on Walt Disney's *Zorro* in 1958; his *Ben-Hur* co-star Francis X. Bushman was as grandiose as ever when he was cast as Mr. Van Jones in a pair of *Batman* shows in 1966. But my knowledge of silent-film stars was still limited. Imagine my surprise when I learned that Neil Hamilton—Inspector Gordon on *Batman*—had been D.W. Griffith's leading man in *America*, made in 1924. I had a similar shock when I read the 1960 *TV Guide* Fall Preview Issue and discovered that the co-star of a new situation comedy called *Bringing Up Buddy* was Enid Markey, who played Jane opposite Elmo Lincoln in the 1918 movie *Tarzan of the Apes*.

Lillian Gish's career never slowed down, and like most New York-based actors she worked on a number of live dramatic television anthologies in the 1950s, including *Kraft Television Theater, The Alcoa Hour, Robert Montgomery Presents*, and *The Philco Television Playhouse* (where she originated the role of Carrie Watts in Horton Foote's "The Trip to Bountiful" in 1953). She also played Mary Todd Lincoln with Raymond Massey as Abe and a young Jack Lemmon as John Wilkes Booth in a 1956 *Ford Star Jubilee* presentation titled "The Day Lincoln Was Shot." In later years she was choosier than some of her contemporaries, but did accept occasional parts on filmed television shows like *The Alfred Hitchcock Hour* and *Mr. Novak* (which made a lasting impression on cinematographer Richard H. Kline, as he noted in an interview with me).

There were many other names and faces I came to recognize on television whose careers went back much farther than I first realized. How was I to know that Gale Storm's perpetually exasperated, silver-haired father on *My Little Margie* had been Janet Gaynor's romantic leading man in a dozen films, including the classic *7th Heaven*? Charlie Farrell went on to star in a short-lived sitcom of his own, *The Charles Farrell Show*, in 1956.

If I, as a budding silent-film buff, was getting a kick out of merely watching these veteran actors on TV, imagine what it must have been like to work with them.

Johnny Crawford started acting when he was eight years old, and at the age of twelve was cast as Chuck Connors' son in the Western series *The Rifleman*, which ran for five seasons (in the days when producers turned out 36–39 episodes a year). Johnny came from a show-business family, and like me, got hooked on silent films when he was quite young, purchasing 8mm home-movie prints from Blackhawk Films.

"I was fascinated with that era, and the assistant directors on *The Rifleman* knew that," he explains. "They hired the extras, and got a kick out of bringing [silent film veterans] on the show because I was so enthusiastic about meeting them. There were a lot of people from that era still around; they were then about the age I am now, and they were doing extra work." Having received an 8mm movie camera for Christmas, Johnny would even shoot impromptu scenes around the set.

Keystone comedy stalwart Minta Durfee, who worked with Charlie Chaplin and Mabel Normand (and was married to Roscoe "Fatty" Arbuckle) was a regular on the show. "She was terrific," says Johnny. "She was jovial, happy, loved being there. We loved each other. She was going to show me where they shot some of the Keystone comedies at Echo Park, and I had my 8mm camera and was always trying to shoot little silent films around the set. But we never did. The last time I saw her was at an event at the Academy and she was one of the guest speakers. Afterwards, I talked to her and she said, 'When are we going to go to Echo Park?' I guess I was just too busy with my

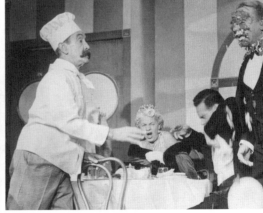

Snub Pollard and Harold Lloyd (as Lonesome Luke) in *Luke's Movie Muddle* (1916). Same mustache, 41 years later: Snub throws a pie at James Cagney (as Lon Chaney) in *Man of a Thousand Faces* (1957).

life, and these opportunities slip away from you."

Another mainstay on the series was Marjorie "Babe" Kane, who worked so memorably with W.C. Fields and Bing Crosby in their early-talkie Mack Sennett comedies. Johnny says, "She was a regular on *The Rifleman*—she and her mother—and they were best friends with my grandmother. They were on the show for several years."

"I didn't know anybody else my age who was into silent films," Johnny muses, "and I had this wonderful, romantic world I could go into. A lot of the crew and the wranglers on *The Rifleman* had also been in silent films; they were only middle-aged and vital. You know, we were only 30 years away. Our gaffer, who ran the lights, was Babe Stafford, who was a director at Mack Sennett in the early talkies when he was 21 years old. He loved talking to me about those days. He brought some clippings he had saved for his scrapbook and gave them to me, out of the trades when he got some directing assignments, noting that he was the youngest director in Hollywood, or that Babe Stafford was assigned to direct Bing Crosby in his next Mack Sennett short. And they had shot them at that studio; we were at Republic, and that had been the Mack Sennett studio."

Some days Johnny would go to lunch with some of his coworkers off the lot and walk a few blocks to a restaurant on Ventura Boulevard. Looking across the street, "I could look over and see the top of the stages at Republic, and you could still see under the paint—they had painted over it but they still needed to give it another coat—'Sennett Studios.' I just loved it. I thought I was the luckiest kid in the world."

One Friday, Harry "Snub" Pollard showed up for work. Few adolescents would have known who he was, but he had been a comedy star at the Hal Roach studio in the teens and 1920s, sporting a distinctive, droopy mustache. Johnny owned some of those shorts, and had enjoyed seeing him in Robert Youngson's 1960 compilation feature *When Comedy Was King*. The assistant directors had told him about Johnny ahead of time, so "he brought his little makeup box to show me, and I remember seeing several mustaches lying there. He didn't look anything like I thought he would—until he put on the mustache!" The actor wasn't very talkative but he appreciated Johnny's interest in him, and promised to bring Johnny some photos and lobby cards when he returned on Monday morning.

It was not to be. Snub Pollard died that night, January 16, 1962, at the age of 72. Johnny was both incredulous and sad. "I worked with him his last day in the business! I was really disappointed because I felt like he was going to be a 'regular.' I went to his funeral at Forest Lawn."

While Pollard had been reduced to working as a day player (he can be spotted in all sorts of movies—including Marlon Brando's *One-Eyed Jacks*),

Closckwise, from top left: With Billy Bevan and Madeline Hurlock in a Mack Sennett short, *From Rags to Britches* (1925); out of character at Columbia in the 1930s; as a Western sidekick in the 1940s; and on *The Real McCoys* in 1959. He used less and less makeup as the years rolled on.

another veteran of silent comedy maintained a certain degree of stardom to the very end of his days. Scottish-born Andy Clyde was a mainstay of the Mack Sennett studio in the 1920s and '30s. Like so many actors of that era, he was a master of makeup; before he settled into the stereotype of the old codger, he played all sorts of characters, from bums to French aristocrats in the Sennett comedies. He headlined his own series of two-reel comedies for almost thirty years, played supporting roles in such feature films as George Stevens' *Annie Oakley* (1935) with Barbara Stanwyck, and was Hopalong Cassidy's sidekick California Carlson on screen and radio in the late 1940s and early 1950s. He had literally hundreds of credits to his name.

As B Westerns and two-reelers faded from the scene, Clyde found work as a featured player on television. He had grown into the role of a colorful old coot, and it was unlikely that any member of the viewing audience wouldn't have recognized him. He won guest-star parts on such shows as *Tales of the Texas Rangers, Wagon Train, The Andy Griffith Show, Gunsmoke,* and *Lassie.* He also had recurring parts in several series: *The Adventures of Rin-Tin-Tin, The Texan, The Tall Man,* and *No Time for Sergeants.*

Everyone I've ever spoken to about Andy Clyde—from Edward Bernds, who directed some of his two-reelers, to fellow *Hopalong Cassidy* cast member Rand Brooks—has said he was "a sweetheart." That sentiment is echoed by Kathleen Nolan, who co-starred on *The Real McCoys* with Walter Brennan and Richard Crenna for six seasons.

Nolan has enjoyed a long career on television, stage, and film, and was the first female president of the Screen Actors Guild in the 1970s. She told me in an interview that she holds a special place in her heart for Andy Clyde. On days when he was scheduled to appear on *The Real McCoys,* "we all perked up 'cause Andy was coming."

Nolan recalls, "I spent a lot of time with him at his house on Bronson Canyon. He had this wonderful house on the corner, and it was like a museum. He had lots of photographs of people and he'd talk about how this one came from the theater, and this one was a stunt person.... There wasn't gossip involved; it was all loving.

Buster Keaton waits patiently for the crew to set up his next shot for a Pure Oil commercial in 1964.

"He never stopped laughing; I never, ever heard him in a bad humor. He was totally supportive and helpful. He was very enamored (not in a romantic way) of Madge Blake, who played his sister on the show, because he thought it was just terrific that she [had been] married, her husband died, and she started in her 50s. He would sort of put his arm around her and say, 'Here's a girl that followed her dream.'"

"He really took me under his wing," continues Nolan. "He also encouraged me to go up to the cutting room; that was before I started directing. He said, 'Go up there and look at that Movieola.' Then I'd come back and he'd say, 'What'd ya learn?'"

"Walter [Brennan] would use cue cards," Nolan remembers, "but when Andy was on the show (and Andy was older than Walter) he'd look at the cue card guy, Barney McNulty, and say, 'What are you doing here?' as only Walter could...and he would be letter-perfect.

"Walter and Andy would laugh a lot and talk about early times, and it was their joy. They would sometimes come in when they weren't working. 'Yeah, I was just in the neighborhood.' I mean, Walter lived in Northridge, Andy lived in Hollywood, and we shot in Culver City!

"I feel so fortunate; we had these incredible people to learn from."

Unlike Andy Clyde and Snub Pollard, Buster Keaton worked as much in live television as he later did in series episodes. Television host Garry Moore idolized Buster and often had him as a guest on his CBS morning show in the 1950s. Comedian and actor Chuck McCann, who as part of the Moore ensemble, remembers watching Keaton rehearse a routine one morning. He was to dive head-first along a counter top into a baking oven, and during rehearsal he misjudged his trajectory and hurt himself. Keaton was unperturbed; he went off by himself and sat down. It was only then that Chuck realized that Buster had torn an alarming strip of skin off his leg. He calmly patted it back in place and prepared to resume his rehearsal. No wonder some of his colleagues referred to him as an Iron Man.

In 1964 Keaton filmed two 60-second spots for Pure Oil in Atlanta that were planned as miniature silent movies. The more inventive of the two appears on the *Industrial Strength Keaton* DVD set and shows Buster, in his traditional porkpie hat and suit, hauling a gasoline hose over hill and dale to help a motorist whose car has run dry. Ad man Rudy Perz wrote the spots, and the account executive for the Leo Burnett advertising agency was Rudy Behlmer, years before he achieved worldwide renown as a film historian.

Behlmer vividly recalls going to dinner with a taciturn Buster and his ebullient wife, Eleanor, the night before filming. He also remembers the comedian's "smoker's cough." (Keaton would succumb to lung cancer in 1966.) On the job, Buster couldn't have been more obliging, doing exactly what was asked of him; he only spoke up once when he had a suggestion for staging a shot.

"It was a wonderful experience for me," Behlmer says. "As soon as you said 'action' he was on, and his timing was perfect. There was a consistency, and yet he was inventive; somehow he managed to do little things pantomimically, with expressions, thoughts and little ideas that he would incorporate. He wasn't told to do that; he did it."

The survivors of the silent film era—many of them trained on the stage—were troupers in the best tradition of show business. They loved performing as much as people loved watching them, even young people like me...and thanks to television, many of them enjoyed a satisfying third act to their careers.

Hollywood's Love Affair with Remakes:
HERE WE GO AGAIN

When 20th Century Fox unveiled its remake of *The Day the Earth Stood Still* in 2008, it seemed clear from the general buzz—and the majority of reviews—that the movie never had a chance. Even if it had been great (which it wasn't), memories of the 1951 original were simply too strong—even after 57 years—for a mediocre retread to win people over.

What must have it been like, then, for moviegoers and critics of the early talkie era who were confronted with one remake after another of great, even beloved, silent films that were barely a decade old? Movies like *Way Down East, Tol'able David*, and *7th Heaven* had made a profound impact on audiences and weren't easily forgotten. But Hollywood tried remaking them just the same, rarely if ever succeeding in surpassing the originals. The fact that those 1930s updates of 1920s classics are so little remembered today says it all.

Cecil B. DeMille poses with the camera used to photograph his original version of *The Squaw Man* (1914).

Sometimes studios and filmmakers would delude themselves into believing that audiences wouldn't remember the earlier pictures; in some cases they genuinely believed they could improve upon the originals. (Studios are often sensitive about the word "remake" and claim, somewhat defensively, that they aren't remaking a film at all but returning to its source material—usually a novel. A friend of mine was working as a publicist for Columbia Pictures when the studio released its ill-fated musical version of *Lost Horizon* in 1973. He was told to avoid the word "remake" at all costs and refer to the picture as a "re-imagining of James Hilton's classic story." Nice try.)

But not every remake was by definition a pale copy of a bold original. Some of the greatest directors of all time remade their own movies, with varying degrees of success. On occasion it was an opportunity to revisit a pet project: John Ford used his clout with Republic Pictures' Herbert J. Yates to remake *Judge Priest* (1934) as *The Sun Shines Bright* (1951), considered by Ford scholars to be one of the director's most personal films. Ernst Lubitsch was on a winning streak with Maurice Chevalier and Jeanette MacDonald and thought the story line of his silent comedy *The Marriage Circle* (1924) would make an ideal musical vehicle for his stars as *One Hour With You* (1932)—and he was right. Cecil B. DeMille didn't have to stretch too far to think of *The Ten Commandments* as his next production in 1956—he had visited the same material in 1923—but this time he staged the story on an even grander scale. And Alfred Hitchcock probably figured that audiences hadn't seen his 1934 British film *The Man Who Knew Too Much* when he remade it in 1956. I happen to like the first one better, but the remake was a smash hit.

Others turned to the tried and true when their careers (or bank accounts) needed a boost: Leo McCarey (*Love Affair* in 1939, *An Affair to Remember* in 1957), Howard Hawks (*Ball of Fire* in 1941, *A Song is Born* in 1948), and most notably Frank Capra (*Lady for a Day* in 1933, *Pocketful of Miracles* in 1961; *Broadway Bill* in 1935, *Riding High* in 1950). On a lesser scale, Mitchell Leisen recycled *Midnight* (1939) as *Masquerade in Mexico* (1946), and John Farrow remade his B-movie sleeper *Five Came Back* (1939) as *Back from Eternity* (1956). A vast number of B Westerns, serials and comedy shorts were also recycled by their original filmmakers.

On the other hand, when John Huston was asked, late in life, how he felt about the prospect of some of his best movies being remade he replied that he always wanted a chance to redo the films that *hadn't* turned out so well—hoping to do a better job the second time around. Unfortunately, that concept has never taken hold.

Cecil B. DeMille was something of a pioneer in the field of remakes. He revisited his first success, *The Squaw Man,* just four years after its 1914 debut. Why would such a prolific and popular director want to repeat himself when he was at what many consider the artistic high point of his career?

Robert S. Birchard, whose exhaustive research into DeMille's career yielded the book *Cecil B. DeMille's Hollywood* (University Press of Kentucky, 2004), explains, "Paramount was reevaluating a number of early properties at the time and either reissuing or remaking them. For example, *The Cheat* was reissued in 1918, and *The Sea Wolf* was ultimately remade in 1920 after two years in the teens equivalent of development hell."

But the art of filmmaking had developed so much in four short years that executives realized the original *Squaw Man*, which had done so much to establish DeMille, Jesse Lasky, and everyone associated with it, looked too primitive to pass muster with audiences of 1918. Still, its name had resonance with audiences, so Lasky proposed that DeMille remake it with the original star of the play, William Faversham. The director thought Faversham was too old, and when the actor had a scheduling conflict DeMille got his way and recast the picture with leading man Elliott Dexter.

It is telling that in the trade magazine *Wid's Daily* (later to become *Film Daily*) the review of *The Squaw Man* on January 12, 1919, made more mention of the source material by Edwin Milton Royle than the earlier film. However, the anonymous critic did note, "Artistry is the keynote of the entire production.... Comparing this with the first screen version of the same film gives an excellent conception of the marked advance of motion pictures as an art. In the opening reels we get some moonlight and garden scenes in which the lighting and photographic effects are remarkably picturesque and pleasing to the eye. Any class and type of audience is bound to recognize the artistic excellence of composition in these, and it helps in creating right from the start the impression of finesse and classy distinction."

Mary Pickford as Tess and Forrest Robinson as Daddy Skinner in *Tess of the Storm Country* (1914).

Like DeMille, Mary Pickford had no burning desire to recycle old ideas, but when she settled in as her own producer at United Artists in the early 1920s she recognized the value in redoing a story she had filmed in 1914, *Tess of the Storm Country*. Like *The Squaw Man* this was a crowd-pleasing melodrama, based on a popular book by Grace Miller White. Mary was cast as a poor girl who lives in a community of squatters, oppressed by a wealthy landowner whose home literally looks down on them. When her father is unjustly arrested on a charge of murder and she is revealed to be carrying a child out of wedlock, events are set into motion that will change the lives of all concerned. This was "the film that sent her career into orbit and made her the most popular actress in America, if not the world," according to the preeminent silent film scholar Kevin Brownlow. Pickford was grateful for its success, but she had no regard for her original director, motion picture pioneer Edwin S. Porter. "He knew nothing about directing," she told Brownlow years later. "Nothing."

In his book *Mary Pickford Rediscovered* (Academy of Motion Picture Arts and Sciences/Abrams, 1999), Brownlow writes, "The second version of *Tess of the Storm Country,* directed by John S. Robertson, gave Mary the opportunity to re-create her favorite role, while bringing the outmoded techniques of early cinema up to date. And nothing demonstrates the staggering advances made in the silent era more than a comparison of the 1914 and 1922 films. The first, raw and theatrical, moving forward in a series of jerks, has much to commend it, but it fails to make any emotional impact on an audience brought up on more sophisticated stories. The second, beautifully mounted and exquisitely photographed, is, by any standard, a work of art. It is hard to believe there are only eight years between them."

Mary Pickford reprises her role as Tess with David Hartford as Daddy Skinner in the 1922 version of *Tess of the Storm Country.*

This marked the only time Pickford ever remade one of her own movies, although she had no objection to other people doing so. Paramount owned the rights to her 1918 hit *Stella Maris* and didn't have to consult her when they produced a new version in 1925 with Mary Philbin. But in the 1930s the canny producer in Pickford generated considerable income from the remake rights to her valuable properties. She sold Fox *Daddy Long Legs* and *Tess of the Storm Country,* which served as vehicles for the next generation's winsome heroine, Janet Gaynor, and *Rebecca of Sunnybrook Farm,* which starred Marion Nixon. These three transactions netted her a tidy $150,000, according to research done by David Pierce, who says, "It is hard to imagine a performer whose work was refilmed more frequently." She then sold *M'liss* to RKO, where it was remade in 1936 with Anne Shirley. Shirley Temple starred in four Pickford remakes, most notably *The Little Princess* (1939). *Poor Little Rich Girl* (1936), *Rebecca of Sunnybrook Farm* (1938) and *Miss Annie Rooney* (1942, derived from *Little Annie Rooney*) all benefited from the high recognition factor their titles held for audiences but bore little resemblance to the original stories.

Pierce's research also reveals that Pickford continued to derive income from her properties even after her retirement from the screen. MGM purchased the rights to her 1929 talkie *Coquette* in 1946, intending to retool it for Lana Turner, and Samuel Goldwyn bought the rights to the 1933 *Secrets* (Pickford's last starring film) for his contract stars Dana Andrews and Teresa Wright. Neither film ever came to fruition.

The thinking in all of this is clear: a great star vehicle that worked once can work again—and again. When Paramount presented its brightest new star, Gloria Swanson, in *Zaza* (1923) an opening title acknowledged the story's long history on stage and even dropped the names of famous actresses who had played the glamorous character in years gone by (including Pauline Frederick, who starred in the first American film version in 1915)—and then prepared its audience for a "new, modern" Zaza. The flamboyant and self-centered French coquette was not Swanson's best part, but the film was still a success. (Claudette Colbert, an even more curious choice, played her in the 1939 remake directed by George Cukor. I'm not sure why this selfish, air-headed character was so enduring, except that she got to wear gaudy and expensive dresses.)

In the 1920s, producer Joseph M. Schenck purchased rights to a number of choice literary and theatrical properties as starring vehicles for his wife, Norma Talmadge. They turned out to be good investments, as five of them were remade the following decade: *Kiki, Smilin' Through, Camille, Secrets,* and *The Dove* (which became *Girl of the Rio*).

As Paramount story executive D.A. Doran explained in a 1947 interview, "We began to run dry [of stories] in 1928, but the invention of sound, to our great joy, allowed us to do them all over again. If we could buy 20 great stories today, we'd take them all and buy some for the future. There are not enough good ones to go around."

The arrival of sound caused many headaches (and heartaches) in Hollywood, but there was a bright side, as Doran indicated: writers, directors, and stars could legitimately recycle their proven hits. Talkies had immediately made silent films seem antiquated—and Hollywood was complicit in furthering that perception.

Richard Bann, who spent a great deal of time with comedy producer Hal Roach, remembers him saying, "A talking picture based on a silent picture's script is not the same film. Look at all the ways it's different, and in addition our aim was to make it better."

Having lived through the television era into the age of home video, Roach also pointed out that moviegoers of the 1930s didn't get to watch their favorite films over and over again. "You have to remember that when we made these pictures, they might play in your neighborhood theater for two days and then be gone," he said. "Audiences did not have a chance to get tired of a picture."

I asked Randy Skretvedt, who is in the process of revising his exhaustive book *Laurel and Hardy: The Magic Behind the Movies*, for his observations about the Hal Roach comedy team's reuse of silent material in their talkies. Because Laurel and Hardy were newly teamed in the late 1920s, their characters hadn't fully ripened; the duo's silent films depended more on gags and situations than the personas of Stan and Ollie. No one could have predicted that their unlikely combination of voices (Laurel's British accent and Hardy's Georgia speech) would work so well, or seem so natural. What's more, their deft use of dialogue added a great deal to the charm and humor of their work.

Duck Soup (1927), for instance, was based on the 1908 theatrical sketch "Home from the Honeymoon," written by Arthur Jefferson (Stan Laurel's father). The talkie remake,

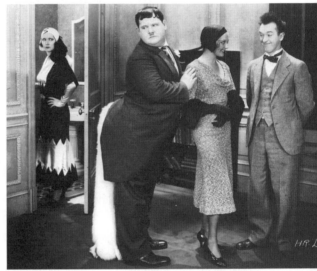

A beautifully posed still from *Chickens Come Home* (1931) with Mae Busch, a compromised Oliver Hardy, Thelma Todd, and Stan Laurel.

Another Fine Mess (1930) was "amplified from the silent version with a new emphasis on the characters of Stan and Ollie," says Skretvedt. "It's a more slowly paced and much richer film than the silent."

Love 'Em and Weep (1927), featuring James Finlayson as a would-be politician about to be disgraced by a past romantic interlude, was remade as the 1931 talkie three-reeler *Chickens Come Home*, with Oliver Hardy taking Finlayson's role (and Finlayson assuming the supporting role of Hardy's butler). Randy observes, "While the silent film emphasizes the situation—not to mention a lot of frantic running around—the talkie emphasizes how the characters respond to that situation."

Cameraman Alvin Wyckoff and director Eddie Sutherland film W.C. Fields (with a false mustache) in *It's the Old Army Game* (1926).

Hats Off (1927) was reworked as the three-reeler *The Music Box* (1932). Skretvedt notes, "In the silent, Stan and Ollie attempted to carry a bulky washing machine up a long, long flight of steps. In the talkie remake, the washing machine was replaced by a piano, possibly because its jangling discords were more suited to a sound film. We don't have *Hats Off* to make a precise comparison, but surviving stills and a cutting continuity indicate that the silent version ended with a 'reciprocal destruction' battle, with a crowd of people swarming onto the streets of Culver City and smashing each other's headgear. (This device would of course be used in many subsequent silent L&H films.) Conversely, *The Music Box* shows us what happens once Laurel & Hardy have actually gotten their charge up the steps.

"A scene where Ollie takes Stan to the dentist, shows him how easy the process is by sitting in the dental chair, and has his own tooth removed by mistake was introduced in the 1928 silent two reeler *Leave 'Em Laughing* and remade as part of the feature film *Pardon Us* (1931). Again, this is made richer and funnier simply through the addition of Stan and Ollie's voices.

"The scene with Stan and Ollie attempting to order sodas for themselves and two girls with only fifteen cents was introduced in the silent *Should Married Men Go Home* (1928). Being a dialogue-oriented sequence, it came off much better in the talking film *Men o' War*, made less than a year later in the spring of 1929."

Those are just a few prominent examples. Roach was absolutely right in thinking that audiences wouldn't mind seeing old routines and gags reused, especially if they were improved upon. And if a film wasn't reissued to theaters, moviegoers would need long memories to recall story lines they'd seen years before. Skretvedt writes, "The idea that a previous film was obsolete definitely prompted the making of *Block-Heads*, which was put into production in the spring of 1938 simply because Roach needed something, anything, to be filming in order to get some financing. Stan suggested a remake of the 1929 talkie *Unaccustomed As We Are* (as the title suggests, their first sound film), because it took place on one inexpensive set, and because it was not likely to be remembered by audiences."

Like Laurel and Hardy, W.C. Fields' screen character blossomed with the coming of sound. Not only did his unique nasal delivery of dialogue cement his persona, but he managed to take material that he'd developed for the stage—and used in some of his silent films—and elevate it to a new level of comedic success in talkies. One could catalogue all the Fields routines that recurred over the years, but several of his silent films were remade verbatim: *Sally of the Sawdust* (1925), based on his stage success *Poppy*, was filmed under that name in 1936. *So's Your Old Man* (1926) became *You're Telling Me* (1934). *It's the Old Army Game* (1926) was recycled in Fields' two-reel short *The Pharmacist* (1933) and then brought to fruition in his masterpiece *It's a Gift* (1934). "The Back Porch Sketch" that Fields introduced on Broadway in 1925 never failed to win big laughs in any of its incarnations, but its performance in *It's a Gift* with T. Roy Barnes as the man looking for Carl LaFong made it immortal.

Hal Roach's *Our Gang* series also successfully recycled silent-film plots and situations on a regular basis, but Richard Bann points out that director Robert McGowan was often restaging his own scenes and was able to get the most out of them.

Such was not the case with another Hal Roach star, Charley Chase, whose greatest silent short subjects were directed by Leo McCarey. The talkie versions of those films pale alongside the originals, not only because McCarey wasn't involved, but often because the reality of a talking world couldn't accommodate bizarre or surreal sight gags. The hilarious scene from *All Wet* (1924) in which Charley repairs his roadster in a watery ditch—apparently remaining under the surface for several minutes—was recreated to much lesser effect in 1933's *Fallen Arches*.

Perhaps the most appalling comedy comparison can be made by watching Harold Lloyd's silent classic *Safety Last* (1923) and its talkie remake, *Feet First* (1930). In the silent, Lloyd's daredevil antics while scaling a building still have modern-day audiences shrieking at one moment and laughing the next. But silence creates an unreality that provides a certain degree of safe distance for us, even as we feel ourselves responding to Harold's antics. Actually *hearing* him cry for help while stranded on a construction platform, inside a burlap sack, isn't funny at all.

In 1930, MGM became convinced that using a proven story was the best way to usher one of its biggest stars into the talkie era, settling on *The Unholy Three* (1925) as the perfect vehicle. The story deals with a trio of crooks. Lon Chaney is the mastermind, a carnival ventriloquist known as Professor Echo who disguises himself as a sweet little old lady; his accomplices are a midget (Harry Earles) who pretends to be a baby and a strongman (Ivan Linow). Because Chaney had to adopt the voices of a wisecracking ventriloquist dummy and a grandmotherly woman, the film would prove that "the man of a thousand faces" was equally skilled in the vocal department. (The same could not be said for the German-born Earles, who was virtually incomprehensible. The fact that the boom microphone was farther from his face than the other actors' probably didn't help.)

The studio had no compunction about selling audiences a movie they'd just seen five years earlier. After all, this would offer them an entirely new experience—with sound. The scenario itself was slavishly faithful to the original. When I interviewed Elliott Nugent, who adapted the screenplay with his father, J.C. Nugent, and also acted in the film, he recalled, "We were talking to Bernie Hyman, the producer, and he kept talking about 'in the

Warner Baxter and Lupe Velez in the 1931 version of *The Squaw Man.*

silent we did this, in the silent we did that.' So we had a Moviola put in our office, and we would run this silent. We wrote the screenplay with the same continuity—we even used some of the old printed titles for dialogue, filled them out a little." *The Unholy Three* was a solid box-office success but Chaney was robbed of an encore: he fell victim to lung cancer and died just one month after the picture's release in the summer of 1930.

At the same time, Cecil B. DeMille was at a career low point. He had moved to MGM and directed two splashy but unsuccessful early talkies, *Dynamite* (1929) and *Madam Satan* (1930). "Haunted by self-doubt and lack of inspiration," according to Robert S. Birchard, he returned once again to his first screen success, *The Squaw Man*. Trotting out an old warhorse of a story did nothing to renew his reputation with the public—or his new home studio. MGM was forced to buy the rights from Warner Bros., which had just acquired them from Paramount the year before. That, and the lofty salaries of his stars, Warner Baxter and Lupe Velez (neither of whom was an MGM contract player), made the film an expensive proposition. In fact, Birchard reports in *Cecil B. DeMille's Hollywood* that Nicholas Schenck, who ran MGM's parent company Loew's Inc., tried to shut down production when he saw the mounting tab but threw up his hands when it became clear that it would cost as much to abort as it would to complete.

Director Leo McCarey poses with ZaSu Pitts and Charles Laughton on the set of *Ruggles of Red Gap* (1935), one of several McCarey remakes.

Yet the talkie version of *The Squaw Man* is one of DeMille's most subdued and effective films. Baxter plays an Englishman who moves to Wyoming to escape dishonor, when in fact he is protecting someone else. There he incurs the wrath of a local despot and marries a timid Indian girl. The climactic dilemma involves him having to choose between the two lifestyles when he is given the opportunity to return home to England.

The Squaw Man unfolds at a leisurely pace, perfectly complemented by Harold Rosson's soft, beautiful cinematography of the Arizona locations, and the remarkable performance of Lupe Velez as the Indian girl. Her underplaying indicates that DeMille actually directed her instead of leaving her to her own devices. Mordaunt Hall offered a perfect summation of the film in *The New York Times* when he wrote, "The seams of age shine through; it is agreeable and expert melodrama." Bob Birchard agrees and says, "You can finally see what attracted DeMille to the property."

Film buffs tend to be dismissive of remakes, but it's useful to remember that some of the best-loved movies of the 1930s and early '40s fit that description. Leo McCarey's comedy gem *Ruggles of Red Gap* (1935) was the third go-round for that Harry Leon Wilson play, as was McCarey's sparkling production of *The Awful Truth* (1937), based on a play by Arthur Richman.

Claudette Colbert, deglamorized as a prison inmate in
Manslaughter (1930).

(Prints of the 1925 version with Agnes Ayres and Warner Baxter and the 1929 talkie with Ina Claire and Henry Daniell aren't known to exist.) Apparently, audiences and critics took such great films as *Holiday, The Letter, Waterloo Bridge, His Girl Friday* (the gender-bending remake of *The Front Page*), *The Four Feathers,* and *The Maltese Falcon* on their own terms and didn't judge them against the early talkies that preceded them—if they remembered the originals at all.

In fact, some of those original pre-Code pictures compare quite favorably to their more famous cousins. James Whale's *Waterloo Bridge* (1931) is more honest and raw than MGM's glossy remake, with a great performance by Mae Clarke as the chorus-girl-turned-prostitute; when Vivien Leigh played the character, she became a ballerina, and her extracurricular activities were soft-pedaled. Lewis Milestone's *The Front Page* (1931) is a visually innovative adaptation of the 1928 Ben Hecht-Charles MacArthur play with a terrific cast (even though Adolphe Menjou was a last-minute substitute for Louis Wolheim, the star of Milestone's *All Quiet on the Western Front,* who died during rehearsals for the newspaper film.) And the first adaptation of Dashiell Hammett's *The Maltese Falcon* (1931) follows the author's work pretty closely—just as John Huston did a decade later—except it's seedier.

While each generation seems to get its own versions of works by William Shakespeare, Jane Austen, Charles Dickens, and Mark Twain, the first half of the 20th century saw the creation of contemporary classics. Modern-day properties like *David Harum, Raffles,* and *Brewster's Millions* soon became evergreens, and popular stories by such writers as Zane Grey, Rex Beach, Harold Bell Wright, Harry Leon Wilson, and Edna Ferber underwent multiple screen adaptations. Other writers, little remembered today, wrote novels that Hollywood turned to time and again. John Fox, Jr.'s *The Trail of the Lonesome Pine* was filmed four times (1914, 1916, 1923, and 1936) and his *The Little Shepherd of Kingdom Come* had just as many screen incarnations. *Under Two Flags* by Ouida (Maria Louise Ramé) was made six times between 1912 (when two separate films hit the screen) and 1936; her other warhorse *A Dog of Flanders* racked up four movie versions. Rafael Sabatini's best-known novels—*Scaramouche, The Sea Hawk*, and *Captain Blood*—all became great hits in the 1920s and yielded equally successful remakes in the decades to follow—although Warners' 1940 version of *The Sea Hawk* with Errol Flynn used only the title; it had little to do with Sabatini's novel or the 1924 feature. Anthony Hope's *The Prisoner of Zenda* became a favorite movie property beginning in 1913. When Richard Thorpe directed his lavish version of the story in 1952, with Stewart Granger, he had a Moviola on the set at MGM and copied John Cromwell's 1937 film almost shot-for-shot. (The idea wasn't original: Cromwell did the same thing in 1938 when he made *Algiers*, the American version of Julien Duvivier's *Pepe Le Moko*.)

But one group of remakes is generally overlooked by film buffs and historians alike: the talkie versions of famous silent films.

Warner Bros. capitalized on the voice and presence of George Arliss with its all-talking 1929 remake of his 1921 success *Disraeli*. Something of a photographed stage play, the early talkie was still audience-proof and Arliss walked off with an Academy Award for his bravura performance as the cunning British prime minister. Then came *The Green Goddess*, apparently shot before *Disraeli* but (wisely) released after, a slavishly faithful remake of the fruity 1923 silent about a cultured but power-crazed rajah, played by Arliss in high-camp mode.

In contrast, Paramount's first sound remake was a complete reinvention of Cecil B. DeMille's silent hit *Manslaughter*. This 1930 film and *The Cheat*,

Irving Pichel fancies Tallulah Bankhead in *The Cheat* (1931).

released the following year, were among the ten features made by legendary Broadway director George Abbott, whose screen work awaits critical rediscovery. His Paramount films from 1929 to 1931 are a mixed lot but reveal an assurance in the technique of sound—and the handling of actors—that remains impressive today.

Manslaughter is the story of an irresponsible Long Island heiress who kills a motorcycle officer and pays the price with a prison term—prosecuted by the man who loves her. The DeMille silent, starring Leatrice Joy, is entertaining but absurd, and the scene depicting the accident is laughably artificial. Abbott wrote the screenplay for the remake, starring Claudette Colbert and Fredric March, who give strong, empathetic performances. The use of a moving camera and authentic, ambient sound (both indoors and out) is as innovative as anything by Rouben Mamoulian, whose pioneering talkie *Applause* had set a high-water mark the year before.

In his autobiography, *Mister Abbott* (Random House, 1963), the great man of the theater devotes little space to his brief film career but asserts, "*Manslaughter* is the best picture I made because it had the most believable story. Claudette Colbert and Fredric March were superb in the leading parts."

When the film was released, *Photoplay* magazine gave it a featured review and wrote, in its colloquial manner, "There may still exist some diehards who cling to the notion that talk has not improved the screen. This will cure them. Vocalized, 'Manslaughter' is so superior to the silent picture in which Leatrice Joy and Thomas Meighan played that it's unreasonable and unfair to compare the two. The Joy-Meighan stillie was a great film for its era. This new 'Manslaughter'...is one of the real achievements of the modern photoplay. It'll play hob with your emotions; it'll thrill you; it'll frighten you. And you'll walk out of the theater with the realization that this Colbert woman is a grand actress, and that movie-makers are really learning the value of repression in talking pictures. This is a picture to see."

Abbott also did well with another DeMille retread, the 1931 version of the 1915 shocker *The Cheat* (which was first remade in 1923), about a cultured Asian, played by Sessue Hayakawa, who "brands" his female conquests. Released on DVD in Universal's *Pre-Code Hollywood Collection*, the talkie is a surprisingly palatable melodrama, even though it changes the male character to a Caucasian (Irving Pichel) with a fetish for Orientalia. It also features one of Tallulah Bankhead's most effective screen performances. (Abbott directed her twice and recalled in his book, "Tallulah's conversation was rough—she liked to shock, and she seemed to want everybody to think the worst of her.... Once when the set was filled with extras waiting for the next shot, she came over and sat down in my lap and said, 'I hope they all think

Advertisement for the 1930 talkie remake of *Tol'able David* with Joan Peers and Richard Cromwell.

we're lovers.'")

Examining reviews of this and other films of the period, one thing seems clear: no one minded a talkie update of an old favorite if it was well done. If it wasn't, or if it seemed dated in any way, then the knives came out.

Virtually every review of Paramount's 1932 release *The Miracle Man*—and most of them were good—recalled the 1919 silent, which featured a tour-de-force, star-making performance by Lon Chaney as a man whose supposedly twisted body was "cured" by a faith healer. The studio sensibly made no attempt to hide the fact that this was a remake. Its advertising proclaimed, "The picture that swept the world—now an all-new, all-talking masterpiece!" That may be stretching the point, but it *is* a very good film that deserves to be better known. Sylvia Sidney and Chester Morris head the cast, with character actor John Wray as The Frog, the part played so memorably by Chaney. (No prints of the 1919 film are known to exist, but fortunately, Paramount excerpted its most potent scene in a one-reel short called *Movie Milestones* that has survived.)

In his notes for a 1962 screening, film historian William K. Everson acknowledged the picture's flaws but perceptively noted, "This *Miracle Man* is a sound and powerful picture. It is still close enough to the silent period to mix its religion and melodrama in that skillful, tasteful way that seemed such a part of the twenties. Its bizarre plot hasn't been altered, and it still shows its kinship to Tod Browning, *The Unholy Three* and *The White Tiger*. Further, there has been no move to update its mood, modernize the motivations or introduce too much logic. The faith-healing of the Miracle Man just has to be taken on trust, and the film never tries to sermonize or explain. Nor has the cynical con-man hero been made more 'acceptable' as happens in so

Rochelle Hudson was a last-minute fill-in as Henry Fonda's
leading lady in *Way Down East* (1935).

many remakes.... Last but not least, the limited but tremendously effective
use of background music is done in the richly emotional style of the scores
that so often accompanied silent films."

The 1921 silent *Tol'able David* made a star of Richard Barthelmess, in
the role of a backwoods boy who proves his manhood in a David-and-Goli-
ath-like fight with a large, loathsome villain. It also firmly established director Henry King, whose leisurely treatment of the pastoral story was exquisite
in every detail. Columbia knew the value of this property and hired A-list
screenwriter Benjamin Glazer (*Flesh and the Devil, 7th Heaven, Beggars of
Life*) to adapt the material for talkies. Director John Blystone was a seasoned
veteran, if not a top-rank director, but he knew how to get the most out of
the story and his cast. And the studio pinned great hopes on its fresh-faced
discovery Richard Cromwell. *Variety*'s Sid Silverman pooh-poohed their bal-
lyhoo for the untested actor and pronounced Joseph Hergesheimer's story
"outmoded," but he underestimated its elemental power. (He also confessed
at the end of his review, "Film got a bad break Friday when the sound went
dead for about 100 feet halfway and then had to fight a disconcerting buzz
the rest of the way.")

The New York Times reviewer wrote, "John Blystone has risen to the
occasion in his excellent direction of the talking picture of...*Tol'able David*,
for...[it] is as fine a screen work for these times as its mute predecessor was
for eight years ago. Moreover, the present version benefits in no small extent
by the power of speech, in that the action is carried on without the interrup-

tions occasioned by subtitles."

Photoplay, which spoke to—and fancied itself the voice of—the fans, was equally enthusiastic. "This is a pretty grand film, even in the light of its great silent version of a decade back. Young Richard Cromwell, newcomer, is no Barthelmess yet, but he has great moments as the beaten little hillbilly, and a fine performance is given by Joan Peers as the girl.... Excellently directed, and a thriller. Young Cromwell's a real comer."

A fluid and well-crafted film, *Tol'able David* was photographed by Teddy [later known as Ted] Tetzlaff and edited by Glen Wheeler; unlike some awkward early talkies, there are no stage waits between lines of dialogue or cutaway shots that are held too long. Cromwell acquits himself well, and Noah Beery echoes Ernest Torrence from the silent film with his brutish, unremitting cruelty. (It's nice to see silent veteran Henry B. Walthall in a supporting role and a young, gaunt Peter Richmond—who later called himself John Carradine—as Beery's brother.)

Tol'able David can't match the sheer physical beauty of the 1921 film and its tangible sense of place, achieved through the use of long, lingering shots of the countryside and its inhabitants. But in fairness, that treatment wouldn't have suited a 1930 picture.

Translating artful silent dramas for 1930s audiences now accustomed to the greater realism that sound brought to the screen was the challenge that faced Henry King when he was given the unenviable task of directing *Way Down East* and *7th Heaven*. *Way Down East* was based on a well-known, and well-worn, play that was first filmed in 1908, and again in 1914 before D.W. Griffith turned to it in 1920. William K. Everson once wrote, "Nobody could quite understand why Griffith had paid $175,000 for the rights to this hoary old tale, but as usual, the old maestro knew just what he was doing." With Lillian Gish as his heroine and a thrilling race-to-the-rescue climax on the ice floes—an addition of Griffith's own devising—the film was one of his greatest successes.

Henry King was now working for Fox Film Corporation, which had enjoyed great success by putting one of its most reliable box-office stars, Janet Gaynor, in remakes of such quaint Mary Pickford vehicles as *Daddy Long Legs* and *Tess of the Storm Country*. She had just completed *The Farmer Takes a Wife* with Hollywood newcomer Henry Fonda when she was cast in *Way Down East*, the tearful saga of small-town gossips, an unwed mother, and an unforgiving father. King took his cast to a northern California farming community to shoot most of his exterior footage. But during one scene Gaynor fell and hit her head, and when the troupe returned to Hollywood a doctor forbade her to work for months. King sought an ingénue who could match the second-unit footage he'd already shot and found her in Rochelle Hudson, but always bemoaned the loss of Gaynor. No doubt her radiant presence would have given the film an enormous boost. As it was, most critics found it hokey and outdated.

Yet the 1935 version of *Way Down East* has much to recommend it. The opening scenes capture the flavor of a small town where everybody knows everybody else's business, and the casting is right on target: Spring Byington as the hard-working farm wife, Russell Simpson as her judgmental husband, The Squire, Andy Devine as their goofy farmhand, Slim Summerville as the local constable who also runs the general store, and Margaret Hamilton as the local busybody. Henry Fonda is understated and sincere as Byington and Simpson's son, who yearns to leave farm life behind, and Hudson is quite capable as the young woman who hires on with the family. When they first meet he offers her a drink of water and they debate the relative merits of water sipped from a rusty tin can or from a gourd dipped into a well. Not many actors could bring the genuineness to such dialogue that these two do.

Howard Estabrook and William Hurlbut's screenplay emphasizes gentle humor and even humanizes the father character somewhat. To some critics' relief, the unwed-mother subplot was downplayed in this version of the story (although that may have been necessary to please the censors).

Where *Way Down East* fails is in its climax, a recreation of Griffith's ice-floe climax; ironically, the silent got it right and the more polished talkie dropped the ball. Henry King was never happy with it. In his oral history for the Directors Guild of America, published as *Henry King: From Silents to 'Scope*, he recalled, "We shot the film in the studio and then on the backlot at Fox, whereas Griffith had shot everything on location. Griffith had ice floes as big as a room floating down the Connecticut River, with Dick Barthelmess leaping from floe to floe, with his breath showing in the cold. I had Henry Fonda jumping from paraffin cake to paraffin cake and sweating like the devil. A picture like *Way Down East* should never have been started under those circumstances, never made on the backlot. It can't be done."

Yet King and his cinematographer, Ernest Palmer, achieved at least one moment of cinematic artistry—without showing off. As Fonda and Hudson race through the oat field, trying to corral the runaway colt, the camera moves along with them, waist-high in the grain. After they collapse on the ground to catch their breath, we continue to see them through stalks of waving hay. It's a striking and unforgettable moment.

(Two footnotes: when Margaret Hamilton walks purposefully toward the farmhouse to deliver some malicious gossip, accompanied by a notable strain of music, one can't help note the uncanny resemblance to her bicycle-riding moment—with that unforgettable Herbert Stothart music cue—four years later in *The Wizard of Oz*. Also worth noting: one year later

Spring Byington, so perfect here as the homespun mother, played a small-town town gossip—not unlike Hamilton—in *Theodora Goes Wild*.)

If *Way Down East* was a challenge for director King, his 1937 remake of Fox's beloved hit *7th Heaven* was doomed from the start. [The silent film used the numeral *7th* while the talkie spelled out the word.] A decade earlier the romantic drama, directed by Frank Borzage, starring Janet Gaynor and Charles Farrell, had been a sensation, and a multiple Academy Award winner. Darryl F. Zanuck saw the property as an ideal vehicle for his newly-contracted French import, Simone Simon, but according to notes on a story meeting on November 6, 1936, "Mr. Zanuck reminded everyone of the fact that we were in a very difficult spot following the memory of the silent version...."

Victor Kilian, Mady Christians, James Stewart, and Simone Simon as Parisians in *Seventh Heaven* (1937).

James Stewart was not yet a major star; he had made his screen debut in 1935 and was on the rise after a careful build-up by MGM. Why anyone thought it was a good idea to cast this quintessentially American actor as a Frenchman—especially opposite a genuine French actress—is impossible to say. But he gives it his all, as he always did, and his Chico—who by his own frequent admission is "a very remarkable fellow," is not easily dismissed.

The film starts off well enough, and Simon is an appropriately winsome waif, but at a certain point it begins to lumber, burdened by its obvious indoor sets and a surfeit of talk. What's missing is the lyricism, the cinematic poetry, of Borzage's lushly romantic silent—something talkies could not easily provide, at least in a mainstream Hollywood production. As Henry King told Tom Stempel in a 1971 oral history for the AFI, "It was just one of those things that didn't seem to lend itself to sound."

Decades later, Simone Simon recalled the unhappy production for Stewart biographer Gary Fishgall and praised her co-star as "a very conscientious actor. He spent the whole day long rehearsing his lines, going up and down the stairs. He had a lot of lines to say. [But] there was no contact between him and me. There was no contact between anybody during that picture."

In 1937 reviews, and in most biographies and career surveys written since, it has been the consensus that Stewart was miscast as the cocky French sewer-rat-turned-street-cleaner Chico. Having just revisited the film, I beg to differ: I think his bold, completely committed performance gives the movie its only value.

Yet even failures like *Seventh Heaven* didn't deter the studios from scheduling more remakes: in 1939 Paramount set out to create a replica of its 1926 smash *Beau Geste*, but it too was merely a shadow of the original.

Even with William Wellman calling the shots, it lacked the mystique that only the unreality of a silent film could offer—an ethereal quality that made scenes in the original unforgettable. Zanuck fared considerably better with his re-dos of Douglas Fairbanks' *The Mark of Zorro* in 1940 and Rudolph Valentino's *Blood and Sand* in 1941, as vehicles for his top male star, Tyrone Power.

But the riskiest remake of all was made thousands of miles from Hollywood, at London's Twickenham Studios in 1935. Producer Jules Hagen purchased the rights to *Broken Blossoms,* a delicate story of goodness and evil based on Thomas Burke's 1917 novel *The Chink and the Child.* The well-remembered 1919 silent starring Richard Barthelmess and Lillian Gish was one of D.W. Griffith's greatest successes, and Hagen was thrilled when the Grand Old Man agreed to direct it himself. The studio hired Welsh actor-playwright Emlyn Williams, whose play *Night Must Fall* was a great success on the London stage, to craft a new screenplay and play the "Chinaman."

But Griffith was in no condition to make this film, physically or emotionally, and his stay in London was tumultuous. Accounts of the debacle vary in detail, but there is no question that he was the architect of his own downfall. According to Robert M. Henderson in *D.W. Griffith, His Life and*

Work (Oxford University Press, 1972), "He arrived on the S.S. *Acquitania* in late May, 1935, full of anticipation and bourbon. Griffith loved England... but...somehow the casting of British players grated on [his] nerves. He grew increasingly irritable. Suddenly he called Lillian Gish at three in the morning New York time, and asked her, somewhat incoherently, to come to London to play the role of Lucy. Lillian, failing to understand the true nature of Griffith's position, suggested that he make some other film and not repeat himself. Griffith asked, pleaded and begged that she come to play the part, and then, without warning, hung up."

The film's leading lady, German film star Dolly Haas, recalled in a 1971 interview with Kevin Brownlow, "Before we started to shoot, I was shown the [original] movie and I felt 'My God, it's so perfect, why, why make it again? How can anyone equal it? Particularly myself—how can I in any way approach what Lillian Gish did?' I brought this to the attention of the people involved and they said, 'But don't you understand? We live in different times now. We have sound, people can talk and films have changed.' My image of the film remains with me always as being one of the great, unforgettable images that this great director could create without sound."

Griffith told her she would have to lighten her red hair, and took her to the area of London where *Broken Blossoms* was set. "We went to Limehouse and I will never forget how he was actually turning into an actor because he said to me 'Now you catch my arm, now you put your hand under my arm.' I didn't ask any questions...." (A dialect coach was hired to help Haas shed some of her German accent and sound as if she belonged in Limehouse or Whitechapel. Ironically, the same woman coached another German transplant, Elisabeth Bergner—and the two actresses sound remarkably alike in their British films.)

Haas enjoyed working with Griffith and warmed to the assignment. "I did fall in love with the part and I asked if it is possible to maybe go back to Limehouse and maybe meet a child that could inspire me and I did. I was lucky enough to be taken and this amazing child I found is very much part of my portrayal of Lucy. She was an exquisite child, she was very religious and she took a liking to me and gave me her most prized possession, a lovely little image of St Francis."

Midway through his stay in London, Griffith was introduced to a French girl named Ariane Borg and decided that *she* should play Lucy. "In a dramatic effort to convince Hagen that his new find should have the part, Griffith had rehearsed the beautiful but inexperienced Miss Borg in a scene from the film, and then staged a reading for Hagen in which he played Battling Burrows himself. The scene was the violent one in which Burrows discovers his daughter in the young Chinese boy's room and beats her unmercifully. Griffith put everything he could into the scene, and the reaction of Hagen was one of shock. He was convinced that Griffith had lost control completely. The scene had an additional and unexpected climax with the appearance of Miss Haas [at the reading]. The producers then terminated the agreement with Griffith as quickly as they could."

To direct, they turned to a German émigré with years of experience in the theater, Hans Brahm. In 1987, film historian Kevin Brownlow talked to another of the film's participants, Bernard Vorhaus, later to become a prolific director himself. "I didn't think the film should be redone," Vorhaus said. "Julius Hagen offered it to Brahm. In two weeks, we were way behind schedule. Hagen wanted to fire Brahm. He came to me and I said I would take over [but] I wouldn't dismiss a refugee from Hitler. 'Let me function as Associate Producer'. [Editor] Jack Harris was worried that some scenes wouldn't cut. I'd ensure it would cut together and would come in on schedule. The concept was all wrong…. Emlyn Williams just looked like a Welshman with mud on his face."

Given this turbulent history, it may be surprising to some that the 1936 film turned out as well as it did. One must be willing to accept the idea of this unabashed melodrama brought to life anew with Welshman Williams as its Asian hero. The obvious use of miniatures during the opening scenes, set in China, is quaint. But Dolly Haas is believable as the wide-eyed, simple-minded heroine of the tale who is abused both verbally and physically by her no-account father, a drunken boxer (Arthur Margetson). The depiction of Limehouse and its denizens is colorful and vivid.

Producer Jules Hagen must have been relieved to rescue the film in any form after its troubled start. Its main title declares that it is based on "D.W. Griffith's masterpiece," but that didn't soften critics or audiences' response. It was not well received.

The movie's aftermath is even more interesting than the film itself: Hans Brahm married his leading lady, Dolly Haas, came to Hollywood, and launched a long, successful directing career as John Brahm. Brahm and Haas divorced in 1941; she later moved to New York and married famed caricaturist Al Hirschfeld. However, she made one more film in England before departing for America, *Spy of Napoleon* (1936). Her leading man—you couldn't make this up—was Richard Barthelmess.

One can't help but wonder if they ever discussed *Broken Blossoms*…or the challenge of trying to remake beloved silent films.

EARLY
INTERVIEWS

Introduction:

SEEING STARS

It's one thing to set yourself up as a publisher at the age of 15. It's another matter to persuade someone—anyone—that it's worth their time to grant you an interview.

I started writing fan letters to people I admired when I was 12 and got some wonderful, meaningful replies. Landing a face-to-face interview didn't occur to me as a possibility until I took over *Film Fan Monthly* three years later. While attending a Wednesday matinée performance of *The Odd Couple* on Broadway I read the *Playbill* biography of co-star Eddie Bracken during intermission. It claimed that he appeared in *Our Gang* comedies when he was a boy. I hadn't known this, and it inspired me to wait at the stage door after the performance, hoping I could catch the actor's attention when he left. Eventually the stage doorman took note of me. I told him what I wanted and he said he'd pass word along to Mr. Bracken. A short time later he returned and said that the star would be happy to grant me an interview if I came back after the Saturday matinée that weekend.

In those pre-Internet, pre-home video, pre-IMDb days it wasn't possible to do much homework before our meeting, but I did the best I could. Bracken couldn't have been more gracious; he spun some stories for me about his career, but I was ill-prepared to ask the right things and didn't know how to pose a follow-up question. He did set the record straight about *Our Gang*, explaining that he was in a rival series called *The Kiddie Troupers*. Then he offered another dubious claim, that he created Francis the Talking Mule! (This didn't sound kosher somehow, but I wasn't going to call him a liar!) I don't remember how long we spoke, but I came away with a taped conversation that was just long enough—and marginally good enough—to publish.

There is a good reason I haven't included that piece in this collection. It doesn't amount to much, but it was a baby step in my budding career as an interviewer.

It wasn't the last time I waited at a stage door, but I soon discovered other ways of contacting famous people: the Manhattan phone directory proved to be a gold mine, as did a periodical I found at my local public library called *Current Biography.* It provided contact information for its subjects, if not their actual home addresses. I quickly learned that agents earned nothing for setting up an interview while business managers (and, even better, publicists) were often helpful.

Since I printed book reviews in *FFM* I had no qualms about calling publicity departments of publishing houses in New York and presenting myself as a legitimate outlet for author interviews. That's how I landed my next subject, and a great one: Anita Loos. Having read her memoir *A Girl Like I,* I felt much better prepared, and she answered my questions in a charming, straightforward manner. This felt like a victory to my 16-year-old self.

When I made my first two trips to Hollywood, in my late teens, I had but one ace up my sleeve: a friendly publicist at the ABC television network named Vic Ghidalia. We had met at a gathering of the Laurel and Hardy organization, Sons of the Desert, and he offered to help me during my California sojourns. The hitch was that he wouldn't know the availability of actors appearing in ABC shows until the day before—or the day of—their employment. That proved to be a formidable challenge since I was dependent on pay telephones (and good timing) as well as friends with cars to shuttle me around. Somehow it all came together.

Technology has transformed our lives so completely that my experiences seem strange and remote, from another planet if not another era. How much simpler it would have been to check the Internet for a list of Henry Wilcoxon's credits at the last minute. How nice it would have been to have a mobile phone instead of having to repeatedly put coins into a pay telephone, only to learn that the person I needed was away from the office—and I couldn't leave a return number to reach me.

Yet I wouldn't trade those experiences for anything, at least from this distant vantage point. They gave me confidence and taught me humility. I think these interviews are still worth reading and hope you will agree.

Conversations:
ANITA LOOS

When I read Anita Loos' charming autobiography *A Girl Like I* (1966), I fell under her spell. A query to her publisher led to an appointment with the legendary writer in her elegant apartment on West 57th Street in Manhattan. I was a young, inexperienced interviewer, so it was a blessing to talk to someone who was so forthcoming and articulate. When I transcribed the recording of our conversation I realized that she spoke in complete sentences—and even perfect paragraphs. I've never had that experience since. Loos went on to write other books, including one about the Talmadge Sisters and another (*Twice Over Lightly: New York Then and Now*) in collaboration with her friend Helen Hayes. She lived to be 92. (Interview originally appeared in March 1967.)

LM: How long were you working on your autobiography?

AL: Oh, I worked on it for about two years. Not consistently, but off and on because in the midst of it I had a play running in London.

LM: Was writing the book an enjoyable task?

AL: Yes it was. I love to write anyway. I look on writing much as crossword puzzles or something of that kind.

LM: You worked at MGM for a while, didn't you?

AL: I worked there for 18 years, and I had a long, long stretch of writing for

Clark Gable, Jean Harlow, Joan Crawford, and a great many of the film stars of those days.

LM: What did you think of Louis B. Mayer?

AL: Well, he wasn't one of my favorite men, although I must say I never had any trouble with him myself. But I was strongly attached to Irving Thalberg, and Mayer persecuted him no end. It was a pretty sordid story.

Clark Gable and Jeanette MacDonald in *San Francisco.*

LM: Did you write stories or screenplays?

AL: I wrote screenplays mostly, from other people's books. I wrote two originals while I was there. I wrote *San Francisco* for Clark Gable and Jeanette MacDonald. You may have seen it because it's on the late-late show about every two months. That was an original. Another one I wrote for Jean Harlow was original. I adapted *The Women*, Clare Luce's play, for the movies. I did so many screenplays in 18 years I can't even remember all of them.

LM: Did you write screenplays with certain stars in mind?

AL: Generally, yes, at MGM we had a star in mind. Although the first job I did for MGM was a book called *Red-Headed Woman*, and I wrote the screenplay and then we found the star for it, who was Jean Harlow. Toward the latter part of my time there I got into the way of being a film doctor, so every film that had some problem in it was handed over to me. I was working on two or three films at the same time. That sort of career, I must say, I had enough of. I was never handed a play to do unless there was something radically wrong with it.

LM: Working as a film doctor, were you on the set a lot?

AL: Yes, I was often on the set. There were even cases where I did some directing. I remember when we did *Red-Headed Woman*, there was a unit going down to the pier at Santa Monica, taking a short scene with Jean Harlow, and the director was busy at the studio, so I went down and directed the scene.

LM: What was Clark Gable like?

AL: Clark was a real man's man. He was never happier than he was when he was out in the woods with a sleeping bag, hunting or sleeping out. His entire interests were all in sports and real male occupations. He was genial; he didn't have a sense of humor, he had a sense of fun. I would say he was about the most 100-percent male I ever knew.

LM: Did he enjoy working?

AL: He must have enjoyed working because he had enormous ambition, and when I first met him at MGM he was just starting, and he really wanted to make a career of acting; but he wasn't like an actor some way. He wasn't a show-off in any way. He preferred to be out of the limelight when he wasn't working. When he'd finish a picture he would go off into the woods somewhere, or down on his ranch, later on, and he'd live the life of a rancher.

LM: Do you have a favorite film from all those you worked on?

AL: I think I liked *San Francisco* the best. I am a San Franciscan and I wrote the film because I adored San Francisco. I had more fun writing it because there was a group of San Franciscans at MGM, and we all got together and sort of had a jam session on the subject of San Francisco. The composer Nacio Herb Brown was a San Franciscan and he wrote many of the songs in the film. Although the theme song "San Francisco," which is now used there as a theme song, was written by a young Yugoslavian composer who just arrived, and he hardly spoke English. It was Bronislau Kaper, who wrote the songs for *Lili*, and a great many more fine songs.

LM: There has been a lot written about Jean Harlow...

AL: Most of it completely untrue, and I go out of my way always to defend her because I knew her as well as anybody could know someone who worked constantly day after day with her, and her whole public image is completely wrong. In the first place she came from a very, very prosperous family in the Middle West, and she was sent to one of the best girls' schools in the Middle West. She was well educated; she wasn't a cultured girl because she wasn't interested in that sort of thing. Many of those film girls who rose from nothing had a vulgar intonation in their way of speaking and she didn't. She always spoke with the cultured accents of a lady. A perfectly scurrilous book came out in which she spoke like she came out of the gutter. All of that was untrue, all of her life she was a victim of her own appearance. She was a terribly nice girl. I adored her.

LM: Did you enjoy working more on sound films than on silents?

AL: Yes, I think so, because it was writing dialogue, which up to that point I had to write as subtitles. Actually my specialty is dialogue, not action.

LM: Is it true that most early films were improvised?

AL: Yes it is. As a matter of fact, the films were practically composed on the set. D. W. [Griffith] would take the bare scenario and work with it. Now this is done in Italy, where they have practically gone back to the methods of the early days of movies.

LM: When you subtitled *Intolerance*, did you know what D. W. Griffith's conception was?

AL: I didn't know what it was about. When I saw it, it startled me. I was terribly confused by it. I must have run it 50 times while I was writing the titles. By the time I finished the titles, I had a feeling of what he was trying to do. When it was completed, I had a great admiration for him.

LM: Do you see many new movies?

AL: I see all the foreign movies. I don't look at the Hollywood movies, not even the ones they make in Europe.

LM: What do you think about censorship?

AL: Censorship doesn't exist anymore. When you go to see an Andy Warhol movie shown in a public theater, you get a feeling that there's no such thing as censorship.

LM: What was it like when the production code came into being?

AL: I was partly responsible for bringing on censorship, because of a film I wrote for Jean Harlow. It was not any particular scene that the censors objected to. It was the fact that a naughty girl came out victoriously at the end of the picture. It was not that the picture was risqué in any way, it was just that a bad girl made good. Sometimes you had to be clever to get your point over, with censorship, so it made an improvement in the films. I know in one case it vastly improved a picture. It

Anita Loos is flanked by Douglas Fairbanks and her husband, John Emerson.

was *San Francisco*, and there was a scene where Clark Gable hauled off and socked a priest, played by Spencer Tracy. The Johnson Office said you cannot have Clark Gable sock a priest, it's unthinkable. So I went away and got to pondering about how I could fix the scene. So I figured out that we would prove at the beginning that the priest could floor Gable any time he wanted to. He was a much cleverer boxer than Gable. That proved that when Clark hit him, he could have killed Clark but he didn't do it, which made his character stronger as a priest, and it was accepted by the censor. In order to prove this situation I opened the picture with a scene of two men boxing and you saw Spencer Tracy sock Gable and knock him out. And then when they got dressed you saw that one of them was a priest. That scene wouldn't have been if I hadn't had to outsmart the censor.

LM: You knew Erich von Stroheim. What was he like?

AL: Naturally he was tremendously bawdy, raucous, witty, and with a colossal sense of humor, terribly good company, and just a terribly interesting man. He was well-read, he had lived all over the world. I met him at the time he got the first job he ever had in Hollywood. He got a

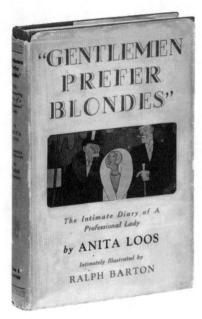

The original edition of *Gentlemen Prefer Blondes* from 1925.

job in a film that my husband [John Emerson] was directing.

LM: Did he write those Prussian roles for his own amusement?

AL: Yes. He adored to be wicked. He adored to be the man you love to hate. And basically he was the most kind, generous, and even-tempered man, but he loved to put on that Prussian exterior and frighten people. As a director he was so obsessed with perfection, with getting everything right that money didn't mean anything to him. He spent twice as much on a film as any other director. He shot miles of film he couldn't use. That was his downfall in Hollywood.

LM: Which version of *Gentlemen Prefer Blondes* do you like best?

AL: I think I liked the latest one, the one written by Charlie Lederer, with Marilyn Monroe. The first one was shot completely silent except for one scene, in which there was sound. Ruth Taylor was chosen as Lorelei for her physical appearance; she looked the part. Marilyn was absolutely perfect in the part, but Carol Channing (who did it on the stage) was a caricature, and she was funnier. Marilyn was exactly as she would have been in life; Carol Channing was far out. I liked Carol better because she was funnier.

LM: I think we've covered just about everything.

AL: My book only goes to 1926 and most of my career has been since 1928, but that's another story. I'll have to pick it up where I left off.

Conversations:
BURGESS MEREDITH

A letter to Burgess Meredith's business manager prompted a warm written reply inviting me to visit him at High Tor, his home in Pomona, New York, named after a play by Maxwell Anderson. I had done my homework and had plenty of questions to ask about specific films, but he was one of those cherished subjects who didn't need much prompting. Although he considered himself a man of the theater, he had a rich film career and was candid about taking commercial gigs in order to subsidize less profitable ventures. When we spoke he was about to direct a production of a new Paddy Chayefsky play, *The Latent Heterosexual*. My father drove me to Pomona for this conversation and took a picture of me with my host in front of an Alexander Calder mobile that held a prominent place in his living room. Some 25 years later I got to interview Meredith for *Entertainment Tonight* at his home in Malibu, California, where we posed in front of the same mobile! (Interview originally appeared in February 1968.)

LM: Didn't you begin as a singer?

BM: Yes, I was a boy soprano, and when I was very little, I think about seven or eight, I won an award for the leading voice of the whole Midwest.

LM: How did that interest change to acting?

BM: It didn't particularly. I didn't particularly get intrigued by acting, but I realized I was rather good at it, as I always took the lead in the play they had at school, in the four years I was there as choirboy. I really didn't have any long desires for the theater…it rather happened, because nothing else happened.

LM: You studied with Eva LeGallienne?

BM: I began with her.

LM: Was that your first professional work?

BM: Yes, but it was scarcely professional. I was an apprentice with her, and then she took a thing called *Alice in Wonderland* uptown to the New Amsterdam theater, and I played the Duck, and the Dormouse and Tweedledee, in my rather exalted entrance into the theater, in the production in 1933. At the same time I made application for a Broadway show called *Little Old Boy*, and that was my first show on Broadway where it was a smashing hit; as a teenager I made this big hit as a reform school kid, and left Eva LeGallienne. And from then on, it was pretty easy sailing.

LM: Your first film was *Winterset*. What did you think of it?

BM: I thought it had its qualities. It was not a brilliant sort of theme film, like *Of Mice and Men*, which will last and never grow old. I think there's something about *Winterset*, not necessarily the acting, which was pretty realistic, but something about the way it was put together that seems to have molded somewhat, so that it doesn't last quite as well.

Burgess Meredith in *Winterset* with Margo and Willard Robertson.

LM: Did you find it an advantage working with the same people with whom you did the play on Broadway?

BM: Yes, we had worked together for a year and a half, which made it a little easier to overcome the obstacles which the movies put up particularly then. [Eduardo] Ciannelli, Margo, and myself had been in New York and the road productions. We shot this at a time when the sound people were very despotic, and they would never accept anything that wasn't perfect sound, and they had a kind of cabalistic hold over everything. Everybody was afraid of the sound people for many years. I mention that because we had a scene to shoot in the rain, and the rain caused the sound people to rush out and say the sound wasn't right, and they tyrannized us terribly while making *Winterset*. It was very hard to sustain a performance because of the tyranny placed upon us. It would be awful if you turned your back or if you had any nuance in your voice; they

With Ann Sothern in *There Goes the Groom.*

claimed it wouldn't be recorded and they were determined that any fading would be impossible to immortalize. I don't think I could have done the performance if I hadn't had the background of playing it in the theater before; I was able to do it under any circumstances, or we were. The fact is that looking back they were good performances, as I remember—I haven't seen the film in 10 years—but to my satisfaction it hadn't aged, it was very modern acting.

LM: At that point, were you content to stay in Hollywood, or did you return to the stage?

BM: Oh no, at that point I was most discontented to stay in Hollywood. I went right back and did another play. I never did sign a contract with any one picture studio, and I was offered a few contracts, although they didn't quite know what to do with me; I was not the typical leading man. I did *Winterset* and got away with it pretty well, but in spite of that I didn't get many good parts offered me after that.

LM: You did something called *There Goes the Groom*.

BM: Oh yes, that was the second thing I did. I couldn't believe it. But I did have one obligation to RKO for doing *Winterset*, and when they gave me that *There Goes the Groom*, I said to the man—the oaf that was running the studio at that time—I told him the part was a big football player, someone like Joel McCrea, for instance, and the man stood up and said, "If it's good enough for Joel McCrea, it's good enough for you," which didn't seem to me to be the point. And so I did *There Goes the Groom*, I remember, in great pain I did that, and I would hate to look at it today.

LM: Then there was something called *Spring Madness*.

BM: Well, *Spring Madness* I wanted to do; that was an MGM picture and it had run on Broadway, and the part that I played was done on Broadway by Dickie Whorf. When they offered me the part I was very delighted to do it. I don't know what that turned out to be, except that it caused a great many people to comment that they liked it. It had a line in it, "When rape is inevitable, relax and enjoy it," and in the film we said, "When defeat is inevitable, relax and enjoy it," but it was done in such a way that people got the allusion.

LM: Next you played with Clark Gable in *Idiot's Delight*. What kind of feeling was there on the set of a film with so many "important" stars?

BM: I know one thing, that there was a great caste system. I would say that it was pretty much you were put in your proper cubbyhole, as to whether you were making $100,000 or 25. Although they still do it out there, Hollywood can't get over it. You see it even in dressing rooms; the dressing rooms get smaller and smaller, with a big one for the star.

LM: Where did you fit in at the time?

BM: Well, I was kind of a maverick; they knew that I didn't like Hollywood, and it wasn't as popular not to like Hollywood then as it is now, and they knew I was a stage actor. I didn't have much of a dressing room, but I was certainly taken in by the leading actors. I actually went out with Norma Shearer. Her husband, Thalberg, had just died a year or two before, and she had never gone out before; so I went out with her, and I remember that David Selznick years later told me that they were

With Lon Chaney, Jr., in *Of Mice and Men*.

very disturbed about that. They knew I was a very disreputable fellow in some ways, and to have the great Queen going out with somebody like myself in a wolf pack didn't seem the right way to treat her. She laughed about it—she is quite a nice woman, and we remained friends for many years. Clark was very nice; I got to know him. We were never friends, but we were always glad to see each other. The aura was that they were big, towering stars we have never seen before or since, and in that sense they made them live up to that. They were certainly kept in great stellar positions, but when you got to know them, they were kind of nice, slightly frightened people.

LM: Your next film, then, *Of Mice and Men*, was a change of pace?

BM: Yes, well it was a better part. I hadn't been offered anything quite that good since *Winterset*. I was very lucky to get that. We did this in the Hal Roach studio, and it was very much an independent production, with Lewis Milestone, who was a very nice and a very lovely, sensitive man, my friend to this day, in charge. Steinbeck was around, too. This particular production was very much on its own; there were no glowering and all-powerful producers over us.

LM: That was a better atmosphere for making a film?

BM: It always is. You've got to leave it to the artist to make the great films. It's never done much, but it should be.

LM: I think *Of Mice and Men* is extremely well done.

BM: Yes, it holds up beautifully.

LM: Do you have one film which gave you the most satisfaction?

BM: No, not really. At times I feel that *Diary of a Chambermaid* was an underestimated film in this country. Jean Renoir directed that. I thought it was a much better film than anybody had any idea of, but for some reason they didn't grasp the notion; then it became a classic, a minor classic, later. It was always appreciated in France, very much so. It was one of my favorites. I think that, and if *Man in the Eiffel Tower* had been cut properly, it would have been a favorite; it heralded an all-new type of picture making. I directed that; and nobody had ever done a single color before that; it was the first time we used a single-color process, or any picture did. That was Ansco color.

LM: Did you want to direct more films?

BM: Yes, I'd like to have directed more films. I didn't quite get around to making the switch successfully in films, as much as I did in the theater, where I did a lot of directing.

LM: You had to direct yourself in *Eiffel Tower*. Did that pose any problems?

BM: Well, that wasn't a problem; I didn't have much of a part. [Charles] Laughton would help me—stand behind the camera for my scenes.

LM: How did you find working with him?

BM: I had a very enthusiastic reception from him as a director, and we had great rapport; we were great friends. We were both startled by the way it was finally cut—it got completely out of our hands. It was an independent production; Franchot Tone put up most of the money for it.

LM: You also produced a few films; what kind of duties did you have?

BM: Well, there was a man out there, Ben Bogeaus, and he was a free-swinging independent producer; he liked me and liked my ideas, and he asked me to produce. I brought two general ideas to him which he bought. One was *Diary of a Chambermaid*, which I also wrote, and the other one was a thing which was torturously called *On Our Merry Way*, but its first title was *A Miracle Can Happen*. When I left to do a film in England called *Mine Own Executioner*, for some reason Bogeaus was persuaded by United Artists to rip out the Laughton sequence in which he read the Bible—one of the most beautiful sequences I've ever seen—because the United Artists people said it was too serious and that Charles Laughton was box-office poison. They went through a lot of rare diseases out there. They ripped that out and I went to David Selznick

With Kieron Moore in *Mine Own Executioner*.

as soon as I could get back, because I had no real power as a producer, and asked him to look at it. He looked at it, and he thought the only good sequence was the Laughton sequence. He offered them a million dollars to sell him the picture as it was, which would give them a slight profit, I think, and a percentage, if they would allow him to redo the rest of the film and keep the sequence in that they were going to throw out. They thought they were going to make a fortune out of the thing; it had all these big names, and they refused it. But it does have in it a kind of a classic—if the Laughton sequence was in it, it would have two classic sequences. The first classic was the segment with Fonda and Jimmy Stewart as musicians. That was written, although it isn't generally known, by John O'Hara. As for the Laughton sequence, it's been offered two or three times, and a lot of money, to show it, but it's so tied up, nobody can get it out.

LM: You worked with a man who is acknowledged to be one of the finest directors of all time, Ernst Lubitsch.

BM: Yes, that was a fine experience, and a haunting experience; today, I think it's haunting because I remember him so much from that time, and I don't know when I had a better time in my whole career than during that period. He and I were very close and we had a fine time together. He was an extraordinary director. He'd act everything out for you, at least he did for me, because he loved the part, and he'd act it out so funny, and so definitely, that I would stand there as an audience. The reason that it didn't bother me (as it might bother me, I should say, because sometimes when somebody acts out a thing for you it's almost impossible for you to reproduce it). He would act it out in such a way, and so hilariously, that he would give you the idea of what he wanted without expecting you to do it, because first of all he had a horrendous accent, and he would stop in the middle of when he was acting my lines and make some crack about my brother, who I was having trouble with then, or some purely personal thing which in some psychic way he knew I was undergoing. He was a very psychic man—and I would fall down laughing because right away he'd improvise in the middle of a scene he was doing for me some very personal thing about my life, with his big cigar in his mouth, and he knew I'd come over and say, "How did you know about that?" and he'd say, "I have ways of knowing." He wasn't well long after that, and didn't do much, but he always wanted to work again with me.

LM: Right after that you did something with Garson Kanin.

BM: Yes, Garson Kanin was my understudy in *Little Old Boy*; he was about my age, and as he zoomed up into the top ranks as a director, he called on me to do *Tom, Dick, and Harry*.

LM: I've heard that he kept the ending of the film a secret from the cast. Is that true?

BM: Absolutely true. Now, I don't know whether he kept it a secret or whether he just waited to see what would be the best ending—which of the three of us would get the girl—because it was absolutely unknown to any of us who would get her, and I think to Gar, although he rather

106

tended towards my getting her, because he was more enamored of this free-wheeling type of character. As a person he was quite a bohemian young man, Garson was. He was very much in control of the whole situation, and I remember during one long love scene with [Ginger] Rogers, as he put it, the scene was all right but there was something wrong with it, namely, I was asleep. I just hadn't woken up yet; it was early in the morning, so he had a man come and blow a huge gun off in the back of my head. I jumped about 20 feet, and then, as he put it, the scene went very well from then on.

LM: Around that time you went into the Army.

BM: Yes, we all went into the Army. I was in the Army, in the Air Force.

LM: You produced some Army films, too, didn't you?

BM: One of those is very much a classic, one I directed. The second one I produced, wrote, directed, and acted in entirely myself, because the British government invited me back to do that, *The Yank Comes Back*. That wasn't quite the success because it didn't have the meaning the first one had. The first one was called *Welcome to Britain*, and its function was about as important a function as you could ever have. It was described to me by a general, General Lee, and he said, "I want you to make a film telling the men how to behave here in England. These are lovely people here, and they don't have much. When the men come in here, they're guests in this island, and they've got to behave as guests. We're allies and we're not conquering them. And at

Ernie Pyle and Burgess Meredith.

the same time it's different from the place they're used to. Saloons aren't saloons here, they're clubs." He said, "I want you to do this film and I've got to have it out of here in two months." Well, I said, I can't do

107

With Doro Merande and Diahann Carroll in *Hurry Sundown*.

it, but I'll do it as fast as I can. I also said, I want to ask you a favor. If I do this film, will you make the same speech at the beginning of the film that you just made to me? He agreed to it; of course he was a little stiff in doing it in front of a camera, but as Dudley Nichols put it, this was a very big step forward in cutting. It formed a whole new type of film, a new technique which I developed there. It had to do with the fact that as soon as the general on film got through talking to me, I turned to the camera and said, "I don't know why he asked me to do this; I've only been here two weeks." Right away that got the GIs, they thought that was very funny, that I was one of them, and then I said, "Come on, let's go over and have a drink." The camera would start to follow me; the camera became an actor. As I started to go into the pub, I stopped and I looked at the camera and said, "Look, before we go in there, don't expect the beer to be cold. They don't like it cold, and noth-ing you can say can get it to be cold. You'll get to like it." So then we'd go in, and every once in a while I'd stop and talk to the camera, which afterwards was done a great deal; people absolutely accepted this as a technique that had been used, because it was so natural, and it really hadn't. It's shown to this very day often at The Museum of Modern Art. It's Jock Whitney's favorite film because he, at that time, was in charge of personal relations for the 8th Air Force. He helped me get some of the equipment together, and he always loved that film, as many people did, and which Robert Sherwood called the most effective orientation film ever made in the war, and Hemingway called it that.

Then I did a third one called *Salute to France*. That was one in which I brought a lot of talent; it was done in secret, allegedly. I produced it, and got Jean Renoir and Garson Kanin, and I would contact all the underground in France and see what kind of a film they wanted. *Salute to France* was the result of the fantastic success of *Welcome to Britain*, which was successful with the soldiers, because it made them aware of many of the things that they were going to face, but its great effect, its extraordinary effect, was that they showed it to the British people, and the British people were just captivated by what we told our soldiers about them. So *Salute to France* was made with a double purpose in mind: first of all, it was to tell the soldiers what they were going to see over there, and as far as we knew, the French had been under cover for a long time, and the great hope was to release it to the French, and have the same success with the French people, we hoped, as with the British. Well, the problem was more difficult, more diverse. I know one thing, we weren't for De Gaulle at that time.

LM: Then your next commercial film must have been *The Story of G.I. Joe*.

BM: Yes. I was called by the White House, from the European Theater of Operations. I had just done *Salute to France*, I was on my way to go back, and [Harry] Hopkins, the right hand man of Roosevelt, called me up. I nearly jumped 20 feet with the White House calling. He said that Ernie Pyle had asked for me, did I want to go? It must have been about twenty seconds, I was out of there.

LM: Had you met Ernie Pyle before you did the film?

BM: Oh yes, Pyle and I were very good friends, and the Army, as soon as I got out, sent me right over to see Pyle in Albuquerque, New Mexico. He was on a short leave before going to Japan, where he died, and was here to supervise the film and I went there and stayed with him a while. Of course we did nothing much but drink, and I remember as he put me on the plane he said, "Don't play me the way I am!" and I was saying back to him, "Well don't think I always act like this!" With that we parted. He came on and stayed with me; one of the last evenings he spent was in my house, before he went abroad.

LM: Did you try to be like the real person in your performance?

BM: I got annoyed by people telling me to copy his mannerisms. I'm not that kind of actor; I wish I were. Some people can do that, but I looked enough like him so that it was fairly presentable to some people who were acquainted with him.

LM: You shot *Mine Own Executioner* in England. How did their filming methods differ from Hollywood's?

BM: Well, that was the black winter, and it was frightfully cold. The English had just had all the bombing and all the trouble, and then they got this terrible winter in which they nearly froze to death. That particular film was done under very difficult circumstances, and I thought they did wonderfully. One wasn't about to criticize them for any shortcomings at that period.

LM: How long were you in production for *Man in the Eiffel Tower*?

BM: I don't remember. I know we spent about three months in Paris, and I worked with a French crew, which was interesting. I used my French as best I could; I remember I used to amuse Laughton—I invented a word, "stoppez," for stop, instead of *cessez*. I think it was great happiness I had on that film; Laughton and I were very close. We enjoyed so finding the great spots that Utrillo had painted, and all the great French impressionists, and setting the camera up like the impressionist painters. They cut a lot of that out, but it was really good.

LM: In the 1950s you did very few films; most of that time was spent directing and acting on the stage?

BM: Yes, that's true.

LM: You did one film called *Joe Butterfly*.

BM: Oh yes, we did *Joe Butterfly* in Tokyo; had great hopes for it but it didn't turn out very well; but it was a very funny character.

LM: Your next five or six films were for Otto Preminger. Do you enjoy working with him?

BM: Yes, he manages to get the parts interesting enough for me. I thought it was a very interesting part in *Hurry Sundown*. I don't know what the rest of the picture was like, but the part was interesting.

LM: Your first for him was *Advise And Consent*.

BM: Yes; that was the last film Laughton did, and I was working with Laughton at that time. We were working on some stage production together, and he more or less urged me to take this thing and got Otto to do it. When this particular bit was being done in *Advise And Consent*, I first got a vision of Otto and we became very good friends; but in the middle of having hundreds of people in this room, this caucus room, and in the midst of directing, I suddenly looked for him, and he was over signing checks! There's nothing that he himself doesn't personally supervise.

LM: Who would you like to work with today in films?

BM: I'd like to work with almost any of the Italians—Antonioni is one.

LM: You've been doing quite a bit of television recently.

BM: Yes, maybe too much, I don't know.

Burgess Meredith as The Penguin with Cesar Romero, Burt Ward, Frank Gorshin, Adam West, and Lee Meriwether in the *Batman* feature film.

Leonard Maltin and Burgess Meredith at the time of this interview.

LM: Is the Penguin on *Batman* a fun role, or just another job?

BM: Oh, no, that's quite a character, I think, almost something out of Dickens. I enjoy playing him. I don't say we sweat a lot of blood over playing him, but I know when I was doing *Hurry Sundown* with Jane Fonda and Michael Caine and everybody, why, the kids by the hundreds came to see the Penguin; they don't know about the others.

LM: You also did the feature film of *Batman*.

BM: Yes; I don't know what happened to that; it just disappeared. They had huge hopes in that. I don't think it was done very well; I think they hurried it a bit, but it could have been a very funny, classic American camp film, if they had a little faith in it.

LM: What about your most recent film work? In the Elvis Presley film?

BM: Oh it's kind of a forgetful Indian. And before that, I did a cameo role in *Mackenna's Gold*. I was sitting around with Edward Robinson and Eli Wallach and Anthony Quayle and Raymond Massey and I don't know who all, and we were all sitting around in these cameo roles, wondering why we'd done it, and Eddie Robinson said, "I wonder what the other films are doing for character men?"

LM: What lies in the immediate future for you?

BM: Well, I haven't many plans beyond the Chayefsky play right now. I want to see what happens to that, and then a couple of films may come up, but the good films never come up when you're free. I would like to probe going abroad and making films because I seem to like their films better.

Conversations:

ROBERT YOUNGSON

Robert Youngson changed my life. In 1958 he produced a compilation film called *The Golden Age of Comedy* and I have an indelible memory of my parents taking me (age seven) to see it. I even remember where: the Guild Theater, right behind Radio City Music Hall. There was a standee of Laurel and Hardy outside. I had already been introduced to Stan and Ollie on television, but I had never seen their silent films or many of the other comedians he spotlighted in that ground-breaking feature. He went on to produce a number of other films in the same vein, and I eagerly awaited each new release. When I obtained his phone number years later and called to ask for an interview, he was delighted that anyone was interested in his career and readily agreed. He lived in a spacious old apartment on lower Fifth Avenue that was filled with movie material. His two Academy Awards held a place of honor in a special display case. Youngson died in 1974, but his influence on a generation of budding movie buffs like me cannot be measured. (Interview originally appeared in January 1969.)

LM: Let's start at the beginning; can you pinpoint your initial interest in movies?

RY: Oh, it began when I was a child. I always had a tremendous interest in motion picture history, and the motion picture past. Back when I was a kid, we didn't have The Museum of Modern Art, and we didn't have any place to see old films, really. I used to rent films from Willoughby's, which had a film rental library; they had a lot of very good things, very good old silent comedies and beautiful prints. That's where I got to see my first old films. Unfortunately, none of my friends had the slightest interest in old silent movies, so I would have to figure out a way of enticing them over to my place to see these old movies. It was sort of a lonely hobby. How it ever started I don't know, except that the interest was there from the very beginning, sort of inborn. It wasn't fanned by anybody because there was no one to fan it at that time. Then shortly thereafter The Museum of Modern Art began operation, and it was just wonderful; they had all original prints—Griffith had donated all his original prints, and Fairbanks. Most of those old original prints, I believe, are now all hypoed and gone, and they show reproductions, which are not the same because you don't have your tint and your tones. These being prints owned by the people who had made the films, they were perfect.

LM: How did this interest develop into a career?

RY: How it all began was in high school; I made a bunch of amateur motion pictures. I went to Harvard Business School and the Harvard Film Society had a contest; I entered a film that I had made in high school. It won first prize, so I sat down and wrote all the motion picture companies, hoping that I might get a nibble somewhere along the line. A man named Fred Ullman, who was the head of what was then RKO-Pathé, had me in for an interview, and gave me a job, so I went right from Harvard Business School into RKO-Pathé working as a newsreel contact man, which meant I had to go out with newsreel crews, arrange stories; then later on I became a scriptwriter for the Pathé newsreel.

LM: When was this?

RY: Well, this all began in 1941, so I became scriptwriter for Pathé News about 1942. During the war I was sent down to a Naval Air Station in Jacksonville, Florida to write Navy training films, as a Pathé employee. Then I came back and continued to write newsreels, and did freelance writing on the outside. Then, under most fortunate circumstances, RKO-Pathé was purchased by Warner Bros., and it became Warner-Pathé. There was a very great and perceptive man named Norman Moray, who was made the head of Warner-Pathé. He was also the sales manager of all the Warner Bros. shorts. He was a very friendly man and one day, I was walking down the hall and this brisk, friendly, gray-haired man stopped me and introduced himself. I told him who I was,

Harold Lloyd with Jeanne and Robert Youngson.

and what I did, and he invited me to lunch. At lunch I told him an idea that I had had for some time, but I had never been able to get off the ground. The idea was to take the Pathé News library, which in strength dated back to 1905 (we had some shots from the 1890s). I wanted to utilize this library to make short subjects, and this was a period when this was not really done. Since then, with television, we've had a lot of so-called library compilations, but this was quite a new thing then. He listened to me, and he said he'd think it over and sometime later I was called in and told to go ahead and produce these shorts. This was a dream come true, so I continued doing my regular job writing newsreel scripts, and on the side, started delving through this great library and making shorts from it.

LM: Did you enjoy your period of working on the newsreels?

RY: Oh yes, it was tremendously interesting, a very vibrant, vital thing, and the years I was working on the newsreels were sort of the height of the newsreel. The newsreels are all gone now, because television has taken their place. Actually, the newsreels aren't gone; there is TV, which is a much degraded form. To digress for a moment, the reason I say this is that our news today consists of seeing a newscaster for about 60 percent or more of the time on the air, and then getting film clips. Of course

115

the old newsreels weren't that way; you had an off-screen narration, but your actual news pictures were the things that counted.

LM: How often did the Pathé newsreel come out?

RY: Twice a week.

LM: What type of time limits were you working with?

RY: Very very tight limits, during the war especially. What would happen was that you would make up a whole newsreel, and then suddenly a big story would break, and the film would come in from the Signal corps, let's say, of a great battle. You would junk all the work you had done and start from scratch, work all through the night and get the newsreel. This was common practice.

LM: If a news story broke on a Monday, how soon would you be able to have it in your newsreel?

RY: Well, we were remarkably fast—of course, not as fast as television. The make-up days were Monday and Thursday. We would make up on Monday, and if the film got to the laboratory on time, in the wee hours of Tuesday morning, prints would start getting into first-run theaters on Tuesday.

LM: Were the shorts you started making mainly from this old Pathé footage?

RY: They were entirely from old footage; on a couple of them like *World of Kids* there was some original shooting that I did, but very little. Those shorts, I'm happy to say, won two Academy Awards and six nominations. They were tremendously successful, and just a delight to work on. I would decide a subject, and then go through great masses of film, screen hundreds of thousands of feet of film, and eventually emerge with that subject. It was a delightful, personal enterprise; it was perhaps in the motion picture industry a rare opportunity to be creative on your own. Under this setup, there was nobody looking over my shoulder, nobody telling me what to do. The only restrictions were certain footage restrictions, whether it would be a one-reeler or a two-reeler.

LM: What was the first film you did that utilized old movie material, as opposed to just newsreel material?

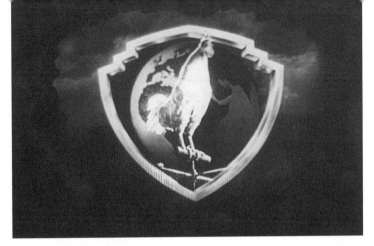

The Warner-Pathé rooster.

RY: That was *Magic Movie Moments*, which utilized the *Noah's Ark* footage. That was interesting—I made a one-reel short out of *Noah's Ark* and then later I did a full feature utilizing *Noah's Ark* material. The spectacle was just marvelous, and it was completed just as talkies came into prominence, and just at that precise time, the interest of the public was entirely in talkies, so they cut down the spectacle of *Noah's Ark* to a tremendous extent and added talkie sequences, which were horrible. They were saying practically nothing, but they were talking; that was necessary in that era in order for a film to succeed. When I made my revised *Noah's Ark* as a feature, I took all those talking sequences out; they just had no value today at all, whereas the spectacle, I thought, had held up extremely well.

LM: What other shorts were comprised of movie material?

RY: *Thrills from the Past* was from an old Warner film called *Old San Francisco*, which had the San Francisco earthquake as the highlight, and *A Bit of the Best* was a condensation of Rin-Tin-Tin in a film called *Trapped by the Police.*

LM: What were your impressions of the Warners film library?

RY: Well, I had complete access, but unfortunately, silent films mainly didn't exist; many of them were just gone. There was a period of time in which there was a feeling that silent films had no commercial value whatsoever. If I may be immodest, I think I had more to do with disproving that than anyone else. It was heartbreaking, there were so many films I wanted to get from the Warner library which had completely been destroyed. The storage of nitrate negatives is a very expensive thing, and as I rather imagined in my mind's eye, the way it occurred,

I suppose someone came in and said, "We have to build some new vaults." Someone else said, "Well, how much will it cost?" "It will cost $500,000." "What's filling up your vaults now?" They looked down the list and said, "Here's this vault filled with old silent negatives—what have they brought in the past 30 years? Nothing! Throw them out; we'll save thousands of dollars." And so much of the history of the silent era is just gone. Basically, the ones that were available were mainly silent films which had been made at the very end of the silent era. At the end of the silent era they added synchronized scores, and these were kept, I suppose, because they figured there was a soundtrack attached to them. All the earlier stuff was gone.

Now that I think of it, I did utilize another talkie film, however used in silent form, and that was *An Adventure to Remember*, which was made from a very early talkie called *Isle of Lost Ships*—this was the second making of *Isle of Lost Ships*, not the Maurice Tourneur version, but one directed by Irving Willat, and it was quite an oddity among early talkie films in that it was an action film. During that early talkie period everything consisted of people just standing around and talking.

Of course, *When the Talkies Were Young* had an appeal, I think, when it was made that isn't anywhere near as great now. When I made *When the Talkies Were Young*, the major companies hadn't released their old films to television, so that people who saw this short were seeing James Cagney, Edward G. Robinson, Barbara Stanwyck, Clark Gable, Spencer Tracy—they were seeing all these movie personalities whom they were seeing constantly in new films, and not realizing how they were changing through the years. All of a sudden here was this short with these people all *young*. It came as a tremendous shock to audiences; and it was great fun to make. Now, of course, that shock effect is gone because on TV you have so many early films.

LM: How did you ever decide which sequences to include in that film?

RY: It was a case where I had hoped to make 10 shorts, or 20 or 30, just like this. It was a tremendous job of selection. What I was trying to do—my main motive—was to show stars at their very beginnings, for example James Cagney in *Sinner's Holiday* with Joan Blondell. It was their first film, in both cases.

LM: Do you remember any films that you almost included, but didn't?

RY: I had already completed a second film, a sequel to *When the Talkies Were Young*, and just as I was completing it, Warner Bros. sold their entire backlog to Associated Artists, and I just dropped the whole project— the film no longer belonged to Warner Bros. One little item that comes to mind [that I included] was Lee Tracy in *Blessed Event*, in which there was a marvelous fast-talking sequence.

LM: May I ask a general question, at this point? When did you first use the Chopin étude that is your theme, and how did it come about?

RY: Well, I had heard that Chopin étude when I was a kid, and when I was a kid I was always having fantasies of making motion pictures, and in my fantasies I had decided upon this as the theme. It took all those years, when I finally made *The Golden Age of Comedy*, to give me an opportunity to use that Chopin étude. I think it expresses a nostalgia, and works very well.

LM: How did your first feature, *50 Years Before Your Eyes*, come about? Was it an outgrowth of the shorts?

RY: Yes; I was the director on that, I wasn't the producer. We had come to the 50-year mark, and I had written reports urging that this film be made. I was finally allowed to make it, but I didn't have the freedom making this that I had with my other films. I was dissatisfied with it; much footage that I wanted to include couldn't be left in because a lot of footage that I thought ponderous and heavy I was forced to include. I don't think it's a bad film, I'm not ashamed of the film, but it's a film that I think could have been much better. In fact, I felt so strongly about my dissatisfaction with the film that I began a series [of shorts) that did the same job the way I wanted to do it. That series started with *I Remember When*, which covered material from before the turn of the century. That was followed up with *This Was Yesterday*, which took the period from the 20th century up until the outbreak of World War I. And there was marvelous footage of the campaign of Pancho Villa in Mexico. I've always considered the newsreel footage that was made on that Mexican expedition, which mind you was made in 1915, so indicative of how far advanced we were in newsreel making. Some of the scenes are striking—there's a scene, for example, of the supply wagons going across the Mexican desert which I think is superior to any scene in *The Covered Wagon*. That film was followed by *It Happened to You*, which was a two-reel coverage of America in World War I, as seen from the home front mainly. There was some battle material in it, but it was mainly a home-front film. And that was as far as I got, unfortunately.

LM: Why did you stop making shorts?

RY: Well basically, because the shorts market was so shot, there wasn't any money in it anymore—not for me, so much, because I would have gone on making them forever. But as far as Warners was concerned, they had a drastic cutting-down of shorts production. Then Warner-Pathé went out of existence, and I turned to making independent features.

LM: How did *The Golden Age of Comedy* come about?

RY: Back in 1950, when *50 Years Before Your Eyes* came out, I traveled out to the West Coast with my parents by car, and as I went from city to city, my picture would be playing in the local theaters. I went to see it many, many times to test the audience's reaction to it, and I had insert-

ed near the beginning of the film a silent comedy sequence with Charlie Chaplin. Invariably this got tremendous response from the audiences, which hadn't had the opportunity to see these old silent comedies in years. I came back from this tour across the country and tried to convince Warner Bros. to let me make a feature to be called *The Golden Age of Comedy.* For seven years I tried to make that picture, but no one was interested. Finally, with some financial assistance from a partner, I made that picture. After I made that, I took it around to all the major distributors; I would sit in screening rooms with these people, and they would roar—they would love it. Then they would say, well, we love it, but it isn't the type of thing for audiences—it's too episodic. They just couldn't see any future in that type of film. So finally I had to have it distributed by an independent, DCA. It was a slow starter—it wasn't acclaimed overnight—but it gradually built into a very successful film. Fortunately for me, 20th Century Fox had taken the foreign rights from DCA, and much to their amazement, it was a tremendous success in other countries. In India, for example, it was the biggest-grossing Fox film of that year. So with this success I was able to go to 20th Century Fox with my next film, and ever since then I have had no trouble finding a distributor for my films.

LM: Had you been gathering material for your *The Golden Age of Comedy* over the years, or did you set out in 1957 to put it all together?

Robert Youngson and Thelma Ritter at the New York presentation of the 1954 (27th) Academy Awards ceremony. Courtesy © Academy of Motion Picture Arts and Sciences.

RY: Oh no, I had been planning the film in my mind for years, and gathering material. Fortunately, I was able to make an arrangement with the Hal Roach Studios to use their material, and I also made use of much Mack Sennett footage.

LM: Did you have any difficulty in obtaining any of this footage?

RY: It worked out very well. It was the same problem I think you would have if you had a sudden inspiration that pebbles on the street were going to be valuable someday, and you went around gathering pebbles off the street. There was absolutely no feeling that these films had any value, at the time; if there had been, there would have been other people making use of the material.

LM: Would it be correct to assume that *The Golden Age of Comedy* is your favorite of the films you've done?

RY: Well, I think it was the breakthrough film; I don't think it's the best. It's very, very hard to single out one film as a favorite, but it certainly broke new ground—I know at that time Laurel and Hardy were pretty much ignored. I remember it was sort of an act of courage to include so much Laurel and Hardy footage in the feature. I kept testing it and it was always Laurel and Hardy that got the greatest reaction. I was determined that I was going to go by the reactions to a great extent. I found that I had to include so much Laurel and Hardy that in a sense the picture was top-heavy with Laurel and Hardy. At that time, they didn't mean much—they weren't even considered first-rate comedians. Look at James Agee's article, "Comedy's Greatest Era," and you'll find that Laurel and Hardy were brushed off. I decided to go ahead and let the film be top-heavy with Laurel and Hardy, and it paid off.

LM: Looking at your four silent-comedy compilations, *The Golden Age of Comedy, When Comedy Was King, Days of Thrills and Laughter,* and *30 Years of Fun,* what would you say was the biggest problem involved in doing these films?

RY: Getting the material. I think the secret of making a compilation is just searching, searching, searching. First, it's hard to uncover; then also, not all silent comedy was great—only a small percentage. To make a poor compilation would be easy.

LM: How much time did you spend on each of these films?

RY: Oh, about a year on each.

LM: How was most of that time spent?

RY: Mostly finding the material and getting it ready for reproduction as part of the film. Next to that, I would say music scoring takes up a lot of time. Most regular feature films just have music bridges, and have long stretches without music. These films can't have a second without music.

LM: When you went to MGM for *The Big Parade of Comedy,* were you subject to any interference from the studio?

RY: I'm happy to say no, none whatsoever. But that is the one film of mine that I do not own. I was paid a salary for that one; MGM financed it, and I received 50 percent of the profits. As part of that contract, however, I was able to make one film on my own which MGM then had rights to distribute, which was *Laurel and Hardy's Laughing 20s.*

LM: *The Big Parade of Comedy,* was the first film in which you used excerpts from sound films. What problems, if any, did this present in contrast to using silent footage?

RY: Very severe, different problems. Sound films are much harder to glue together. I have found that pacing in old films is much different from that of today; consequently for each of my films I have test screenings. I find where the dead spots are, and I pull a lot together. When dealing with talkies this becomes a lot more difficult, with dialogue and music on the soundtrack—if you cut, there may be a sudden jump in the music, so that presents a serious problem.

At the New York presentation, 1954 (27th) Academy Awards ceremony, from left: Danny Kaye, recipient, Honorary Award; Nancy Kelly, acceptor, Honorary Award; and Robert Youngson, winner, Short Subject (One-reel) (*This Mechanical Age*). Courtesy © Academy of Motion Picture Arts and Sciences.

LM: Your latest films have been devoted to Laurel and Hardy; do you think you could have done such a film at the time of *The Golden Age of Comedy*?

RY: I could have done a wonderful Laurel and Hardy film, but it just wouldn't have sold. Outside of kids there seemed to be no adult interest in them at the time; certainly there was no critical interest.

LM: In your new film, *Four Clowns*, you give Charley Chase equal billing with Laurel and Hardy and Buster Keaton. Do you think this will mean new recognition for him?

RY: Well, Charley Chase is in a position now where Laurel and Hardy were 10 years ago. And hopefully—I think I even hear murmurs of it now— he will come into his own.

LM: Is there any specific "missing" footage or silent material you would like to acquire?

RY: Actually, I can say that if anybody, anywhere, has any 35mm comedy material, I would like to buy it from them—anything of possible value. I would like to see a lot more of the Educational Comedies of the 1920s; some I have seen are bad, but there are some that are quite good. And whereas the Laurel and Hardy comedies have managed to survive, we're not nearly as lucky with Charley Chase. I've looked at just about everything that exists on Charley Chase from the silent days, and I think this is about it—unless somebody else has a print of something. There is no problem with rights, because if there are rights I can arrange to buy them from the copyright owner. The only trouble is that so many copyright owners have rights but no films. I hope we can uncover more film and preserve it.

LM: Well, you have done more than practically anyone else to achieve this end, and all film buffs are grateful to you for it.

RY: Thank you. You know, everybody has to have a goal in life, and that's my goal, to preserve as much of this great comedy material as possible.

Conversations:

JOAN BLONDELL

On my second trip to Los Angeles I got to interview a number of people, mostly character actors who were happy to talk about their careers. Joan Blondell was an exception, the most challenging interview subject I'd ever encountered. I met her on a lunch break from the ABC television series *Here Come the Brides*, in which she played a saloonkeeper in turn-of-the-20th-century Seattle, a role she felt suited her well. (She also said it was "a cinch" to do.) She was pleasant enough to be with but offered terse responses to most of my questions about the 1930s and finally asked, "Isn't this kind of dull talking about way back there? Who wants to hear this?" I tried to convince her that many people would be interested and

Photo of Joan Blondell taken by Leonard Maltin at the time of the interview.

forged ahead. She later penned an autobiographical novel about her colorful life growing up in show business called *Center Door Fancy* (1972). (Interview originally appeared in September 1969.)

LM: Was there a "family" feeling among the Warners stock company in the 1930s?

JB: Oh yes, so much so that we seldom said hello or goodbye; it was just sort of a continuation.

LM: Did you ever get scripts or characters mixed up?

JB: We would make little funnies like "It's the same script, we just changed clothes."

LM: Were you ever working on two pictures at the same time?

JB: Oh indeed, many times. At one point in my life I was in four different pictures in four different theaters in L.A. at the same time. That was hard, continuous and hard work. They got their money's worth out of us.

LM: We read somewhere you did 20 months straight work?

JB: That's right—it was 32 pictures in 27 months.

LM: How much time would you spend on a "big" picture like *Gold Diggers of 1933*?

JB: That's an awfully long time ago, I don't really remember. A couple of months, I guess; a certain amount for the story, and a certain amount for the numbers. You would rehearse the numbers while you were working on the book end of it, and then do the numbers one after the other.

LM: Was it an easy adjustment for you from stage acting to screen acting when you came out here for *Sinner's Holiday*?

Blondell with Dick Powell and Warren William in *Gold Diggers of 1933*.

JB: That wasn't an adjustment at all. That thing should have been called *Penny Arcade*, because that was the play that Jimmy Cagney and I starred in on Broadway. They brought us to pictures to do that here, and then they changed the name of the picture to *Sinner's Holiday* and they gave Cagney's part to Grant Withers, and my part to Evalyn Knapp. That's how their brains worked. So that was kind of a vague thing to us.

LM: Were you and Cagney given a big build-up as young stars?

With James Cagney and Edward Woods in *The Public Enemy*.

JB: The minute they saw us work, after the second day of shooting, they signed us right then and there to a five-year contract. They saw us work and they saw we knew what we were doing, because we had come from the stage.

LM: Could you compare working for Warners in the '30s and doing a new film like *The Cincinnati Kid*?

JB: There's no difference; work is work. The only thing about the portion of my life that I spent at Warner Bros. was that I knew everybody in the cast. It was like working with your brother or sister.

LM: Does that make working easier?

JB: Not necessarily; it was just that we are all friends. Sometimes you haven't met the people yet and you work with them; it's no harder, it's just different.

LM: When you weren't working on a picture, did they keep you busy with publicity work?

JB: We never had time off—never. We were either on the set or in the portrait gallery, or having a layout at the beach or up in the mountains—always working. They got their money's worth.

LM: Did they give you time off when you became pregnant?

JB: Very little. I did five pictures with Ellen and seven carrying my son. They kept shooting me higher and higher. They had me in back of everything—desks, barrels, anything.

LM: Was there a point when you fought back and decided that you'd had enough?

JB: Yes, I went into the hospital once, just walked into the hospital and called my doctor from the lobby and said, "I'm stuttering and I can't stop blinking my eyes. I can't work another day." I was just suffering from exhaustion; I had about 48 hours' sleep.

LM: Then you went back?

JB: Sure. You know, I 'm known for doing this. [flutters her eyelashes] Well, that wasn't being cute—that was because I was exhausted and couldn't keep my eyes open!

LM: Do you mind if we toss out a few titles of films you've done to get your impressions?

JB: No, go right ahead.

LM: How about *Make Me a Star*, with Stu Erwin?

JB: That's a long time ago. I don't remember much about that; that's when I was doing them fast and furious. In fact, there were many I didn't see ever, and I never saw rushes, and a few times I've seen them for the very

With Bobby Sherman and David Soul in *Here Come the Brides*.

first time on the Late Show. Several times I've thought, "I don't remember doing that at all."

LM: What about working with Busby Berkeley?

JB: He was marvelous. He was a ringmaster, there was no question of that, but everyone was young, and happy; it was kind of hard, really. The hours were very long, but he knew exactly what he wanted and had everything coordinated in his mind. There was nothing rattled about it at all. It was just done—one, two, three—precisely.

LM: Why didn't you sing more in your films?

JB: I didn't want to, particularly. I wanted to get into the acting end of it more. I did several silly numbers like "The Girl at the Ironing Board"; a few of them.

LM: How about *Stand-In*?

JB: I enjoyed that—with Tay Garnett directing.

LM: Was there any problem in going on loan-out like that after working with the same people for such a long time at Warners?

JB: Listen, anybody that's been in vaudeville as a little child, until I was 17, playing a different town every single week, a different theater; you're hardly uprooted by going across town. That didn't mean a thing; a movie was a movie.

LM: Was the Hollywood-party image of Hollywood a phony one in the 1930s?

JB: Definitely. Worse than today. There was no way humanly possible of knowing your lines, being on time, working that steadily and looking right if you went out at night. Very seldom did anyone go to a club, but if you did go to a club, you were so popular that every newspaper would come and snap you and the next day you'd be all over the country in a nightclub. If you didn't go again for eight months, you'd be snapped all over again. Mostly we went to each other's houses going with our own group, but it was an impossibility to have a wild life.

LM: Were there any roles you went after or particularly wanted to do?

JB: Not particularly; I wasn't that ambitious. I enjoyed a home life more than a theatrical career. I just took what they gave me, because I wanted to get home quickly.

LM: Do you have any memories of working with Michael Curtiz?

JB: He was on the cruel side—a cruel man, sadistic, with animals and actors, and swung that whip around pretty good. He overworked everyone. But, he was amusing, and he turned out some good pictures.

LM: And Errol Flynn, who worked on that same film?

JB: Oh, I loved Errol. He was a dear friend of mine, and quite unlike his publicity. It started out by his being a lady-killer, and getting everybody pregnant, and being the father of somebody's child in Kansas City. It amused him no end. I don't mean he wasn't a ladies' man, that he didn't like the ladies, because he certainly did. He most of all was just a guy who liked to tell stories, have fun, have some drinks, and be with his friends. He had this reputation of destroying the virtue of young ladies, which was hardly true, since they flung themselves at him.

LM: How about Warren William, who co-starred with you quite often?

JB: He was an old man even when he was a young man. Always very quiet, and wearing slippers. He didn't mix very much.

LM: Bing Crosby?

JB: Crosby was very aloof—he was probably that way from the day he was born.

LM: *Nightmare Alley* was one of your most unusual films, a really bizarre movie. It didn't make money when it was released, but now it has quite a reputation.

JB: A very interesting picture. And Tyrone Power was a darling; I felt awful when he died.

LM: That was directed by Edmund Goulding.

JB: Yeah, that nut.

LM: In what way?

With Katharine Hepburn in *Desk Set*.

JB: Well, he had to get up and act it out for you first, and your big problem was not to give an impersonation of him doing you.

LM: How about Kazan?

JB: I loved working with Kazan; I guess he was my favorite, along with Tay Garnett, who did *Stand-In*. I love Tay. He knows what he wants, and he lets you go. That's the way Kazan was; there were no big meetings, or going into closets to figure out what your mood was. You just did it. He chose you because you were the right one for that role and then let you go.

LM: One of our favorite pictures is *Desk Set*. Your scenes with Katharine Hepburn in that are just marvelous.

JB: It was marvelous working with her. I loved her, loved working with the two of them. They were great together; not only professional, but there was such a wonderful relationship. He was marvelous with her, and she with him. It was a terrific experience to be with them—and no effort at all.

LM: One film of yours that seems to be shown quite often is *Good Girls Go to Paris*.

JB: Let me tell you how different censorship is now. The title was originally *Good Girls Go to Paris, Too*, but the censors made them cut that off.

Conversations:

MITCHELL LEISEN

Because I was a contributor to *Action!*, the publication of the Directors Guild of America, I received a copy of their annual members' directory, which proved to be a gold mine. Not only did it tell me who was still alive

but how to reach many retired filmmakers. A letter to Mitchell Leisen resulted in an invitation to visit him at a dance studio he maintained in Hollywood. My friend David Chierichetti drove me there and struck up a close friendship with Leisen. This led to a book-length career study, *Hollywood Director* (1973), which I edited as part of a paperback series for Curtis Books. An unsung and largely forgotten figure when we spoke, he has come into his own in the decades since—although writers like Billy Wilder and Preston Sturges insisted that they pursued their directing careers because they were dissatisfied with Leisen's treatment of their screenplays. He couldn't have been more gracious to David and me, and even invited us back a few nights after our first meeting to screen 16mm prints of some of his rarest films. (Interview originally appeared in January 1970.)

LM: Could you give me some background on yourself—where you were born and that sort of material?

ML: Well, I was born more years ago than it's worth mentioning—1898, as a matter of fact—in Menominee, Michigan. Much to the scandal of the country, my mother and father were divorced when I was four. People didn't get divorced back in those days. We moved to Kansas City and then St. Louis; I spent most of my life in Kansas City. Then I started to study art at the Art Institute in Chicago and architecture at Washington University.

LM: How did that lead to Hollywood?

ML: On a vacation. A rather amusing story, as a matter of fact. I happened to be staying with Ruth St. Denis and Ted Shawn, who were very good friends of my family, and Ted asked me out to dinner one night at Lois Weber's, who was the only woman director at that time. I sat next to a very charming woman at the table, and I know I talked quite a bit about myself. A couple of days later I saw her at the Old Ship Cafe with Cecil DeMille and I went over to ask her how a mutual friend was, and she said, "I'd like to have you meet DeMille," and he said, "I'd like to have you come to work for me; I've heard about the fabulous things you do." Well, if the planks had opened up I would have gone right into the ocean. So I went out and I did three sketches; I'd never made a costume in my life, and they wanted me to do costumes. However, I made three sketches which were bought by DeMille. A year later I asked Jeanie Macpherson—the lady who had gotten me the job—"What in the world did you ever tell him about me?" and she said, "Oh, I don't know." I said, "Whatever gave you the idea that I could do anything?" She said, "You had interesting hands; I knew you could do something." So that's the true story of my beginning in Hollywood.

LM: Did you just design costumes, or did you do sets as well?

ML: I did costumes at the beginning, for about a year, and then I went to DeMille and I said "Look, I'm supposed to be an architect, not a dress-maker," and he said, "Well, I'll put you with my brother William, as a set dresser." So I became a set dresser, or an interior decorator, as they call them today, and eventually became an art director. I held down five jobs with DeMille, and finally little Manny Cohen (at Paramount) took five of us—Henry Hathaway, Charlie Barton, Al Hall—and made directors out of us. All of us made it but one: Arthur Jacobson never made it. We all became pretty well known directors.

LM: What was it like working for DeMille?

ML: Hell.

With Cecil B. DeMille and Jean Arthur on the set of *Easy Living*.

LM: Was he a taskmaster?

ML: If you learned to think as he thought, you got along all right. To him everything was in neon tubes eight feet high, in capital letters: LOVE, PASSION, LOVE, REVENGE! There were no nuances at all. And when he saw my first picture he came to me and it was almost pitiful, because I was doing what he couldn't. You know, he had that big spectacle, and he tried to make what he thought was going to be a light comedy—it was the most tragic thing I ever had to sit through. And he could never figure out—he always thought my pictures were the greatest pictures ever made. He could not work with nuances or subtlety.

LM: He wasn't a penny pincher, though, was he?

ML: On other people's money he wasn't, but not on his own. When we finally went to Paramount to do *The Sign of the Cross*, he was using his own money, and then, boy, the pennies were pinched. I was with DeMille for about 10 years. I worked on *King of Kings, Sign of the Cross, Volga Boatmen*, so many others.

LM: Were you with him when he went to MGM?

ML: Yes, he did his first talkies there. And those were very hectic days, because they only had one soundstage. Our sets were put in and ready at 9:00 in the morning; they were snatched out from under us at 6. At 6:30 there was a set in for a short subject, which quit at 7:00. At 7:30 that was gone and the set was in for a company that worked all night. So the sets had to be very flexible, to be brought back in in a hurry.

LM: Did you have anything to do with the zeppelin in *Madam Satan*?

ML: Yes, and I had a nervous breakdown doing it. He stalled for four weeks on that zeppelin because I was in bed; finally they let me come back to work for an hour a day with a trained nurse. That's when we did the storm with the zeppelin, which was quite something. We were doing it in color, which was real difficult. I invented something there that is still used today. We had to get the wind on the deck, and we couldn't have the sound of wind machines—we didn't know how to dub yet, it was all direct sound—so it suddenly dawned on me and I went up on the roof and took the ventilators off the roof—big electric ventilators. I hung them on ropes from the ceiling, blowing onto the decks of the zeppelin. That's how we got our wind effects. Later on I had a picture of mine, *Thirteen Hours by Air*, where we worked at Alhambra Airport. I had to have a blizzard, so I built tunnels clear across the airfield—the airport wasn't in operation then—put my wind machines on the far side of the tunnels, and got my blizzard without any sound.

Probably the most interesting thing I had to do was in *King of Kings* when Christ appears to the blind girl, which is also the first time we see him, and his face gradually forms by the rays of light. We said, "How the hell are we going to do this one?" It couldn't be a trick, so I devised a scheme of using six layers of very sheer soufflé—the finest silk gauze I could get—and I airbrushed rays of light onto them. Then I lifted each one individually and started with all the lights on; as I faded the lights out, one after another the rays decreased until finally his face appeared. I used that many times; I used it in *The Girl Most Likely* in color, which was another little problem, because every time the right boy kissed her, the girl turned pink. So I had her surrounded by pink clouds revolving; I did it on sheets of glass. They wanted me to do *Blithe Spirit*; I said it was very flattering, but you know Noel Coward is going to direct it himself, so why waste my time and your time?

LM: On your first films you were listed as assistant director, weren't you?

ML: No, co-director, with Stuart Walker.

LM: How did you divide your responsibilities?

ML: Well, we were working in booths at the time, and I just told Stuart—he had been 28 days over schedule—I said, "You go sit in the booth and listen. If you don't like the way they're reading the lines, then come out." We made the picture in 18 days, and he never got on the stage. So then a little script came through called *The Eagle and the Hawk*; it was the only thing I ever really wanted to make. I went in to talk to the producer, and he said, "I've got Bill Wellman here," and told me to get out. But then I got a telephone call from the producer, and he said, "Wellman doesn't like it at all, and he wants to change it. I would like to do it with you, but I'm not sure you know enough about dialogue, so I would like to have Stuart Walker as dialogue director." Stuart insisted on getting full credit, and I was to get credit as co-director. That made the studio so damn mad they said I could have any picture I wanted. I said I want *Cradle Song*, and this was Stuart Walker's pet ambition to make that picture; I took it right out from under his nose. After two weeks they said, "What else do you want?" and I said *Death Takes a Holiday*.

LM: Paramount Pictures of the 1930s always had intriguing opening titles. Were you responsible for the opening sequence of *Death Takes a Holiday* where the names appear under the players as they are first seen on-screen?

ML: Oh, yes, now there's a little subtlety there which I don't know whether you dug or not. Everybody is introduced at a wine festival. Everybody's gay and happy, with loads of flowers—except Grazia. She is in the church. I tried to set up from the very beginning the personality of this girl. Maxwell Anderson did the script for me, and Max said, "Grazia has no motivation; she's the toughest character to write because she

Mitchell Leisen as himself in *Hold Back the Dawn*; Brian Donlevy at left.

has no motivation." And I said, "I don't agree with you; she has every motivation in the world. She doesn't want to live. She wants to die— she goes out in the garden one night and catches pneumonia, and her family can't keep her alive. That's the whole story." Now, Kent Taylor and Freddy March looked almost like twin brothers, so I cast Kent as the live lover, and Freddy as Death. There was very little between the two of them. In one scene in the film I had March, as Death, and Sir Guy Standing, as the Duke, sitting as close as you and I, actually on the stage, and yet Death was transparent. That was a little chore which turned out to be very tough, because each setup took hours and hours. I took a 30-percent transparent mirror, and a black-velvet set, with chairs and things matched into the actual pieces on the stage. So if I wanted Death transparent I simply lifted pieces of the black setup, and if he sat in a chair, you could see the arm through it.

LM: So actually it was a reflection.

ML: It was a reflection.

LM: Where was the dividing line?

ML: There was none. The whole lens was covered by this mirror, on a 45-degree angle. You shot through the mirror at the scene, so you could see through it, and at the same time get enough reflection to make him seem transparent. Of course, you had to keep Guy Standing out of the way so he wouldn't be too.

LM: Your next film, *Murder at the Vanities*, was very offbeat.

ML: That was Earl Carroll, and I did a very simplified version of the show. I wouldn't allow Mr. Carroll on the stage, but I'd see him sneaking around, peeking. He raised such a stink in the front office that we did $70,000 worth of numbers, elaborated it, and made a real Earl Carroll show out of it. That was probably the most nude picture made up to that time. The girls had so little on it wasn't even funny. One scene with green fans, an ocean scene with the girls coming out of the water, they had two little ivy leaves as pasties, and about four more with a few strings of fringe. The first day they wouldn't even take their bathrobes off unless all the men were off the stage except me, the cameraman, and the head electrician. The next day they were sitting down talking to the carpenters.

139

LM: Were the chorus girls Earl Carroll's or Paramount's?

ML: Half and half. Ann Sheridan was one of the girls.

LM: How closely did you work with your writers?

ML: Constantly. Arthur Hornblow was my pet producer, and we would have daily story conferences. Any scenes that would come in we would go over and fight it out. Billy Wilder and Charlie Brackett did most of my scripts before Billy became a director, and he would scream and yell if you changed an if, and, or a but. The first day on the set [of his first film] I saw him rewriting like crazy, and I said, "What's the matter, doesn't it work?" Because it can look fine on paper, but if an actor couldn't say it, there's no sense in forcing him to. It's much easier to change the dialogue to make it easier for him to say. Preston Sturges is another one who would blow his stack if you changed a word of his dialogue, and he also—when he became a director—rewrote everything.

LM: So it was a collaborative effort all the way down the line?

ML: Oh, yes, it isn't today, because the writers have their teeth into it much more. But we'd have 16 writers on a script; if we thought they were exhausted we'd get a new team. We had Dorothy Parker once—on *Hands Across the Table*—and I think she gave us one line.

LM: I've always loved *Easy Living*, and one thing that impressed me in particular was that incredible Automat sequence. Was that a full-scale set built in Hollywood?

ML: Yes, that was my idea to reintroduce slapstick comedy into high comedy. The idea appealed to me that if all those doors flew open at once (in the Automat), all the bums in New York would rush in. We had every stuntman in town working on that scene, stacking up trays and sliding around. And there were things in the hotel with a dog, and falling into the bathtub. We had a very cute love scene; there was a long, circular couch—in those days you didn't dare show two people in bed together—so I laid them with their heads opposite.

LM: On *The Big Broadcast of 1938*, was it possible to direct W.C. Fields?

ML: No. Mr. Fields was the kind of a guy who had to chisel a story open to

get his routines in. And I'd say "Bill, just say one line to give me a cue to go on." [He said,] "Anything you want, son, just tell me what you want me to say." Do you think he'd say it? He'd say everything but. Then he'd find out we had a space made for the routine. He'd say, "I'm going to go to my dressing room and study up on the routine." I'd say, "Bill, you've only done the routine six times—you did it in your last picture." "I did not, this one is different." "What's different about it?" "In the other picture it was a bottle of gin, this time it's a bottle of bour-

W.C. Fields, Dorothy Lamour, and Mitchell Leisen on the Paramount lot.

bon." He'd come back on the set two hours later and say, "I've changed my mind. I don't think I'll do that routine after all. I'll do another one." Just to screw you up. Finally I went to the front office and said "Look, get him a special director to direct his stuff and I'll only pick him up where we need him." Well, we had shot Kirsten Flagstad in New York singing the Valkyrie, and Bill heard about it so he had to come out and get into the act. He came in and said, "Who's that?" And someone says, "That's Madame Flagstad." "Oh, I thought it was a screeching parrot." I went down to the front office and I said, "We can't do this, we can't insult Kirsten Flagstad." And they said, "Oh, we'll just put it in for the preview to please the old man [Fields], then we'll take it out." I said, "I'm sorry, it'll be over my dead body." Bill LeBaron, head of the studio, said, "Just for one showing, then we'll take it out." So I went down to the legal office and I said, "You've got a suit for a million dollars on your hands. Bill LeBaron insists on putting a scene in the picture where the old man calls Kirsten Flagstad a screeching parrot, and as far as I know one performance is all that's necessary." That film was burned—five minutes later. There's kind of an amusing story about "Thanks for the Memory." The boys—Rainger and Robin—had written a song, and I had a habit of visualizing a song to see if it was going to work, and this wasn't what I was after at all. I said, no, I wanted something like the Île-de-France with all the gulls around it. So they wrote another song,

141

and the tempo was not right. I said, "Fine, but I'm going to ask you one thing. I'm going to make a direct recording of it, and I don't want you to come near the set until I call for you." So I had a 90-piece orchestra, three cameras—one on Shirley Ross, one on Bob Hope, and one on the two of them, and I shot the number. I sent for the boys and we did a direct recording of it; at the end, they were both crying. They said, "We didn't know we wrote that!" I had slowed it up quite a bit.

LM: Did you supervise the musical scoring on your films?

ML: Oh yes, I always sat in. I went in one day and they had a 90-piece orchestra going full-blast, and I asked Victor Young, "What the hell is this?" and he said, "It's a rehearsal for the ballet scene in *Masquerade in Mexico*." I said, "Victor, there are three guitars in this scene, and you've got 90 pieces!" He said, "We've got 'em, we might as well use them." I said, "You've got them, but you're not going to use them." I can't read one note of music, but I always had the reputation at Paramount of being able to say, "Fellows, there's something wrong in there." I had the opening of *Swing High, Swing Low* with the Panama Canal locks, and there again they had orchestrated a terrific thing and I said, "No, this has got to be cacophony—chains dropping, the sound of the locks opening, the little donkeys with their engines pulling the boats through." So I said, "Get ahold of Victor," and I said, "Take a look at this, Victor. I want Mickey Mouse for this." He composed from the podium, right then and there, a hell of a thing, and we finished about 1 a.m. It cost a hell of a fortune.

With Claudette Colbert and Ray Milland on the set of *Arise, My Love*.

LM: How was John Barrymore to work with on *Midnight*?

ML: He was wonderful. He had his wife, Elaine Barrie, and she kept a tight rein on him. She was in the picture so she could keep an eye on him. One day, when we'd been shooting about three weeks, Elaine came to me and she said, "You know, John thinks this is a wonderful picture—he read the script last night." This was my introduction to idiot cards, flying back and forth all over the place, and boy, he could start one and pick up the next like nothing. We had this one scene where he had to walk down a narrow corridor, and with the cameras and lights and things, there was just no room for idiot cards. So I said, "John, I'm afraid you're going to have to learn this." He said, "Oh? Do you want me to recite the soliloquy from *Hamlet* for you?" and he did. So I said, "Then why the hell these idiot cards?" He said, "My dear fellow, why should I fill my mind with this shit just to forget it tomorrow morning?"

LM: You worked with Claudette Colbert quite often, didn't you?

ML: Yes; she gave other people trouble, principally about her clothes, but I thought she had excellent taste, and I never argued with her. I never had any trouble with her—she was divine. One time she did a scene, and I okayed it, and said, "That's perfect." She said, "Uh-uh. I can do it better." Now, a director has no right to tell an actor or actress if he thinks he can do it better that he can't do it. And we took it over—it was a crying scene—we finished it and she said, "Now that's good." I said, "It stunk." She said, "What do you mean? I felt that." I said, "That's the trouble, Claudette, you felt it." I said, "All right, I'll prove it. I'll get a rush print on both takes, and you be in the projection room with me tomorrow morning at 8:00." When we came out she said, "You're right." I said, "Because you were out of control—you weren't controlling the scene. So you couldn't direct it where you wanted to go. You've got to stay in control."

LM: You remade *Midnight* very soon after its original release, as *Masquerade in Mexico*.

ML: Yes, within six years—I was surprised, looking at the dates just now.

LM: Do you think it went off as well as *Midnight*?

ML: No, you had Barrymore, Ameche, Claudette Colbert, as against Dorothy Lamour, Arturo de Cordova—please!

LM: Your next film was probably one of your best—*Remember the Night*.

ML: It's one of my pets. Barbara Stanwyck has a very bad back, and had to wear that wedding dress with the corsets. She'd be dressed and on the set at half past eight in the morning. I'd say "Barbara, for God's sake, come on, I'm not going to use you for an hour; why don't you loosen up those corsets?" She'd say, "No, you might need me." I'd come on the set at 8:45, having lined up the sets the night before, and a voice would come out of the fly gallery saying, "Come on, you sonofabitch, let's get this show on the road—where the hell have you been?" It was Barbara. She's a perfectionist if I ever saw one. If you watch people on TV, they can't talk without moving their heads, or their hands are going. You watch Barbara. Her hands never move, and her head never moves.

LM: Was that you playing yourself in *Hold Back the Dawn*?

ML: Yes.

LM: You played yourself several times in films, then.

ML: It was a gag—I could deduct my wardrobe costs. Until Hitchcock started to do it, I always appeared somewhere in a picture, just walk through a scene, going clear back to *Cradle Song*, where they are building a railroad; you can see me walk past the camera.

LM: *The Lady Is Willing* was made for Columbia, but it looks just like a Paramount film, with you directing, and Dietrich and Fred MacMurray starring. How did that come about?

ML: It was a package deal. Oh, Marlene scared the daylights out of him [MacMurray]. He was so scared of women it was pitiful. I never allow the press on the set if there's a difficult scene for the actor or actress, and that came about because Marlene had broken her ankle in *The Lady Is Willing*. She tripped over a cart on the floor and had a baby in her arms. To protect the baby she turned herself around so she landed on her back, and broke her ankle. She started work two weeks later with a walking cast. The first scene she had, with the baby in her arms, was a crying scene. And when Marlene started crying, the baby started crying too. Well, this reporter wrote that Marlene had made the baby cry, that the baby was afraid of her, and from that time on, I said "No reporters without my permission."

LM: Why was "My Ship" omitted from *Lady in the Dark*?

ML: The head of the studio, Buddy DeSylva, hated Kurt Weill with an undying hate—loathed the song, and he got it out of the picture. It was the best thing Ginger [Rogers] did—it was filmed. She sang it *a capella* against a foxtrot from a gymnasium. She was sitting all alone outside the gym, and sang it *a capella*. We blended it together so the foxtrot made a background accompaniment. And he couldn't stand it; he said, "Take it out." I said, "Over my dead body—it's the basis of the whole plot. When she suddenly remembers that song, her problems are all finished, but it didn't mean a thing to him. Then he discovered that her lover was supposed to be a father image. Well, he said, "I am not going to have incest in any picture made by Paramount," and I said, "Then why did you buy this story? That's the whole plot!"

LM: Was it difficult working in color?

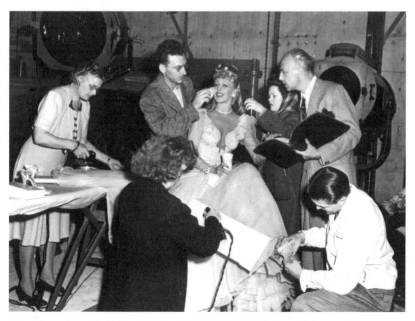

Ginger Rogers is attended to between shots of *Lady in the Dark*, with director Leisen at right.

145

ML: Time, time. It's not so difficult now, but the lights used to be murderous. For instance, in the blue dream in *Lady in the Dark*, all the women have red hair like her [Rogers'] mother. We used 155 arc lights with four layers of blue filter to make the air blue, then she had to be lighted separately so she didn't pick up the colors. Well, you could take it about a half hour and then you had to go off the stage, because you couldn't see blue anymore. Your eyes got tired and there was no longer any blue there. It was the same thing with the gold dream, the wedding-cake dream; that was all done with amber lights and all the girls had amber make-up on. To see those girls with their red hair, blue faces, and red lips go into the commissary, people would throw up. Those dresses were so big that we cleared out the sub-basement of Stage 18, and put in dressing rooms. We had a freight elevator to take them up, and we could only get three girls into that big freight elevator at one time. Those dresses were 14 yards around the bottom. We rehearsed with blue wrappers, to get the lighting, and in that I discovered that to make the blue more intense, I threw some jade green and a touch of lavender spots here and there to intensify the blue, just as we used orange in the gold dream.

LM: You tried to be very authentic in *Kitty*, didn't you?

ML: *Kitty* was a very interesting picture; we worked over a year in preparation for it. I sent back to the National Gallery of Art, and got the exact list of paintings exhibited that year, which was the year the Louvre was first opened. We had 40 Gainsborough paintings copied, I had 10 different artists. They were exactly the same size as the originals, same colors. But the "Blue Boy" was the big problem; we could not get anybody who could paint the "Blue Boy." It was unbelievable. Finally the make-up guy at Paramount painted one, and that was the one we used. I don't know whatever happened to all those paintings, but they were hijacked by everybody at the studio.

In *Kitty* Paulette [Goddard] had to be a cockney (in the original book she's a whore, but we made a buckle-thief out of her) and I couldn't get anybody who would admit she was a cockney, except Ida Lupino's mother, Connie Emerald. So I moved Connie into Paulette's apartment, and said, "Talk morning, noon, and night. Don't let her speak English at all." By God, she did. Ray [Milland] talked cockney with her, I talked cockney with her on the set. Now she had to become the Duchess, so I moved Connie Emerald out and moved Constance Collier in, and we changed the whole pitch of her voice; the first time you heard her speak as the Duchess, it was fascinating. We did the same thing in *To Each His Own*; I lowered her voice. Also, there's a trick, as a director, that I used. The first line spoken in a scene sets the tempo. So I used a formula of "Ready, right, action!" not just "Action!" And I would set the tempo of the scene by the way I read that line. I've watched directors say, "Go ahead!" and the actors wouldn't know what was going on.

Barbara Stanwyck recreates her role in *Remember the Night* for radio's *Screen Directors Playhouse*, with director Leisen, in 1949.

LM: You were known to pay a great deal of attention to women's styles in your films. What did you do in *To Each His Own* along this line?

ML: In *To Each His Own*, the girl ages during the picture. Olivia [de Havilland] had been sick and lost 17 pounds, and I insisted on shooting the picture in continuity. So we started when she was thin, and with as attractive a make-up as we could get on her, flattering her as much as we could. As the picture progressed, I fed her up every day and she gained back the 17 pounds, and she wound up wearing a Frankly Forty foundation garment. They wanted her to have gray hair. I said, "She's only 40, she doesn't have gray hair!" And we used a more unflattering lighting. That's all we did.

LM: How do you compare making films to working in television; the main difference is speed, isn't it?

ML: Speed. The last ones I did were all hour shows, where you had six-day shooting schedules, but even those six days you're going like a bat out of hell; start at 7:30 in the morning. You've got to keep going.

LM: Is it possible to be creative with those kinds of restrictions?

ML: I think I did, because of the past experience. I utilized everything I'd ever learned about directing pictures. I had it all at my fingertips. These new guys can be four days behind schedule because they don't know where to put the camera, what to do.

LM: You did several *Twilight Zone* shows, including one with Ida Lupino that's quite good.

ML: Ida was so funny in that she was directing at that time. She said, "I want you to understand one thing: I'm the actress and you're my director. And you make me do what you want me to do. I'm going to steal from you like mad!" And she was just as docile as could be.

LM: Many people have criticized the studio system of the 1930s and '40s, saying that is was restrictive and didn't allow creativity. Do you agree?

ML: No, not at all. It might have been in some cases, but I was a top director at Paramount, and if I snapped my fingers I got what I wanted. No arguments about it.

Conversations:

HENRY WILCOXON

While I was visiting Los Angeles in the fall of 1969, I kept in telephone contact with my friend at ABC Television's publicity department in New York. One day he asked if I would be interested in speaking to Henry Wilcoxon, who was shooting an episode of *Marcus Welby, M.D.* on the Universal studio lot. Of course I would! I didn't have time to do much preparation but Wilcoxon was a charming man and enjoyed telling stories as we lunched at the Universal commissary. He was 64 at the time but his body was spry and his face still bore the classic features that first struck Cecil B. DeMille in the 1930s. (Interview originally appeared in February 1970.)

LM: Why don't we start with some background material on yourself?

HW: Well, I come from the London stage. I had many years of theater in England. My first really important work was with the Birmingham Repertory Theater, in every type of role. I must have played 70 or 80 leading parts. It was the finest theater experience in human memory; we had a fabulous bunch of youngsters in the same company together. We had a young kid named Laurence Olivier, and another called Ralph Richardson, and another named Robert Donat, and another young man, Cedric Hardwicke, along with Edith Evans, and May Whitty. Just a bunch of raw talent. It was really a great experience. The policy

With Claudette Colbert in *Cleopatra*.

of the Birmingham Rep was to put on three seasons a year, with eight to ten plays each season. Two-thirds of them would be revivals, and the rest would be new plays, so you would have three new plays per season, with nine or ten new plays a year. Now out of those ten plays, one, and if they were lucky two, plays would be of hit quality, and they would bring those plays into London for a London run. So sometimes there would be as many as four Birmingham Rep plays running in London at the same time. As an example, the Birmingham Rep used to run the famous Bernard Shaw Festival Season up at Malvern, and put on all Bernard Shaw plays. I was in the first three of those, and we tried to get Shaw to write a new play each year, but of course that couldn't be done. The second year Shaw was writing this play, *The Apple Cart*, but it wasn't ready in time for our season, so we had to get a new play by an outside author, and we got a play by a fellow called Rudolph Besier, *The Barretts of Wimpole Street*, which turned out to be quite a hit. I was under contract to the Birmingham Rep for seven years, but that includes both my work up in Birmingham and in their plays in London. It was really fabulous experience. This is not to say that I didn't do plays for other companies and producers, which I did. I played several leading parts in London; in fact, I was doing the lead in a play called *Eight Bells* when Benjamin Glazer, who was a producer at Paramount, saw me, and he knew DeMille was looking for someone to play Mark Antony in *Cleopatra* with Claudette Colbert. He arranged to have me do a test, and that was sent out to Hollywood, not specifically for the part of

Mark Antony. The way it worked out was that they were running this test of a young British leading man for the producers and directors at Paramount. DeMille, as I said, was preparing *Cleopatra* at this time, and he happened to have some footage showing horses in action, which he wanted to buy for a scene in the picture. So on his way to lunch he stopped in at the projection room with this footage under his arm, and he asked the projectionist to put on this reel when he was done with what was being run. So he was waiting in the projection booth, and he heard this voice, looked through the window, and I was doing this test. He said, "Who is that?" and they told him it was a young actor Paramount was thinking of putting under contract. He said, "Forget the horse footage, run that for me when they're finished." So he went into the projection room, ran that, turned to his various assistants and said, "There's my Mark Antony; get him out here!" And that's the true story.

LM: *Cleopatra* is such a good film; I think it's one of DeMille's best pictures.

HW: I like *Cleopatra* very much, but I think I like *The Crusades* a little better. I think *Crusades* is one of the best pictures DeMille ever made. It really holds up; it doesn't date at all. As you know, Loretta Young played Queen Berengaria, and I played Richard the Lionhearted. But they were both very good pictures, no doubt about that. You know, it's a funny thing; I haven't seen *Cleopatra* with Burton and Taylor, but I do know that the picture cost a great deal of money. I believe the studio admits to it costing $35 million; others have estimated over $40 million. But just as a matter of interest would you care to guess how much the original *Cleopatra* cost to make?

With DeMille.

LM: A million?

HW: $750,000—you were very close. Of course, to make that same picture today would certainly cost you $10 or $12 million, even the way he did it, in black and white. On *The Crusades* there's also something funny. You know, I've been in show business now for almost half a century,

151

and I've talked to many thousands of people, and it's amazing, that there is one scene in *The Crusades* that almost invariably causes people to say "I remember that scene when…" And that's the scene at the Council of Kings when you have these two very strong men pitted against each other. Richard makes some crack, and Saladin says, "The English king's wit is as dull as his sword." And Richard says "What! My sword dull? Bring me an iron mace." They bring this massive iron mace, and he says, "Now set it between two stools," and they take these two huge oaken stools and set the mace across. Richard draws his sword and wham, he cuts it in two. They he says, "My sword dull, eh?" Sala-

With Carole Landis in *Mystery Sea Raider.*

din looks at him and says, "The Lion King has shown the strength of his arm, not the sharpness of his sword," so he goes to Richard's queen, and very graciously borrows a flimsy silk scarf that she has. He balls it up in his hand, throws it in the air, and as it's coming down, he holds his sword with two fingers, almost like a lady holding the handle of a teacup, and draws it across this thing floating down, and the two pieces fall on either side. Everybody remembers that scene. It's a good scene, because you have the conflict of these two powerful men: one who's a rough, tough sonofabitch, which Richard was, the other a cultured, magnificent man like Saladin. You have this terrific conflict between them, and yet there's an admiration for each other in this scene. Then you have this beautiful girl who is Richard's queen—and he uses her scarf. And it's so visual—seeing him cut this thing in half.

LM: Did you have any difficulty in adjusting from stage acting to screen acting?

HW: Well, there's a difference, but it's much easier to adjust from stage technique to motion pictures than the other way around. Because in motion pictures you don't ever learn to time an audience, to get the feel of an audience. Particularly this is true in comedy, where if you get one audience, and they're enjoying themselves but they're not laughing too much, then the actor will pick up his cues much faster and not wait for the laughs. Whereas you might also get an audience that is very, very demonstrative, and they laugh a lot; if you haven't made allowance for that, they're liable to be laughing over the next line. Also, on the stage, the part belongs to you, and nobody else, but in motion pictures a lot of it belongs to the director, to the writer, to the cutter, and a lot of others. In all of show business, the most important person—many people think the star or the director is most important—the writer is always the most important person in show business, always has been and always will be.

LM: Did DeMille work closely with writers?

HW: Oh yes, and he did a lot of his own writing. He always said that the secret of success in show business is one word: preparation.

LM: How did you get so closely allied with DeMille?

HW: Well, he brought me out to play Mark Antony in the first place. There was an immediate rapport between us, and our relationship was more than director and star; there was a great friendship, and a great mutual respect. I loved the old buzzard. You either hated him or you loved him, there was no half-way measure at all. He liked me because I never "yessed" him, and contrary to popular opinion, DeMille hated yes-men. There were a lot of people around him who were yes-men because he was such a powerful producer-director, but they wouldn't last. He'd always say, "I don't want 50 little DeMilles running around—it's bad enough to have one!"

LM: At what point did you begin to assume behind-the-camera responsibilities with him?

HW: I was in the Navy during World War II, and when I came out I was lucky enough to still be starring in films. I co-starred in *Samson and Delilah* for him, and it was during that film that he said, "I think you'd make a very good producer, Harry. Why don't you join me as co-producer?" So I did, during that picture. And for the next 13 years of his life I was co-producer on such pictures as *The Greatest Show on Earth*, and of course *The Ten Commandments*.

LM: What were your duties, co-producing with a man who was supposed to be so meticulous about his films?

HW: Does your tape last about 10 hours, because I could tell you about my duties with him. I'm very proud to say that he leant on me very heavily for a lot of things. I used to do everything—some writing. I used to sketch, so I did a great deal of costume design, and even on some of the sets I did the basic design for them. My ability to draw and sketch quickly would be very useful to him, because we'd be in a conference, and he'd be trying to make a point, and I'd see the person wasn't getting what he meant. So, while that would be going on, I'd sketch very quietly and then tear off a piece of paper and give it to him, and he'd say, "Here, this is exactly what I want." I remember he used to say, "If you get a dozen men, and you tell them that in this shot there's a house with a fence around it, one man will visualize a white picket fence, another will visualize a split-rail fence, another one will see a hedge, another will see a brick wall, etc. But if you have what you want on a piece of paper and say 'Gentlemen, I want a fence like that,' everybody knows, and you save yourself a couple of dollars."

With Mel Ferrer, Richard Anderson, and Stewart Granger in *Scaramouche.*

LM: He has been accused of being a great military commander but ineffective in working with intimate scenes of several actors. What do you think about this?

HW: I don't think that's true. It is true that when he was handling very large, vast numbers of people, he did assume almost the quality of a general in the field, and as a result he got better results out of those guys than any other man on earth. He would always address the entire group of extras, and say, "Ladies and gentlemen, I want you all to realize one thing: I don't want any extras on my set. I only want actors and actresses. During the making of this picture, if I come up to you and I say, 'What are you doing, and where are you going?' and you can't tell me, either you, or the assistant director, who is responsible for your segment, will be fired. I want you to think, and act. When you're crossing the square,

I want you to be able to tell me that you're crossing the street to the sandal maker's to get your sandal repaired. Or I want to know you are going to pick up your little son." Or whatever. And that is why, when you see a DeMille crowd scene, every extra walks around the scene at the same speed. Nobody is hurrying past anyone else. Nobody is sauntering between other groups of people. Now on the second part of your question, as far as the intimate scenes are concerned, DeMille would lean very heavily on his actors. If you're a good actor, he wouldn't bother to say a lot of things; he would just generally give directions, but he felt that he didn't have to impose his thought on theirs. He liked the actor to own the scene he did, if the actor was strong enough. When he had good actors, he left them alone. When he originally cast an actor in a role, and that actor was set, he would ask him to come and see him. They would sit together, and DeMille would tell the actor the whole script from the point of view of the character the actor was playing—so that the character was the hub of the whole picture. If that guy only had two scenes in that picture, all of this background material was in his head. So DeMille did all his directing in the office, and made sure that the actor knew what he was, what kind of character he was, whether he was a wealthy man or not, whether his father and mother were members of a minority group; he knew what his social status was, he knew all these things, even though he might have had just one line.

LM: Did you work with other directors while you were at Paramount?

HW: I was almost exclusively with DeMille for most of my time at Paramount, and even after Mr. DeMille died, the DeMille unit asked me to go on and finish the story that DeMille and I had started to prepare six months prior to his death, namely, the story of Lord Baden-Powell, the founder of the Boy Scouts. That picture I'm sure will be made; in fact, there is some activity on it now. They asked me to carry on, get a full treatment, and I did. I stayed on for another three, three-and-a-half years, until I had a shooting script and a very full treatment. Baden-Powell had one of the most incredible lives—he was an incredible guy. Let me say at the outset, it's not a Boy Scout story. The story finishes when Baden-Powell, the youngest general in the British army, and probably one of the most successful ever in military history, gives up a brilliant careers in order to start a worldwide organization dedicated toward youth and peace, and that ain't a bad story. He had such a fabulous life, including the famous Siege of Mafeking, where he and his tiny garrison were besieged, and by sheer bluff and guts and a sense of humor,

Henry Wilcoxon in *The Ten Commandments*.

he managed to bluff his way through this army of 12,000 to 15,000 men, all armed. That's just one part of this story—it's like a fabulous African western.

LM: Did DeMille have an actor in mind for this film?

HW: Yes he did, and I had the guy fly out from New York on that say-so; I never told him why, but I was able to talk him into coming out. I just promised him that he would have a part in a DeMille picture. I had known him from the days when he would come out with me on my boat, before he was even in pictures. It was David Niven. David came out, I met him at the plane, and he said, "You've got to tell me what this part is," and I said no. He said, "But we've been friends for years," and I said, "I've been friends with DeMille for years, and I promised him I wouldn't tell you. And anyhow, I want him to tell you." His plane got in very early in the morning, so I took David to his hotel and then I called Mr. DeMille and said, "He is here." He said, "Bring him out to the house, Harry. Has he had breakfast?" I said no, and then I told David, "Mr. DeMille wants you to have breakfast with him; is that all right with you?" He said, "Yes, I just want to find out what this part is." So we got in the car and drove up to the house; it was a beautiful day. We sat him down, and DeMille took his time, made small talk—he was almost Oriental. He said, "I saw you in such-and-such a picture, it was an excellent picture. Tell me about that picture." And Niven was biting his nails, so finally I said to Mr. DeMille, "Sir, I think David is going to lose his mind if you don't tell him." So he said, "I'll tell you one thing. When you play this part, not that this would make you scared, I promise that you will be knighted by the royal crowned heads of England." This helped David a lot. He said, "Sir, please what is it?" He said, "The part, David, is that...of...Lord...Baden-Powell of Gilwell." And David sat there for a moment; DeMille said, "Well, what do you think?" David was crying; he couldn't talk. When he regained his composure, he said, "Do you know, Mr. DeMille, that Baden-Powell has always been my great hero, all my life? My God, what a part—I'll do it for nothing!" This was about 12 years ago.

LM: Can you fill me in on *The Buccaneer*? DeMille was listed as producer on that, wasn't he?

HW: No, it was production supervisor.

LM: And Anthony Quinn was director.

HW: That's right.

LM: How much did DeMille have to do with that film?

HW: Not enough. It's not one of my favorite stories; the whole thing was a disaster. I don't like name-calling: I could give you many reasons why. You mentioned Tony Quinn. I want to say that Tony is, if not my favorite, then one of my favorite actors. And that's all you'll get out of me. (laughs)

LM: Besides this *Marcus Welby* episode, have you done much television work?

HW: I've done a number of guest-star things in series like *I Spy, Big Valley, Daniel Boone, F.B.I., Wild, Wild West*—about a dozen.

LM: It's much faster work than you must be used to.

On television's *Marcus Welby, M.D.* with Robert Young.

HW: Yes it is. On the other hand, I've done a few Republic Pictures, too. You know, the old Republic Pictures would run for about 70, 80 minutes, and they would make them in seven days, even faster than TV. Some of them were very good pictures, some of them were just ghastly. I remember I did one called *Prison Nurse* with Marian Marsh, and another called, oddly enough, *Woman Doctor*, with Frieda Inescort. She was so funny. I did *Tarzan* [*Finds a Son*] with Johnny Weissmuller and Maureen O'Sullivan, and Frieda played the British woman on safari;

I played the white hunter. Dear Frieda wore her pith helmet and veil absolutely straight. We'd tell her to wear it with a bit of a tilt, to take the curse off it, and she'd say, "No, no, they always wore them absolutely straight." I remember we had a dinner scene in Tarzan's tree-house where Cheetah, the chimpanzee, fell in love with Frieda. It was embarrassing as hell; we kidded her a lot about that. I had to sit next to her in one scene, and I was passing her something. Cheetah came up and growled, as if to say, "How dare you?" I'll never forget, in that particular *Tarzan* we were all captured and put into one of these huts. Of course, the natives were getting restless, and the tom-toms were going. Naturally, someone came up with the line, "I don't mind the wait, it's those constant drums that are driving me mad." And then I said, "It's when they stop that you should start to worry." It was a good story, though.

There was a scene where Tarzan had gone out somewhere or other, and I was supposed to cut a hole in the back of the hut: I would go through first, and then I was supposed to help Maureen through, and carry her out. So we'd shot it, but for some reason it had to be retaken. They retook it maybe three months after we had originally done it. And Maureen was always pregnant. She was only five months pregnant when we did it the first time, but now she was eight months pregnant, and everything was showing—they had to keep giving her baskets of fruit and things. At any rate, I cut the hole in the hut, and I got out, and then I had a great struggle getting her out of there—I was carrying both of them. This was in the days when if an airplane came over, they cut. So sure enough, a plane came over, and I said, "Uh-oh, it's the stork." So now, when I meet that young lady over there, I can say, "I carried you before you were born." [Directly across from us in the commissary was a photo of Mia Farrow; in fact, Maureen O'Sullivan was pregnant with son Michael at the time.—Ed.]

LM: You also did *Mrs. Miniver* at MGM with William Wyler. Is it true that he made many takes of each scene?

HW: Yes, he took a lot of takes. An interesting thing about that: I played the minister, as you may remember, and at the end of the picture I give this sermon in the blitzed church. We finished that picture, and right after that, while they were cutting it, Pearl Harbor came along, and suddenly we were at war. I was in the service, and they ran this picture and suddenly realized that the sermon I made was much too pacifistic. They needed something much more Winston Churchill-ish, so they had to get hold of the Navy Department for permission for me to come back. The Navy gave me permission for two days' absence; I flew from wherever I was to Los Angeles. William Wyler and I stayed up all night rewriting that sermon, and finally, with coffee running out of our ears, we opened the curtains; it was broad daylight. It was about 7:00 in the morning, and I had to be on the set at 9. I took a quick shave, got made up, and had the thing in the can by noon. Roosevelt liked the speech so much that he had it re-printed, and translated, and they had it dropped in leaflets from planes all over Germany, Austria, and occupied France.

Gary Cooper and Henry Wilcoxon in *Souls at Sea.*

I'll tell you an interesting sidelight about a picture I did called *Souls at Sea*, with Gary Cooper and George Raft. I had a nice part in that, and afterwards, I went to England to make a picture—I also wanted to see the coronation of George the Sixth. I had wonderful seats right by the Abbey, special seats, which were a difficult thing to get. I got this frantic phone call and telegram from Paramount saying, "Get on back, we've got retakes to do." I was absolutely livid; I said, "I can't, I've got these seats at the Coronation." They said I'd better come back or they'd get the Screen Actors Guild after me. So there wasn't anything I could do. I said, "Look, I'll be leaving within 10 days anyhow," but they said, "You'd better come over right away, and if you do, we can get you on the *Queen Mary* and you'll get here that much earlier." So I got on the *Queen Mary*, disgruntled as hell, got back, flew back to Hollywood, and made the scenes. A couple of days later I was listening to the radio, and the reason I was listening at that time was because of some reservations I had had to come over on the zeppelin Hindenburg. And I heard the guy saying, "Jesus Christ, it's on fire—" I'm sure you've heard that broadcast. I'd had reservations on that zeppelin, and I'd been mad as hell at Paramount—they saved my life! So, retakes can be good—they have their good points.

Conversations:
GEORGE O'BRIEN

One morning a friend phoned me to say that George O'Brien was in New York visiting his daughter Orin, who played double bass with the New York Philharmonic. He even provided me with a phone number. The next morning I found myself sitting in a noisy hotel coffee shop with a 71-year-old man of boundless energy who described himself, accurately, as "a man of a few thousand words." He was friendly, animated, and happy to draw on his memory to cover a lifetime of filmmaking, military activity, sports, and  globe-trotting. Among his favorite subjects were his parents (his father was a famous police chief in San Francisco and O'Brien still had strong ties there), his children (daughter Orin and son Darcy, who was then teaching English and went on to write a *roman à clef* about his actress mother [Marguerite Churchill] called *Margaret in Hollywood*), and John Ford. Pleased with the frequent revivals of his pet film, O'Brien had recently sent a gag telegram to Ford telling him, "Am now appearing at five theaters with *The Iron Horse*." (Interview originally appeared in May 1971.)

LM: Why don't we start at the beginning?

GO: *The Iron Horse*, my first starring role—I think it wasn't planned that way. I was, I guess, the last of the litter. Jack Ford had tested everybody at the Fox company for this lead, and when I was called, I'd been doing stunts and working extra. I'd been on the camera first, assistant camera boy. But somewhere along the line I became enthused about this sort of acting. When I was called, Jack Ford said, "I understand you've had several tests, one for *Ben-Hur* and one for *The Leather Pushers*." I said yes. He said, "What was the trouble?" I said "Well, June Mathis was very kind, so was Jimmy Hogan, who was the director of the test, but I'm unknown, and they wanted a box-office name for *Ben-Hur*." He said, "What about *The Leather Pushers*?" I said, "Well, Ricardo Cortez is a friend of mine, and we did an exhibition of boxing, and when we got the report from the studio, the man in charge, who I assume didn't know too much about boxing and probably very little about *The Leather Pushers*, told me that he thought it was very good but what they wanted was an actor who could look like a boxer, and not a boxer who could look like an actor." So the big so-called opportunity came when Ford said "How about taking the test today?" I said sure, and at that point I was on my way out, in my own mind. I figured "I'm going to give this about another six months." I'd already had about three years. So he said, "Go over to wardrobe," and he called for his assistant; his assistant went over with me and got a buckskin suit. He gave me a test, turning left, turning right, and so forth. Some of the cameramen I used to work with were around there working, all wishing me good luck and telling me that they had about 58 other established actors that they'd tried. But after we got going I more-or-less sensed what Ford had in mind. I think what he wanted was a sort of hungry kid; the part was a pony express rider, and you don't come off as a pony express rider if you're well-groomed and well-fed. I was about 23 years old at the time, and you know the old saying, "If you're hungry you'd fight Jack Dempsey."

But the main thing was that during the pictorial test he called to a beautiful young lady who was walking across the stage, who was Gertrude Olmstead. He said, "George is making a test for the part; would you do a little scene with him?" So he wrote right there on the set a little love scene; I've only got five minutes but I had to come back to see her, and all that kind of stuff. She was wonderful, and you know, if people compete with you it's much better. This brings you up. It's like any kind of athletics; if you're forced, you'll break a record—if you're not forced, you won't. We did the scene, and Ford was talking on the sidelines. "All right now, George, you know they're after you, so kiss her goodbye and go to the door—no, don't go to the door, go through the window." The window was open, a big window. I did this, and I think I added a little bit more because she was so helpful. She held me just a little bit as I turned to go, which was very good, and I turned back to her again. He said, "OK, print it. Well, as far as I'm concerned, you can have it, but we've got to get the OK from New York and all that sort of thing." So I went on going about my work, looking for extra work or stunts, came back about three months later, and I figured they must have forgotten me. I was now 59 of the actors he'd tested. Then another call came to come down, and he made me wrestle Fred Kohler, who I'd just met. Fred and I tossed each other around. Then he asked me to pick up his glove, on horseback. Luckily I'd had all this experience. He said, "I want you to do some vaulting for me," you know, the pony express stuff, so I did, and the last time coming by, the cinch broke underneath; the horse went one way and I went another. But I got up—youth again—I bounced. And then he assured me that as far as he was concerned, I had it. And again I went on my way, and signed up with Frank Lloyd as one of the many slaves on the galley ship in *The Sea Hawk*. Wonderful job, in Catalina a few months—$10 a day and all you could eat, all the time watching behind the camera, because I really wanted to be a director. I came back from Catalina, and Frank Lloyd and the rest of the company were going to do some interiors, then they were going to pick us up again. In other words, we were off salary, but they still had us signed for the job. So I

Fox publicity photo with Lois Moran.

went home to our little house, where Mervyn LeRoy and I were renting a room from a nice man and his wife; Gary Cooper was living there. I walked in the door, and Mervyn yelled at me, "George, quick! Fox wants you." So I got on the phone with a very nice gentleman from the casting office, Jim Ryan. He said, "George, I've been trying to reach you. Hurry down here. Have you seen Ford?" I said no. I went down to Ryan's office and he took me to Ford's office; Ford stood up and said, "Have you talked to Mr. Wurtzel?" I said no—you know, everybody assumed. He took me to Sol Wurtzel's office, and he read me a five-page night letter from William Fox saying to sign me for five years, with a six-month option; "...and I caution you again: this is entirely untried, an entirely new man, unknown. You will take 90 times the scenes if necessary." And Ford said, "That won't be necessary." Well, from there we went away, and it developed into a tremendous thing.

LM: How long were you shooting [*The Iron Horse*]?

GO: We were about six months; we went to Montana; we went to Mexico; [and] Montana for the buffalo. We spent most of our time in Nevada, on a railroad siding. We slept in railroad cars. Of course your old crowd says, when you go back to Hollywood, "Say, we hear it's terrific," and all the time you're hoping. The opening night your mother and father come down. My mother was asked by Jimmy Starr, the columnist, "Margie, who's your favorite actor?" She said, "Tommy Meighan." And they roared. He said, "What about George?" And she said, "Oh, he's my son."

LM: How would you describe Ford's direction on your first film?

GO: To me, he was a coach. You see, I was young enough to want to go all out. "Let me do it, Coach." Impressionable, if you want. People like Duke, John Wayne, and Maureen O'Hara claim he has eyes in the back of his head. Because you'll be over working out some business for a scene, you'd get in the scene, and he'd say, "Here's what I'd like you to do—not what you were trying to do over there." And you'd say, "How did he know that?" Then he'd come over and put his arm around you like a coach, and say, "Nice going." That's all you need sometimes.

Also, I think Ford, myself, John Wayne, we started from humble beginnings, and when we realized we were up against it, we went to work. And work in those days meant practically living in the studio. I slept in my dressing room many times. The Guild wasn't strong then, so there weren't labor problems. Today, if they keep you too long in wardrobe they give you a check. Dolores Del Rio and I in *Cheyenne Autumn* didn't understand that. When we got these checks she said, "George, I don't understand this check," and I said, "I don't either, Dolores." So we went to Wingate, the production manager, and he said, "Oh, that was for the two fittings you had at wardrobe." I've been fitting on cavalry coats for years, but these are the rules. And I like it—not for me, but for the fellow who is me 40 years later, who has only got one cup of coffee left. I think that with Jack Ford, it may be theatrical to say, "He lived it," but he did, and we did. And this is the way he liked it. You'd sit around at nighttime on location and talk over the scenes. He'd pick you up on a Sunday morning after church, go down to the studio and run some film. There are those who still do it. On *Cheyenne Autumn* I had promised to do three weeks, but I stayed on the picture two-and-a-half months, because every day, even though I wasn't working, I'd come over.

LM: I'd like to know about the making of *Sunrise*.

GO: Murnau, the German director, decided he wanted me after he saw *The Man Who Came Back*, which was my second picture. William Fox at that time gave a carte blanche contract to Murnau; not so much money, because I'm one of the few people who saw Murnau's contract. But again, the enthusiasm was there. He had, as they said then, far-out ideas on camera techniques, and Charles Rosher and Karl Struss, who I knew very well. I would sit for hours while they were lining up a shot. It was all closed in. We worked about six months on it; Janet Gaynor, Margaret Livingston, Murnau, and myself had lunch and dinner every day when we worked at the studio. He had it like a family.

LM: You had to maintain a mood, didn't you?

GO: This was it. And we were on location at Lake Arrowhead for a long time. There was great physical strain.

LM: How much of the film was on location and how much was studio?

GO: We built a whole village up at Arrowhead. The interior of the church, the dance scene, the Luna Park, that was in the studio.

LM: Wasn't some of that built in forced perspective?

GO: Yes. Charles Rosher would set his camera up, and the set would be in perspective, slanting up. We danced on a slanted floor, if you recall the peasant dance. In order to help me with my mood, Murnau would explain each situation; I had studied German in school, as part of chemistry, and I made an effort, but I didn't have to, because Murnau went to school in England, and he spoke better English than I did. But every once in a while he'd be lost for a word. He was explaining to Margaret Livingston what kind of woman she was. He was going along

O'Brien was not shy about showing off his physique.

fine, and then he went as far as he could; he couldn't think of the word streetwalker, he couldn't think of the word slut or prostitute. It wasn't coming to him, so he turned to me, and I kind of nodded, and he said to Margaret Livingston, "You are a...you are a...sonofabitch!"

LM: Do you remember much about *Fig Leaves*?

GO: Howard Hawks was more or less getting his footing, or getting his stride, at this time. It was one of the far-out films, but of course the studio was behind it or they wouldn't have let Hawks make it. But the work that went into the prehistoric scenes. There's one scene where I'm reading the "newspaper" and Olive Borden is trying to read the ads on the back of it, and I rip the stone in half, terribly annoyed, and give her half. Then we go out on our way to work and a dinosaur comes by like a subway.

165

LM: Was there any chance for improvisation on the prehistoric scenes?

GO: Constantly. That's why it was great working with Hawks—very flexible. "Let's try it this way." Which was wonderful.

LM: You worked with so many great directors. What problems did you face when you worked with someone who was less gifted?

GO: Well, Ford, in his days under contract to studios, had to take people and get a performance out of them. Now I, under contract, occasionally had to do a story that I didn't believe in too much. But I always believed the customer, in this case the studio, which was paying me 52 weeks a year, and some years I only worked 24 weeks. That wasn't a bad life, so why shouldn't I give in a little, once in a while? You can call me a company man, or an establishment man, but I was just embarrassed if I'd say, "I won't do that." What I did was try to get with the director, who, after many worldly experiences I found was partly shy, sometimes tense, and sometimes in awe of the fact that he had the number-one box-office star of Fox who would carry him into a lot of theaters. So, answering you directly—sure, there were times, but call it Pollyanna or whatever you like, when I saw that this fellow was forcing too much, I sometimes would take him to lunch, particularly if he didn't have a big credit, and I would say, "You know, this can be a sleeper, and I was thinking about what you said the other day...." Many doctors have told me that if you let people talk enough they can cure themselves, because they'll tell you what's wrong and what they think ought to be done. Now sometimes

With Dolores Costello in *Noah's Ark*.

people would come to me and say, "I understand you're going to have so-and-so on your next picture," and I'd say, "That's right," and they'd say, "Boy, he blows higher than a kite." One of the greatest experiences I ever had was coming back here [New York] and doing *East Side, West Side*, with a man who did have that kind of reputation, not for swearing at you, but for being rather brittle and sarcastic, Allan Dwan. The first morning I came in 15 minutes early; he came in and I said, "Allan, how are you?" and he said, "George, I'm delighted." And we hit it right off. I listened, and paid attention, because I saw this man had it.

LM: You worked with a legendary character, Michael Curtiz, on *Noah's Ark*.

GO: Yes, indeed. Some said he was a madman, but I don't think so. But I lost both my big toenails in the flood scene; he had me tied up. Then, when I was to be blinded with a hot poker, he said, "George, I want to come very close, my boy. I want the audience to scream." And I'll tell you, I could feel the heat of that thing. I screamed bloody murder. And I went through the rest of the picture blind; that was an experience. The Westmores were wonderful; they hadn't yet developed whatever it is they use now for blind people, and they used spirit gum, the stuff you use to put whiskers on. I had 14 sties in both eyes. I had to be led off; once you put it on in the morning it was murder to take it off, because your eyelashes would come off with it! So I was blind and chained to this thing when the first flood started, and rock and debris and wood from the top of the chutes fell down. Dolores Costello, who was in the picture, was out of it for two months; she caught pneumonia from all the water.

LM: What was your first talking picture?

GO: Well, there was half a talking sequence in *Noah's Ark*. Dolores Costello, who had a delightful voice, said, "George, have you had any tests?" I said no. She said, "This is going to be a test." We had already heard over at Fox that we were all going to be replaced by stage actors, and the directors were, too. So the scene was written, kind of a semi-love scene. They took the platter and went into the projection room; Jack Warner came in, the director came in [Roy Del Ruth directed the talking scene], they ran it, and I was amazed. I thought it was my brother talking. You see, you don't hear yourself. Warner turned around, and said, "It was great," and Del Ruth said, "Great." So we went right back and made the whole sequence. It was a good sort of pat on the back.

Then right after that I made *Salute*, up at West Point. That's where we took John Wayne, Ward Bond, all the guys from USC and made actors out of them. *Salute* came out, and the same thing took place; various directors around the studio started to bid for me. So I was assured right away. Out on the first Western, *The Lone Star Ranger*, we had to carry the cable under our legs while the horse was going along; they were still inventing things. On a long chase, they hid the microphones in the bushes, and Barney Fergus (the sound man) would say, "George, how close are you going to that bush? My main microphone is there." I'd say, "All right, Barney, where's the other one?" and he'd say, "The other one's over here." Then the director would say, "Now, George, I want that awful fast coming through there," so I didn't want to be looking for microphones in the picture, and I came close one day. I didn't touch it, but I hit a rock or something, and the rock bounced, almost blew poor Barney's brains out. Then they started covering the microphones with shammy, because the wind sounded like the ocean waves.

LM: How quickly were your RKO Westerns made?

GO: My pictures would take from three to four weeks. My pictures with Sol Lesser, which were released by 20th Century Fox—we would be gone for a month, sometimes over that. We went to Utah, Monument Valley, Arizona, Montana, Colorado, sometimes where the story called for. The RKO ones, we went to Foxborough and Sedona Valley, and there's quite a resort there now called Old Oak Creek. But three weeks, maybe, including one or two interiors. The RKOs had very few interiors; in fact, we took some mobile sets with us. Or we wrote the story so I had a little lean-to in the rocks, or something.

LM: How much were you involved in the production of those films?

GO: All the time. I worked with the writers; I always sat in with them.

LM: What kind of things did you try to project in your characterization?

GO: Well, if I was a marshal, or a sheriff, or an F.B.I. man, I tried to model it the way my father believed in people. He was a very anti-violent man; in fact, the recent chief of police of San Francisco told me, "Your father was one of the first in the United States to be called a progressive police chief." So I used a lot of these things, and also from my early days as a kid riding with sheriffs; when I was 19 I was on a manhunt myself, with two of my father's mounted men.

LM: So you tried to be basically real.

GO: Yes I did, definitely.

LM: Where did you discover the various leading ladies who appeared with you, like Laraine Day, Rita Hayworth, and Marjorie Reynolds?

With Janet Gaynor in *Sunrise*.

GO: Some of them were under contract to the studio, on a stock contract, like Laraine Day. Some of them were under contract to another studio, like Rita Hayworth, and the studio was glad to get rid of them for a while to pay the overhead. I believed if they were sort of Johnny-come-latelies, fresh out of kindergarten; after talking to a person for a while you can tell if they're sincere in their work. So if I was willing to do scenes over and over with them, and the director was willing to spend the time, they had to definitely have some sort of inclination to try hard. Of course, you run into that in any business, you run into people who just want their salary and that's it. But I'm happy to say that practically every one we took with us and worked on, and spent extra time rehearsing with, has turned out pretty well.

LM: Do you have a favorite of all your films?

GO: I guess I'd have to say *The Iron Horse,* because it was a success and it could have been an awful flop, and Ford and I would still be trying to make a living someplace. So it did two things: it gave me my opportunity and it gave Ford his opportunity, because up until that time he'd been making Harry Careys. So you see how things happen. If Ford and the Fox company had been happy with one of the 58 tests they made, I'd probably be off sailing a ship someplace. Then I would also say something that wasn't George O'Brien, the characterization in *Sunrise*, because I like to think that everybody sees what I saw in *Sunrise*, a chance to prove that I could concentrate on something besides my ever-lovin' personality.

Conversations:

RALPH BELLAMY

Ralph Bellamy was a stalwart of stage and screen for half a century and a pioneer of live television. Still vigorous at 66, he was happy to talk with me during a lunch break from filming an episode of ABC's *The Most Deadly Game*, in which he starred with Yvette Mimieux and George Maharis. Like other actors of his generation he had a ready repertoire of stories to share, and I was grateful to hear them. (Interview originally appeared in September 1971.)

LM: Do you mind if we dig into the past a bit?

RB: Go ahead.

LM: How did you come to make *The Secret Six*, in 1931?

RB: I was in a play in New York which lasted two weeks, I believe, called *Road Side*. It was Lynn Figgs' first play—he, you know, wrote *Green Grow the Lilacs*, which became *Oklahoma!* The play didn't go, but I got five picture contract offers, and Arthur Hopkins asked me to accept the one from Joe Schenck, who was head of United Artists at the time. I did, although it wasn't the best contract. I came out here and right off the bat he loaned me to MGM. That cast was Clark Gable—that's the one on which he got his MGM contract—and the leading man was Johnny Mack Brown. Plus Harlow, Beery, Lew Stone, Marjorie Rambeau. I was a gangster.

LM: Had you been playing heroes on Broadway?

RB: I hadn't done much on Broadway; I had only done two plays on Broadway up to that point. The bulk of my experience had been in stock—not what they call stock today, but real old stock companies. I had my own for a while. I played leads in stock, which meant you played a different play each week, ten performances—seven days a week, three matinées—of fairly current Broadway plays.

LM: I suppose after that experience movie technique didn't faze you.

RB: It's a different kind of approach; each medium has its differences, but this is a big one. The transposition from the stage to the camera, when you first have it, is a rather awesome thing. You've got to reduce everything, or at least not treat it so broadly, as you have to do on the stage because of the gallery, the back of the house. You do just the opposite. It's a thing you have to get used to. Everybody was getting used to it at that time. At that time I heard for the first time a phrase I've heard many times since. I'd just come out, and I was dining at a restaurant which is no longer here on Hollywood Boulevard called Henry's, which was a popular place at the time. Gable came in, alone, and he said, "What do you think of this thing out here?" and I said, "I don't know yet." Gable said, "I just finished a picture—I got $11,000 for playing a heavy in a Bill Boyd Western. Eleven thousand dollars! No actor is worth this. I got myself a room at the Castle Argyle, I bought myself a second-hand Ford, and I'm saving every nickel I'm making, because I'm not going to buy anything you can't put on the Chief." That was the first time I'd heard that phrase—don't buy anything you can't put on the Chief.

LM: So then you were loaned to Paramount for *The Magnificent Lie*?

RB: No, I broke the contract with Joe Schenck, because he told me after he got me out here under contract, I had 30 weeks guaranteed out of 52, which allowed him to lay me off 22 weeks, which he did after *The Secret Six*. He didn't think I was for pictures, so I said "Well, let me out of the contract." So that was freelance. I freelanced for a while, then I got a Fox contract and worked there for a while.

LM: They really kept you busy there.

With Wallace Beery in *The Secret Six*.

RB: Oh yes. Spence Tracy was there then; we did two or three together. They wanted us both to stay on another year at the same salary and we both said no—we were in everything they were doing.

LM: Do you remember another picture at MGM called *Toast of Broadway* with John Gilbert?

RB: Yes. Sound had just come in, and all the studios had to refinance. Nobody was prepared financially for sound, and to get refinancing, MGM quickly signed a contract with Gilbert, who was their hot man then, for either three years at two million dollars or two years at three million dollars—I forget which; he told me this story—so that they could go to the banks and say "We've got John Gilbert, and we need X millions of dollars." They got the money, but when they put Jack under a microphone, he came out with a thin, piping voice. It really wasn't too bad, but it wasn't good. Well, they did everything to try and get out of the contract with him. I remember he said to me, "I know what they're doing. They're giving me second-rate pictures"—which this one was—"but I've got such a contract that I'm going to do it. I'll clean out the spittoons and sweep the floors for the duration of the contract." Which he practically did. He was quite a guy; I liked him.

LM: What was your part like in the picture?

RB: I was a ranch foreman, and he was the fellow from New York who owned the ranch. I had ridden back East; I learned at an Army base in an Army saddle, but I'd never been in a Western saddle. They said "Can you ride?" and I said "Yes." I'd done it, and I could. But the first shot with Jack was coming in from making the rounds of the ranch, the two of us riding. I had a ten-gallon hat, boots, and everything. We were to ride through the gate, up to the hitching post, and dismount—a silent shot. So the director, Harry Beaumont, said "Go out around the corner there, and when we call you, come in at a fair pace, tie your horses up and leave." So we went out, and we were on the side of the hill. I had never neck-reined a horse, and I couldn't turn the horse around. Jack was dying laughing. Suddenly, I kicked this horse around, got it facing practically downhill, and in the distance—they used those loud, big clappers—the horses, which were picture horses, had heard the director, knew what they were supposed to do, and the next thing I knew, I was coming through the gate with both hands on the pommel, my hat off, my hair flowing in the breeze, feet out of the stirrups—the horse came up to the hitching post and stopped dead. Jack was fifty yards behind me, and everybody was dying laughing. They printed it, and I saw it on the screen.

LM: Do you recall another early picture called *Forbidden*?

RB: Well, that was Capra's first big picture, and Stanwyck's first big picture—that was at Columbia. Columbia—that opens up some stories. I have some firsts over there. I didn't have an agent at that time, and in Harry Cohn's office, he and Sam Briskin, who was his right-hand man, literally had me backed into a corner, pointing fingers at me, to talk about this deal. I didn't even know enough to be flattered about it; I thought this was the way they behaved. Anyway, we had a handshake deal for me to do these pictures. I went home and Dan Kelly, who was then the casting director at Columbia, called and said, "Mr. Cohn says if you're going to do that picture with Capra and Barbara Stanwyck, you've got to do one first with Fay Wray." I said, "Well, it's possible; let me see the script." So they sent me the script, I read it, they called and said, "What about it?" I said, "The one with Fay Wray is a very physical, strenuous thing; go to sea for a week—water, lifting people, going under water in barrels—and it finishes the day before the one with Stanwyck starts, and I'm in every scene with Stanwyck." This was before the Screen Actors Guild. "I would have to have a stand-in." So Kelly said, "We've never had a stand-in on the Columbia lot." I said, "I will have to, and I would think anybody would have to, to do those two pictures back to back." He said, "I'll call you back." He did, and said, "Mr. Cohn wants to see you." I went to the office, and he said, "What the hell is this, you New York actors coming out here. Stand-in! I've never had a stand-in on the Columbia lot, and we never will have." I said, "I'm not pressing anything, I'm just telling you that I couldn't do justice to you, the part, myself, or anybody concerned, without a stand-in." So we batted this around, and I didn't know Harry very well at that time, and I finally said, "Well, Mr. Cohn, why don't we just forget both pictures, and maybe some time later on we can find something we can do together." Which you weren't supposed to say to Harry Cohn. We talked a few minutes more, and he said, "You can have a stand-in on one condition: don't tell Jack Holt!" I said, "I don't even know

With Harry Holman and Barbara Stanwyck in *Forbidden*.

Jack Holt, and if I met him, I don't think I'd say, 'I have a stand-in and you haven't.'" He said, "Don't give me any of that, get out of my office and do the two pictures." I did, and I wound up under contract to him. Then, like at Fox, I was in everything they did. In those days, again before the Screen Actors Guild, we worked what they were pleased to call six days a week, but it really was seven. You'd come to work Saturday morning, the usual time, and work all day, all night, through the night, until the leading lady fainted Sunday noon, or some catastrophe started. Now, some of my friends were arbitrarily stopping work at 6:00. I thought, "If anybody has a right to do this, I have." So each afternoon around 5:30, I would say to the assistant director, "Don't let the director get into a setup that includes me after six, because I'm not going to be here." This went on for about a week, and a boy came on the set one day with a note: "Stop in my office today when you finish work—Harry Cohn." By now, I knew him pretty well, and I must say I got on with Harry, I liked him for what he was. He said, "What the hell is this walking off a set? Something new, isn't it?" I said, "I don't walk off a set; I walk on every morning, on practically every set you have here, I've been doing it for a long time, and I believe that if that's the way it's going to be, I have to have that amount of rest."

He said, "You're under contract to me, you'll do what I tell you." I said, "Harry, I can't do it. If that's the way you feel about it, let's tear up the contract." Which again, you weren't supposed to say. So we talked some more, it got pretty rough, and finally he said, "All right, you can quit at 6:00, on one condition: don't tell Jack Holt!"

LM: What was Frank Capra like as a director?

RB: Just great, just wonderful, He was flexible, and gentle, and perceptive. He used what you had, as any good director does. He knew how to get the greatest degree of what you had to offer, providing what was called for in the script. That's a picture that might stand up today.

LM: Barbara Stanwyck is terribly good in those Columbia pictures.

RB: Barbara Stanwyck is terribly good in anything. And it's easy to explain: it's absolute simplicity and complete honesty. There isn't a phony note there.

LM: I'd like to know more about some of the things you did at Fox.

RB: That one picture you mentioned, *Surrender*, we started on the old Western Avenue lot, and they were completing the Fox Hills. We shot the first half on Western Avenue, and moved over and used the new studio for the second half. I guess we might have been the first ones to use the new studio.

LM: What was it like to play a scene with Spencer Tracy?

RB: Just great. This was real acting. Neither one of us held, or as far as I'm concerned still hold, with the theories of the "method," or any of the procedures or patterns that are dealt to young aspiring actors. There is no definition of acting. No one can say what acting is; and no one can teach you to act. I dare say you can be helped by joining some other people and doing things together, but acting is the result of first an urge, then a knack, and hopefully a talent, and an awful lot of experience.

LM: We now come to *Air Mail*, certainly one of your best films, directed by John Ford. One great asset is its feeling of authenticity; was it shot at an actual air field?

RB: It sure was. We went up to Bishop, California, for that; the airplane expert was Paul Mantz, and a fellow working for him was Jimmy James. Jimmy James was one of the nine remaining 45 mail pilots; they were a colorful, roustabout lot. Wonderful people, but crazy. We had a scene in which Pat O'Brien was supposed to be flying in to our airport, and his reputation had preceded him as being a wild sort of uncontrollable kind of guy. The scene called for a one-man circus up in the air, and then a 10,000-foot dive through a one-ship hangar, leveling out and landing. Well, this meant that Jimmy James, who was doubling for Pat in the airplane, would have to fly upside down in an open-cockpit plane, do barrels, outside loops, inside loops, everything they knew in those days, and then this 10,000-foot dive. Well, up at Bishop, which is high-mountain area, the weather was unpredictable, and we always had it on the schedule to do if the weather were right, but it would be windy, or up-and-down drafts, and they'd say, "Not today." One morning we got out there about 7:00, and Ford said, "Where's Jimmy?" Somebody said, "We haven't seen him, but he probably won't be here, because he was up all night shooting craps, drinking. "All of a sudden, off in the distance goes Jimmy James in his plane. This was a particularly bad day, with up-and-down drafts. We tried to signal him from the ground to come down, but he paid no attention. Then he started an ascent, and went to 10,000 feet. We couldn't stop him, so finally Jack said, "Get the camera set up; if he's going to do it, I guess we'll have to take it." He said to me, "This weather is so wild, why don't you go out about 30 feet in front of the hangar, mark center, and start flagging him down?" At the same time, I'd be marking center for Jimmy. So he started this dive, and I'm 30 feet in front of this hangar waving a flag, and he's aiming right at me! I suddenly realized, "Where am I going to go?" I never ate so much dust in my life; I suddenly fell to the ground, threw the flag away, and he did it.

LM: Another good picture around this time was *Picture Snatcher*, with James Cagney, in which you played a drunken city editor.

RB: As a matter of fact, we met on that picture. It had two distinctions: He was the only man I ever hit, and it was the only time he ever got hit hard enough to have a lasting effect. I had to hit him someplace in the story. The usual trick, as you know, is to put the camera over the shoulder of the person who's throwing the blow; you throw the fist past the chin— it doesn't matter what distance, as long as it covers the chin and passes it—when they put a blow in, and the fellow who's receiving the punch snaps his head, it looks as if he's hit. Jimmy said to me, "Aim at my face, I'll get out of the way." He was a boxer. I said, "I don't want to do that." He said, "It's my fault if anything goes wrong; I'll get out of the way. Aim at my chin." So I did, he didn't get out of the way, and it broke a tooth. I guess a lot of people have been in fights—I never had been, never had hit anybody in my life. I remember it now graphically, and I think it hurt me more than it did him. He's wound up my closest friend over all these years.

With Cary Grant and Irene Dunne in *The Awful Truth*.

LM: What are your memories of *Spitfire*?

RB: Why don't we just drop that? I did it for no reason except I loved Katie Hepburn. Well, I can tell you one good story there. Katie was about to do a play in New York called *The Lake*, with Jed Harris. She actually wanted me to do it with her, but I decided not to. This was during the time of shooting *Spitfire*. It came to the last scene, and she was to go to New York to start rehearsals with Jed Harris the next day; another good friend of mine, John Cromwell, was directing. We'd finished rehearsing this last scene, which we couldn't do the picture without, and she said, "Now, John, before we start to shoot this, I want to bring up a point. We're a day over schedule, and when I made this contract, everybody being aware of the fact that I had to be in New York in rehearsal on such-and-such a day, there's a penalty clause in here of $10,000 a day over. It's a day over, and before we shoot this, I'd like to have the $10,000." In 15 minutes, Myron Selznick, her agent, Pandro Berman, who was running the studio, everybody in town was on that set. Katie said, "I'll be in my dressing room. When you get ready with the check, come see me." Not too much time went by, back came Katie in a gingham dress. John Cromwell said, "OK, let's rehearse it once more. We got out in front of the camera, and Kate put her hand in the pocket of her gingham dress and said, "There's the check."

LM: Among the other distinctions in your career, you worked with Anna

177

Sten in *The Wedding Night*. Samuel Goldwyn was very much involved in the production of that film, wasn't he?

RB: He sure was. I remember, this was a story about Connecticut tobacco fields, and Polish people. She was Polish, and I was. I forget how Gary Cooper got into it, but everything was all right until Gary came along. I don't remember the story very well, but the point was made that this was an isolated ethnic group which stayed with their language, stayed with their customs, their dances, and everything. I had to learn Polish dances; I can't even foxtrot but I had to learn Polish dances. So I was playing it as indicated in the script, and then Goldwyn came on the set, just before we were going to do a long take. When we finished it, King Vidor and Goldwyn had a long conference and Goldwyn left the stage. Vidor came up to me and said, "You, I guess, have upset Mr. Goldwyn." I said, "Why?" He said that Goldwyn said, "Vy is Bellamy playing it vit an accent?"

LM: Working at Columbia, in the midst of all these B pictures, you did *The Awful Truth*, which was one of your all-time best films.

RB: Oh, that was wonderful. One day I was telephoned at home by Dan Kelly, and he said, "Mr. Cohn is sending a script over called *The Awful Truth*. He wants you to read the script and look at the part of so-and-so, which was written for Roland Young. Don't pay any attention to it, because it isn't going to be that kind of a part." I said, "Well why are you sending it over, and why am I supposed to read it, if I'm not supposed to pay any attention to it?" He said, "I don't know, that's the message Mr. Cohn gave me." I read it, and it was a pretty funny script—it was from a stage play, as you know. Then I was called and asked to go to Cohn's office. He said, "What do you think of the script?" I said, "I think it's a very good script for Roland Young." He said, "Never mind, it's not going to be that kind of part." I said, "What's it going to be? Why did I read it?" He said, "Just to get your reaction." I said, "Well, you've got it." That was the end of that; I'd forgotten about it, and one day I got a call from Mary McCall Jr., a writer, and she said, "We're good friends; would you do something for me? Come over to my office. I've got *The Awful Truth* here, and I'm supposed to make a character out of the part that was written for Roland Young, and tailor it for you." I said, "Sure, I'll come over." And she said, "What do you think it should be?" I said, "I think it's fine the way it is, and I think Roland Young would be just great in it." She said, "But I'm supposed to make him

Western. We talked about this a bit, and we had the damnedest thing arranged. I think I, in a New York hotel, came down a fire escape into a window, and that was my entrance; she wrote it, and we thought we'd had a good afternoon. Then I was at somebody's house, a cocktail party, and Dwight Taylor saw me and said, "Oh, we're going to be working together." I said, "Yeah? On what?" He said, "*The Awful Truth*." I said, "Are you collaborating with Mary McCall?" He said, "No, she hasn't anything to do with it; I was given the script. It's going to be great, I've got a great part for you." I said, "What is it?" He said, "I'm not going to talk about it." So weeks go by, and I meet Dorothy Parker and Alan Campbell. They said, "Isn't it wonderful, we're going to be together." I said, "On what?" She said, "*The Awful Truth*." I said, "Oh, I didn't know that. What happened to Dwight Taylor?" She said, "We don't know anything about Dwight Taylor. Harry Cohn sent us the script. And we've got a beautiful part in it for you." But they wouldn't talk about it. So, time went on, and Dan Kelly called, and said, "Report to the studio Monday morning to do *The Awful Truth*." I said, "To play what? Where's the script?" He said, "I don't know, I guess they'll get it to you." I said, "Who else is in it?" He said, "Cary Grant and Irene Dunne." So I tried to get Harry, and I got him the Friday before, and said, "I've got to talk to you about this. What am I playing?" He said, "Just leave it to Leo McCarey. Leo McCarey is a great director, and we're going to be all right. I'm not going to tell you anything." I said, "How am I going to play a part if I don't know anything about it?" He said it would be a westerner, from Oklahoma. I said, "That's not much of a lead. Would you mind if I go and see Leo?" He said, "Go ahead." So I

With Cary Grant and Rosalind Russell in *His Girl Friday*.

called Leo at his house. Did you know Leo? He always had a big grin, and those bouncing eyes. I went out to his house, and I said, "I want to talk to you about *The Awful Truth*." He said, "It's gonna be great!" I said, "But what's the part?" He said, "Oh, don't worry, don't worry." It all seemed so indefinite, and nebulous. So then this call came to show up Monday morning, and I said, "What kind of clothes?" They said, "Just bring a lot of clothes." I was being nasty, I got made up, and all the

clothes I could carry I brought onto the set. Leo came over, said hello. I said, "Leo, I don't know what the part is, I don't know how to dress it; I was told to bring a lot of clothes, so I've got a lot of clothes." He said, "What have you got on?" I said, "Odd jacket and trousers." He said, "Let me see it—just the thing!" It was just the way I came to the studio. He said, "Come over here," so I went over, and he had Irene sitting at a piano in front of the camera, and she was saying, "Leo, I can't;

With Margaret Lindsay and Ann Doran in *Ellery Queen's Penthouse Mystery.*

you can't ask me to do this." Irene and I said hello, and Leo said, "Can you sing?" I said, "I can't get from one note to the next." He laughed, "That's exactly what I want!" He said, "You're an Oklahoman." I said, "What kind of Oklahoman?" He said, "Just be an Oklahoman for the moment; I'll tell you about the rest of it later. Do you know 'Home on the Range'?" I said, "I know the words, but I can't sing it." He said, "It's perfect! Irene, do you think you could do it?" She said, "You know I don't read music very well," and Leo thought this was funny. The camera was all set up, and Leo said, "Let's try one." The camera's running, she's playing, "Home on the Range," and I'm singing it, and it's just awful. We finished, there's no place else to go, and nobody said, "Cut." We finally looked up, and McCarey was doubled up under the camera. He said, "That's it! Cut, print it." Irene and I didn't know what the hell we were doing. She was mad, I had no idea what the part was. Cary came in, did a scene, and he was put off. At the end of the day, Irene was in tears, Cary went to Harry Cohn and said, "I'll make you one of two propositions. Either let me play Bellamy's part as it is written for Roland Young, or let me out of this, and I'll do another picture for you for nothing." I didn't know where I was. No script at all. Next morning, McCarey came in, and he had a piece of paper a few inches long; he said, "I've got something here I think would be very funny. You come in here, and you come in over there, and then we'll see what happens." So there we are coming in doors, and the dog is running through, and everything. And he's chuckling gleefully. Well, a couple of days later we saw what was happening. We shot that in less than six weeks, without a script. Leo knew all the time what he was going to do, but he was the only one who did. After a couple of days, we were willing to be putty in his hands.

LM: I guess you played your part too well, because it typecast you for a while, didn't it?

RB: It was one of those things; I guess there hadn't been anything written for that type of character for a while.

LM: *His Girl Friday* comes to mind right away. How did that line describing your character as a Ralph Bellamy type come about?

RB: I was off one day, and I came on the lot to say hello, because we were having a good time on that. I ran into my friend, by now, Harry Cohn, and he said, "Let's go see the rushes in my projection room." I went up to his private projection room, and we saw the previous day's rushes: I hadn't been in them. The scene you're talking about, I think, is where they've sent someone to pick me up and get me in some kind of trouble, and Cary says, "He'll be in front of a building and he'll probably have a raincoat and umbrella." The guy says, "What does he look like?" and Cary says, "Sort of ordinary looking, like that guy in pictures, Ralph Bellamy." When this came out, Harry said, "What the hell are they doing down on the set? This wasn't in the script!"

LM: One of the notable things about that picture is the frantic pace of the dialogue. Did that require a lot of rehearsal?

RB: We all had worked together before. But you had to take the cue, instead of from the last word, from two or three words before the last word of the speech. Just a matter of concentration. It was a pretty good picture, as I remember it.

LM: How about *Trade Winds?*

RB: That was shot entirely against background plates. Tay Garnett had gone around the world on his yacht, and shot plates. Freddy March, Joan Bennett, Ann Sothern, and I did almost the entire picture against background plates of Siam and Singapore. Incidentally, Freddy told me he took a percentage on that picture—it cost nothing to make—and he said of everything he did in Hollywood, he made more on that. That was one of the few times, when the picture was over, I got a note from Walter Wanger saying, "Nice to have worked with you." He could have done it by phone, or on the set, and I don't think it had ever happened to me before; I thought it was quite nice.

LM: Although you've done a lot of films, many people identify you most closely with the short-lived Ellery Queen series.

RB: Yes, that's very strange. I think I did four, and everybody calls it the Ellery Queen series. They were just inexpensive pictures, overseen by the two fellows who wrote the stories, so there would be some accuracy technically.

LM: Then at Universal you broke new ground by doing some horror movies.

RB: I did one that involves my favorite story. Whatever it was [*The Ghost of Frankenstein*], everybody on the lot was in it—the Frankenstein monster, and the Wolf Man—and also everybody in town was in it. We finished a scene one day on the set, and I can't remember the name of the director, a little fellow who wore riding britches, a puttee, a scarf, and had a megaphone almost as big as he was. We finished a scene, and he said to Cedric Hardwicke and me, "We have to go down to the backlot for a staircase, to shoot a silent shot. Why don't you sit here and relax?" So Cedric and I had a pleasant hour, two hours, and finally decided to go down and see how they were doing. There was a lot of hollering and running around, and the assistant director finally went to this little director and said, "We're ready." He picked up the megaphone, and almost bumped the assistant as he turned it around. He said, "Get Evelyn Ankers at the top of the stairway." It was just a silent shot, to let the audience know the geography, that they're downstairs now instead of upstairs. Now it's quiet, they've got Evelyn Ankers at the top of the stairway. He starts to pace back and forth, with the megaphone, and he says, "Now Evelyn, you're all alone in this dim, dark, dank, dingy, ancient, oozing, slimy castle, at four o'clock in the morning. Your mother's been carried off by the Frankenstein monster, your father's

Ralph Bellamy as Franklin Delano Roosevelt in *Sunrise at Campobello*.

been killed by the Wolf Man, the servants have fled, your lover is being chased across the moors by the dogs. I want to get the feeling from you as you come down this stairway that you're fed up with it all!" Anytime Cedric and I saw each other anywhere in the world, and it was a lot of places, across a room we'd say, "You fed up with it all?"

LM: Why did you leave Hollywood in the mid-1940s?

RB: To go to New York to do the play that won the Pulitzer Prize, *State of the Union*.

LM: Weren't you fed up with it all?

RB: No, I went before that. I know what you're talking about, when I was sitting in Mark Hellinger's office and saw this script: "A charming but naive fellow from the west, a typical Ralph Bellamy part." That's when I made up my mind that I would go east. That was before I did *Tomorrow the World*.

LM: Then you did a lot of stage work, and hardly any films, until *Sunrise at Campobello*, which I guess you've talked about to death.

RB: Yeah, and everybody's read about it to death too.

LM: And after that, nothing until *The Professionals*?

RB: That's right. I've never seen it, incidentally. I understand it's good.

LM: More recently, you did a very fine film, *Rosemary's Baby*.

RB: That was a good picture. I thought it was excellent, of its kind.

LM: And Roman Polanski?

RB: Just great. A strange little fellow, but extremely talented. Then I've just done *Doctors' Wives* for Columbia, which we shot up near San Diego.

LM: Which brings us to your newest project, *The Most Deadly Game*, a new series on ABC. What kind of role do you have?

RB: It's about three people. The fellow I'm doing is an older fellow interested in criminology, who is united with two other people, played by George Maharis and Yvette Mimieux, who share his interest for various reasons. And out of this a relationship has begun. My fellow's interest is more in the psychological level—what causes a person to commit a murder. The resolving of it is basically up to the other two, but they work together and solve it. I hope that sometimes we will be unsuccessful, to make it believable. The ingredients are all there, so it seems to be up to us to pull it off.

LM: You did one of the first major TV series in 1949, didn't you?

RB: Five firsts, as a matter of fact: it was the first live half-hour dramatic weekly network show on the air, *Man Against Crime*. It got the first award given by what became the Emmy Awards. This is my fourth series. I did *Eleventh Hour* for a year, and last year, I guess everybody will forget, I did *The Survivors*.

LM: Does one medium give you particular pleasure more than others?

RB: The stage. Anybody who'd done all of it will say that, if they're honest. The difference is the audience: The audience is like meeting a new person, with a collective personality, every night.

LM: Do you have a favorite of all your film roles?

RB: Well, it has to be FDR, even though the picture wasn't successful; but I can't separate the picture from the play, which was our trouble with the picture, really. I knew the Roosevelt family, all but Anna and John, all through the White House period. I did a lot of extensive work with Mrs. Roosevelt before we went into rehearsal, and at the Institute for the Crippled and Disabled, where FDR got his braces and wheelchair. Then, in an effort not to do what at best could be called a good nightclub trick, an imitation of FDR, I learned his speech pattern with a voice coach, then threw it away. There were only a half a dozen places in the play when I would strive an exact imitation. For the rest of it, he had what was very helpful to an actor, a cadence. When he spoke, he would speak a phrase; he would never break a phrase, which was a very helpful thing. I certainly used his mannerisms, but I was not trying to do an exact dupli-cation of FDR, and I didn't, the point

With Ruth Gordon in *Rosemary's Baby*.

being that he having been so recently among us, a lot of people at that time still had a vivid mental image of him. If I could appeal to each individual mental image, enough to keep it alive, that would be the greatest I could achieve—much better than trying to play the whole thing as a nightclub impersonation.

LM: And it remains your favorite role?

RB: Sure. Jimmy Roosevelt gave me this ring; it's an exact duplicate of FDR's ring, given to his father by his mother in 1850. He had it on in every picture you ever saw of him. Jimmy just wrote me and said, "Would you consider seeing that sometime in the future the ring gets to the collection of memorabilia at Warm Springs?" I said, "If you want to wait a long time, I'm going to be around a while; it'll be 35 years or so, but I'll see that you get it."

Conversations:

MADGE EVANS

Madge Evans had three distinct careers. Starting before even she could remember, she was a child star in movies. Her adolescent years found her a successful Broadway ingénue. Then, in the 1930s she became a star in Hollywood, working, ironically, with people she already knew from the stage— Spencer Tracy, the Barrymores, and James Cagney, among others. She left acting when she married playwright Sidney Kingsley in 1939 and remained inactive although very much in contact with show business through her husband's work. While most  of her movie roles at MGM were cut from the same cloth, Miss Evans had several opportunities to prove herself an actress of skill and sensitivity, as in *Dinner at Eight, David Copperfield,* and *Hallelujah, I'm a Bum,* among others. Still a beautiful woman, she was joined by her husband for a most pleasant interview at the Kingsleys' home in New Jersey. (Interview originally appeared in December 1972.)

LM: Why don't we start with how you got into films in the first place.

ME: Well, I was a child actress. As a matter of fact, I was a child model before I was an actress. I was the Mellin's food baby.

SK: Madge puts us all to shame. She was earning a very handsome living before you were born, and when I was not even in knee breeches, because at the age of two she was already a celebrated model doing nudes.

ME: That's quite true. I did quite a lot of commercial photography in New York, and at that time Fort Lee was a very active film area. Mary Pickford and many others had already gone to California, but Fort Lee still had Theda Bara and the Fox Films, and I was with World Films. The first work I did, at least the first my mother told me about, was as the Mellin's food baby. I may have done something before that, but I don't remember most of this; I only know it by hearsay. Then I started doing film work. For instance, William Farnum made *The Sign of the Cross*, and I was one of the little Christian children being fed to the lions.

LM: How old were you then?

ME: Oh, about two or three. Then I started playing small parts in films, and by the time I was about five I had a contract with William A. Brady, who made the World Films. The stars in those days were Alice Brady, Montague Love, Robert Warwick, Henry Hull, Clara Kimball Young. I became a child star. There were Madge Evans dresses, and Madge Evans hats. It was very amusing. On the label of the hat it had a sort of photograph of me in replica, printed in silk, and underneath it said "Madge Evans Hats for Little Ladies." That was all at Fort Lee until I was about 10, and then I went out to California and made two color films there, in a color process called Prisma. I made *Heidi in the Alps* and another shorter film. *Heidi* was a full–length picture that showed at the Capitol in New York and was quite sensational, because it was one of the first color films. After that I stopped working in films, more or less. I made a couple of pictures during summer vacation when I was about 14, but I didn't want to live in California; the whole industry by that time

Madge Evans in MGM publicity photo.

had moved out there. My interests were in the theater, and Mr. Brady gave me letters of introduction so I could get started. When talkies came in, I made short subjects at the Vitaphone studio, because it was nice to pick up extra money, but my main interest was in the theater, and I hoped to stay in the theater. At that time, of course, they were signing up everybody for talkies. You had only to step foot on the stage if you were young, and you had plenty of places interested in you, but I wasn't interested in it, and I didn't even make tests. I was in a play of George Kelly's called *Philip Goes Forth* and there were two young actors in it, Harry Ellerby and Ralph Ernie. They were both very good, and

With Ramon Novarro in *Son of India*.

they got excellent notices, so Paramount and Metro wanted to test both of them. Ralph Ernie had a small part, but Harry Ellerby had plenty of scenes and Ralph was his understudy. Ralph Ernie asked me to make the tests with him in one of Harry's scenes, because it was a much bigger part, for both Paramount and MGM. I only did it for him, and then they both offered me a contract! I suppose it sounds rather fantastic, but it just happened that way; they didn't offer him one at all. For one of the few times in my life I was a good businesswoman. I kept juggling one against the other. I would say, "Paramount will give me so much," and Metro would say, "Well, we'll call the Coast." It ended up with Metro giving me the better contract, and I took it. It had options for six months; six months the first year, and then yearly options. We didn't even give up our apartment in New York because I was so sure that it was going to just be six months.

There is one important point about all of this, and it is often neglected—at least, I don't see it mentioned. In telling this to you I've mentioned money a couple of times. You know, this was the Depression era, and I was very lucky; I worked. I was in the theater, and there were many plays being produced. For instance, in one season I was in a play that Florenz Ziegfeld produced for Billie Burke; I played her daughter, and it also had Arthur Byron and Reginald Owen. That closed up after about 10 weeks. It wasn't a success, but I went immediately into another play called *Our Betters* by Somerset Maugham, with Ina Claire, so I was very lucky. But all around us there were men selling apples on the street, so if you weren't personally involved in having a difficult time, you were very conscious of the situation. Spencer Tracy, for instance, did not want to go to California at all, but he had a wife and a little boy. I was in a play with him by Owen Davis, who was a very well-known playwright; it was produced by Sam Harris, and it had all the auspices of a hit, but it was just no good.

After that, Spencer Tracy went to California, and I think most of us went for purely economic reasons. Then practically the first thing I was greeted with in California—I don't think I had been working at Metro more than three or four weeks when we were all called up to the executive projection room by Mr. Louis B. Mayer and told that the world was in a frightful condition, and that as part of the elite, financially speaking, we would all have to take a 50 percent cut for 10 weeks. Well, Wallace Beery got up and said he didn't see how a hundred actors and actresses at MGM taking 50 percent of their salary was going to save the country. I thought, "I came out here for security and money and this is the first thing to happen," but it did. There was a story at Metro that Wallace Beery never took the cut, but most of us did.

SK: I think the point that Madge is making is that underneath all the glamor of the era, it was a very troubled and shaky time. Today the young people look back on it as an era.

ME: They talk about it as the golden era. Yet there was always this uneasiness; we were making fairy tales, and we knew it. I think they were quite self-conscious fairy tales.

LM: Perhaps more so at MGM than at some other studios. What was the first film you did for them?

ME: The film I went out to make, which was already in production, was *Son of India*, with Ramon Navarro. Navarro, John Gilbert, and Billie Haines had been their big stars, but they were just finishing up their contracts, which was a very sad thing. I had no adjustment to make for films, because I had been in the theater. It was much harder on these men, who had been in silent films. It was terribly hard for them to talk; they used to have dialogue coaches on the set, and they made such a thing of speech that I think they terrorized them. After *Son of India*, I made a murder story called *Guilty Hands* with Lionel Barrymore and Kay Francis. While I was making that, they had another film called *Sporting Blood*. They were quite pleased with me in the first film, and they liked what they were seeing of me in *Guilty Hands*. Meanwhile, Clark Gable had made a film at Warners on loan with Barbara Stanwyck called *Night Nurse*. It was a small part, but already it was getting big repercussions; they thought Clark was going to be very big and they put him in a film with Greta Garbo, *Susan Lenox*. Now they had this film called *Sporting Blood*, and they thought, maybe Clark isn't going to be too good, and maybe I wouldn't be such a good ingénue, but here is *Sporting Blood* where they could use us both and see. So while he was making *Susan Lenox* and I was making *Guilty Hands*, we worked on Saturdays, Sundays, and holidays making *Sporting Blood*. All the long-shots for that film were done by doubles they took down to Kentucky. Had Clark and I been in the same picture, they could have arranged schedules easier, but with two different films it was difficult.

LM: Did you have any say in the selection of roles?

ME: I had no say whatsoever; all one could do was go on suspension. You just quit, went home and stayed home, and started negotiating. Myrna Loy did that, but I can't think of anybody who really had complete choice of roles. What they could do was to up their salary to such an extent that it was no use putting them in those awful B pictures.

LM: Were there roles you tried to get?

ME: Oh yes. They were talking at that time of doing Sinclair Lewis' *It Can't Happen Here*, and I wanted desperately to be in that, because I had read the book and I liked it enormously. When they finally announced the cast they had given the part to Virginia Bruce, but the film was never made. I wanted very much to be in *Holiday* with Katharine Hepburn. I had made two films with George Cukor, and I had known him in New York. He wanted me, but I was under contract to Metro and that was being made at Columbia. I wanted to be in *Night Must Fall*, but Rosalind Russell got the part, so there were things I wanted very much to do and didn't get.

LM: What did you think of the directors you worked with?

ME: I think the two best directors I ever worked with in California were Robert Z. Leonard, who was known as Pops, a darling man, and George Cukor. I made two come-dies with Robert Leonard, *Piccadilly Jim*, and a play that had a dreadful title but was a pretty good film in its time called *Lovers Courageous*; both of them were with Bob Montgom-ery. He was a very good director for women, and comedy. Cukor was also a very good woman's di-rector. I liked very much working with Jack Con-way, a very good man and a good all-around direc-tor. A lot of people found Woody Van Dyke diffi-

With Clark Gable in *Sporting Blood*.

cult, but I didn't. I liked him very much, and I liked making films with him because he had been a cutter and his great position at the studio came about because he brought in his pictures so fast. He never took 10 shots of anything. He never let a scene run over, because he could cut with the camera. He knew when he was going to go to a close-up, so he cut the long shot and made the close-up. A lot of actors and actresses didn't like this, because they felt they couldn't get rolling, but I didn't think I could get rolling anyway, because they did a long shot and then they took five hours to light the close-up, so I could never get what they were complaining about. He was a good director; sharp. He knew what he wanted.

LM: Did you have much rehearsal time, or was it on the set?

ME: It was always on the set, and nine times out of ten the dialogue was given to you that morning. They were constantly rewriting. They had dozens and dozens of writers, and they were always hiring someone to rewrite a scene, so you would go home at night, learn a scene that you knew was to be shot the next morning, and when you got on the set you were given three pages of dialogue which was entirely different. The only time you really ever had any sense of rehearsal was if you were in a Thalberg film. It wasn't that there were any advance rehearsals, but he would come on the set and watch rehearsals, and then there would be great conferences while the actors sat around. He was a very quiet man; he would confer with the director, then the director would come back and the scene would be redirected. One film I made that Thalberg did was *What Every Woman Knows* with Helen Hayes. We'd been shooting for about six or seven days, and he stopped production because he didn't like the wardrobe that Adrian had designed. Everything was thrown out, and we all made clothes tests. Then we went home and when they were ready, they called us.

LM: Wouldn't he also go back to a completed picture and reshoot some scenes?

ME: Oh yes, he did a lot of that. Working for Irving Thalberg, or for David Selznick, was entirely different from working in any other film, because they had complete control. They would go back, reshoot, replace ac-

With Roland Young in *David Copperfield.*

tors. In *David Copperfield*, for instance, they replaced Charles Laughton as Micawber. After they'd shot 10 days or so, Laughton was taken off the film, because Selznick didn't think he was funny, and they got W.C. Fields.

LM: Did you have a family feeling at MGM?

ME: Yes; it was really a stock company. You're easier when you've worked with someone before; you're more relaxed. They know you; you know them. They had a slogan, "More stars than there are in heaven." Howard Dietz added, "And more greed than there is in hell." But that was in the front office. The actors, as a group, got along very well. The only one who kept to herself, but was not in any way unpleasant, was Garbo. We all had a great admiration for her, as a matter of fact, and there was a wonderful woman at Metro in those days named Polly Moran. Garbo was crazy about Polly Moran and used to send for her when she wasn't working, to talk in her dressing room. There was no sense of caste. I think the only one that everybody stayed away from a little was Norma Shearer, but that was because she was the boss's wife, you know. Of course, we were all of us crazy about Jean [Harlow]. She was a lovely girl, and there was no jealousy. There was no desire to tear each other down. At least if there was, it was never overtly expressed.

LM: They certainly kept you working.

ME: Oh my God. The first year I was at Metro I made 11 films. My contract guaranteed me 40 weeks out of the 50, and they paid me for 49 weeks. That meant I had two weeks, if they closed production, doing stills, and things like that. That was not counted; that was free time. So during my first year, I was probably at the studio every day, but there wasn't anything else to do anyway.

LM: Fred Allen once said of California, "No matter how hot it gets during the day, there's still nothing to do at night."

ME: Well, it's true. There wasn't anything to do except make pictures.

LM: One very good film you made away from Metro was *Hallelujah, I'm a Bum!*

ME: That was an exceptional picture; it started with Lewis Milestone di-

With Ina Claire and Joan Blondell in *The Greeks Had a Word for Them*.

recting, but Jolson didn't think Milestone was good for him. We also had Roland Young playing the Frank Morgan part. Jolson didn't think either one was very good, so that stopped production. They got Chester Erskine to direct it, and Frank Morgan to appear. That really wasn't a very happy picture, because they had found all the great old comics, Harry Langdon and Chester Conklin, and they were being treated like bit players, because Jolson was very much the star. They may have had bits in the picture, but my God, they were wonderful in their time. The changeovers were difficult, although I liked both Roland Young and Frank Morgan. They were both very funny, delightful men, but still, when someone you know is replaced by someone else, it's awkward. I think the nicest part of that film was Dick Rodgers and Larry Hart, although Jolson wasn't pleased with the songs he had. I must tell you something about that. I'm tone deaf, I can't carry a tune. Of course Sidney, being married to me, knows this very well and a few years ago we were with Richard Rodgers and Sidney made some joke about my not having a voice, and Dick said, "Madge sang in *Hallelujah, I'm a Bum!* As a matter of fact, I have a tape of it." So we had dinner and he put on this tape. In one scene [cut from most release prints] Al Jolson sings the story of Cinderella; he says, "Are you listening, Princess?" and I say, "Um-hm." That was my singing career, singing Rodgers and Hart songs.

LM: Another interesting film you did on loan-out was *The Greeks Had a Word for Them.*

ME: Yes, that was for Goldwyn. Lowell Sherman directed it and George Barnes was the cameraman. That's when he and Joan Blondell fell in love, so a great deal of the picture is slightly out of focus.

LM: What was Sherman like as a director?

ME: I don't think he was much of a director, but he was a delightful man. I liked him enormously. He didn't take directing very seriously. That was a rather hectic picture, with him not taking the directing seriously, George Barnes falling madly in love with Joan so he could hardly see anybody but Joan. Ina Claire was very much in love with John Gilbert (this was before they were married), and every time she got into a costume that she thought she looked well in, particularly the bridal costume at the end of the film, she disappeared from the lot, because she had driven off to Metro to show John Gilbert how enchanting she looked. I went into that film very quickly, because Carole Lombard was supposed to do the part I played, but she became ill and I replaced her.

A glamour shot.

LM: *Dinner at Eight* was certainly one of your best films, at MGM.

ME: That was a great cast; it's a sad thing to think that most of the people from *Dinner at Eight* are dead, even the young ones like Phillips Holmes. It was about the third time I worked with John Barrymore, because I worked with him in *Peter Ibbetson* as a little girl, and of course Lionel had played my father and Billie Burke my mother in a play of Noel Coward's called *The Marquis*. I had known George Cukor in New York when he was with Gilbert Miller. So that was a very happy film for me to be in, very happy. That film was departmentalized; it wasn't a picture in which we all got together, but it was a nice picture to work on. I think I had a couple of scenes with Billie Burke and Lionel Barrymore, and a scene or two with Marie Dressler, and that was it. I worked mainly with John Barrymore, and I loved it. I was terribly in awe of him and he was very nice to me; it was getting toward the end.

LM: That was before his decline?

ME: Well, it was beginning. He had trouble with his lines; not as much trouble as W.C. Fields. But he was very sweet with me, and he could be very cutting when he wanted to be, but he wasn't.

LM: What was Lionel Barrymore like?

ME: Lionel was always nice, but I don't think he had the same sense of humor John had. Lionel, of course, was very ill; he was in great pain. He had given up the theater for about 10 years. He wanted to be a sculptor and he'd been in Italy working. I don't think either John or Lionel really liked acting very much. I think John liked aspects of it, but I think Lionel didn't like it at all. I remember in *David Copperfield* he had a line of dialogue about little Emily in which he was supposed to say "the bright-eyed little bird." George Cukor said to him, "For God's sake, I've never heard such a vicious denunciation of anyone in my life," because he had kind of a way with talking, and he was very tight with pain and dislike. They had to change the line. Of course, *David Copperfield* was a nice film to be in, too; very nice.

LM: I see that you did one loan-out to Warner Brothers for *The Mayor of Hell*.

ME: Yes, with Jimmy Cagney. I had known Jimmy quite well in New York, because he came from George Kelly's plays, and so did I. When we went out to California, we lived quite close to the Cagneys for some years, and I used to see a great deal of him, but that was the only film I ever made with him.

LM: Did you feel, as many film buffs do, that there was a different atmosphere at Warners than that of MGM?

ME: Oh, completely. They were all completely different.

With Al Jolson in *Hallelujah, I'm a Bum!*

SK: Each one reflected not only the man that ran it, but a kind of tradition that had been built up in them.

LM: *Broadway to Hollywood* is such a typical MGM picture, where you and Frank Morgan and Alice Brady are supposed to be vaudevillians, yet they always cut to a long shot for every singing or dancing number.

ME: That was a very funny thing. Nobody sang, nobody danced, nobody did anything really. Even things you could do, you didn't do; it was done by a double.

LM: Did you see your films at the time they were done?

ME: Not all of them, no.

LM: Would you see them in the screening room, or at a premiere, or what?

ME: Sometimes if there was one you were very interested in and they were previewing it, you'd find out. They didn't tell us when they were previewing. I don't know if they thought we would applaud ourselves or send in favorable cards or something; they didn't trust us. It was very hard to find out where the initial previews of the film were, and they used to take them to all kinds of places like San Bernardino that took you an hour or more to get to, so I didn't see many of them, and afterwards when they were cut and released, you would have gone to see

them out of the sense of just having finished it, is it any good. But by the time they were out in the world, you really didn't want to, nine times out of ten. You'd want to forget the whole thing.

LM: It seems that whenever MGM had a programmer at this time, it starred you, Robert Young, Nat Pendleton, or Ted Healy.

ME: Yes, first it was Robert Montgomery, then Robert Young. I made a picture called *Fugitive Lovers* in which we went cross-country with a background of the Three Stooges; they were marvelous.

LM: How did you happen to be loaned to Gaumont-British for *Transatlantic Tunnel*?

ME: They had borrowed someone to come over here, so it was sort of an exchange. It was a very nice experience. We stopped every day at 4:00 for tea. They brought a great cart on the set with tea and sugar buns, and all the prop men and electricians joined in; it was an absolute break. They stopped a good hour and a half for lunch, which we didn't do. They didn't work late. It was very nonchalant. It was very easy, very relaxed, and they were making good pictures.

LM: How did you come to leave MGM?

ME: I had a seven-year contract, and they couldn't loan me out if they were going to exercise their option. They wanted to loan me out, and I said no. That ended the contract, and I was very happy because I wanted to come back and go on the stage again, and I also wanted to be in New York, because Sidney was here and he wanted to stay in New York. It seemed like a very nice arrangement, but of course, we didn't know we were going to have a war so soon. We were married in 1939 and Sidney was in the Army in 1940. I wasn't quite prepared for that, but that's the way it happened.

LM: You made two last films for other studios before you left. How did you like working with James Whale on *Sinners in Paradise*?

ME: Well, this was not his kind of film. He was much too intelligent, much too good a director for this kind of nonsense which was all about people cast adrift on an island, a dreadful picture and he was much, much too good for it. He hated it, and also being a rather up-tight Englishman, he showed that he hated it. You could just see that every time he came to a scene, he was saying, "Oh, my God," and that doesn't make anybody feel either confident or happy.

LM: And you worked for Republic Pictures.

ME: In a film called *Army Girl* with Preston Foster and a very good director, a very nice man named George Nichols [Jr.]. Mr. Yates, who was president of Republic, had at that time decided to go into more ambitious productions, and I think we must have been all of three weeks, instead of three days. We went on location and other elaborate things for Republic.

LM: When you made a B picture at MGM it wasn't really like a B, was it?

ME: It wasn't a B in the terms of a Republic Picture, or what was then snobbishly known as Poverty Row. At Metro even a B picture took three, four weeks, and of course you still had the good cutters, the good cameramen, the good clothes, the good casts, because they threw anybody into a B picture.

LM: So that was your last film, and they never lured you back?

ME: No. When Sidney was in the Army, RKO offered me a contract, but it would have meant going back to California, and he was in New York, stationed at Governors Island. We kept thinking that he was going off every five minutes, so I wanted to wait. I didn't think much about it; I don't mind.

LM: Have you had any other film offers since then?

ME: Well, Sidney Lumet wanted me to be in a picture recently, but I'm not interested, really. Sidney Lumet is a dear friend of ours; he was one of the Dead End Kids on the stage, and he's always been close to my Sidney. He didn't believe me when I said I didn't want to work.

LM: But you certainly crammed a lot into your career when you were working.

ME: I did, and I'm like anybody else. I would love to do something really great today, but you get past the period of just wanting to work to keep busy. If someone like De Sica offered me a walk-on, I think that would be a terribly interesting experience, and something that would be exciting to do. I would like to work with Stanley Kubrick. But something like that hasn't been suggested to me, and for the rest I'm very content and happy.

LATER IN-DEPTH INTERVIEWS

Conversations:

JOHN CROMWELL

John Cromwell is something of a forgotten man in Hollywood history. Never regarded as an auteur, he nevertheless piloted an impressive number of first-rate films, including *Sweepings, Of Human Bondage, Little Lord Fauntleroy, The Prisoner of Zenda, Algiers, In Name Only, The Enchanted Cottage, Anna and the King of Siam, Dead Reckoning, Caged,* and *The Goddess.*

When I approached him for an interview in the early 1970s, he was more interested in talking about the political atmosphere of the time, and his concern that we might some day relive the horrors of the witch hunt and blacklist that he suffered through. Asking for anecdotes about movies of the 1930s and '40s seemed frivolous

John Cromwell in a 1940s magazine ad for Lord Calvert whiskey. As the caption indicates, he was a "Man of Achievement."

in comparison, but he eventually warmed to the subject. Our conversation roamed freely, though we covered only a fraction of his long career.

He insisted on taking me to lunch before we did our formal interview and I'm sorry I didn't have a tape recorder running then. I do recall him saying that there was no way to improve upon Julien Duvivier's *Pepe Le Moko,* so he copied it as closely as possible when he directed its Hollywood remake, *Algiers.* Other nuggets are lost to memory.

Several years later, Cromwell appeared in front of the camera, working with his second wife, noted stage actress Ruth Nelson, in Robert Altman's *3 Women and A Wedding*. Cromwell died in 1979 at the age of 91. His son, the versatile actor James Cromwell, carried on his name and profession. (Interview originally appeared in 2007.)

JC: I'm afraid I'd been like most other people in the theater in New York at that time about movies, treating them with a good deal of scorn. I suppose there was a reason why people in the theater would react that way, because it seemed like such a funny, haphazard medium. And you really had to put a lot of work and preparation into life in the theater. So [movies] seemed like a silly little toy and really hadn't accomplished much artistically.

When the little gadget [sound recording/microphone] was discovered, no one was at all sure about how this thing would work. There were rumors about its uses and the theater [people] saw a possibility of infringement on what they considered their proper status. The rumor around the theater in New York at that time was that there wasn't much to this; you know, you put up a camera and then photograph a play. When I [went] out to California acting in a play and was invited to roam around the studio and see what I thought, I said to myself, "No, I think that the secret to this as far as me and the theater are concerned is contained in that little black box they put up there. I was determined to find out more, to get on in the business.

Actually, when I had my first interview with Ben Schulberg at Paramount about a contract, I really thought I would be coming out to learn silent motion pictures. I just vaguely had heard [what] was going on, but not enough to be wise to what it really was.

My contract with Paramount was contingent on a play that I was going to do, a newspaper story, and we opened a week after *The Front Page* and suffered the consequences. So, I was Hollywood bound much sooner than I ever expected to be. But the reception in Hollywood was more than cordial because at that particular time, they really felt more dependent on directors, I think, than anyone else, because [of] a knowledge of how to handle dialogue. To the Hollywood people, learning about the camera didn't amount to a great deal because they could put a movie director with you and cover all that. It was this old devil dialogue, as I called it, [that they were concerned about].

Cromwell and his wife, actress Kay Johnson, meet director George Archainbaud and his wife on the tennis court in the 1930s.

The first thing that struck me was the absolute paralysis of fear that [talkies] had cast over all of Hollywood. And when you come to think of it, there was very well-founded reason for it because from the producer down, they all had their situations to meet. A producer had to think how the devil he was going to prepare his studio for shooting sound pictures. [They had] this great backlog of silent pictures that stayed on the shelf for six or eight months every year, all dependent on whether the public was going to laugh this thing [talkies] out of existence or accept it, you see.

Then just the logistics of converting the studio—tremendous in every department. Imagine that all the electrical had to be torn out and discarded, a camera had to be developed, the new kind of film had to be used, the different set designs and then material. Who the devil were they going to get to write stories? Well, all this was the producer's job, and it was something. Of course, the actors were the quickest to be frightened out of existence. They didn't know whether their voices would pass muster. They didn't know whether they could learn lines and speak them the same every time. They didn't know how they were going to look. People didn't know whether they were going to have a profession to follow or not. At first, it must have been very worrisome. And then gradually, as things happen, it became funny and ludicrous, particularly the story material.

LM: What did you perceive to be the biggest difference between silent films and talkies?

JC: The silent motion picture is a purely subjective medium: people went to these pictures and wrote their own dialogue, and it was damn good dialogue, too, because it fitted them exactly. That's why they were so successful. The extraordinary thing to me was that almost immediately audiences seemed to say, "All right, here I am. Show me. Tell me what I'm gonna hear," and became objective. I will never forget going to see a new picture at the Beverly Hills Theater [when] a leading man very passionately said, "I love you," to the leading woman, and the audience absolutely fell on the floor laughing. I was so astounded because I hadn't thought of it that way at all. And the panic that seized the studio—they immediately ordered no more love scenes. And, of course, the creative people said, "What do you mean, no more love scenes? That's what movies are!" (laughs) How the hell could you get along without a love scene? "Well," they said, "You can't say 'I love you' anymore." That was the first thing we had to solve, some way to show that a man was passionately in love and yet he never could say it. Those were all the ludicrous things that happened.

The director poses with his stars, Joel McCrea and Barbara Stanwyck, on location for *Banjo on My Knee* (1936).

It was extraordinary how fast all these problems were solved. The enormous speed they made in overcoming the whole camera difficulty. The first cameras we had were great six-by-four feet by six-feet-high booths that [had] great thick walls of acoustical material. No ventilation, and the glass that your camera shot through in front. It took about six or eight stage hands to move these things. So, you really could only use about two of them successfully to shoot; one was what we call a full shot, and the other some close-up or a two-shot or something a little closer.

LM: Were you shooting two cameras simultaneously then?

JC: Oh, yes. We started that almost right away. I think I only used these booths on my first picture, I think, which was a little number called—

LM; *Close Harmony.*

JC: *Close Harmony.* A little innocuous kind of picture, 'cause I thought I would start simply and not stick my neck out too far. By the time we got to the second picture, they had a camera developed for one man. It was on a tripod, it was an enormously cumbersome thing. It took two or three men to carry it, as I remember, and could be moved slightly by an operator, but was rather precarious business. I think probably by the third to fourth picture they'd almost solved the problem as regards movement and all that.

LM: Did you have to work at night? Were you involved in that Paramount fire?

JC: Oh, yes, it was my picture that was to open that stage, and it was the night before we were to begin.

LM: Which picture would that have been?

JC: Well, it was a picturization of a very successful play called *Burlesque* that the studio called *The Dance of Life.* We were all ready to go on this brand new, marvelous stage that Paramount had built. Somebody phoned me that night. Fire broke out [on the new stage]. It didn't burn to the ground because all the outside walls were acoustical stuff. That all burned but the walls themselves stayed there.

So, there was consternation naturally as to what the devil they were going to do about this. My old friend Sam Jaffe was a studio manager at Paramount; he was a brother-in-law of Ben Schulberg's, who had gotten him the job. A very enterprising guy, a wonderful studio manager. He somehow felt that this was his responsibility. He was called at home and told the studio was on fire, and he rushed down there and here was this brand new stage going up in flames. He paced up and down, [wondering] what the devil would they do? Because [they] just couldn't stand still too long [with] actors' contracts and everything. And finally, toward early in the morning, he hit on a solution. Why the devil can't we shoot at night? During the day they had aeroplanes, traffic noises, fire engines and everything—and at night, you had nothing. No planes. An occasional fire, but [no traffic].

So, he rushed to the top brass with this solution and [when he later told me] his story, he said they finally called him in and said, "You know, it's marvelous what you've done for us; you really have saved us." Well, he could calculate about how much he had saved the studio by this as well as they could, you see. I think they offered him $5,000 or something like this as a present and, of course, he was absolutely indignant. And when they saw that this didn't please him, they made some other offer like more salary or something of the sort. He refused it all and didn't take a thing and very shortly after that, left the studio and became an actor's agent. That's how I got close to him a little later, because I became a client of his.

I must say that I never acclimated myself to shooting at night—it just couldn't be done—but we managed to live through it, and [it was a] most successful picture at the time. I saw it not long ago.

LM: What do you think of it today?

JC: They showed it at The Museum of Modern Art and there was an enormous crowd there, much to my amazement. They put on a demonstration that embarrassed the bejeezus out of me. I didn't know what to make of it. As a second effort, I thought it was pretty good, not bad at all, but as a picture, it was really pretty bad. Fortunately, I recognized it. It took me quite a while to do anything that I thought deserved much consideration except tolerance.

LM: What about story material. How much choice did you have at the time?

JC: Well, you had hardly any. I was very much interested in reading [Frank] Capra's book, which I thought was extremely entertaining. I don't think anyone really had the choice [of material] that he had—no one, really. The more experienced movie directors seemed much better prepared to know how to manipulate events. They did a great many pictures that they liked doing but, in the main, new directors didn't have any of that power or choice.

LM: Were you considered an outsider, being from New York?

JC: Yes, I think so. I've always felt that, practically through my whole career. I don't know exactly what it was, whether they expected men from the theater to be awfully cocky and superior simply because of this matter of dialogue. Well, it [turned out] that dialogue wasn't so important; it was just like everything else and you picked up how to use it.

That was their biggest hurdle, I think, because they had to do a great deal more homework than they were accustomed to doing, to save yourself from going miles over budget and schedule. You had to prepare yourself for what you were going to do with a particular scene, therefore you had to become a greater judge of how the dialogue could be fitted, could be broken up, whereas

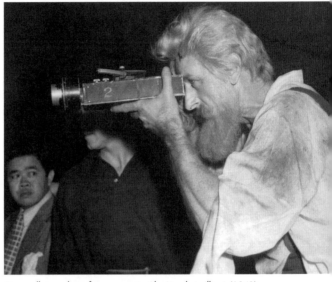

Cromwell, in makeup for a cameo in *Abe Lincoln in Illinois* (1940), checks a shot through a viewfinder as cinematographer James Wong Howe looks on.

in a silent picture, it all went in a director's head. All he had to do was just roll and he could do practically anything because there was nothing to stop him doing just as he damn pleased. That sense of responsibility that always fell on a director was the greatest asset that he had. I think studio heads never got over the fear of taking a director off a picture [and] putting another director on, or interfering almost in any way, because there had been too many instances of that wrecking a picture.

LM: How did you develop a pictorial sense?

JC: I suppose it can be developed. I felt that I developed finally a certain sense of composition. I was aware of it anyway. It seems to me you never got accustomed to the terrific range of the camera and its effect; I know I never did. What the choice of shots can do to a scene. Just put a whole different aspect on the whole business. I was always terribly interested in the stories more than usual, because my experience in the theater had always been in close cooperation with the playwright. At that time, it was very much the way to put on a play. To become a producer in the theater, you had to really learn something about play writing so that you were able to be articulate with an author, in telling him what you wanted. So when I came to pictures, I was pretty well prepared in that direction. Once I found out that pictures were a completely visual art... I'll never forget the sign that DeMille had in his office: "Say it with props." That was just one way of expressing that it was a visual medium.

LM: How much did you rely on your cameramen?

JC: Oh, I had to rely an enormous amount, particularly at first, and I never was able to learn much about lighting. Because it seemed to me that every cameraman I had was so different from the last one, in his techniques and the way he accomplished things, that it was almost impossible to learn unless you just took time out and devoted yourself to it for a year or so. So, I had to be completely at their mercy. I would talk mostly about how I felt about a scene or a sequence and what it meant to me in terms of lighting, as near as I could tell, and rely entirely upon them. But I was very lucky. I had some wonderful cameramen, in that they were men that never let you down, never betrayed you, you know?

LM: Who were your favorites of the ones you worked with?

JC: Oh, I suppose Jimmy Howe, the most. I remember one of the early ones at Paramount was Charlie Lang. And Arthur Miller at Fox. I never worked with the best of all, from what I understand; that was Goldwyn's cameraman—

LM: Gregg Toland.

JC: Gregg Toland. Never worked with him. But oh, so many of them. I remember one at RKO that did a few pictures with me named Roy Hunt. He was a most inventive guy. He invented almost all the early portable camera carriers.

LM: At what point did you feel that you really were in charge of the production all the way through?

JC: I would say it's the first one that I did with David Selznick, *Little Lord*

Fauntleroy. I think it might have been because everything about it seemed to be the best that I'd had yet. All the story preparation, all the casting, everything about it was done in such an orderly, professional, highly artistic way. The shooting was fairly easy and it all came out very well.

LM: And you were involved in most phases of production?

JC: Oh, sure. I did five pictures with David and we got very close. I was always a great admirer of his comments. He had such a superior story mind. He knew what he was talking about and at that time, this was quite rare in the producing. You would find it in individual ones, but not to the extent that he was. I suppose that's why he almost insisted all the time on writing himself. When we did *Since You Went Away*, it was his idea originally to base this picture on a little bit of a book that came out during the War about the letters of a wife to her husband, telling what was going on at home. Oddly enough, this had never been thought of as a war picture. A war picture was always the other way around, it was what hubby was doing out there on the battlefield and its reaction on little tots at home. This was just the opposite, no battlefield at all. And oh, the extraordinary experiences.

David ran into this little book and immediately bought it and he did the script himself. But David was about as badly disorganized an artist as I have ever seen in my life, and he couldn't discipline himself to certain things. He'd get great ideas [but] the muse didn't move him except at night, so he wrote this whole script at night. [He] had two stenographers and he'd dictate all night to them. I had started with 20 pages when the picture [began shooting], and I would meet him every morning coming into the studio. He'd read me and hand me what I was to do that day; we'd sit down for half an hour or more and go through it. Then I'd start to work and, I'd usually have to wake him up several times a day to get some interpretation.

LM: How long did it take to film?

JC: Oh, three or four months.

LM: That was a very long picture.

JC: Yes, it was. But he was very resourceful as a writer. David was inclined to be too lush emotionally and let it get beyond him and I'd always caution him about this. When he still didn't understand what I meant, I'd say, "Well, let me—let me read the scene to you," see, and I'd put in just enough acting to make my point. And he saw quickly what I meant. Then he would change his ideas, you see. But, usually he would come to a scene and say, "Now that's what I want," after we'd worked and worked on it. And he'd go in the other room and write the scene again, come out with it, and give it to me. Through that kind of process, we would arrive at what we were gonna use.

I often said to him, "David, [have] you ever really tried directing? Your mind works that way so much and if you would try directing, you would find that things change. You recite [scenes] as a writer, that's one thing, but when you bring in all the other problems of a director, it shapes your thinking about the scene itself and about the story." I said, "I think that's one of the reasons why when a writer can turn himself into a director, that's it. This is that kind of medium. A fella who directs ought to write the story." That would make it a hundred percent his. Right in the midst of this I got a touch of flu and I had to stay at home one day, so he phoned me and said, "Everything's going all right, fine." Later in the afternoon he called me again and said, "John..."And that's all he ever did with trying to direct. He found out certain things weren't quite as simple as he had always imagined. I think it was a good experience for him.

LM: Talk about interference and how the director really has to be in charge when it comes to shooting.

Cromwell is perched alongside the camera as James Stewart and Carole Lombard emote in *Made for Each Other* (1939).

JC: Well, there was a story about that with David, too (some years earlier) on *The Prisoner of Zenda*. He came out on the set one day. We rehearsed a scene and he called me back and he said, "John, I don't like the way you're doing that," and he went into a long harangue and I said, "David, don't think that I'm trying to be stubborn or anything like that, but you haven't said anything in your objection that changes my line of thinking about the sequence and this scene's relation to the scene that follows and the scene that I've just shot. And I can't put it together that way." Well, this developed into one hell of an argument. He got pretty stubborn, and I could get good and stubborn, too. I felt so frustrated because I couldn't convince him, and I knew what that might lead to. So I just walked off the set, and I started walking and I walked all over the studio. I don't know how long I was gone, maybe a half hour or more, and finally got back to the set and my assistant came and said, "Mr. Selznick has gone back to his office and he said you go ahead and do the scene the way you want to do it." I said, "How long did it take him to make up his mind to that?" He said, "Oh, that was about five minutes after you left."

This is what I was talking about earlier. It's very easy to see if you have to place the responsibility for the way the thing really comes out in somebody else's mind. You've got to be awfully dumb to keep pecking and interfering, 'cause you ruin your whole property. That's been done so many times, and one of the first things you learn in movies.

LM: I'm curious about your relationship with Selznick because some directors couldn't work with him at all because he interfered too much.

JC: No, he could do that. We established a very good relationship right from the beginning. I did his first picture, when he was an assistant to Ben Schulberg at Paramount.

LM: Film buffs feel that each studio seems to have had its own special style. If you clipped off the titles of a Paramount film, an RKO film, and an MGM film from the 1930s, you could tell which was which. Do you go along with that?

JC: Oh, yes, very much. I had to write something about that at one time and to me, they all had a personality. A very distinct personality that had something to do with their physical makeup but mostly with their philosophy and the kind of pictures they tried to do. I'm sure anybody could tell an MGM picture when they saw it. Or any studio at all, really. I think they were all, you know, quite distinctive, quite individual.

At Fox, for instance, [not just] anyone would pick material. It would be entirely Darryl Zanuck. Buddy Lighton was doing *Anna and the King of Siam* because they knew [he was] an extremely independent guy; he wouldn't do anything that he didn't feel down deeply about. Zanuck must have seen his studio as a certain type. He must have reflected to himself that "I don't want this studio to lose a kind of broadness of vision. It's good to hang onto a man like Lighton who has tastes in a different direction. He's a very competent producer; you don't stub your toe with him much. The thing he will do, the studio can afford to pay for. [It] probably won't make any money but [we] can afford to pay for it as part of [our] whole concept." You see?

He hadn't done a picture for so long and then finally, I guess, they started to put pressure on him. And Buddy ran into this story. *Anna and the King of Siam* was a casual bestseller, may I use that expression. It was pretty good, it was in the Ten Best for not too long, but it had great individuality and great color. [Buddy] got crazy about this story and said, "I'll do this." He got his favorite writer, Talbot Jennings, and they went to work, and I think they were working on the second draft of the story when I entered into it. I had worked with Talbot and I had done several pictures with Buddy and we got along beautifully. Then there was Irene Dunne, who I had worked with. The only unknown quantity was Rex Harrison. That didn't work out so well, but otherwise, everything was just marvelous, one of the best experiences I ever had in Hollywood.

LM: Talking of studios, some of your most offbeat and unusual films were the ones you made at RKO in the '30s.

JC: Particularly what?

LM: I'm very fond of *Of Human Bondage*. It's a lovely film.

JC: That, again, of course, is an olive. They must have thought we were absolutely crazy to try this story, you see. It rather astounds me, [though] this never occurred to [me] at the time, [and] now it seems so obvious. They refused to accept *Of Human Bondage* because of the character of the leading part, who was a cripple to begin with and suffered from this affliction that had been visited upon him. It took the form of what he thought was a deep, deep love for this poor, unfortunate gal who just kicked him around like nobody's business. This just destroys the hero image for the audience. They won't have anything to do with it. All pictures at RKO at that time had rather a perfunctory procedure. You went out with your best cut and previewed the picture and made a lot of notes and came back and [revised] the picture, and it was released; that was the end of it. We had six previews on that picture, trying to get out the bad laughs. We couldn't see it in the projection room, but get it in the theater and they'd just howl with laughter. She'd turn on him again and he would say, "Yes, dear," something or another. They just wanted to murder him. Finally, by manipulation and cunning we were able to get around it, [but it wasn't a popular] success. I don't think it ever paid for its cost at all.

Assistant director Eric Stacey and Cromwell show set visitor Sabu the shooting script for *Made for Each Other.*

LM: How did it come to be made in the first place?

JC: It was a little difficult at that time to tell where those original ideas came from. Whether they [it] might have been the producer—

LM: Pandro Berman?

JC: Yeah, Pandro Berman. He'd been a bright boy around RKO in several different positions and was extremely good, efficient, and was growing and it was the kind of thing that just at that point in his career, he would be quite liable to choose. Because he thought he could make a mark for himself with that picture and I think it did an enormous lot for him, for his career.

LM: What do you think of Bette Davis's performance in it?

JC: Well, it was terrifically interesting to me because it was like something suddenly revealed, and you saw all these pent-up and much-used aspirations coming to life, you see. Here she was, a little stock girl at

Warner Bros. going along, playing nice little acting parts. As a matter of fact, the one man that believed in her over at Warners at that time was George Arliss. He always had her in pictures, if there was any kind of a part, because he recognized this talent. I happened to see we were stuck, and Pandro and I got along very well and particularly our idea [of] casting off type. He believed in it and so did I.

You know, you always sent down to the casting department when you got stuck and said, "We want somebody like so-and-so for this part," and they'd read the script. So up comes this list, and it seems to me that every picture this list came and it's the same old list. We were getting awfully close to the deadline and I was going to pictures every night, and I ran into this Arliss picture. I'd never seen this gal before and she was just plain. And I said to myself, "Jeez, it seems to me that girl could act if she got the chance." I didn't even try to get in touch with Arliss and get his opinion, which I know would have been full of praise for her. But we asked her to come over and see us. Pandro and I had a talk with her. We said, "Here's the script. Read it and come back if you can tomorrow. We're kind of approaching the deadline. Let us know what you think."

Now, in the meantime, any number of actresses that we had approached that fitted our requirements had turned it down, and said, "Oh God, no, that'll ruin my career. This bitch? I'd be tagged with that the rest of my life, I'd never be able to do anything else. No sir." She came back the next day and we said, "Read the script?" "Yes." "How do you like it?" "I think it's marvelous." I said, "Would you like to play the part?" And she said, "On one condition." We said, "What's that?" "No compromise." Now, she hadn't been out here very long, so there was a lot about Hollywood and all that she had to absorb and see how it worked. And she had run up against, time and time again in her own experience, with other people that they get right in the middle of a story and if they saw a quality coming to life in several scenes, they'd say, "Why don't we change the end of the story and use this?" It didn't matter in most of the usual material, but when you pick a story as famous as this one, you can't monkey with those things, because they come down on you like a ton of bricks. So she said no compromise; she wanted a statement in the fact that we wouldn't turn around and pretty up this love story.

We assured her that was not the intention and that the script would be shot almost 100 percent as she had read it. She had no fear at all and so we went on from there. My wife knew much more about her background than I ever did or ever found out. She came out of Boston, you know, and with all the inference of Boston upbringing and [had] quite a bit of experience on the stage. But she saw her opportunity. She saw what she could do with that part, and it was just marvelous [that] we got her. We didn't want a conventional Cockney accent. We wanted what people don't know too much about, called a city accent. It's reserved for the part of London that's around what they call the city. And we found a woman in Hollywood who knew all about it and immediately engaged her to help Bette in this thing. Then, almost in every scene, you just see her putting together what she had devised in her mind with the idea of a characterization that would really make her. So, it was an extremely interesting thing to watch.

LM: I also like a little film that you did at RKO called *Village Tale,* a very unusual, quiet film.

JC: [*Village Tale* was written] by a man named Philip Stong and at the time that he was writing these novels about that middle section of America—Iowa, I think it was. [Stong also wrote *State Fair.*—Ed.] He had lived among these people and was able to write about their particular individuality and wrote extremely well. I was crazy about them. The trouble was that they were that in-between thing. The attraction was in the characters and the way they behaved; there wasn't much plot. There weren't many situations, so you'd give it to the ordinary leading actor and he'd say, "Oh, no, this story doesn't interest me." It was very difficult to get anyone to have any enthusiasm about it. That's why I was able to get only what I would call secondary casts.

LM: How about *The Fountain?*

JC: Which also was the same kind of material, only it was Canadian, you see. [These films] appealed to me because it was the kind of thing I loved to do. They didn't do me any good—did me a lot of harm, as a matter of fact, because they were just looked on as "another picture." You were as good as your last picture and that wasn't good enough.

LM: But was it was a satisfying experience for you?

JC: Oh yes, very. Because [it was] very real and valid material. Real people. Not the usual concoction that you got from most studio writers.

Cromwell coaches Myrna Loy and Warner Baxter for a scene in *To Mary—With Love* (1936).

LM: Do you think those could have been made anywhere but RKO?

JC: I doubt it. That's the kind of studio it was. It was like the wild west, the studio was, because it was so going in any direction and all directions. It was like the problems that came up [when] I was given a story that I loved doing which was *Enchanted Cottage*. I suppose [I loved it] because it was such a challenge. I'll never forget Dudley Nichols, who was at the studio at that time, calling me in and saying, "Jesus, John—loved your picture." He said, "I worked on it and I couldn't lick it. We had to give it up and I think it's just a marvelous job."

There again, [it was] just a crazy thing that happened. We couldn't get a writer that seemed to satisfy us at all. It came down to Herman Mankiewicz and ordinarily, he was the last guy in the world you would put on this fantasy. He just adored it. He just adored the assignment and worked like a son of a gun and did, I think, a beautiful script. But those kind of things could happen at RKO and it seemed they were always happening that way. I had some funny experiences there. But it was a nice place to work because everyone was so exceedingly independent. Nobody bothered by anything.

LM: That was probably because they changed regimes so often. Why did you finally leave after your second stint there in the late '40s and early '50s?

JC: I had just signed the best contract that I'd ever had—to do one picture a year at more money than I'd ever had before. I called off that first picture [I was offered] at RKO, *I Married a Communist*. The second year I got a very good picture to do over at Warner Bros. about women's prisons [*Caged*, 1950], one of the best pictures I ever made. Then the third year I did a [remake] of the play that I was in when I first went to Hollywood and got my first contract, *The Racket*. And I've forgotten about the fourth year, Finally the contract was canceled and by that time I was tired out. I finally made up my mind that I was going to go back to New York and go into the theater, and got this offer to come back in the theater and took it.

LM: Even when you were doing a lot of pictures, you returned to New York, didn't you?

JC: Oh, no. The way that came up was when I got fired by Sam Goldwyn [in the late 1930s]. I had a contract out here to do three pictures, one with David Selznick and one with Walter Wanger. Selznick's was *Prisoner of Zenda*, Wanger's was *Algiers*, and Goldwyn's. Goldwyn came and he fired me, [so] here I was with this time on my hands.

I was an old, old friend of Freddie and Florence March's, and just at that time they came to me with this play that they had discovered with the idea that Freddie had some time off, [so] why not go back and do it in New York? I read the play, liked it very much. Freddie and I each put up $20,000 and as soon as I cleared things, we went back to New York and put on this play, which was also a very enlightening experience. We had a dreadful time with this play on the road. The author was quite a good picture writer [Horace Jackson], and this was his first play; it was about Addison and Steele. Very literate and quite amusing. Jo Mielziner did the sets and the costumes and we had Dame May Whitty. There weren't many parts: Florence and Freddie and, I think, a couple of other men. Very well acted. I remember Montgomery Clift, it was his first part in New York. He was 16 years old then, and played this little bit. But we had everything happen to us on the road and finally we opened in New York.

We had been warned about this. We were the first Broadway people who had gone to Hollywood and made good and came back to do a play. And brother, that didn't sit well at all. (laughs) Here were all these people who, for one reason or other, hadn't made it in Hollywood, and they didn't like the idea of people making all this money and coming back and taking the attitude of, they thought, "We'll show you how to put on a play, see?" That's what it amounted to because they just crucified us. It was just dreadful.

LM: What was the name of the play?

JC: *Your Obedient Husband*. It wasn't any great shakes but, as I say, it was literate, it was about something, it was terribly amusing. It had gone beautifully on the road. Full of laughs but there was something wrong with it and we couldn't get this bastard to fix it. He just lost his head and thought he was doing Eugene O'Neill or something. So we ran about three weeks [Actually, it was just one week.—Ed.] and we had probably the best public relations man that I can remember in all my experience in New York. That was Dick Maney. We called him particularly because we didn't know how to handle this. The three of us were just burned up because a lot of people who were supposed to be our friends had not given us a very fair deal, and we would like to express ourselves about that before we left. So, our idea was [to] take a big ad in the paper and say, "you son of..." And we were each trying to top each other with the vituperation of our idea.

Dick Maney listened to all of this. We finally turned to him and said, "What do you think?" And he said, "Well, I'll tell you. You're dear people and I understand so well how you feel and I think, believe me sincerely, you have every reason to feel that way. But, I think it's rather a silly thing to do and I have a suggestion to make." He said, "About a month before you opened, a cartoon came out in *The New Yorker* and it was two aerialists, [where] the fella lets go and is supposed to catch the other fella's hands? Well, in the picture it's obvious that he'll never make it, you see that he's gonna go down, and the [caption] was, 'Whoops, sorry.'" We laughed our heads off. He said, "I suggest you just take an ad and I'll get the rights to use this. You print this picture and put your three names down at the bottom of it and let it go at that." Well, of course, it was a stroke of genius. People from that time can remember this so well. Oh, it just created a sensation.

LM: So it was back to Hollywood. What can you tell me about *In Name Only*?

JC: [A] really funny thing that happened in that picture. It was, you know, soap opera, but I loved working with Carole, and she was interested in Cary. I was perfectly amazed when he took the part and nothing was said about meeting or talking about the script; he's the guy who first thought up the idea of paying $25,000 to get out of a contract because he turned sour on the story. [I was sure he would see] at one reading what his part amounted to, you know, a guy between two dames fighting over him. Can't do anything but take the worst beating in the world, and I thought surely—was that smart? Nothing happened and I was absolutely amazed. Finally, just two days I think it was before we were to start rehearsal, this call came from Cary. He was quite upset about the script, and he wanted to talk about it. I thought to myself, "Oh, here it comes." I didn't know what we were gonna do because we hadn't been able to get anybody. I had had a couple of other choices before him and they had seen through it right away. Berman was working on another story, I remember, and he said, "I'll have George Haight there for you."

So [his assistant producer] George came up to my house. We met; I remember, about 10 o'clock in the morning, Cary came. We sat down and I was trying to think of all the bright things I could say in defense of this script to answer his questions, but he said, "All right, on page 10, it says, 'Now, you surely don't expect me to believe that.' But, I think that's a little strong. I think it's, 'Now, you don't expect me to believe that?'" It was just as inane and silly as that. I couldn't believe my ears. I could see that he had his script all marked and pages turned down so I knew they all meant something that I was to hear about. Instead of betraying my relief by a quick answer, I acted like a fool. I put on a show and I said, "Mmm, well yes, I think..., don't you, George?" He played right into it and we said, "Well, yeah, that's much better, yes, right.... Now, what's next?" We went through the whole script and that's all there was. When we got all through, Cary got up and said, "I feel so much better about the whole thing."

LM: His performance is quite nice in it, too.

JC: Oh, yes, fine—nothing for him to do! (chuckles) At the end [of production] he left. He was going to London on a trip or something, and he said, "John, send me a wire after the preview; tell me how the picture went." I said, "Sure, Cary." So, I had the preview and—you must remember a leading man in Hollywood named John Boles?

LM: Mmm-hmm.

JC: He was just the last word in everything perfect, so much so that he was kind of a laughingstock because he wasn't much of an actor. I sent this cable and I said, "Picture went very well. Audience seemed to love it and I have to tell you that you are the new John Boles." I thought at last he'd get a good laugh, you see.

LM: Which of the stars you worked with do you think were both stars *and* actors? For instance, there are some people who say that Gary Cooper was—

JC: Oh, well, Gary Cooper. I followed him pretty closely. I did an early picture with him at Paramount, and his good common sense about himself, which he never lost. That was the marvelous thing about him, because he just made his mind [up] early, he wouldn't be an actor and he wouldn't try. He tried to do it his own way and gradually through experience he evolved a kind of technique of his own which expressed his feeling. I think his scene at the end of the picture about the baseball player [*The Pride of the Yankees*] was just as fine as any actor that I know of could have done it. This to me was the sum of his work on the screen, what he had evolved in the way of technique. There it was expressed and it was absolutely beautiful, just beautiful.

LM: What about Barbara Stanwyck?

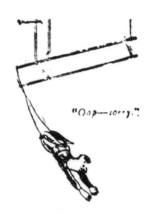

"Oop—sorry."

Courtesy, The New Yorker

**Fredric March
Florence Eldridge
John Cromwell**

From the "News of the Stage" column in *The New York Times* edition of Saturday, January 15, 1938: "*Your Obedient Husband*, which arrived at the Broadhurst on Monday, goes at the end of eight performances. (Apparently Mr. March and his family can take it. Their card on the subject is printed in an adjacent advertisement.)"

JC: She was such a wonderful actress. I had tried to get her for a play I was doing in New York, and I think it was timed a little wrong. It was just after she had read this play *Burlesque*, which was a much better part than I had to offer. So, she didn't do it. But I'm a great admirer of her work.

LM: Carole Lombard?

JC: Oh, Carole was just a joy. Wonderful, wonderful gal, a wonderful woman. She was enough of an actress, you know, to display her personality and her great charm. But I don't think she ever did any more than just fulfill the ordinary aspirations of somebody in that position. I think she was interested in other things in life than just being an actress.

LM: Jimmy Stewart.

JC: Jimmy? I'd seen him a lot in New York on the stage. A delight to work with and a very fine actor. Very.

LM: Irene Dunne.

JC: Well, Irene was another one of those naturals, a great talent. [There came] a point where I developed a philosophy about acting. I think you sum it all up by saying, "You're just as much of an artist as you are a person." The two are very much related, I think. I think that the fine artists, particularly in acting are a result of what they amount to as a person, in their philosophy and everything else. I think those are quite related to each other.

Conversations:
PEGGY WEBBER

Peggy Webber may not have been a household name, but directors as diverse as Orson Welles and Jack Webb regarded her as a Rock of Gibraltar in any medium. Both met her when she was a fledgling radio actress in the 1940s, and continued to call on her for the rest of their working lives—Webb for episodes of the TV shows he produced and directed, Welles to dub entire female roles for *Caligostro/Black Magic* (she replaced Valentina Cortese's voice) and *Chimes at Midnight*.

Another radio colleague, actor-turned-producer-director William Conrad, hired her to loop lines for *Bonnie and Clyde* and other films when he was an executive at Warner Bros. in the late 1960s.

Her father's itinerant life as an oil wildcatter made it difficult to put down roots; it also helped make young Peggy a self-starter. Born in 1925, she began performing in theaters, between movies, at the tender age of two and a half. At age 11 she presented herself at San Antonio radio station WOAI with scripts she'd written and was promptly hired to stage plays for children on Saturdays. When the family moved to Tucson, Arizona, a few years later, she stormed station KVOA and won her own show on Sundays. Her high school drama teacher in Tucson also gave her great encouragement after seeing her do an audition piece that included impressions of such current movie favorites as ZaSu Pitts, Edna May Oliver, Shirley Temple, and Stepin Fetchit.

Peggy and her mother moved to Los Angeles from Tucson after her father died; she had already graduated high school at age 16, and enrolled in the School of Speech at USC, where theater courses were taught. The co-director of the department, William DeMille (Cecil's brother, Agnes' father), urged her to stay in school, but having already had professional experience she wasn't content merely to study. Before long, she was working on the air and attracting the attention and respect of her colleagues.

That never changed. In addition to her own considerable acting and voice-over career, for over 25 years, Peggy Webber ran California Artists Radio Theatre (CART), producing and directing both new and classic plays for airplay—and for live audiences in Los Angeles. CART's repertoire is available online at www.cartradio.com, and their work is rich and vital, just like Peggy, who has remained indefatigable past age 90.

Although her screen career was sporadic at best, she worked with such titans as Welles and Hitchcock, and performed on radio alongside some of Hollywood's leading lights. She paints a vivid picture of the days when radio played a major role in many movie actors' lives. (Interview originally appeared in 2010.)

LM: You were just a teenager when you broke into the radio business in the early '40s. How did you do that?

PW: We arrived in Los Angeles and the next day I went into every building at Hollywood and Vine. I didn't know what I was doing but I went in. [If I saw] anything that looked like an advertising agency I would go in and I'd give them my name. I'd try to audition for anybody who would let me. I did that for days. I found an apartment for my mother and me for $21 a month on Sunset Boulevard, just beyond CBS. They've torn that building down; it was a brick building. We were upstairs, they had a wall bed that came down. I got to meet Bob Carroll [later one of the key writers of *I Love Lucy*]; he was the first person to talk to me. He belonged to the radio station and was just a guard. He had a little box out in front and he was to answer questions. He had red hair and was wearing his uniform, so I told him I had just come from KVOA in Tucson, Arizona, and I want a job and what do I have to do? He said, "I will notify you when there's an audition." Then he took my name and he did. He contacted me; I don't remember how, but he did.

Basil Rathbone and Nigel Bruce strike a mock-serious pose at the NBC mike.

I auditioned for [radio producer] Ted Wick and I did my routine with the impersonations. He and Edna Best and Mercedes McCambridge were in the control booth; I didn't know them, I didn't know who they were. But they came out laughing. Edna Best hugged me and Ted Wick, who worked for Selznick, said, "I'm putting you in my next show. It's a little girl who's trailing across country on the railroad by herself; she's 12 years old." And Edna Best said, "I'm doing *Sherlock Holmes;* I'm going to hire you, too." And they both kept their word. Mercedes McCambridge came over and hugged me and said, "You're going to be a big star in radio." And that was my beginning.

LM: And you were still attending USC?

PW: Well, I wound up getting more work and more work until I was doing 21 shows a week—and we needed the money. So what I did was to drop out temporarily. I finished three years at USC; I only had another year to go and I [completed my degree] later.

LM: You were 18 or 19 at this time?

PW: Yes. And I got the lead in [a radio serialization of] *Casablanca,* the Ingrid Bergman part. Over 40 well-known actresses turned up for this part. I had been to see Ingrid Bergman in *Casablanca*, and I sat and watched it over and over and over, and I could do her voice, I could impersonate her.

LM: Who was playing Rick?

PW: Eddie Marr, who was a nobody. As far as radio was concerned, he was busy, but he never played big parts. This was the *Dreft Star Playhouse*. We did 30 [15-minute] episodes of *Casablanca*. They sent pictures all over the United States and they made a big fuss about it. There were very good actors in it; there was a fella named Tom Sawyer. He played the husband who was the French patriot.

LM: The Paul Henreid part.

PW: That [*Casablanca* series] was one of the things that really got me going. When I did that, Ken Murray called me to do *Which Is Which?*, which was all impersonations. The audience had to guess whether you were really the actor behind the screen or whether you were impersonating. I fooled them a few times; I was a regular on that show. Then Harold Lloyd had a comedy hour and I was a regular on his show, *The Old Gold Comedy Theatre*, and a number of evening shows that I was doing all the time. *This Is Your F.B.I.* was one of them, for [director] Jerry Devine.

LM: And you got to appear on *Sherlock Holmes*.

PW: [I thought] I had died and gone to heaven. I was locked in with Basil Rathbone and Nigel Bruce and all these great British actors. They were the most marvelous actors, all of them. I just drank it in; I couldn't get enough of it. We even got to eat together at a restaurant on Melrose.

LM: Tell me about Basil Rathbone and Nigel Bruce.

PW: They were constantly ribbing each other and teasing each other. When they'd get on the air, they're try to break each other up, and Nigel Bruce just loved to torment Basil Rathbone. I guess he thought he was too much of a stuffed shirt, but he wasn't; he was a wonderful man. Very dignified and very generous and very kind. Nigel Bruce just had this great sense of humor; it was a wicked sense of humor. He would do all kinds of things. He'd purposely mispronounce a word or do something to get under Basil Rathbone's skin (laughs). And I got to work with all of the English actors and actresses who were great character [people]: Frederick Warlock, Alec Harford, Mary Gordon, Alma Lawton, and sometimes Gloria Gordon, who was Gale Gordon's mother.

They were very particular; they didn't bring in any of the Hollywood crowd very much. Ben Wright got in later but not at the beginning. I was 16 or 17, I think, when I did the first show. I graduated when I was 16 and when I got the first job, it was either at the end of '42 or the beginning of '43.

LM: Did Edna Best direct that series?

PW: She did a lot. Then her new husband, Nat Wolf, came in and did some. Of course, she had been married to Herbert Marshall and I began to work a great deal with him.

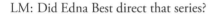

Two actresses who channeled their talent behind the mike: Edna Best (above) and Helen Mack.

LM: Tell me about Edna Best. She'd been an actress, of course.

PW: She was my heroine. She never lost her temper. She always had a sense of humor. She was intelligent and she didn't bother the actors ever. She cast the right people in the right parts and she didn't have to do anything about directing, really, except time-wise. I was so complimented that she allowed me to be with her and with them. Helen Mack and she were my dreams.

LM: So Edna Best had to ride herd over Basil Rathbone and Nigel Bruce.

PW: She enjoyed them and she knew that this was their way of relaxing.

LM: Helen Mack is another actress who turned to radio directing.

PW: Helen was married to Thomas McAvity; he directed too. And she loved her home. She had great warmth in her home; everything was a little bit old-fashioned but it made you comfortable. She was open to new ideas. She tried to do a couple of shows where she starred me; she wanted me to do a series. She put me in a lot of things. I worked with Arlene Francis when she did *Anne of Scotland Yard*. I played the secretary in that, and I did *A Date with Judy* and she

With Herbert Marshall, the star of *The Man Called X*.

directed that. Wherever Helen Mack went, I would be hired. And the same with Edna Best.

LM: There were virtually no female movie directors at the time.

PW: No. And it was rare in radio. I worked for hundreds of directors but they were all men, and these two women were just gems. They were good fellows, you know? They were full of fun; they could tell jokes with the boys and it was fun to be with them.

LM: I know it's a cliché question, but do you think the fact that they were both such good actresses—

PW: Made a big difference. Absolutely. I do think that's important. To be a director you should have been an actor first.

LM: Did the working radio actors welcome you and take you in?

PW: Yes, I guess because I was so young. I know Hans Conried [jokingly] said to me, "You were only 12 when I first worked with you." And I said, "No, I wasn't. I was not 12." He would shout at me down the halls, "Are you still stagestruck?" [Years later] I was making a movie

Peggy stops at an advertising agency in between radio broadcasts in the 1940s. Agencies produced most leading network shows in those days.

on the Paramount lot, and he was doing something with Jerry Lewis. They were in a convertible riding around on the lot and they had a loudspeaker in the car and he said, "There's that Peggy Webber! She's stagestruck!" (laughs) Then Jerry Lewis stood up and said, "You're my favorite actress…" And I thought, "What did you ever watch or listen to that I was in? (laughs)

LM: So despite your age your colleagues accepted you as a professional peer?

PW: They did. They didn't let me know if they felt that I was a kid. But the fact was that I worked so hard—Parley Baer told me that. He said, "I never saw anybody who worked so hard." Well, I *had* to work hard. I didn't know anything, so I had to work hard to learn fast so that I could compete with these good actors. They were great actors and I had to really bone up; they called it woodshedding in those days. I was the most famous woodshedder of all time. From the minute I got the script, I'd be marking every word and going off in the corner and trying to be better. They used to make fun of me. After I left and went to Japan,

Jack Webb wrote me letters and he said, "You should see Jack Kruschen doing an impersonation of you—you'd fall out." (laughs)

LM: I've heard you on some of the *Dr. Kildare* shows with Lionel Barrymore and Lew Ayres. They'd been through a lot by the time they reunited for this show.

PW: That's right. [Again, there] was a constant battle going on between the two. It was similar to Basil Rathbone and Nigel Bruce; they were always needling each other. They would have an argument going on about some subject like the cat being altered or not being altered. Lew Ayres felt they should all be altered and Lionel Barrymore said, "They have nothing else to live for. Why would you want to take away the only joy they have?" (laughs) That would go on even into show time. But I loved Lionel Barrymore. He was an honest man. He said what he felt from his heart and had no baloney.

LM: You also worked on *Mystery in the Air* with Peter Lorre.

PW: He was a great actor. He was from the German theater, you know, and he was really a fine, fine actor. I asked him if he ever went to the rushes to see himself. He said, "Never! I would never go to look at myself in the rushes!" We had audiences with that show and once when we were doing a show, he [accidentally] dropped his script. I think it was "The Horla" and he got so worked up the foam was coming out of his mouth. (laughs) "The little horla! The little horla!" From then on, we had to ad-lib it because he no longer had the script. It was a live show too. In those days, with live shows, God help you if you fluffed.

LM: He seemed to get carried away on all of those shows.

PW: He did. He was great fun, though, because he loved what he was doing and he loved throwing himself into the character.

LM: How would you land a steady gig as opposed to one-shot appearances at this time?

PW: I was working on a show with Burgess Meredith. He was the lead and I had the romantic lead opposite him, playing an Australian war bride. When it was over, that's when Jack Johnstone, who was the director of *The Man Called X*, came up on the stage—it was an audience show—

and said, "I want you to be the leading lady for *The Man Called X.*" I felt, you know, so elated that he would choose right at that moment to come up and say that. And I did do about two-and-a-half, three years of *The Man Called X.*

LM: That's my cue to ask you about the star of that show, Herbert Marshall.

PW: The greatest gentleman that I've ever known. He was a beautiful man. He lost his leg in World War I, and he would wear a handkerchief tied around his forehead during rehearsal because he was in such pain all the time. Sweat was dripping into his eyes and he couldn't see the script. He had a manservant, a Filipino, who knew when he was just exhausted and when it was too much. He would come in and say to Johnstone, "He needs rest now." Then he would go out and get him ice and cold drinks, things like that, and get him feeling better. He was a darling man; I loved Herbert Marshall.

And I [also] thought Errol Flynn was a fine gentleman. I was probably too young to appeal to him; whatever it was, he never, never made a move, and I'd heard from other people that he moved on actresses. I wasn't that attractive so I probably didn't have to worry about it. (laughs) He was just a really nice man.

LM: Where'd you get to work with him?

PW: He had his own series [*The Modern Adventures of Casanova*]. He was just a darling. There were some actors, maybe one or two in all of radio, who had dirty minds. And those two, as a young person, when I was 16, 17, I didn't want to be in the room with them. (chuckles) They would be the ones who'd stop me out in the hall and say dirty things, but there were only two. One had been a doctor. He had evidently performed abortions and was kicked out of being a doctor. He hung around for a while. The other fellow was very clever, could do all kinds of accents and he was someone that a lot of people loved. Richard Crenna loved him, you know, and he was—I think for the boys, it was fine. Whenever I would come into a room, they would say, "Shut up, the kid's here. The kid's here." And everybody would stop; they wouldn't talk dirty anymore. Then when I'd leave, they'd say, "OK (laughs), she's out; now let's finish that story." But they always were very respectful that I was young and innocent. I always appreciated that but it didn't prepare me for the world.

LM: You were part of a community.

PW: [There was] a coterie of men that were in Jack Webb's initial company: Stacy Harris, Jack Kruschen, about six of them altogether. They always worked on all the shows, and one fellow who was quite a famous actor took me out and said, "Gee, I'm afraid to touch you." I said, "What are you saying?" He said, "Jack Webb and all those guys told me that if I laid a hand on you, I'd have to answer to them." So I felt very protected by that bunch.

LM: Do you remember when you first met and worked with Jack Webb?

PW: I think it was when they brought [his] show from San Francisco because I did a couple of the *Pat Novak for Hire* shows [in the late 1940s]. But it didn't work out and he then began freelancing. I worked *Escape* two or three times with him. I think we worked *Romance* and *Adventure* but I know I worked [*This Is Your*] *F.B.I.* with him quite a lot. I used to do at least one *F.B.I.* a month and he was usually on during that period of time. [One night

Publicity pose from the 1940s.

in 1949] he said they were doing an audition of something that he thought would go; it was sustaining [unsponsored] and they were going to record it around midnight. "Peg, why don't you stick around?" We had just finished the [*F.B.I.*] show and he said, "I know it's kind of late for you to be hanging around but I think it's going to go, I think it's going to be a success." I said, "Of course, Jack, I'll be glad to do it. I'm flattered." So I stayed and he offered me a contract. I had, like, three lines in this; it was all about men and I played the police operator or something on the phone. He stayed after because he was so excited; he was talking to the sound men and he said, "Stick around, Peg, I want to

With Michael Raffetto in the television version of *One Man's Family*.

talk to you." I stayed and I remember the sound table was up high. He brought me over there and pulled out this paper and he said, "I'm going to sign a contract with you." And the show hadn't been accepted yet. He didn't have any money. He wanted me to play his mother and I said, "Jack, I don't want to sign a contract; I'll do it any time you call me." And he looked so upset. He thought, "She thinks she's too good for me" or something, and he got really upset with me. I didn't hear from him for two or three weeks. I thought about it, because he had said how he wanted me to be a part of this, so I called and I left my name with his secretary. He called right back and he said, "I've got a great part for you." And from then on, I was in the show.

LM: I've listened to many of those shows and heard you play suffering wives, girlfriends, and of course, Joe Friday's mother, even though you were in your mid-20s.

PW: That came in pretty early. I think he'd worked with me [on] other shows where I played old ladies and he thought that was funny. Because I lived with my mother and he lived with his mother, I had a sort of inside track of what it was like. When we'd go live on the air, tears would come down his face, he'd be laughing so hard at things I would be saying that sounded probably like his mother—or my mother. He would just get such a kick out of it. He had Jim Moser write this part for me early on.

LM: How did you come to do those character parts when you were that young?

PW: Well, I think George Fogle gave me the biggest break. He had a show called *Press Club* on CBS with Marvin Miller. I had started doing his soap operas; he had three or four soap operas and I was working on all of them. He hired me for this *Press Club* which was sort of an elite group of people from Chicago, and one girl I could tell was having trouble. I don't know if she was sick, or what, but she just wasn't doing her part, and he asked me to take over for her. I think that was the first time that I really played an older part where it was going to be heard by people. Although from the get-go, you know, when I did those impersonations, I was doing Dame May Whitty and Edna May Oliver and all those older people. It's hard for me to recall now what was the first. It seemed like I was always playing some old lady. And I had to have quite a variety of them 'cause I couldn't do [them] all the same. (chuckles)

I had a step-grandmother who showed up late in my life. My mother had been raised as an orphan pretty much and this woman showed up when I was about 16 and wanted to put me through college. That was where we got the money for me to go to USC. I impersonated her a lot, and her sister was an Irish woman. They all came from Nova Scotia. The sister spoke with a thick Irish accent whereas the grandmother took after the French side and so she had more of the French. Between the two of them, I learned a great deal about old ladies and how they thought. And my own mother was very eccentric, so I could impersonate her.

LM: Obviously, you had a great ear and a gift for mimicry.

PW: I did in those days, now I'm deaf. (laughs)

LM: Tell me some of the actors you worked with who impressed you.

PW: Alan Napier could give a tremendous performance out of a nothing piece of you-know-what. He could turn it into something brilliant.

This was true with a number of fine actors who had had theater training. Of course, Jeanette Nolan always impressed me the most. Jeanette was magic. She wanted to be an opera singer and she could hit those notes. She could scream and she'd curdle your blood, hitting it at just the right moment and the right sound.

Lurene Tuttle had her moments, too; she reminded me of Helen Hayes. You know, Helen Hayes was a truthful, warm fire that could hit the true notes. She could build a scene, she could build a climax in a scene; I don't think I ever saw her do a bad job. Virginia Gregg was a very fine actress. I only worked a few times with Bea Benadaret, but the times I did, she was very good.

As far as movie people were concerned, I was often surprised with people like Ann Blyth. She was a very good actress, a very fine actress. And you know who else? Tim Holt. I thought Orson Welles must have been very perceptive. We did a Western series and Tim Holt was the star, or maybe he just came in to star in that one show. But he just floored me, he was so brilliant. Agnes Moorehead was brilliant. Lionel Barrymore was brilliant. But then, we all knew they were brilliant.

LM: Did you ever work with Ronald Colman?

PW: I didn't. I would have loved to, he's one that I didn't work with. Vincent Price was always wonderful. Brian Aherne was usually very good. Olivia de Havilland surprised me. Deborah Kerr—she was wonderful. She always gave a great performance. There were people who really knew better but, I think, were thrown by reading the words [rather than memorizing].

[Among the radio people] Howard Duff was quick, very quick, didn't need any rehearsal. Same thing with Bill Conrad. Bill Conrad didn't need rehearsal. And Hans Conried. Bill Conrad and Jeanette Nolan and one or two others prided themselves in not marking their scripts. They wouldn't put their circles and all this stuff. Of course, when I was young and first coming in, I just knew that if I fluffed early that I was dead, so I had to be sure that I had everything marked. Gradually, I noticed that these people weren't marking their scripts. They put their feet up and they played poker or they'd do something to show how nonchalant they were about the whole thing. I gradually became relaxed myself because you kind of got into the groove. I had to learn to become the character, which was something that took maybe five years. I could do the character, but to become the character was something else.

LM: Because you started out as a mimic, so that was a facility that you had.

PW: Yes. But now, when actors come up to me and want help, I tell them become the character, be the character. That's the secret. Then you don't have to worry.

As Lady Macduff in *Macbeth*.

LM: When did you first work with Orson Welles? He did so many different series in the 1940s.

PW: I was on my soap opera and the phone call came through. I guess he was doing a show over at CBS. I was at NBC and, of course, here is my idol; I worshiped Orson Welles. They called me from the from the booth; they said, "Orson Welles is on the phone." I was apoplectic 'cause I had to do a show. I was just five minutes or ten minutes from going into doing my show. I answered and he said, "Can you get over here right away?" And I said, "Yes, but I've got to finish the show I'm on." He said, "As soon as you're finished, get over here!" I walked in, and I had the lead opposite him and it was a Russian play of some kind. I never had time enough to look at the script to even know what the name of the script was, but everybody in the cast had champagne glasses and we threw them against the wall at CBS in the auditorium. It was an audience show, and that was the final thing in the script. We all threw our glasses and they all broke. He did his usual thing with the script, where he drops the script and the audience [gets hysterical]. The light goes on and the script is all over the floor; he did that every time. That was his routine to get the audience all keyed up. And he would slash and slash and slash [the script] just before you'd go on the air; that was pretty scary. But, generally speaking, Orson loved actors and he didn't give actors a bad time. He teased those that he loved, you know, like Dick Wilson. But when we were working on the movie, he was very cruel to the workers, the sound men and the grips. If they weren't paying attention, he would then whiplash them with words they had never heard before. It just would pour out of him. He'd say, "How dare you do this?"

With Ben Alexander and Jack Webb in a television episode of *Dragnet*.

When he would come on the set, everything would change. You didn't have to know that Orson had come on the set. All of a sudden, you know Orson's there somehow because everything suddenly went to pieces, everybody was jumping and everybody was doing their thing. He loved old actors; he was very kind to old actors. He brought one old actor in and he couldn't remember his lines. He was so patient with him and so sweet.

He was very kind to Jeanette [Nolan]; he always greeted her with a kiss and told her how wonderful she was. He was a lovely man, and bighearted. He took us all to dinner every night; we'd all have a Chinese dinner. We would go to Wong's. James Wong Howe, the cameraman, had his own restaurant in the Valley, and we'd all go together. He was on a diet because he wanted to get very thin by the end of the picture and he was losing weight. He never slept; he was taking pills all the time. He had Shorty, the little man that he got out of prison, who was his servant, and Shorty would come running. He'd say, "Shor-teee!" You'd hear this voice. "Yes, boss! Yes, boss!" And he'd bring his tray with these little pills that he had to take to keep awake.

LM: That low-budget production of *Macbeth* that he made for Republic Pictures in 1948.

PW: Twenty-one days. Three years to edit. The minute that I read it he said, "That's it! That's it! Go down and record it." We recorded our voices so it was a soundtrack we were acting to, because he didn't want to stop if airplanes went overhead or anything like that. I went down and record-ed it without really getting into the part, so I'd hear this reading coming back [at me] and I'd think, "That's not the way I want to do it; I don't want to say it that way." Well, I had three years to change [everything] so it was OK.

We all came in for years. For two years, I did every-body's part, with Scottish accents, English accents, mid-Atlantic-Irish accents, standard accents. We tried everything and he would make a whole edit with one kind of accent, and then come back six months later an do the whole thing all over again in another accent.

With Jack Webb and Harry Morgan in the late 1960s version of *Dragnet*.

I saw the final cut, which was good. I was always dis-appointed that he turned over [the shooting of] my close-ups to Dick Wilson. And I was very upset because my wig didn't sit right. It was somehow askew when they took the close-up of it. I know if Orson had been doing the close-up he would have seen it. He did my one big scene; he did come in and run us through it. Then he set the camera and he sat on the dolly and then did the reverse shot. But he didn't stay for the actual filming of it; he stayed for the rehearsal of it. He liked my playing the old witches; he enjoyed that.

LM: Your vocal performance as the witches?

PW: Yes, the funny voices. But I was so distraught by hearing my voice com-ing back at me and having to mouth my speeches to something that I recorded five minutes after I read it for him. That did kind of throw me. It was a complicated time. But he was awfully good to all of us.

LM: I would think so. He really leaned on the radio people because he re-spected and trusted them.

PW: He did and so did Jack Webb. He used to say to me all the time, "The best actors in Hollywood are radio actors."

LM: There are all these stories about Jack Webb not letting anybody see their scripts beforehand when he did the *Dragnet* TV show and making people read teleprompter.

PW: He did; he wanted the teleprompter. [When] I came back from Japan, he was so proud. He showed me this and he said, "Look what I did, look what I did. You don't have to learn your lines, you can just read it like you did in radio." And I thought, uh-oh, he doesn't understand. Then I memorized for that [episode about the] Spanish mother that stole the baby. ["The Big Mother"—Ed.] I memorized it thoroughly. But he kept saying, "Your key light is in the teleprompter, so you've got to look at that." Because I had memorized it, I didn't read it. Ever after that, he would scream, "Read it! Read it!" He would say, "I've got it timed so that it's right." But it did bother [me]. You need to know your part.

If you're a good actor you learn the part. He usually didn't cast you until the day before so you didn't know what you were playing. But I did know on "The Big Mother" and I think that's one of my best pieces on film.

LM: On the radio show, do you remember the kind of direction he gave early on to achieve the effect that he wanted?

PW: Yes. That first night [when we did the audition] he said, "I want you to stand back from the microphones." Murphy was our engineer, and he said, "Murph will ride the gain but you stand back; I don't want you getting into the mike. I want it to sound like we're overhearing a conversation. I don't want you to be acting and projecting into the microphone." And that was what he achieved. Then he was very, very strong about sound effects; he wanted the sound effects to be perfect. They had to be authentic because he could tell the difference and so could I. But he wouldn't let me rehearse. We'd do the first reading and then he'd say, "I'm putting you in the sound block. When it's time for you to come in, I'll let you come in." He would do that to me because he said I gave better first readings. He didn't like my readings after I got too involved. But I loved him; I thought he was a great fellow.

LM: Tell me a little about your theater work in Los Angeles.

PW: [In the 1960s] I began producing stage shows [at The New Hope Theater] so I could be home with my children. I put them to bed and then I'd go do my shows. We had a theater right across the street. We lived in Rustic Canyon, and it was the old Uplifters Ranch. It had been a theater; I had to go downtown to City Hall [to get permission to] turn it into a theater again. I had to put acoustics in and that took two or three years of bargaining with the city people. We were doing shows on a regular basis out of there. I had Lee Marvin and Jimmy Whitmore and John Dehner and all the "good ones." Jeanette's son [Tim McIntire] played the lead in *The Corn Is Green*. Doris Lloyd played the schoolteacher. Marlon Brando's sister Jocelyn was my next-door neighbor; she played Major Barbara for me. Earlier, I had done the show with Robert Ryan for [director] Lamont Johnson.

Lee Marvin [lived next door and] was my children's godfather; his wife was their godmother. He and I starred in two live television shows and we did three other television shows [including Marvin's *M Squad*—Ed.] and we did stage plays together. We were very good pals. He was a darling. When I [first] worked with him, I didn't want to get to know him too well. But after I knew him, he was the salt of the earth. He would jump over the fence and pull out a jackhammer and work on our septic tank or if we were making ice cream and it wasn't working, he'd jump over the fence and he'd say, "I'll show you how to make that work!" He would come to all of our parties. As a matter of fact, every afternoon when he wasn't filming, he and his wife would come over for the cocktail hour with my doctor husband. I'd be putting the kids to bed, fixing their dinner and all that stuff and they'd be drinking and drinking at the bar. (laughs) I'd finally come in after everybody was swacked. Then we'd all go to whatever restaurants were open at the time and have an extra dinner.

LM: Was your New Hope Theater successful?

PW: *Under Milkwood* by Dylan Thomas was one of our big hits, where people sat on their suitcases around the block to get in. We did Dickens' *A Christmas Carol*. Ted Cassidy was the Ghost of Christmas Future, Ford Rainey was Marley, and Richard Hale was Scrooge. We also hit *Time* magazine with Sean O'Casey's *Bed Time Story* and Lady Gregory's *Rising of the Moon*. *Time* had an Irish reporter covering entertainment at that time. She was from Dublin and loved what we offered. We had evenings with people like Groucho Marx getting on stage and singing with the Gilbert and Sullivan shows. And John Dehner and me spouting Bobby Burns' poetry, impromptu.

Lee Marvin and I hosted The Old Vic [troupe] during the run of *Milkwood*. We served prime rib dinners and had an open bar. It was The Old Vic's second visit to Los Angeles. The first time the party was held at our adjoining homes, in Rustic Canyon, where Lee built a gate between our properties to that the party could flow between the two houses—and it did flow for two nights and days.

LM: Why didn't you pursue more film work?

PW: I don't think I was really the type; I don't think I photographed that well. And I never had a good agent. My agent was a sound effects man at CBS. Rosemary DeCamp told me once—she was so darling, we were doing some show, and she said, "You know how I got started in movies? There was a fellow who wanted to start an agency and I was his first client. He went out and worked like a dog to get me jobs." She said, "That's the way you have to do it. You can't go with some big agent that's already successful." So this fella who was the sound effects man approached me about a week or two later. He said, "I've been watching you and I want to start my agency with you. Will you join me?" This was like some prayer that had been answered. So he got me lots of work at first. My first role was at Universal in *Little Miss Big* as the cockney maid, in 1944. Also *Her Adventurous Night* with Ella Raines.

I did a lot of second-rate movies. The only time I ever looked good [on film] was the Jack Webb episode where he directed it and I was the Spanish woman; he knew my bad angles and he knew what I could do; he was familiar enough with me. You have to have a director that cares about you.

I had a good role in *Submarine Command* opposite William Holden. I had the lead in *The Screaming Skull*, for Alex Nicol. I played a small scene as a Jewish woman praying in a temple in *The Greatest Story Ever Told*. Sir Carol Reed gave me the lead opposite Tony Quinn in dubbing the American Indian film *Flap*. I looped the whole lead femme role. I looped for many other films. I was the mother of Nicolas Cage in *8MM* and have dubbed dozens of other films.

LM: Tell me about working with Alfred Hitchcock and Henry Fonda on *The Wrong Man*.

In *The Screaming Skull.*

PW: Hitchcock made the part more important. He improvised the scene into something important after he engaged me, and he gave me very big close-ups. For the two or three days that we shot the key scene he kept telling me to stay afraid. But he was very positive about my rendition of the office girl who puts the finger on Henry Fonda. Fonda was always a special love of mine. He told me to learn how to take naps between scenes; he said it was the secret of his success. I do not have much more to say about that film except I liked the story very much, and I wished I could have had more time with Hitchcock. He seemed to trust my instincts. He made me trust myself, and just let the camera go with the flow in my scenes. I liked Hitchcock and I think he liked me. He tried to get me for his film *The Birds.* Doovid Barskin was my agent and he left town in a hurry when he was told that his father was dying. He left no forwarding information and he did not pick up his phone messages. So after two or three weeks Hitchcock gave up trying to reach me. Doovid kept that secret from me for a year.

LM: I've heard it said that some radio actors had a hard time in films and on television because they weren't accustomed to blocking. I've even heard it called "radio feet." Do you agree with that?

PW: I do, but I think sometimes that's the fault of your director, like Jack [Webb]. When they got into having to turn out a show every week, he'd say, "Don't move. Just stand there! I don't want to see you move! We've got you already lit, we don't have time! Stand there!" (laughs) So you'd stand there and say your lines and look like a fool. There were actors in New York who were known as very fine actors and when television came in, you could see it was all [about] their voice. They didn't become the character.

243

Conversations:
ARTHUR GARDNER

At the Golden Boot Awards dinner in 2006, my friend Rob Word introduced my wife and me to our table-mate, a friendly, white-haired man named Arthur Gardner. I was aware of his long partnership in the production company Levy-Gardner-Laven, which was responsible for such long-running TV series as *The Rifleman, Robert Taylor's Detectives*, and *The Big Valley* as well as many feature films. What I didn't know until we started to chat was that he had started out as an actor, and had among his credits *All Quiet on the Western Front* and the notorious *Assassin of Youth* (also known as *Marihuana*)!

I arranged an interview at Levy-Gardner-Laven's office space, which the team's surviving partner shared with Batjac Productions in Beverly Hills. One couldn't hope to cover the many facets of Gardner's career in one interview, but we touched on a number of highlights. Arthur was 96 when we first spoke; he died in 2014 at 104. (Interview originally appeared in 2007.)

AG: I was a nervy kid. As soon as I was done with school I saved up and when I was 18, I came out here. I knew that Carl Laemmle had owned a furniture store in Oshkosh, so I wrote him a letter. My name was Arthur Goldberg, and I told him I was from Wisconsin, and so on. The next day I got to my rooming house and the landlady said, "You got a call from Universal Studios." I spoke to Mr. Laemmle's secretary—I'll never forget her name, it was Lillian Russell and she said, "Mr. Laemmle gets a thousand letters a day, but I told him I thought he should see you." She showed me into his office; he was just a little man, but he spoke to me and said, "I want to introduce you to my son, Junior; he's running the studio." I went to see Junior Laemmle and sat in his office all day; he didn't see me. Then I sat there all the next day, and he didn't see me. Junior's secretary came out and said I'll take you down to the casting director's office, Fred Datig, and Fred Datig put me to work as an extra.

[At first I worked] in silent films, in *The Collegians* series. They paid us $3 a day and a box lunch, sometimes $5 a day. For one scene they had dummies attached to either side of us, so for each one of us they had *three* extras. They gave each extra a dummy with a hat pulled down over his face. When he said, "Action!" we would move the dummies as we moved to conform to our movements. So the studio was getting us for a dollar a day! I got some other bit parts.

LM: Do you remember any of the pictures you were in?

AG: I was in a film called *Broadway*.

LM: That was a big production.

On his way to Hollywood, 1929—and a Collegian at Universal shortly after arriving.

AG: Yes, a big picture, and they must have had about 200 extras in this nightclub scene, so I was thinking, "What would a guy like me do in a nightclub?" so when the camera passed by me I pretended to throw up!

[The director] Paul Fejos was a Hungarian and his English was very

In the front row, soldiers-to-be in *All Quiet on the Western Front.* (from left) William Bakewell, Lew Ayres, Ben Alexander, Owen Davis, Jr., and Arthur Gardner.

fractured, and he was a very excitable man; talented but excitable, and when he wanted something he would scream at the top of his voice and wave his arms.

LM: But then you moved up to an actual speaking role in one of the most important movies of that time. How did you wind up being cast in *All Quiet on the Western Front?*

AG: Every day I'd hitchhike to Universal and back, so I was standing outside the studio and a car stopped; the driver was wearing glasses. He asked me where I was going and I told him Hollywood, and that I had to get home before dark because it was my mother's yartzheit [the anniversary of her death—Ed.], I asked him what he did and he told me his name was George Cukor and he was working as the dialogue director on *All Quiet on the Western Front.* I said, "*All Quiet on the Western Front?* They're hiring juveniles to play the students." He arranged for me [to be hired] for $75 a week. I worked about twelve weeks on that film.

LM: What can you tell me about that experience?

AG: It was marvelous; it was terrific. Everybody was friendly. Cukor, who had been from the stage, took care of all of the dialogue. [Director Lewis] Milestone didn't pay any attention to the dialogue portions; he had all the action, and everybody was friendly. [Leading actor Louis] Wolheim was a dream—this old, seasoned Broadway actor. We all sat down and he threw stories at us. The entire picture was a pleasure.

You remember the scene where the soldiers swam across the stream and the French girls were on the opposite side? We shot it at night, and it was bitter cold. They asked for doubles for the main actors. The first guy to apply was me, of course. We all jumped in the stream. First, they showed Lew Ayres and the others walking into the water, and then we swam across the stream, and emerged on the other side and then they had Lew and the other cast people come out on the other side. [The Los Angeles River] is all concrete now, but back in 1929 it was a stream with dirty water in it, flowing out to the ocean. It was on the old MGM backlot, a tremendous backlot. I would volunteer for anything.

We had a man Laemmle had brought from Germany to teach us how to drill like soldiers. I was always fooling around, and I said something or other and this man said, "Look, you dirty Jew, you ought to pay attention. You're fired!" And he fired me. So I went to Mr. Cukor's office, up a flight of stairs, and I said, "I know I was wrong, but he still had no right to call me a dirty Jew." And Cukor and Lewis Milestone had the man fired. Milestone was just great to me.

At one point the production manager came to us and said the studio was having money problems and they'd have to cut us back to $50 a week.

LM: How much were you paying for rent?

AG: Eleven dollars a month.

LM: So you were doing fine!

AG: Yes, but there were times when the money wasn't coming in and I didn't eat for three or four days at a time. By now I was living at the Hollywood "Y" and I used to walk on Hollywood Boulevard to these restaurants that had glass fronts, you know? You could get ketchup for free out there, so I asked for a glass of hot water and I made myself tomato soup.

When *All Quiet on the Western Front* opened at the Carthay Circle, I think, I think the opening price was $2.75. I couldn't afford to go to the opening! I think at that time I was busted. But I saw it about a month later.

Michael Owen, Gardner, and Luana Walters in the infamous *Assassin of Youth* (1937).

LM: Was it exciting to see yourself on the screen?

AG: Of course it was exciting, thrilling. Then I got an agent, and he said "Arthur Goldberg? That's no kind of a name for movies," so I was walking on Sunset Boulevard, and I was approaching Gardner Junction... [And the rest is history.—Ed.]

LM: What was it like to live in Hollywood in the early 1930s?

AG: It was really a small town. Hollywood Boulevard was like the main street of a small town. D.W. Griffith couldn't get himself a job, and the old Hollywood Hotel was on the corner of Hollywood and Highland. It was a big wooden structure and had a big wooden porch. You could walk by there any day and see him sitting there with his feet on the railing. Nobody knew who he was, [but] I knew who he was. Charlie Chaplin would have dinner on Hollywood Boulevard with his family; there was a little restaurant right near Vine Street. I couldn't afford to eat there, but I walked past it. Nobody bothered them. I never intruded on them.

LM: Did you study acting at all?

AG: No. I just thought I was a natural actor because I was in my high school play!

LM: Did you take it seriously?

AG: Sure, I took it seriously. I was an actor for about eight years. I played the lead in a half a dozen films, and at that time the WPA formed a theater, because all the actors were starving. So I went down and I applied because they needed young people. It was a blessing; they paid $96 a month. I joined, and you had to go on relief to get it, so I was a little bit ashamed to do it, but there were about 10 of us who did it. We were at the old Mayan Theater downtown; they opened that and we staged plays there. And they also had a Jewish theater. As a kid, I was bar mitzvahed and I spoke a little Yiddish, so I did some plays there too.

I played the juvenile lead in a Warner Bros. picture called *Waterfront*, then I played the lead in one of the worst pictures ever made, but one of the most infamous films, *Assassin of Youth* (1937). [Also known as *Marihuana.*—Ed.]

LM: People still watch that today because it's so campy.

AG: Campy? My god, is it campy.

LM: But I presume you took it seriously at the time, as an actor.

AG: Of course, I did. We must have shot it in six days.

LM: And you must have pleased Elmer Clifton, who directed it, because you worked for him again some years later on a film called *The Hard Guy* at PRC. That was considered the bottom of the barrel, wasn't it?

AG: The bottom of the barrel! (laughing) They were always killing me off. In *Waterfront* (1939) I was killed by Ward Bond. I was going through some old stuff and I came across a letter from my father. When my grandmother saw the movie in Chicago and saw my leg severed in the picture she screamed at the top of her voice, "Oy vey, Arthur!" and almost fainted!

Allen Jenkins and Dick Foran with Gardner in *Heart of the North* (1938).

LM: Were there any actors you got to work with whom you particularly admired?

AG: I worked with an actress at MGM that I admired, not especially for her acting ability but for her body, Lana Turner. [The film was *Dramatic School.*—Ed.]

LM: Then your career took an unexpected turn; how did that come about?

AG: There was a woman who used to run a bridge club, and I was a bridge player; my grandmother had taught me how to play. She needed some bridge tables, and I was pretty handy, so I made some tables for her and then played at her club. One of the other players was Frank Kozinski. [Who later changed his name to King.—Ed.] He and his brothers had made a lot of money with slot machines.

LM: Was this sub rosa?

AG: No, it was perfectly legal, right here in Los Angeles. One day Frank told me he was going to go into the movie business with his brothers. He said he had a budget of $16,000, and I could have my choice of jobs: I could play the lead or work as the assistant director; the pay was the same, $75 a week for two weeks. I said, "I want to be assistant director."

So then I said, "There's a friend of mine who's been doing bit parts around town, and he's a good actor. You should use him in the lead." That was Alan Ladd, so he got the part. [The film was *Paper Bullets*, also known as *Gangs, Inc.* (1941).—Ed.]

LM: As you continued working behind the scenes on these films—like *I Killed That Man, Rubber Racketeers*, and *I Escaped from the Gestapo*—you still did some bit parts in these films, didn't you?

AG: Yes, I did.

LM: To save a buck?

AG: To save a buck! I can't say enough about the King Brothers. They were a very close-knit family. Frank was the real brains, but he always gave credit to Maurice, who was the older brother. Hymie was the youngest, and he contributed the least to the team.

LM: What kind of experience did you have to be an assistant director?

AG: I'd been on sets; I knew what they did. I knew what everybody did.

LM: And you had *chutzpah.*

AG: I had more *chutzpah* than you can imagine.

LM: Tell me about directors like Phil Rosen.

AG: They were efficient. They were guys who could get a film done in six days; they were mechanics. Joe [Joseph H.] Lewis was one in a million—a great guy and a great director. [Many years later, in the television era] we made 175 episodes of *The Rifleman* and he must have directed about a third of them. He was tough, but not abrasive. He was just a very creative man, and when he knew he had to shoot it in three days he did. He had a great way of handling actors. Of course, the camera to him was like his right hand.

Gardner (at right) records sound for a 1944 Army film featuring Van Heflin (on porch).

LM: Then came World War II.

AG: I was 32 and I had an infant son, so I knew I was going to be drafted. I heard that they were forming a unit at Warner Bros., so I made an appointment and met Ronald Reagan, who had a little office with just enough room for a desk and a chair on either side, up at the Talisman Studio. He was very nice, but he said, "We're full up." He said he'd take my phone number and let me know if anything opened up.

Eventually they split the First Motion Picture Unit between Hollywood and New York. They told all the guys who were staying here that they could drive their own cars to the new headquarters at the Hal Roach studio. They drove down Hollywood Boulevard and people cheered, as if they were going off to war. They were going to Culver City!

I did my basic training in Florida, and my wife came down with me. Then I was transferred to an army base in Missouri, and I was classified as a radio operator. My wife had a relative who was an officer at Wright Field, and he arranged to have me transferred there, but the only way he could do it was to designate me as "kitchen police," KP. That's where I met Johnny Sturges. They had a lot of good people.

With William Holden in an Army training film.

LM: But eventually you made it back to Culver City and worked at "Fort Roach."

AG: We made some good pictures there. We took over the entire studio. There was a man named [Sidney Van] Keuren who used to work for Hal Roach, and he was the head of production. I knew every inch of that studio. Of course, they had one soundstage that was strictly off limits. You know what was in it? They had built a gigantic map of Japan, on the floor of the stage, and had overhead cameras photographing it, to train the men who were going to drop the bombs, so they would know exactly how to recognize their targets.

LM: Was there any military discipline there?

AG: Not really. They tried in a half-assed way. I don't remember ever saluting an officer. Clark Gable was a producer [there] and an actor; he was a terrific guy. [Also] Van Heflin, Bill Holden. I played small parts in the training films.

LM: Was it after the war that you teamed up with Jules Levy and Arnold Laven?

AG: The three of us were in the Army together, and we said when we get out we're going to have our own company. We trusted each other with everything. We each had different strengths: Arnold was very artistic, Jules was the toughest guy with a dollar or a nickel that you ever heard of, and I was in between. We never did anything without the three of us conferring—a solid partnership.

[We made our first picture when] the story editor at Monogram said, "You guys are looking to make your own movies, right? I know about a story..." So we got a script written, and that was *Without Warning!* (1952). We had a preview at the Pantages Theater and the motion picture editor of the *Times* said, "These guys have made a film that will make a million dollars." So Howard Hughes' assistant called and said Mr. Hughes wanted to see the picture. We sent over a print, and he offered to buy it from us for RKO for $150,000. We said, "We don't want to sell the movie, we want to release it." So that was that. Then we got a call from Nate Blumberg, who was running Universal, and he offered us the same figure, $150,000. We said we didn't want to sell; we wanted to release it. Sol Lesser [called] and we went to meet with him. He offered to pay us $150,000 for our half-interest in the film, so we said yes. Then he tried to sell it to RKO and they said "We made them an offer; we're not interested." Finally, United Artists was getting started, and they agreed to release it—and it died!

LM: Proving again that this business is always a crapshoot. How did you move on from there?

AG: We got a call from Edward Small. He wanted to meet us. He had a commitment from Edward G. Robinson to make a movie for $50,000. He normally got $250,000, but he had been let go from Warner Bros., and was suspected of being a Communist, so he agreed to do this [picture called *Vice Squad*]. Then there was a part for a woman; she was all through the picture, but we figured out that we could shoot all her scenes in three days, so we hired Paulette Goddard.

Eddie was great to work with. He had it in his contract that he wouldn't work past six o'clock. Well, one day we had to go into overtime, so Jules and I went out and bought some expensive cigars. Then we told Eddie we had this situation and we'd have to work just an hour, or an hour and a half overtime; would he consider doing it? He thought for a moment and said, "I'll do it if you get me some particular cigars." We handed him two boxes full of them and he was happy. UA opened the picture in New Jersey and we were a hit!

LM: After making more movies with your partners, you all went on to enjoy great success in television. I know you also helped launch a few careers along the way.

AG: A couple of guys we gave their first chance at doing anything important: Sam Peckinpah and Steven Spielberg. When we were thinking about the *Rifleman* script, someone, I can't remember who, told us about this fellow named Sam Peckinpah, who had written a couple of things. He had an idea that might suit us for our pilot script. We'd already written one that we didn't like, so we got in touch with Sam Peckinpah, who was a very eager young guy from Fresno. He came in and he had a short story he had written. We read it and said this might be the basis for the pilot script. We signed him and we paid him $2,000, which was the minimum [at that time]. That was in early 1958. We started to shoot and he was very, very eager to be on the set. Arnold Laven directed the pilot, and the first two or three shows. Peckinpah said, "I have an idea for another script, and I'd like to direct." Arnold said, "If you want to direct, stand behind me and watch me." Sam wrote another script and after about ten shows we gave him a chance at directing. Arnold stood behind him and gave him tips. That was the beginning of his career.

At that time he was married and had children; we thought he was a happily married man. Then we hired him to write a screenplay for us; his writing habits were very peculiar. Our offices were at the Hal Roach Studio at the time. We'd leave the office around 6, 6:30. We had a little office for Sam. We had a tape recorder put into his office, and he would stay there all night and dictate his screenplay. In the morning our secretary would pick up the script and type it. This went on until he completed the screenplay, called *Glory Guys*. We made it in the '60s. It starred Tom Tryon and Harve Presnell. It was a Western and we shot it in Mexico. From then on Sam started to get jobs, and as you know, he went crazy. He left his family. I don't know what happened to him.

We then moved our offices to the Goldwyn studio and we would have lunch at the Formosa and bump into Sam there; he was warm, but he was wild. It's a shame because he was very, very talented.

LM: And how did you cross paths with Steven Spielberg?

AG: It was in the [early '70s]. Mike Medavoy was an agent at the time, and Jules and I got a call from Mike saying, "I know that you have this script, *White Lightning*. I have a young fellow that I think would be perfect for it; his name is Steven Spielberg, and he's done a lot of television at Universal. Why don't you send a script over to me and I'll give it to Steven?" The next day he said Spielberg read the script and he'd like to meet with you. Steven came out and met with Jules and me; I think Arnold was directing a feature [at the time]. He was a nice, pleasant young man, about 22, 23 years old. He said, "Have you any idea for a cast?" We said the cast was set, and we've got Burt Reynolds, and his face fell. We asked, "Don't

Producer Gardner on the set of *The Big Valley* with its star, Barbara Stanwyck.

you like him?" Here's a kid who had never directed a feature. Jules and I alternate [as producers] on our features; this one was mine. So Steven and I, for about two weeks, talked back and forth; he had some very good ideas on the script. Burt Reynolds had just finished a film called *Deliverance* so Steven and I went out to Warner Bros. and they ran the film for us, and Burt was marvelous. That's when he said, "I like him." We signed a contract, I think for $50,000 for Spielberg and 5 percent of the profits.

Then one day we got a phone call; it was Mike Medavoy again. He said, "Fellows, I know you have a contract with Steven but he has been preparing a picture here at Universal called *Sugarland Express*, starring Goldie Hawn, and he has written part of the screenplay, and Universal has just given him approval to make it. I know you have him under contract, but if you could release him so he could do this, it would be a big, big favor to me and him. Maybe he could do another film for you." So Jules and I looked at each other; we said, "We'll call you back." Here's a guy who we like but he didn't like Reynolds to begin with, and he's got his own screenplay, but it would be foolish of us [to force the issue] because he'd be doing it under pressure. So we decided to let him go and we hired another director. That picture made more money than any feature we've ever done.

Conversations:

MARC CONNELLY

One evening in 1978, I was surprised to see playwright Marc Connelly as a guest on *The Dick Cavett Show*—surprised because I hadn't realized he was still alive! In fact, the then-88-year-old survivor of the fabled Algonquin Round Table lived just blocks from me on Central Park West in Manhattan. I wrote a letter asking if he would be willing to talk about his film career and he agreed.

I was a great admirer of *The Green Pastures* (1936), the screen version of his Pulitzer Prize-winning play (and the only film he ever directed) and wanted to learn more about it. It derived from a book by Roark Bradford that interpreted biblical stories through the eyes of simple black people down South, and Connelly was enchanted by its ability to "present certain aspects of a living religion in terms of its believers." It took a lengthy search to find the right man to play De Lawd, an elderly resident of Harlem named Richard Berry Harrison who'd never acted before. One must appreciate the magnitude of the play's success, and Harrison's contribution to it, to understand Connelly's dismissal of the movie and its leading actor, Rex Ingram.

Many of the plays Connelly wrote with George S. Kaufman—including *Dulcy, To the Ladies, Merton of the Movies*, and *Beggar on Horseback*—as well as *The Farmer Takes a Wife* (written with Frank B. Elser) and *The Wild Man of Borneo* (co-authored by Herman J. Mankiewicz)—were turned into movies, but I was chiefly interested in talking with him about the few occasions when he actually worked on screenplays himself.

What I didn't know, until he mentioned it at the outset of our conversation, was that, like his great friend Robert Benchley, he had also written and starred in a series of humorous short subjects in the earliest days of talkies.

They were produced by RKO, but I have never found a trace of them. Connelly told me that he had prints stored away, and I tried to pin him down, gently pointing out that The Museum of Modern Art might be a good home for them, but he evinced little interest. Connelly died two years later in 1980, but I still have hopes that at least one of the eight shorts he made in 1929–30 will turn up some day. (Interview originally appeared in 2008.)

LM: How many of those shorts did you make?

MC: I think I made six of them. I made them…mostly in '29.

LM: What was the nature of them?

MC: They were two-reel comedy shorts. They were original. Some of them were scripts that I had done originally as little skits for Dutch Treat shows, the annual Dutch Treat dinners we used to write for. One was *The Traveler,* which is a fairly well-known thing; it's been done a great many places all over the world. About a traveler who arrives in Grand Central Station, makes friends with the porter, and is told that he can either sit in back in seat 27 or here in the smoking car. It turns out he's going all the way to 125th Street. And he makes friends with the conductor and so on; they have quite a chat and so on. And, there was *The Bridegroom* and there was *The Burglar.* I think there were six characters all together. They're all wrapped up somewhere over in New Jersey.

LM: Did you appear in them?

MC: Yeah, I was in all of them. I wrote them for myself to do, yes.

LM: Who directed them?

MC: I directed them.

LM: Where did you shoot them? Do you remember?

MC: Down at 24th Street. In the old studio down there.

LM: What was your impression of working in film?

MC: It was pleasant. I did it with the people I wanted, mostly with old friends. Some of them were with well-known people: Heywood Broun, actors like J.M. Kerrigan and Russell Crouse; people like that.

LM: Did you want to continue in that vein?

MC: Well no, because about that time *The Green Pastures* came along and I started rehearsals of that in the early 1930s. And I got so involved I didn't want to do any more.

LM: Did you have any involvement at all with the silent films that were adapted from your plays?

MC: No. I went out to Hollywood in 1926 with Beatrice Lillie, who was an old friend of mine. They'd asked her to do a picture, and she said she'd go out if I'd do the picture. So, we went out together, and I wrote a picture for her out there which was quite successful, *Exit Smiling*. It's still in existence, as a matter of fact; they ran it in England, at some festival there. I haven't seen it since it was first done. I remember it had a subtitle in it that was hilarious and I wish I had written that. I was credited with it, but I didn't write it. The boy who wrote the subtitles for the picture wrote the thing and I remember it very vividly. It was, "She wanted to be an actress. She had created the role of nothing in *Much Ado About Nothing*." (laughs) That's a lovely line.

LM: That was made at MGM, wasn't it?

MC: It was MGM, yes. I wrote the picture on the lot.

LM: And what were your first impressions of the place?

MC: That it was insane. That it was filled with egomaniacs. Frightened. Terrified, intimidated, all afraid of someone superior who might, more or less, end his career like *that* if he made some false move. I didn't give a damn about it, because that wasn't my field. I was out there just to do one picture.

LM: Was that an original work or was it adapted from source material?

MC: Yes, that was an original thing I wrote for her.

LM: What can you tell me about the technique of writing for silent film? Did you write full dialogue or was it mostly descriptive?

MC: Yes, I wrote dialogue. Oh, sure, you write dialogue for a silent script just as you write for a play but they have things done in mime mostly, of course, but it's condensed and [put] into short sub-titles.

LM: Did you stick around while it was being filmed?

MC: No. No.

LM: Do you remember seeing the finished picture when it came out?

MC: I think I saw it. I don't remember too vividly whether I saw it or not.

LM: I've always been curious, did you see the adaptations of your plays like the silent film of *Dulcy* or *Merton of the Movies,* and do you recall anything of your reaction?

MC: I think I saw some of them, but I don't recall them at all.

LM: Did they pay well in those days for screen rights to plays?

MC: I don't know what we got. Nothing comparable to what they pay today. I suppose they paid, oh, twenty-five, fifty thousand dollars. I think *Merton of the Movies* got some fantastically high sum, incredibly high in those days, I think a hundred thousand, something like that.

LM: When they bought the rights to a play of yours, did they also have the

Connelly makes a curtain speech at a theatrical evening called *The Post-Depression Gaieties,* with chorus girls from *Anything Goes* behind him.

right to do remakes? I notice most of them were remade as talkies, and sometimes two or three times.

MC: I think the contracts varied. It depended on the stipulations that were achieved by your lawyer. Of course, the movie company grabbed everything possible. It depended on how much they wanted the property, and how agile and insistent your lawyer was on retaining certain aspects of it.

LM: I've read that Edna Ferber had the canniest contracts of all.

MC: Oh, Edna. She was nobody's fool.

LM: The first screenwriting credit that I have for you, aside from the silent film that you did, is *The Green Pastures,* but you also got to co-direct it with William Keighley. How did that come about?

MC: Well, I directed it up to the last two or three weeks. I was getting up at five in the morning and getting to bed about three in the morning, because there was so much to do. I was looking at the rushes and rehearsing and having production meetings and so on. I just couldn't handle it, so they gave me a man to help out the last two to three weeks. That's the reason he came in as a co-director. I directed the whole bloody thing except for the last couple of weeks.

LM: How did you get to direct the film? Was that a condition that you put on the sale of the screenplay?

MC: Well, I directed the play, you know. I've always directed my own plays. I've done that since the late '20s. I've directed everything I've ever written. So I automatically went with the play as its director.

LM: So that was your first experience directing a major Hollywood production within the studio system.

MC: Under the days of Mr. Jack Warner, the late beloved.

Connelly and his cinematographer, Hal Mohr, on the set of *The Green Pastures.* (1936).

LM: Can you tell me something of your experiences going out and trying to prepare?

MC: Well, I remember about the second day I was there, I encountered Mr. Warner somewhere. He greeted me in a very jovial way and asked me if I could come down to court the following day and be a character witness for him. Which I thought was rather odd that I, a newcomer to the place, who had known him about 24 hours, should be entitled to be a character witness. It seems he was being sued by this bastard Jimmy Cagney. And I got out of that one very easily by saying "Well, unhappily, Jimmy Cagney is an old friend of mine. And I shouldn't like to get involved in a thing like that." But imagine him asking me a thing like that. He was a preposterous sort of creature. He had an amazing blindness about himself. He regarded himself as a man thwarted by his commitments as a big producer from being a very successful actor and comedian. He loved to tell stories. And he told stories that wouldn't have got a hand at a rotary meeting, you know. He regarded himself as a comedian—as a humorist—and it was really rather pathetic. He was a humorless man.

LM: What was the biggest challenge for you in adapting your play to the screen?

MC: The biggest challenge was not blowing up completely when I discovered that [I wouldn't be] allowed to make the picture down South, which was the original idea. I didn't want to transpose the thing merely to a studio stage, I wanted to make it down South. I wanted to make a good picture out of it. Unhappily, their contract was such that I was obliged to abide by it, so I had to make it at the studio. Which meant merely transposing the play to the screen. That was all. Instead of amplifying it, and using the South and expanding and experimenting and making it the kind of picture that would have been fresh and original and would have been in an entirely different dimension from what the stage play was. I don't say that it would have been better, or even as good, but to me it would have been interesting to have done it down there using the real background of the old sharecropping countryside.

LM: Were the sets based roughly on what you'd had on the stage? Or were they different?

MC: Oh, I brought my own stage designer out there. I brought the man I

A unique logo and title card: this was a prestige picture, and Warner Bros. wanted everyone to know it.

wanted to do it; he designed the sets.

LM: What was his name?

MC: His name was—it will come to me in a moment. The play was done, of course, by an outstanding, preeminent—our greatest scene designer—

LM: Jo Mielziner?

MC: No, no, the man Jo said he adopted as his godfather.

LM: Jones?

MC: Yes, Robert Edmond Jones. He designed the scenery for the theater. No, [the film[was done by Allen Saalburg. I brought Alan out. Alan had never designed a picture before, but I knew he could do it, and he did a highly competent job of making the studio's sets for the play.

LM: How much control did you find you had in all the day-to-day creative decisions?

MC: Oh, an amazing amount. I had control up till the last three weeks.

LM: How did you decide on Rex Ingram?

MC: Well, that was the end of an unhappy search. Because, Mr. Harrison [who created the role of De Lawd on stage] had died, of course. Ingram was a competent actor. Competent's the word; that's about all.

LM: Were you happy with Eddie Anderson?

MC: Oh, Eddie Anderson was an artist. Sure. I'd have taken him for anything that required warmth and simplicity and humor. He could do anything. A darling human being. He played Noah for me.

LM: How closely did you work with your cameraman?

MC: Not very closely. He was a stiff man, a man named Hal Mohr. I don't know why I should remember his name because usually there's a kind of Freudian release from names that you don't remember happily. But, this fellow was rather stiff, and I didn't find him at all sympathetic toward work.

LM: What did you think of the finished film?

MC: I never liked it, really.

LM: Really? Why?

MC: Oh, because it was spiritless. It was mechanical. It was...

LM: Well, you see, I come to it not having seen the stage play, so I have a different perspective.

MC: It didn't have the electricity, it didn't have the dynamics, it didn't have that extra charge that it should have as a play.

LM: Why do you think that was?

MC: Well, partly, it was because of Ingram, I think. Ingram did his best, but Ingram, after all, was an actor. Whereas Harrison was an incredible artist as well as an incredible human being.

LM: Do you think any of it had to do with the different dynamics of the theater and the film medium?

MC: Well, of course the effect achieved in the theater is about 85 percent human. Fifteen percent is, at the most, mechanical. It's almost the opposite in the movies. It's about 85 percent mechanical, 15 percent human. The use of close-ups and staying on a face and getting whatever human reactions you can get from a face. Oh, you might get 20 percent of the human commitment from the screen but, that's about all you can hope to get, I think. Pictures can be made by an artist. A beautiful picture can be made by an artist. But it isn't the same as theater. And I'm not denigrating pictures, I'm not for one moment minimizing their values or their impacts—they can be wonderful—but the theater happens to have its own individuality, its own personality, and it moves closer to the heart than the movies ever can. Because the theater can get right to the heart, it always has. Ever since man invented it. After all, it's the best social instrument man's ever invented, and it's been the wellspring for practically every religion he's ever had. Every orthodoxy he's ever invented has drawn on the theater for its machinery.

LM: Did you feel that way about the film when it came out? Or is this in retrospect?

MC: No, no, no. I simply looked at the film as a director. That was all. I could see whether the bolts and the nuts all worked together, and the grooves were correct, and the joints, and the thing functioned. It did function all right. It just didn't have, to me, it couldn't have, the spiritual value that the play has had.

LM: Was Mr. Warner pleased with it? Do you recall?

MC: Oh, Mr. Warner was pleased with anything that turned the dollar on. Hell, he wouldn't know if anything was good or not.

LM: Did he make you an offer to direct or write other pictures?

MC: Oh, yeah. He asked me to do other things, yes.

LM: Why did you decline?

MC: I didn't want to put Warner's name on anything I had done.

LM: But a year later you did work for MGM doing *Captains Courageous*.

MC: Oh, I did *Captains Courageous* in '35. *Captains Courageous* was a peculiar situation. That was the first real picture I had a chance to work on. When I went to MGM I was known to people out at MGM as a personality. I wasn't though, which was fortunate for me. Plus the producer, a guy named Buddy Lighton, was being let out; this would be his last picture. And, Victor Fleming, the director, was an arrogant man who wouldn't talk to anybody there. He had an intellectual, completely

The director coaches "the barnyard babies" on the set of *The Green Pastures*.

valid, contempt for nine-tenths of the people there; he wouldn't talk to them. So, the three of us were left completely alone and we cooked up a picture. And we had a hell of a lot of fun just cooking up a picture. Cooking up in the sense of Nunnally Johnson, who said pictures weren't written, they were concocted. Well, we concocted a picture. The three of us. Each contributed his part. And, the result was it was a pretty successful picture. And, both of them were darling people to work with. We screamed and yelled and did everything that collaborators should do. Always about *it,* never about each other. We got along fine. We were all good friends. I came away with enormous admiration for both of them, and Fleming, of course. Lighton had his contract renewed because they suddenly saw that he—maybe—had a merit. Actually, it was this petty jealousy on the part of other people that were easing him out there. That was the only reason he and, as I say, Fleming just didn't give a damn about any of them. Oh, God, Fleming's contempt for them—it was just wonderful. It was contempt of a fine musician for somebody who couldn't hold a flute in his hand. He looked at these people with such disdain and such authority. He couldn't be bothered with them. He didn't have time to sneer at them, so he just avoided them. He had too many important things of his own to do.

LM: And was successful enough to survive.

MC: Well, he knew himself, was a hell of a workman, of course—damned thorough workman. First-class man.

LM: Tell me how you approached adapting that story.

MC: The early part I took out of my own childhood; the business of Harvey at the school, where he gets into trouble—that was all out of my own boyhood. The business of the boy in Coventry and so on. You see, what Kipling did. Kipling turned a cute trick. He took what would have been two short stories and made them into one story. He wanted to do something about American railroads and at the same time wanted to do something about the Gloucester fishermen. So he combined them into one story [with] the father crossing the country by [the] miracle of American railroad system, and then running and finding the kid. Well, I cut out the chase across the country, but I had to make a three dimensional background childhood for the boy. So I invented that. Then I got them to bring in Charlie Connelly, who used to write about the fishing boats around Gloucester. I had never known him before; he's no relation, I'd only heard of him. I'd never met him until he got paid. He was a cute little fellow. He was a great authority on the schooner itself, and he supplied me with all the stuff I needed for that. He knew everything there was to know about the fisherman.

LM: Were you there while it was being made?

MC: Just the beginning of it. Then I was back doing something else while they were shooting it, so I saw a good bit of it. That was loaded with stars. My God, they had about 95 stars in that thing.

LM: It's a beautiful film. Were a number of your New York companions working out there at the time?

MC: Oh, yes, a great many of them.

LM: That was the peak of the New York migration, wasn't it?

MC: Oh, yeah. Well, we had a small group. I've written about the Butterworth Athletic Club—[Charles] Butterworth, Oscar Hammerstein, Harry Ruby, and that whole crowd.

LM: What was your view of working in Hollywood at the time? Was it slumming? Was it easy money?

MC: It was easy money. God knows, I made money. Wodehouse was there one whole year without doing a single thing. He wrote a couple of Jeeves novels while he was waiting for the sign. (laughs) And I saw a lot of Bill Faulkner, he was a good friend of mine. Bill came and used my house all the time. And that pipe of his, too. Whenever he wanted to get a good reply, he would take a puff. "Mr. Faulkner, do you want to work at the studio or would you rather work at home?" "I think I'd rather work at home." (pipe-puffing motion; laughs)

LM: Then you returned to New York for quite a long stretch.

MC: I had come back and forth actually.

LM: The next picture I see credited for you is *I Married a Witch,* which was directed by René Clair.

MC: Oh, yeah. Well, that was a short rewrite thing actually. The chap who originally wrote it [Thorne Smith—Ed.] wrote the original version. He wrote several comedies, some of them quite amusing, too. He had gotten mad and walked off it, or blew up or some goddamn thing; anyway, there was a mess up [and] they called me in. I used to write the thing, then [go to the] back door, hand René two or three minutes of dialogue, and then I'd scoot back. Instead of handing the thing in, as was the protocol, so some mastermind could look to see that you hadn't written anything to get Paramount sued. I would slide down the back stairway and hand it to René, and he'd give it to Freddie March or Bob Benchley or, what was the name of the—

LM: Veronica Lake?

Set visitor Bette Davis watches as Connelly makes an announcement on the set of *The Green Pastures*.

MC: Or Veronica, and they'd play the scene and I'd be up trying to knock out another scene. I'd get about four or five minutes shooting a day. That's how the goddamn thing was really written.

LM: Incredible. What was Clair like?

MC: Oh, charming—quiet and polished. I was going to say reserved; he wasn't reserved, but he was a curiously dignified, terribly likable man. The story of how he got the hell out of France about five minutes ahead of the Nazis, who were after him, is an awful story—how he got down through Spain and got out. It was amazing. He was very, very gallant, very brave guy. And God knows a very competent director. Awfully good director. We used to go to the theater together.

LM: Was he confident working in Hollywood?

MC: If he was working with people whom he liked, yeah. I know he liked me, as a human being. We got along fine but we were sort of working in the back alleys together.

LM: How apt that you should be working on a picture that Benchley was appearing in.

MC: Well, Benchley is one of my dearest, oldest friends, yeah.

LM: I see that you're credited as one of the writers on an MGM picture called *Reunion in France.*

MC: I don't remember that.

LM: How about *The Imposter?* Does that ring a bell?

MC: Who was the director?

LM: Julien Duvivier.

MC: Yes, I knew Duvivier. He was an excitable little man. I don't know whether or not I worked on that or not. I might have done a little doctoring on it. I doctored several.

LM: How did that come about?

MC: They'd just call me and ask me to do, maybe some little repair work or something like that. Which I tried to do.

LM: There was a time at MGM when practically no picture came out with one man's name on the screenplay. It was always four or five people.

MC: I did a lot of doctoring on those things. I did that a lot at MGM.

LM: Can you remember any examples? Any titles you worked on?

MC: Oh, the Edison pictures. [*Young Tom Edison* and *Edison, The Man*— Ed.] I worked on those. I wrote a speech for Edison to make.

LM: Who would call you in for that? The producer?

MC: Yeah. I would presumably be working on a picture. I was out there on an assignment.

LM: And while you were there, they would come to you—

MC: And say, "C'mon, c'mon, help me finish my little..." because I was good at stopping nose-bleeding. They'd say, "C'mon, bring your handkerchief." That was their motto.

LM: Which producers did you work for, and did you respect any in particular besides Buddy Lighton?

MC: A couple I had enormous contempt for. One was—oh, I'd wish I'd been there to see him get his comeuppance. His name was Sidney Franklin. Mr. Franklin found himself with Mr. Charles Brackett and Mr. Billy Wilder, borrowed from Paramount. One afternoon, he summoned them to his office. Brackett looked down and said, "My name is Brackett. My partner's name is Wilder. And yours is, right now, Sidney Franklin. We are terribly well-known, and we are both quite rich, and you are a very unimportant little pipsqueak of an upstart of a producer who doesn't know one goddamn thing as far as we've been able to find out. And we wouldn't work for you for anything. Goodnight, you little squirt." They walked out on Mr. Franklin. What a preposterous little creature, this Sidney Franklin. Oh, and he used to sit there with an authority. He had it all. I don't know what he had read, but he had read about the calm of authoritative men. And I think he had what he thought was calm. It was nothing except a photographic attitude. That was all. Well, he gave me an awful lot of anal pain. I got along with most of them.

LM: Was your main contact with the producer as opposed to with the writer or the director?

MC: Well, I had very little to do with the director. Usually we just wrote the script and that's the last you saw of it. But most of the directors I knew were good friends of mine. People like Lewis Milestone.

LM: When you were working on a screenplay or even doctoring something, were you ever doing it for a particular actor's talents or as a vehicle?

MC: No, my concern was only as a storyteller, to see that there was a flow, that there was a progression, and that the thing had, please God, some cumulative dramatic value.

LM: Did you feel it was a different procedure from writing a play?

MC: The difference: technique. Of course, in a living theater you have more time for nuances. You can do more. I love the living theater because

Connelly got to write for his friend Robert Benchley in *I Married a Witch* (1942) with Veronica Lake and Fredric March.

there's a greater freedom there. I suppose in movies today you can do almost anything you want to; you have the freedom that you didn't have ten years ago, probably, so maybe you're as free as the theater, but the theater has been, over the years, completely free. It's been devoid of the censorship that the movies had to face and thwart whenever it could.

LM: Did you have problems with censorship when you were working on screenplays?

MC: Oh, I found a lot of it.

LM: Do you remember any problems where you were thwarted by censorship from things you wanted to include in the screenplay?

MC: Well, there was a time when "damn" was regarded as a thing to stop a picture's production. You couldn't do it. I remember the days when that was taboo. Even "darn" was looked at with raised eyebrows. Most of the eyebrows came down eventually. Now, of course, you can say anything, you can say any monosyllable you can think of and get away with it.

LM: Was there any problem with the Breen Office on *Green Pastures*?

MC: Oh, no. Never had any.

LM: What about *I Married a Witch*? That was kind of saucy for this time, wasn't it?

MC: No, I don't remember any problem with it. If there were problems I suppose René may have had to face them, but I don't remember any.

LM: I don't know anything about two films that you worked on in the '50s with a man named Fred Pressburger. Can you tell me about them and how they came about?

MC: *Fabiola* was something, already done. I just helped re-edit it a little. I had nothing to do with the making of it or the writing of it.

LM: And another one called *Crowded Paradise?*

MC: Don't remember it at all.

LM: Finally, how did you come to be a movie actor in later years?

MC: Well, I began in the theater. When actors were ill, I've gone on and acted. I act. I did *Our Town* here and in Europe, various other things. I did *Tall Story, Velasco,* and I did it in the pictures also. I went out and played my partner there. I've done several plays. Played in stock.

LM: Whose idea was it to put you in *Spirit of St. Louis?* Was that Billy Wilder's?

MC: I don't know, it might have been Jimmy Stewart, it might have been the producers. It might have been Josh Logan, I don't know. Possibly because of my priestly general overtones. They might have suggested

Connelly recreates his Broadway role in the film version of *Tall Story* (1961), with Jane Fonda, Ray Walston, Anthony Perkins, and Anne Jackson.

it. I got in a big argument with Josh on the picture of *Tall Story*. And, he confessed I was right, too. He said, "What was wrong with it?" And I said, "Well, goddamn it, nothing was wrong except you took all the humanity out of it." Which he did. It was a shame, too. He just made it mechanical. He took all the humanity out of the professor, and the boy, and the girl, and he just made it absolutely routine. How he could suddenly have blinded himself or become blind up to the basic requirements of the story?

LM: Had he done it on the stage?

MC: No, he didn't do it on the stage.

LM: That was Jane Fonda's first movie, I believe.

MC: Oh, yeah, Jane is lovely. Well, I said this about Jane Fonda. It was remarkable to see her when she wasn't rehearsing, or in a scene, standing practically as close to the camera as she could get, watching every shot. Learning her business. That kid was there to learn something about the movies. That's what I thought about her. [She said] "All right, start talking." And I said, "What'll we talk about?" And she said, "Sex." It was a funny thing because her father and Anthony Perkins' father had got their start in shows that I'd had a hand in. Isn't that funny? I put Henry—

LM: Oh, in *The Farmer Takes a Wife*.

MC: Ozzie [Osgood Perkins] was in *Beggar on Horseback*.

LM: I'd like to ask you about somebody you mentioned briefly before who intrigues me but I know very little about, Charles Butterworth. On-screen he always brought his own particular humor to whatever character he was playing.

MC: One of the dear guys of the world, real sweethearts of the world. A sweetness awfully hard to describe. Gentleness, lived for fun, for humor. Very diligent, very hard working, but just ready for laughter. Charlie was both an amused and amusing person. Do I mention [in my book] about taking a horse to his house?

LM: I don't recall that, no.

MC: Mr. Benchley and I were on our way to Charlie's one evening for a birthday party and we didn't now what to get him. A cart went by taking old horse on his way to the chicken factory. So we stopped it, and we bought the horse, paid twenty dollars or something for it. Led it up the steps, into the parlor. "Charlie," he said, "don't say a word." He stood there with the horse and said, "You've been reading my mind, haven't you?" (laughs) Our "old pet."

LM: Did he ever write? He seemed to be a natural humorist.

MC: Oh, he was. No, I don't think Charlie ever wrote anything. I was working on a play down in Palm Springs and I had a house right next to his. I had rented Paul Lukas' house for the year, or whatever the hell it was, and Charlie would come down on weekends. One weekend he came down, and I said, "Well, what's happening?" He said, "Oh God, you won't believe it. No mail's being delivered. They've turned off the water, electricity, none of the facilities are on, streetcars have stopped running." I said, "Everybody's Pecking, Pecking, Pecking." You're too young to remember that song.

LM: I do know it.

MC: He had a lot of the qualities Mr. Benchley had. Really. He had a gentleness that was kind of like Benchley's.

LM: Can you shed any light on Benchley's attitude towards performing? At first, I know, it was a lark, and then, gradually, it became his career.

MC: He was happy to make a good livelihood by it. His salary went up all the time when he got good parts. He didn't mind it; it was easy for him. He realized he didn't have to act; all he had to do was to memorize the lines and then say them. One time, somebody went up to Ethel Merman on an opening night and said, "Are you nervous?" She goes, "What the hell are you talking about, if I'm nervous? I know my lines." (laughs)

LM: That's the whole thing, right?

MC: Why, certainly.

Conversations:
PAUL WURTZEL

Paul Wurtzel was part of a family with deep Hollywood roots. His father, Sol Wurtzel, ran the West Coast operation of Fox Studios in the silent-film era, under the heavy thumb of William Fox, headquartered in New York. He later supervised all of 20th Century Fox's B-movie output until the late 1940s when he set up Sol M. Wurtzel Productions and made a string of low-budget films for Fox release. Paul worked on all of those films as assistant director, sometimes also getting credit as associate producer. He later spent several years working for Howard Koch and Aubrey Schenck's Bel-Air Productions, turning out still more programmers. His long experience in the B movie world served him well as a unit production manager in television, where he worked on literally hundreds of episodes of shows like *The Fugitive* and *The F.B.I.*

Paul was proud of his family history and donated most of his father's papers to the Academy of Motion Picture Arts and Sciences. His late sister, Lillian Wurtzel Semenov, collaborated on a book called *William Fox, Sol M. Wurtzel and the Early Fox Film Corporation: Letters, 1917–1923* (McFarland, 2001) drawn from surviving correspondence between the two men.

Age 87 at the time of our interview, Paul was still close to many of the people he had met and worked with over the years, and was happy to draw on his memory to provide a clear, no-nonsense look behind the scenes of studio moviemaking in the 1940s and the early days of television. Paul passed away in 2014 at age 92. (Interview originally appeared in 2008.)

LM: How old were you when you first visited your father at the studio?

PW: I don't know, maybe, eight or nine. I remember he took me over—they were doing a picture and they had a group called the Singer's Midgets. He wanted me to meet the Singer's Midgets. And Tom Mix was my godfather. I never got along with my father because he was always tied up in a knot. He worked, like, 18 hours a day; we never saw him, you know. Nobody worked as hard as he did; he was so terrified of William Fox. I remember going to the barber shop. Western Avenue had a lot of little shops right outside the studio. They also had a restaurant called the Munchers on Western Avenue; that's where most of the employees would go.

LM: Did you ever work at the studio as a kid, on summer vacations? Or just hang out?

PW: No, 'cause I was mostly at military school [the Black-Foxe Academy]. I boarded there. The two Charlie Chaplin sons were there when I was there, and two of Buster Keaton's sons—that sort of movie crowd. They sent Mickey Rooney there and he lasted about two weeks. He was a tough little bastard, a little feisty guy. Sam Goldwyn, Jr., was a good friend of mine when I went there. I'm trying to think of picture guys. A guy named C. Ray Stahl; his father John Stahl was a director.

LM: When you graduated, was it inevitable that you would go into the family business?

PW: Well, no. My father said, "You're not emotionally fit to be in the picture business." (chuckles) "What I'd like you to do is go to a university and study agriculture and then we can buy a farm and you can be a farmer." I wasn't too happy about that. Anyway, I went to UCLA; that was before the war broke out. Then war started. My father tried to get me to enlist before the draft took over into the Coast Guard. They wouldn't let me in 'cause I had had this back surgery. I said, "What if I'm drafted?" And he says, "If they draft you, they're crazy." I got called on the draft and they rejected me so I lucked out, I guess.

LM: Did you complete four years at UCLA?

PW: No, two; then I went to work at Fox as a second assistant. I wasn't doing too well at UCLA—I wasn't interested—so they got me a job at Fox

Sol M. Wurtzel in his office. Note William Fox's picture looming over him.

and I started there in '41.

LM: Since your dad had been William Fox's guy, how did he fare when Darryl Zanuck took over?

PW: They got along great. In fact, I found a postcard from Zanuck after [20th Century Pictures and Fox] merged—I guess it was '34—saying how much they liked each other. I gave it to the Academy. I was amazed because they got along fine. I don't know if you've been in the projection rooms [at the studio]; I don't even know if they're still there in the executive building. [They are as of 2008.—Ed.] My Dad's was on one side of the entrance and Zanuck's was on the other. They both had their own projectionist. I'd go there a lot; my Dad would take me and I'd sit in the dailies. You know, they had to look at dailies from three or four pictures, 'cause they had to fill out like 26, as I recall, a year.

LM: By the time you went to work at Fox, your dad was in charge of all the Bs. As far as you know, did Zanuck even look at them or was it entirely your dad's domain?

PW: No, it was all his unless there was some actor he wanted to look at. I always remember Zanuck had a sawed-off polo mallet, and he had a unit manager named Ben Silver; he looked like Zero Mostel, a big fat guy.

He would throw bottle caps on the floor and Zanuck would hit them with the [mallet] into the screen.

LM: While watching the screen?

PW: Yeah. He was practicing his polo.

LM: What did being a second assistant director entail?

Director John Ford, Sol M. Wurtzel, and associate producer John Stone at work on a film in the 1920s.

PW: You learn from the ground up. I knew nothing at all, any more than my father knew about making movies [when he started] and he got on. They stuck me with Stan Hough, whose father was Lefty Hough, who was John Ford's prop man for years. The first thing that they [did was they] made me start drinking. I'll never forget the first location. We had to be at Fox Hills at four in the morning to take the bus up to Lone Pine; we were doing a Western. These were my Dad's pictures—they didn't dare put me on a Zanuck picture. (chuckles) Anyway, we're standing, waiting to go and one of the cowboys, a stunt guy who became famous, Frank McGrath, pulled out a pint and said, "Here, take a drink." I said, "Jesus, it's four in the morning." "Do you want to go home or do you want to do this?" So I had to take a slug of bourbon at four in the morning. But they were wonderful guys and they were the real thing, those guys. A guy named Jim Tinling was the director. They called him the Chinese director: Tin Ling. He was a great guy and it was a great experience, it really was, and then I just kept going.

LM: What did you have to do that the assistant director wasn't doing?

PW: It's the same today, I'm pretty sure, except you've got walkie-talkies. We used a whistle and a red flag and a white flag. And you ran—you had to run 'cause you're making a B picture (chuckles). You give the actors the call, go get 'em, make sure they're in makeup, take 'em here, put them in the car. You give 'em their dialogue. One time much later, I was working with Glenn Ford and he was in his own world. We'd say, "All right, Glenn, tomorrow you'll be in makeup at eight o'clock and then on the set at nine and here are the scenes we're doing," They'd hand it to him, the call sheet and everything, and he'd come in and he never knew anything. [And he'd say] "Well, the assistants never told me anything." So the first assistant on this particular film said, "Okay, you give him a carbon copy; you make a carbon copy and make him *sign* it." That's what we had to do. That guy was a famous assistant director, Ben Chapman; he was the production manager for Quinn Martin when I was working on the F.B.I. show.

LM: Tell me about making your first B Western up at Lone Pine.

PW: George Montgomery [was in it]; it's when he just was getting started. *Riders of the Purple Sage*. What's-his-name [Zane Grey] wrote it, and about every eight or ten years they'd remake it. I forget who the first Rider was, William Farnum maybe, and then when I got it, it was George Montgomery. The chief wrangler had been Tom Mix's guy, in charge of all his livestock and wagons, named Sid Jordan. He was one of the wranglers with us; he was about 65. We were out looking for a certain location where they had a big rock they're supposed to shove over. He not only did it with Mix, he did it and then he punched holes in the cliff and he climbed up. And the holes were still in the cliff! So we went and shot the same place. Did you ever read a book called *Tom Mix Died for Your Sins*?

LM: Yes.

PW: Well, the guy that wrote it interviewed me and I said, "He was my godfather and I met him but Sid Jordan, if he's still alive—he's got to be 90-something—he can tell you anything." Somehow he tracked him down, and Sid told him all the stuff.

LM: You earned your money on those pictures, didn't you? You had to really go, go, go.

PW: Oh, yeah, all the time. We had a guy named Cliff Lyons who became a second unit director. Tough guy; he was like one of the cowboys, and Frank McGrath who became a pretty well known actor on *Wagon Train*. Frank was always getting me into trouble, when we'd shoot out street lights in Lone Pine and then he'd be picking fights with cops. I mean we were crazy people. George Montgomery I loved; he was a great, great guy.

LM: In those days everybody stayed at the Dow Hotel in Lone Pine, right? [It's still there—but now it's called the Dow Villa.—Ed.]

PW: The Dow, exactly. And I went back; later, when I was working on a pilot for *Kung Fu* and the director wanted something spectacular. I said, "Lone Pine! Nobody ever goes there anymore. Mount Whitney, the rocks where they shot *Gunga Din* and all those movies." I said, "Go up there and you're gonna get some great stuff you'll never see." We went back and I stayed in the Dow Hotel again, years later.

LM: What kind of problems would come up that you'd have to solve as a second A.D.?

PW: Well, weather, and how many lunches [you needed]. At Fox you used to get box lunches which were made three weeks ago. (laughs) You'd always have to count 'em, and be sure. One time we were going out to a location [and] one of the electricians died on the bus. We had to stop, and I had to call the studio and say the electrician died. I think it was this guy Ben Silvey, who was Zanuck's guy. And he says, "Be sure and cut off one box lunch." I swear.

LM: You couldn't make that up. When you were working at the studio, would you ever get to use a set that was built for an A picture for a B you were shooting?

PW: Yeah, but you had to change it so you wouldn't recognize it. I worked at MGM on a comedy series called *Colonel Flack* with Alan Mowbray. We had the two cheapest producers. The [studio] let us shoot the big sets from the huge musicals, but they were all struck out and they wouldn't pay to put drapes up. You were shooting on a big set and we only had three electricians on this show so they couldn't light anything.

LM: Did you ever get to work on A pictures at Fox?

PW: [One day] they sent me down to the car. "You go down, pick Mr. Lubitsch up; if he has to go to the bathroom, bring him back to his office." So I went on the stage and said, "Mr. Lubitsch, I'm here to take you up to your office." And he had the camera and it was set up on an old photograph. So they shot the insert and we got in the car and [I said,] "You know, Mr. Lubitsch, we have an insert department," and he says, "Every shot in my picture is the most important."

LM: He wasn't going to let anyone else shoot a moment in his film?

PW: Yeah. I [also] worked on a couple of Laurel and Hardys they made. One with Vivian Blaine.

LM: I know they weren't happy making those films at Fox. Did it show?

PW: I've got one photograph of Laurel and Hardy, both of them signed it. And it says, "Paul—nuts to you and Dante, too." Dante was the magician [in the film, *A-Haunting We Will Go*]. They did their best, you know, they really did. Hardy would always just sit there and do whatever he was [asked]—he was terrific; I loved him. And he was a great dancer. He was the lightest guy on his feet you ever saw. They were both very nice.

Monty Banks and his wife, Gracie Fields, stroll on the Fox studio lot with Darryl F. Zanuck.

LM: Did you work on *Great Guns*, when they were directed by Monty Banks? He'd been a comedy star himself in the silent film days.

PW: My father *had* to use Monty Banks; he didn't want to use Monty Banks, but Zanuck was making a deal with Monty Banks' wife who was a British actress—

LM: Gracie Fields.

PW: Yeah. So Zanuck would say, "I want you to have Monty Banks as the director." And Laurel and Hardy hated Monty Banks. So [my dad] got blamed for that.

LM: Can you remember some of the other directors you worked with at Fox?

PW: One of the greatest was Edmund Goulding. He was fantastic. I got to know him very well, he was very top, [when he was making *Claudia* with] Dorothy McGuire and Bob Young. And Kazan—I worked on two pictures with him. *A Tree Grows in Brooklyn* and *Viva Zapata*.

LM: *A Tree Grows in Brooklyn* is one of my favorite movies; that was Kazan's first film.

PW: He didn't know what to do with the camera. So the cameraman, Leon Shamroy, who was an old friend of mine [and] the best around, wanted a co-direction credit, which he didn't get. But he really helped Kazan a lot. I mean, Kazan caught on real quick. Joe MacDonald did *Viva Zapata* and he was a real rock.

LM: What did you observe of Kazan and the way he worked with actors? They loved working with him.

PW: 'Cause he was an actor, I guess. He was a great guy, he really was a terrific guy. He was good with the people and the crew liked him.

LM: Let me ask you about that. When it's the first day of a production, how would a director set a tone or establish his presence?

PW: They come in and they're uptight, too, you know—really uptight, especially in those days, working for somebody like Zanuck or my father, who was a hammer. It depends on the guy's personality. [Then] they ease off. At first you don't know anything. "Oh Christ, this guy—we'll never get a laugh out of him," and you find out he's got a [sense of humor], once they know that the crew's on their side. Some of them just had a bad attitude—you know, "I'm working; you guys can work too"—then [the crew] just pull back. They can kill a guy. But I think they respect who they are from what they've done.

Walter Lang was a good guy but he was focused on what he [had to do] and that was it. I worked with a guy named Gregory Ratoff and was the second A.D. I went out to go to the bathroom, I remember, and there was a red light went on outside so you wouldn't [walk in when they were filming]. I came out of the bathroom and here's Ratoff standing, waiting to pull the door and the red light is on. I said, "Mr. Ratoff, you know they're in there." He says, "No, no, no, they're shooting, I can't go in." I said, "Well, you're directing the picture!" (laughs) They shot while he went to the can! I guess my cousin rolled the camera. I couldn't believe it, but he owed Zanuck money from gin rummy games. That was the story, you know; Zanuck would give him jobs so he could pay off his gin rummy debts.

LM: He must have been quite a character.

PW: Oh, he was. On that Laurel and Hardy movie we had a live lion on the set. Ratoff was next door doing some movie, so he came in and he's talking to me. And I said, "Oh, look at the lion." He jumped behind me, grabbed me, and held me in front of him. And he backed off the stage holding me in front of him. He was a character.

LM: Who were some of the most colorful assistant directors you worked with?

PW: One of them, Eli Dunn—his brother was married to one of Fox's sisters, so he got his job from the top guy. Most of my father's family went to work for my father; we had about nine or ten of us at Fox at one time. And three of them named Paul Wurtzel.

LM: Really?

PW: My other two first cousins; why I'll ever know. One was eventually head of the effects department and the other was in construction. And I was the assistant. So we got all screwed up all the time, you know.

LM: I realize it's an obvious question, but were you treated better or special because you were part of the family?

PW: Maybe. Probably. But a lot of them [would say], "Hey jerk, shut up." They didn't take any crap from [anybody]. I never tried to give 'em any but I said to one wardrobe man, "Don't you think the cuff…" and he said, "Hey, that's my department, you stay out of it." So they set me straight. A couple of grips--I remember Hank Gerson was one

of them—he just said, "Get out of the way! Go back and we'll tell you when we're ready." Some think it was great that way instead of kissing your ass, you know.

LM: Leon Shamroy was the king of the cameramen at Fox, wasn't he?

PW: I loved him, he was the most obscene guy you'd ever want to meet. He was always saying these terrible things with children, "You little son of a bitch…" But he studied art; he studied the famous artists and their lighting; he started working in the lab in New York as a young guy.

LM: I would imagine there was no room for temper tantrums. Was that tolerated at all?

PW: Well, not that I ever saw it in my father's outfit. *He* used to do all ranting and raving. I mean, he was embarrassing even to me; he was just terrible. I don't know how he ever lived as long as he did. They had in those days mineral water called Pluto Water with a red devil on the bottle that he used to drink; it was a laxative. And he smoked these goddamn cigars, boxes every day. I still can't stand cigar smoke.

LM: How would you get on an A film? Because they didn't have work for you at that moment in the B unit?

PW: Yeah. Usually you were just sent out to be a second second assistant. Luckily I got on *A Tree Grows in Brooklyn* because my cousin was the "first." Peggy Ann Garner was wonderful [in that], wasn't she?

LM: An amazing performance.

PW: And Jimmy Dunn. When they went to fit him for the waiter's tuxedo, they sent him to wardrobe and he came back and showed me, it was one my father had donated to the wardrobe instead of throwing it out! He said, "Look," and it had my father's name in it. And he wore that tux in the show.

LM: Again, you couldn't make that up. After the War when your father set up his own production company and you worked on all those films: *The Crimson Key, Tucson, Miss Mink of 1949, Night Wind*, etc. He seems to have hired people he'd worked with before that he felt he could trust.

PW: Always. Always. The directors.

LM: Like James Tinling, who directed *The Riders of the Purple Sage*.

PW: James Tinling he hired, and Jim went back to drinking then.

LM: And William Claxton.

PW: We had a chauffeur for my mother; she couldn't drive. His name was Jack Cox, and his son or adopted son or stepson was Bill Claxton. Bill was a couple years older than me, but we used to know each other and we went deer hunting. Finally when he got out of school, Jack asked my dad if he could give him a job at the studio and my dad put him in the cutting room. He became an assistant cutter and worked his way up. Then when my dad started making these, he brought Bill in and made him a director. He went on to do a lot of Father Kaiser stuff, tons of stuff, and he turned out to be a pretty good director, apparently. Nice guy, too. But that's how he got his job.

LM: And Malcolm St. Clair, who in the 1920s was considered to be an aspiring Ernst Lubitsch.

PW: Did you ever see him? He looked like—who was that French comedian?

LM: Jacques Tati?

PW: Yeah, sorta like him; he was funny looking. He did the charcoal sketch of Michael Romanoff that used to hang at Romanoff's on a piece of newspaper. Then my dad gave a job to a guy named Henry Lehrman who made these Lehrman's Knockout silent comedies and he [had been] a monster [in his heyday]; nobody liked him. They gave him some job; we didn't have the money in the budget to do anything but he would sit on the set with Mal. I'll never forget one day it was raining and Lehrman apparently came to work on the bus, and he'd been a big director. I was standing there and he came over to Mal and he said, "Hey Mal, will you give me a ride home?" And Mal said, "Well, I don't know..." He said, "I'll give you a dollar if you'll give me a ride home." I mean, it was the saddest thing.

LM: I've always admired the fact that Zanuck and your father were loyal to these guys.

PW: My father gave Allan Dwan a comeback. A lot of those guys.

LM: Another director on these Wurtzel Productions of the late 1940s is unfamiliar to me: Arthur Pierson.

PW: Yeah, nice guy. He was a dialogue director and they let him direct. I forget the picture he directed; was that the one with Marilyn Monroe in it? *Dangerous Years*. I remember when they brought her on the set. Fox wanted to see some film of her 'cause they were signing her up and Ben Lyon, who was the head of casting, called my dad and he said, "Look, we need some footage. We don't want to just do a test, can you write a part in?" So they wrote a part in as a waitress in this one show.

LM: So, to ask the obvious, when she walked on the set did you see something special?

PW: No, I didn't. I never have since. I could never figure it out. I really couldn't. Because I ran into her other times on the lot after she got going and got big, but I never could figure it out.

LM: Apparently Benny Kline photographed all of your father's independent productions.

PW: Benny was hard of hearing. He was a real old-timer, you know. We'd be shooting and we had a mixer who was a great guy. And Benny, during the take, would be moving [something], a rattling [sound], and he couldn't hear. The mixer would always say, "Jesus, stop it, stop it, Benny!" So one day we're shooting a scene, and I see the mixer take the earphones off and get up. He walked right through the set, right through the scene like a stranger. And the director says, "Cut! What the hell, what are you doing, Hutch?" And he says, "Well, if Benny can rattle and make noise during the take, I can walk through the scene." Benny was a great guy. My Dad and Benny used to play gin rummy.

LM: Were those films shot at Fox or did you rent studio space?

PW: No, we shot 'em at Western. He went back to where we started.

LM: Was that still owned by Fox?

PW: Yeah. We moved in there. We used the cutting rooms and we used the administration offices. His bungalow had been torn down long before and made a backlot.

LM: There was a backlot there, too?

PW: Oh, yeah. In fact, when I worked on *Twelve O'Clock High* for TV they had a whole English street that we used to use all the time on the west side 'cause it was ran east and west. And then the Grandeur Room. You know about Grandeur, don't you?

Young Paul Wurtzel, embarking on his film career, is flanked by Sam Schneider and Stan Hough in 1941.

LM: That was Fox's widescreen process from the early talkie days. You mean, there was a specially equipped Grandeur Room so they could screen dailies of movies like *The Big Trail*?

PW: Yeah. The 70 millimeter. We used to use it as a stage, 'cause they didn't use it as a projection room anymore.

LM: Amazing. Did you ever go on location for those films your dad produced on his own?

PW: We went to Vegas and we shot the Flamingo when it first opened. We went up there and we didn't even take lights with us, that's how cheap it was. Don Castle was the actor.

LM: *The Invisible Wall?*

PW: *Invisible Wall.* We shot around the pool and we used all the showgirls. Got in trouble with the Screen Extras Guild. Then we shot inside once without lights. We shot a cab coming and going in the front and it's in the middle of nothing. [Bugsy] Siegel wasn't there; he got killed right after that.

LM: I get the sense that when you worked at a studio in those days it was like an extended family.

PW: It really was. See, when I was at Fox you had a baseball team, you had a basketball team, you had golf tournaments that the major studios would enter. And they'd hire the best athletes. We had ex-prizefighters; Freddie Steele was an electrician, carrying lamps around. And they used to hire these guys; a lot of drivers were top baseball players. It was great. [The studios would] fight each other for movies but they'd get together and they loved sports. I remember one golf tournament at the Rancho,

Father and son have lunch at the private dining room at the Fox Hills studio.

we had a world champion prizefighter. They gave him a job as an assistant and after the golf tournament they got a crap game going and somebody caught him cheating at dice. And they beat the crap out of him. (chuckles)

LM: What kind of hours would you work?

PW: When I started you worked every Saturday night 'til midnight and you'd have Sunday off and then you were back. The hours in the old days were terrible and that's when they finally put a stop to it 'cause it was too much. On television now they're back to [that same level], so they pay the penalties. At the Western Avenue studio there was a hotel on Santa Monica Boulevard, the Green Hotel, and it was full of hookers. So they'd give guys meal checks and they'd go down to the hotel and these hookers would take the meal checks and get the five bucks.

LM: Was working in filmed television just an extension of working in B movies?

PW: I remember I worked on one of the first anthology series for a guy named Frank Wisbar called *Fireside Theatre*. They used to try to do two in a week; you never made it all the time. I worked on a bunch of stuff like *Dear Phoebe* with Peter Lawford, *Colonel Flack*, and various others. Then I got with Quinn Martin in '60 and I was with him almost 18 years. I got lucky there, you know. And he did a lot of good stuff.

LM: I can't resist asking you about working on *Macabre* with William Castle.

PW: Oh yeah, Bill Castle. He was very nerve-wracked, a very nervous guy. Very high strung, always perspiration, but we got along fine and ran all over town trying to make the damn thing. And Bill Castle, if we did it on schedule, was gonna give me a big bonus, which, you know... (chuckles)

LM: You're still waiting?

PW: I'm still waiting.

Conversations:
DICK JONES

Dickie Jones achieved immortality when he provided the voice of the title character in Walt Disney's *Pinocchio*. He was 11 years old and already a seasoned screen veteran when Disney cast him in 1938. By the time that movie reached theaters, Dick's credits included *Queen of the Jungle, Daniel Boone, Black Legion, Stella Dallas, On Borrowed Time, Destry Rides Again*, and *Mr. Smith Goes to Washington*. (In the latter, he's the page who shows

James Stewart to his assigned seat on his first day in the Senate.) He also appeared in a number of Westerns, serials, and *Our Gang* comedies (although he never became a series regular) and later took over the starring role of Henry Aldrich on radio before serving in World War II. In the early days of television he acquired a new generation of fans playing sidekick to *The Range Rider* (Jock Mahoney) and star of *Buffalo Bill, Jr.*

When I talked to Dick—no longer Dickie—Jones, he was a straight-talking, straight-shooting fellow, a proud father and grandfather, who had moved to a career in real estate and was still married to his teenage sweetheart Betty after 61 years. It was a colorful life for a Texas boy who started out as a rodeo performer, billed as The World's Youngest Trick Rider and Trick Roper. Dick died in 2014 at 87. (Interview originally appeared in 2009.)

LM: When did you start riding?

DJ: I can honestly say I have no idea when I started riding. I've got a picture of me standing, tipping my hat with the bridle in my hand of a small, spotted horse, pony-size. Not a pony but he wasn't big enough to be a horse. I'm in half-English puttee pants [jodhpurs] and hand-tooled cowboy boots and I'm standing there taking a bow—at the age of four.

LM: What did your parents do?

DJ: My father was a newspaper man. He started pushing the rolls of paper around and [then was a] press operator. He went to editorial and became a managing editor of the McKinney paper; it was a small paper and he got to be the editor-in-chief of the *McKinney News*. McKinney used to be 30 miles out of Dallas, now it's a suburb of Dallas. My mother was just a Meglin Kiddie mother. [Referring to the famous troupe of child performers run by Ethel Meglin, who also had a chain of talent schools.] When Hoot Gibson said, "That kid oughta be in movies," my mother said, "Whoopee!" And away we went.

LM: Do you think she always had a show business bug?

DJ: It must have been that she had a show business bug because she kept hauling me into Dallas. I was on the radio with the Rambling Cowboy, who had a radio show where he sang and told stories. I was called the Little Cowboy Rambler, and I strummed the ukulele and yodeled and that kind of junk. This is all just recollection and stuff that people have told me.

LM: What did your father make of all this?

DJ: Paid no attention to it; he was too busy slurping up the booze.

LM: Oh, dear.

DJ: Yeah. He was quite an alcoholic. But he got dry. He got 13 years and got a gold lighter before he passed on.

LM: Where were you performing when Hoot Gibson saw you?

DJ: Dallas Centennial Rodeo in Dallas. I think it was 1932 or '33. I was a contract act performing with the trick riders. I'd ride around in the arena, around the circle, do a hippodrome, stand up in the saddle, fall off the side and do a Cossack drag and stuff like that.

LM: What's a hippodrome?

DJ: Where you stand up on top of the horse with both hands free. It's a girl's trick, where they lean up over the ears and their fancy costumes are blowing in the wind. A hippodrome was the opening for the *Annie Oakley* TV series. [Stuntwoman] Donna Hall came charging out and shooting the guns, doing a hippodrome, standing up on top of the horse.

LM: Would you perform just on weekends? Were you going to school?

DJ: I don't imagine I was going to school. My schooling all sort of went behind everything else.

LM: So Hoot Gibson came down to appear at this Dallas Centennial.

DJ: Yeah, he was the headliner.

LM: And he said to your mother, "This kid oughta be in the movies."

DJ: Yeah. Now, that's the publicity version of it. There must have been more talk than that because the next thing I knew I was living in Newhall, California—it's now called Canyon Country—at the Saugus Arena, which used to be Hoot's ranch. It's where the Saugus Raceway was; after the rodeo died on the vine, it became a three-quarter midget track. And the house that I stayed in next to the old barn, it's still standing. The barn's gone. I used to ride "the horse has never been ridden," Tumbleweed. I used to ride him around in the paddock, just exercise him.

We stayed there for two years while mother was in Hollywood trying to get a place for us to live. Hoot took me around and introduced me to different places and I got a job with Buck Jones, first crack out of the box. Never worked with Hoot. Worked with all the others, though.

LM: Do you have recollections of Hoot?

DJ: No. No.

LM: You were awfully young.

DJ: Yes. People ask me, "What do you think about so-and-so?" They usually want to know about the women. I say "At that age I had Mom."

LM: So your dad stayed behind in McKinney?

DJ: Yeah, and I didn't see my dad again until, let's see, I went back to New York. When I got drafted, the day before I went into the Army he came up. I got a big kick out of showing him around New York. Then after I got back, and Jocko [Mahoney] and I started doing the rodeo show, he came down to Houston when we did that stock show. It wasn't much of a relationship between me and my Dad.

Cowboy Dickie Jones and William Boyd as Hopalong Cassidy in *The Frontiersman* (1938).

LM: So from knocking on doors, and Hoot Gibson opening some doors, you got work in movies.

DJ: The first job that I really had was in *Wonder Bar* with Al Jolson. I saw Al Jolson from the top of Stage 13 and that's the closest I got to him 'cause I was flying around on wires in that scene, "Goin' to Heaven on a Mule." I was in blackface with white robes on and the wings and stuff like that. And I was up there for a long time. Ms. Horn was the resident school teacher at Warner Bros. One day she says, "I counted up the days that I had you for school, and you could have had a five-year contract at Warner Bros. here." But my mother never would let me go under contract. She made a couple of errors that cost me, but that's the way she did it.

LM: On the other hand I don't think you were idle very much.

DJ: No. And it was difficult for me because I didn't like going to school on the set. I wanted to get back to the public school. I wanted to be a real boy. I'd go back and I'd have all my work done and I wouldn't be be-hind. The other kids would look at me, like, "What are you, some kind of a freak? You're never in school and you come back in and everything's okay?"

LM: Do you remember being in *Babes in Toyland* (1934) with Laurel and Hardy?

DJ: I remember the studio more than being in the film because I would sneak off the set and go out and play on the pirate ships out in the backlot. And I thought it was fun riding on the pedestal of the wooden soldiers as they'd march.

LM: So you were one of the kids clinging to a wooden soldier in the film?

DJ: Uh-huh. Somebody got a picture, freeze-framed it, and I got a real good photograph from it.

LM: Were you living in Hollywood by this time, and do you remember where?

DJ: I don't know which came first. [There was] the courtyard on Wilton—six or seven little bungalows, and in one of them was the Sons of the Pioneers: Leonard Slye [who later became Roy Rogers] and two of his

Randolph Scott, Moroni Olsen, and Miriam Hopkins hover over Dick in *Virginia City* (1940).

boys. That's where I first met Roy. Then we lived at another apartment above Hollywood Boulevard; it was a two-story brick building. And then we ended up getting a house close to the Carthay Circle, below Wilshire. Olympic, I think. Yeah, Olympic. A little two-bedroom, one bath house. Cost all of $7,000. (laughs)

LM: Was that more permanent? Did you stay there?

DJ: We stayed there longer than any other place I'd been in. I went to half a dozen grammar schools; I went to two junior high schools. And I went to L.A. High for two years and then back to New York. So when I finally got on my own and [my wife and I] bought a house, I said, "This is it." We stayed in the house in Burbank 14 years. Then we built a house out in Northridge; we moved in it in January of '64 and [have] been in there since. I don't like moving around. (chuckles)

LM: Forgive me if this is a naive question, but did you make friends with any of the other young actors you worked with, or were things too transient for that?

DJ: I had casual acquaintances with them. I never buddied around with 'em, never palled around with them. I was a kid and I couldn't transport myself around until I pulled a sneaky and I got a driver's license at 15. It was gonna be a limited license and I said, "Well, what if I'm at the Warner Bros. studio and they're working me 'til 10 o'clock at night. How do I get home?" [The inspector] says, "Oh." He was gonna restrict me to daytime driving; then he said okay and they gave me an unlimited driver's license. But no, I didn't pal around with them even after I had transportation. They would do their thing and I would do my thing, and I didn't like some of the things they were doing. I lost a couple of friends, screwing around with that crazy stuff. I don't know how I didn't get on it, but I didn't. I didn't make many close friends.

LM: Are you talking about drinking or something else?

DJ: Well, back then the hardest thing was heroin, and they would mainline it, but it started off with marijuana. All the kids were smoking marijuana; the powdered coke didn't come in until, I think, after the war. They were either hooked on heroin or they were smoking a lot of marijuana. Alfalfy—Alfalfa Switzer—he was a procurer for the stuff. Scotty Beckett overdosed, and we lived across the street. I knew him well.

LM: That was one of the saddest stories of all. I'm so glad you didn't go down that road. Did I hear that you attended a professional children's school at one point?

DJ: When I broke my leg playing football at L.A. High School, I couldn't manipulate those stairs and the big corridors. So they sent me to Hollywood Professional School on Hollywood Boulevard east of Western, and I lasted three days. I couldn't handle those Hollywood phonies. I made the acquaintance of some real lovely ladies there like Gloria De Haven, but I didn't get along with the guys too well.

LM: You probably auditioned opposite these same kids all the time, didn't you?

DJ: Yeah, we'd go on so-called cattle calls and when it was callback time and it'd be whittled down to one or two, Dickie Moore and I knocked heads all the time.

LM: I remember at one event we were chatting with Sammy McKim and you said the two of you also competed for parts.

DJ: Well, it whittled down to where it was maybe between Sammy and I for *Pinocchio*. We worked the longest time together on *The Great Adventures of Wild Bill Hickok* (1938) with Gordon Elliott. Started out here at Columbia Ranch and then further out in the Thousand Oaks area and then went to Kanab, Utah; we were there a week or so. We were together a long time on that one.

LM: Would your mother travel to all these locations?

DJ: Oh, yeah. You had to have a guardian with you, and my aunt could never stand in for her because she was only 10 years older than me. She was busy at school.

LM: Pretty early on you played John Wayne as a boy.

DJ: Yeah, in *Westward, Ho!* (1935).

LM: Do you remember ever meeting him on that shoot?

DJ: I remember Yakima Canutt more than anything, 'cause Yakima Canutt was the one that kidnapped me and threw me up in front of him on the saddle and away we went. And then I got even with him again in *Rocky Mountain* [in 1950]. I said, "I waited a long time to get even with you." (laughs)

LM: Would you hang out with the wranglers and the cowboys?

DJ: Yeah, they made me look good so they were my friends. They weren't snooty like the actors were.

LM: Once they saw you knew your way around a horse, I guess that pleased them too.

DJ: Well, they weren't worried about me. They always made sure that I got a good horse that had a good gait, wouldn't cross-fire, and would stand still for dialogue. I got along with 'em good. I was fascinated by the stunt men and I would always try to figure out how they would do their "gags." I was [also] fascinated with the character actors, like John Carradine.

LM: What are your recollections of the atmosphere and the kids when you worked in the *Our Gang* shorts?

DJ: Alfalfy Switzer was a pill. He thought that he was the greatest thing that happened to the motion picture industry. We never got in any fights or any arguments or anything like that. Spanky was a fun kid. I had a crush on Darla, and that crush continued when I got back out of the service. I took her dancing a couple of times. A beautiful lady. What a loss. She'd sing the blues like I can't imagine. She didn't emulate anybody, she had her own style. Real good. Love lost.

We just had fun [on *Our Gang*]. I enjoyed the directors more than anything else. Gordon Douglas—I worked with him in a couple of Westerns.

LM: Did you have favorite locations? Were there places you looked forward to going?

DJ: I liked Lone Pine the best because if I got off work early, I'd go fishing. But then [years later] after we went up there and stayed for 13 weeks and did 26 shows, I wanted to get away from Lone Pine.

LM: Any recollections of George O'Brien, from working with him on *Daniel Boone* (1936)?

With Alfalfa, Spanky, and Porky backstage in *Our Gang Follies of 1936*.

DJ: Not really. He didn't pal around with kids, let's put it that way. He was a nice guy. I remember he had a great big huge barrel chest. And strong as an ox. Picked me up and held me just like a paper sack.

LM: You worked with some of the top directors in Hollywood, but I don't know if they took the time to connect with you. Did any of them make a particular impression?

DJ: I liked Michael Curtiz. He liked goobers—clouds. He said, "We wait for the goobers." He'd watch 'em. "The goobers are coming," he says. "Let's get ready; okay, roll 'em. And we have speed—now." (laughs) And he's matching clouds.

LM: But Curtiz could be a real taskmaster. I find it interesting that you liked him.

DJ: He put me in a spot that when I think back on it kind of scares me. [In *Virginia City*] he wanted me to do the jerk out of the wagon when the horses reared up. He says, "We'll shoot it where we'll have two guys. The minute that you're below the hub of the wheel, they'll jerk you out from under the wagon and then the horses will go on and hit the log, as if you got run over." Well, the first guy missed me and the second guy got me out just in time. I think back on that and, whew! Close, but it was fun.

LM: The welfare worker must have been snoozing when that was going on.

DJ: No, the welfare worker had nothing to do with what you were doing in front of the camera or with the director. She turned you over to the second assistant and the second assistant turned you to the assistant director. You'd listen to all of them but you'd take the last word from the director for what you did.

One director, he didn't like me and I didn't like him. He says, "Get that kid with the ants in his pants in the back!" And that was me. I had ants in my pants. Henry Hathaway.

LM: He was tough on grownup actors too.

DJ: And one actor didn't like me one bit because he kept flubbing his lines and I'd feed 'em to him. Hopalong Cassidy.

LM: Well, in fairness, a lot of actors wouldn't have liked having a kid reciting his lines back to them!

DJ: (laughs) Yeah. And the first time that he let on that he didn't like that, I just rubbed it in even more. (laughs) I knew the script inside out and sideways, went through his lines and underlined. Gene Autry used to do that, get an actor that only knew the cue word to start talking and Gene would never give him the line!

LM: That's funny.

DJ: Terrible (laughs) to treat your fellow actor that way.

LM: Do you have a clear recollection of meeting Walt Disney?

DJ: I remember him being a very quiet, very nice man. I remember the luncheon when he informed my mother I had been selected to do the voice. He said, "How would you like to do the voice of Pinocchio?" and I said, "Swell, when do we go to work?" It was just a job, as far as I was concerned. It was spread over about a year and a half. Of course, I was excited to be chosen over a couple of hundred others that were trying out for it.

LM: I think Walt said that he liked your voice because you sounded natural and unaffected.

DJ: No, he didn't say that. He auditioned adults trying to imitate children, and he wanted an authentic youngster—their enthusiasm, their

299

Dickie and Cliff Edwards examine a storyboard before recording a scene from *Pinocchio*.

voice—the same thing that Clifford Goldsmith [said] when I did Henry Aldrich.

LM: And Cliff Edwards, who did the voice of Jiminy Cricket?

DJ: He was a good goose-button dart thrower, and he was easy to work with. He would come down to my level, instead of being up on his high stool, and I enjoyed it when he'd bring out his ukulele and strum little ditties, and do his do-do-da-da stuff. He was a fun person to be around. And he always wore a hat with the brim back, all the time, always wore that.

LM: What was the process like of performing just with your voice?

DJ: It was a combination of radio and motion pictures. There was no script; it was a storyboard, like the funnies in the newspaper. They'd say, "OK, this is what we're gonna shoot today," and it'd be up on the wall, and we'd look at it, and then they'd give us the words. To get the detail and the authenticity, they would photograph with a 16mm camera, just our nose and our mouth and our chins. Then there were a couple of scenes where they wanted to get the flow of the human body motion so they dressed us up in costumes and actually filmed it, like we were doing a motion picture. The one I remember was Walter Catlett (who played Honest John) and [the man who played] Gideon and I went up and down over a rolling road, and we did, "Hi-diddle-dee-dee, an actors' life for me." We danced along and they photographed that, and we were in costume.

LM: Well, no one will ever forget that film—or your voice. Let's talk about some other people you crossed paths with back then. You worked for John Ford on *Young Mr. Lincoln* (1939).

DJ: I forgot all about working for John Ford. I said to myself, gee, of all the directors, I would love to work with John Ford. But I did, on *Young Mr. Lincoln*. That was just a one-day blip where you had to look hard to even see me.

LM: How about Frank Capra on *Mr. Smith Goes to Washington* (1939)?

DJ: That was a good picture to work on; he was very good. Frank Capra would talk to his [actor] before rolling the film to get him in the mood and bring him up to speed to what had happened, what transpired beforehand. About time he says, "Are we ready? Roll 'em, speed, action," you're in the mood and you're doing it. Very, very good. Like a painter. That was a great job, we were on the set about 90 percent of the time, 'cause our schoolroom was just right around behind the Senate. They built the Senate, and we all sat there and watched how they worked back there in Congress. It was just amazing; we got a lot of history out of that. I [also] fell in love with Jean Arthur. I think that was the first lady I ever asked for her autograph; she gave me a great big autographed picture.

LM: You told me you also liked Ann Todd, who played your sister in *Destry Rides Again*.

DJ: And then turn right around a couple of years later, she was my sister in *Brigham Young*. That was a tough one. We spent a lot of time out on that flat dry salt lake just outside of Lone Pine. The wind was blowing the dust and the sand, and if that wasn't bad enough, they brought these great big, huge fans out there and made it more of a dust storm. Boy, that was tough work. And when you got out from in front of the camera, they gave you goggles to keep the sand out of your eyes.

LM: Now let's talk about some cowboys. You got to work with Buck Jones.

DJ: He was my favorite; he was a man's man. And he was a good cowboy until he started to act. (chuckles) He wanted to be an actor so bad he couldn't see straight. But he was a real nice guy, real nice to me. The first time I worked with him was *Smoke Tree Range* (1937) and whoever the wardrobe man was gave me a dorky little fedora, made it look like a cowboy hat. [Buck] says, "Kid, that's no cowboy hat, " so he gave me this beautiful white Stetson [with a] big four-inch brim. I looked [silly] underneath a 20-gallon hat, but it was a beautiful hat and I had it for a long time. Made good friends with Mrs. Buck Jones. She used to call up and say, "Mr. Jones?" And I'd say, "Yes?" "This is Mrs. Jones." And I said, "Oh yes, Mrs. Jones…" I'd go down on his boat and have a lot of fun. I was supposed to be on his boat the day that he was killed in the fire back there in Boston. [Jones died in a terrible conflagration at the Cocoanut Grove nightclub in 1942.—Ed.]

LM: How eerie. So many people admired Buck Jones, on and offscreen. I know you were also fond of Bill Elliott.

DJ: Yeah. He turned out to be a real cowboy; he loved to ride cutting horses. I remember the first time he put on a pair of chaps and wore his gun backwards. That was in *Moonlight on the Prairie* (1935) with Dick Foran. Before that, he had been a dress extra.

LM: Oh, you spot him all the time in movies of the 1930s.

DJ: Little thin moustache and slicked hair down and a high, stiff collar and tails.

LM: You mentioned the schoolteacher at Warner Bros. Were there things about each studio that you particularly liked or disliked? If you got a call to go to Universal or you were going to Fox or Paramount, did it make a difference to you?

DJ: Some of the little ones like Monogram and Katzman, that was kind of third-rate. I liked Columbia. Mrs. Barkley was the schoolteacher, she was great. Really great. She wanted me to be a student. She really worked me hard to get my work done. And you know Fred Krone, the stuntman? She got him a degree. He worked so much at Columbia, she worked him real hard and he got a bachelor's degree, a correspondence course type thing. I remember working at 20th Century Fox, going to school there, and I had Linda Darnell as one of my school chums. And Jane Withers was there. That was a real nice schoolhouse, just for the kids, until I didn't get to work there anymore.

LM: Why was that?

DJ: I got blackballed.

LM: By whom?

DJ: Zanuck. I was signed to do *Home in Indiana*, and my mother thought that [doing the] *Henry Aldrich* [radio show in] New York was better than that, so we jumped the contract I had already signed and I never worked at Fox again. Never even got a call to go on an interview.

LM: Wow.

DJ: My mother did some interesting things in my career.

LM: You're listed in some credits for *The Major and the Minor*, but I don't remember you in it. There's a scene where the cadets at the military school mingle with some girls at a dance.

DJ: They had a guy double me for that because I had a broken leg and couldn't dance. I think that they cut my part completely out of that just like they did with *This Gun for Hire*. I did Alan Ladd as a kid in

With Buck Jones and Helen Twelvetrees in *Hollywood Round-Up* (1937).

the dream sequence. I never made it past the first showing and I cannot find an original print of that thing. They cut that whole dream sequence out, which explains how he got that big lump on his wrist.

LM: When did you go to New York to work on the *Henry Aldrich* radio show? Was that before World War II?

DJ: No, it was during the war; I was only 15 when I went back there. Well, I was almost 16 'cause I was only there two and a half years.

LM: How did the *Henry Aldrich* job come about?

DJ: Oh, that was a big test [of many actors]—from back east to Los Angeles. I was in AFRA (American Federation of Radio Artists) because

I had done a couple of the *Lux Radio Theatre* shows. So they just put my name on the list and tested. Everybody else was trying to imitate Ezra Stone [the original star of the popular radio show]. And Clifford Goldsmith, who wrote *Henry Aldrich,* said, "No, no, no. We can't keep changing the actor; we're going to just change Henry Aldrich completely." So he says, "Use your own voice. Act this way, think about it this way," and he took me up to his place on

Martha's Vineyard, and we stayed there for five or six weeks. Every day he worked with me. I was the third Henry Aldrich. Ezra Stone was number one. Norman Tokar, who played Homer, became the second Henry Aldrich. And then when Norman Tokar got drafted, I got in there. And then when I got out of the service, they wanted me to come back and do Henry Aldrich as a sitcom for television. I saw the way they were working and I said, "This is not for me." I came home to California. Boy, can you imagine doing one of those sitcoms back then when they didn't have five or six cameras working? No, thank you. Dick Crenna stuck it out and worked for about six or seven weeks on it; he finally gave up and came home.

LM: Had you done much radio besides *Lux* out here?

DJ: No. I have claustrophobia and I hate working inside studios. That's why I got along so well in Westerns outdoors. *Pinocchio* was actually the worst, because that was working in closeted areas. Most of the time they'd have to spend half an hour trying to find me 'cause I'd be around the studio somewhere.

LM: So, when you got out of the service...

DJ: I came back and started nosing around, trying to get an agent to get me started again. And that old adage, "out of sight, out of mind"—five years gone. [I] might as well have started all over again. The first job I got was that thing at Republic with Vera Hruba Ralston [*Angel on the Amazon*]. God, I'll never forget that. I felt like such a jerk.

LM: It must have been tough those first couple of years.

DJ: Yeah. And I got married during that time. I didn't have a job; I got tired of driving home after taking her home. I said, "This has got to cease," so I made real good friends with her mother, and her mother said, "OK."

LM: Where did you live?

DJ: At first we stayed there at Betty's house.

LM: Because you had no regular income at that time.

DJ: No, I was working—at a gas station. Then I started working as a carpenter; I worked apprentice to get a journeyman's on that, and I was doing pretty good. I was making $35 dollars a week, if it didn't rain. We had [our first child] Melody and paid for it out of $35 dollars a week. Boy, you can't have a baby today at that price. I worked all kinds of jobs 'cause I had a sexy brunette wife and babies to feed. I stood in the unemployment line one time and that was so degrading, I said, "No way! I am healthy, I'm not going to do this; I'm going to earn my keep." And I never did stand in line again. Then getting that job with Gene Autry—I don't know what happened but right after that I got all kinds of calls.

LM: You were even in one of Republic's biggest pictures, *Sands of Iwo Jima*.

DJ: You've got to look quick. I made more money on that show than any other movie I was in.

LM: How so?

DJ: Allan Dwan cast me. I got my script. I did wardrobe and when they said, "No, we're going to cut that out." Boom, the contract was null and void, but they had to pay me off, so I got the full three-weeks guarantee up front. A couple weeks into production, I get a phone call and the assistant says, "Mr. Dwan wants you to come down here and do this part that you were hired for. It's been cut down to where it's just one scene, so if you would, we'll give you a daily and transportation and take you down to [Camp] Pendleton." So I signed up for the thing and the daily minimum was far greater than the three weeks' guarantee was. So I went down there one day, I sat around on the set for a couple of days and then the weekend came and they still had to keep me down there. Then the next day I think I worked overtime and then they took me back to the barracks. I was down there for two-and-a-half, three weeks and I was getting overtime, golden time, meal penalties. By the time I got through I made a helluva lot more than the three-weeks contract was, but all they wanted me for was to come unglued and run out and get shot and react to being shot with a machine gun on a bungee cord. That was my first experience with a bungee cord and needless to say it almost cut me in two.

LM: Because it sprang you backwards?

DJ: Yeah, and I was running real hard and I didn't think about keeping it taut, so when it let go, there was maybe three feet of slack for it to really hook up and wham, it almost broke me in two.

LM: Why'd it take so long to shoot such a simple thing then?

DJ: Well, that's the way that movies were made back then.

LM: Was it that you waited so long just to get to shoot the scene?

DJ: Yeah, guys just sat around on the set and waited and waited. They kept changing the angles, and actors couldn't remember their lines, and Dwan wanted to do it this way and then changed his mind right in the middle of it. That's the way they made movies back then.

LM: Then you landed a really good part in *Rocky Mountain*.

DJ: *Rocky Mountain* was my favorite. I enjoyed working with Errol Flynn. He was one hell of a good actor.

LM: Where was that shot?

Script girl Irene Ives, director George Archainbaud, Gene Autry, Dick, and Arthur Space on the set of *Last of the Pony Riders* (1953).

DJ: The whole thing was shot outdoors in Gallup, New Mexico.

LM: There's not a studio scene in the movie.

DJ: That's right, nothing was done indoors. We were about an hour-and-a-half drive, every day, in the middle of the Indian reservation. The Indian constabulary couldn't figure out how [Flynn] got drunk by four o'clock every afternoon. I found out later on that before we went down there, he got with the location manager, found out where all the shots were going to be done, and he buried his booze and stuff there a month before.

LM: Did they have you spend time with the dog, to bond with him?

DJ: I think it was six weeks I was on a minimum salary to wrangle the dog. [Director William] Keighley and I went to the pound and spent a couple of days scouring over the dogs and found one that was likable, [one with] lots of pep. Keighley thought he'd photograph really well and said, "OK now, this is your dog. Nobody else touches him, nobody messes with him, nobody feeds him and he stays with you 24/7." That created quite a problem when we went down on the train, 'cause they wanted to put him in the baggage car. They said, "This train does not roll until the dog is sitting in this kid's lap." Then, when we went down to the hotel, they said, "We don't allow animals in the rooms [but] we're going to make an exception to this one." And he stayed right in my room all the time. After the whole thing was over with, Warner Bros. called up and said, "We want to use your dog." And I said, "What for?" "We're using all these stock shots for *Cheyenne,* Clint Walker's [TV show]." Because they used all of the chase stuff, the Indian stuff, and the wagon wreck that we shot for *Rocky Mountain* in *Cheyenne.* They also used some of it in *Maverick.* So they'd come to my house early in the morning in a limousine and pick the dog up, walk him out to the limousine, put him in the thing, and off they'd go to work. And about six o'clock at night, they'd come back and trot him up on his leash, and I could see the neighbors looking out through their windows, wondering what in the hell's going on.

LM: How long did you have the dog?

DJ: Oh, 10 or 15 years.

LM: Wasn't Yakima Canutt in *Rocky Mountain?*

DJ: Yes, he was, and I finally got even with Yakima Canutt, because [in] 1935 he kidnapped me out of the wagon in John Wayne's *Westward Ho,* took me off, and made me a hardened outlaw. So I said, "I'm gonna get even with you one of these days, Yakima Canutt," because I ran into him a lot of times.

LM: How did you do it?

DJ: Well, he was doubling a bad guy and I shot him.

LM: There you go.

DJ: To give you an example of how precise Yakima Canutt is, when the Indians overtook the stagecoach at the beginning, they wanted the wagon dumped. Keighley and the cameraman figured out the best photographic place to turn the thing over. So Keighley went out there and said, "OK, this X marks the spot where I want that stagecoach upside down." And Yak says, "Can do." And then the assistant cameraman came up and says, "You can't do that because that's where we're going to put our backup camera." And Mr. Keighley says, "If Yakima says you can't put it there, you don't put it there." He says, "Well, I'm going to put it there anyway because that's the best shot." So here they come and it's a dummy sitting in the booth, Yak's driving the team from 20, 30 feet off to the left, out of camera range. He's driving the six of them and when it comes to the spot where he wants to dump it, he pulls the lever and the horses go loose, the coach goes up on its nose and boom-boom, two rolls and bang—shatters itself right on that camera. There went a 35mm Mitchell [camera]. He was the best rigger in the business.

LM: You got to do a little fancy riding in *Rocky Mountain*.

DJ: I made out pretty good on that, 'cause every time I made that run and dropped off the side, I got adjusted for it, because I said, "Hey, I don't want to do this thing because if this horse stumbles, he falls on me." And they said, "Well, we'll adjust you for it."

LM: Meaning they gave you a little bump in your pay?

DJ: They gave me full stuntman's pay.

LM: Good for you! Would you tell me a little bit more about Errol Flynn?

DJ: He didn't go down till a couple years after *Rocky Mountain*. I couldn't keep up with

Dick Jones in his favorite film, *Rocky Mountain* (1950), with his dog, Spot.

him walking; just his stride was twice mine. He was going to throw a cast party after we got back to Los Angeles, so he says, "I want you and your better seven-eighths, Miss Betty, to come to my cast party." I said, "She would really enjoy that 'cause she's a big fan of yours." He said, "Oh, really?" And he said, "I'll tell you what, we'll set the time and when you get to the gate, push this signal into the gate opener, and I will personally greet her at the door." So the day comes, and it was a hot day; Betty's all dressed up in a nice little summer dress, looking good. We pull up in front of the house, and I get out of the car and walk up to these great big huge double doors. We ring the doorbell and the big ol' gongs go off and here he comes. You hear the clacking of the door opening up and the levers opening the thing, like a prison cell. It swings wide and he's dressed in one of those died-with-their-boots-on Cossack uniforms with the jacket over one shoulder and the epaulets on this side and high boots up to his knees. He just pushes me aside and says,

"And this must be Betty." He grabs her hand, picks it up, and kisses her on the hand, and she fainted right there. She just says, "O-o-o-oh…" clunk. He says, "Gee, I hope she's not hurt."

Dick and Errol Flynn in *Rocky Mountain*.

LM: What a great story. Just to be clear, had you ridden in the five years you'd been away from the West Coast? Did you ride at all in New York?

DJ: Uh-uh.

LM: And were you ever on horseback when you were in the Army?

DJ: No.

LM: So, you hadn't ridden in five years.

DJ: Yeah.

LM: Was it just like getting back on the horse? (laughs)

DJ: Felt like riding a bicycle. Once you learn how, you never forget. It just came naturally to me. I don't know why; I don't like horses. Never did like horses.

LM: Really?

DJ: Dead serious. I never had a horse at my house. Never lived around 'em.

LM: But you know how to handle them.

DJ: No, I knew what I *couldn't* do. And I learned when you're trying to do a gag, don't extend yourself to something when you haven't got a "what-if" figured out. In other words, don't go past your ability.

LM: Did Jock Mahoney approach it the same way when you did the *Range Rider* TV series?

DJ: No, hell, no. [If] it's there, he can do it. (chuckles) Oh man, we had so much fun. We'd stay up at night and conjure up things and say, "Well, has this ever been done?" "No, but we're gonna figure out it can be done." We did stuff that's never been on television before. Our timing was identical. We could say, "OK, one, two, three" and walk around the block and come back and we'd still be on the same count.

LM: Amazing—but then, he was an amazing guy to watch.

DJ: There were things like—I'm doing a fight up on the stage [coach] and he's down here. The guy clobbers me and I just launch myself off 'cause I know Jock's gonna be there to turn and catch me, "Go get him, Tiger," and throw me back up there. Things like that.

LM: Did the two of you do a lot of touring?

DJ: Yeah. That was one of the things that Jocko told me about the very first day we worked. He said, "We're not going to make any money on this show. Our money's going to be made at the tours. And we're not going to do any one-nighters because we can't pick and sing." So we figured the best way would be to do the rodeo stuff. We started off at the Houston's Fat Stock Show. Went from there to Little Rock and then to Madison Square Garden; we were there for three weeks, eight shows a week. And boy, did we tear up furniture. They had moving vans bringing furniture in. We'd set up a living room or a bar in the middle of the arena and come out and do our saddle fall and come up, get to the [microphone] and say, "This is the way it's done in motion pictures and we'll show you how." Then Jock and I'd take off and he says, "We don't use breakaways 'cause you get hurt with breakaways," and he took a chair and just slammed it. We'd just tear the place up. Then we went straight up to Boston Gardens. Then the next year, they wanted us back. So Jocko said, "Well, we'll come back to Boston Gardens on a percentage." They said, "What do you want for base?" And he says, "Twenty-five percent over the record that Gene set." We packed that thing, I think it was three weeks plus a whole bunch of matinées they threw in. We had that thing sold out every single performance and walked away with a bundle. Then we went to some big, big fairgrounds on the way back. Instead of driving straight through from Boston to Los Angeles, we get something in the middle. Jocko would go ahead and be the advance man. He knew how to talk and get things done. But I knew the horses and I knew the equipment we need; I took care of that and I rode with the truck.

[One night] I'm all packed up, we're all set to leave that evening in Houston, zipping up the last bag. Jock comes running in with what looks like a big bag of laundry and he says, "You got room for this?" I said, "Yeah, if I can take it apart." He says, "OK." So I zip it open—it's nothing but bundles of one-dollar bills—$10,000. He says, "That's your share!" And he's out the door. And I said, "Thanks a lot, I gotta rassle $10,000 on the road going back to California; it's the middle of the night." He thought that was funny.

LM: He was quite a character, I know. The pace of doing *The Range Rider* must have been just incredible. How much time did you have to do an episode?

DJ: Well, we'd do two a week. In six days.

LM: Three days each.

DJ: No, not each; we were working them at the same time. We'd have the actors work two shows. Jock and I would have two scripts, two stories. Just read the page once and you get the same thing over and over again. It's the actors that had to make wardrobe changes and change their character; Jock and I were just the same no matter what it was, but by changing the actors and [moving] the camera ten degrees, you got a new scene. It was very well laid out. They had it all down to where you'd start at daylight when the first rays of sun would hit and get warm enough to photograph it. And we'd follow the sun up to—

LM: Panic Peak.

DJ: Panic Peak, thank you. It would be a long day and then at Pioneer Town if we didn't get two, we'd go in and work indoors at the big barn, [which] was a soundstage. We'd work 13 weeks straight through with just a day off to play, rest, and repair. We'd do 26 shows, and they would take 13 weeks, all of 'em. It was go, go, go, go, go. But, I think the actors had the hardest part. I remember Walter Reed said, "You and Jocko, you come out of the barn and you're on your horse and you're gone before I even get to my horse." And I said, "Well, Walter—you're an actor."

LM: Your cameraman had to be pretty sharp to follow all that action you did.

An action scene in *Rocky Mountain*—for which Dick got full stuntman's pay.

DJ: No, he had an easy job, and he told me about it. I think the very first scene, we'd come together right up to the camera and we're talking and he [Jock] says, "We're going to do this, do that, do that," and he gets on his horse and he's gone. And I get on my horse and I finally catch up to him over the hill someplace. The camera operator comes up to me and says, "Hey, kid. What's the name of this show?" And I said, "*Range Rider*." He says, "Are you the Range Rider?" I said, "No, that long drink of water is the Range Rider." He says, "Well, let me tell you something. See this viewfinder here? My job is to keep those crosshairs on the star, the Range Rider. And if you want to be in this picture, you better whip up and get in his hip pocket." So I thought about that and I said, "Aha, that's right. I can't dilly-dally around." When he goes "whoosh" and gone, so I had to be "whoosh" and gone *with* him.

LM: Did you and Jock continue to tour even after you had finished shooting the show? The show went for two years, right?

DJ: Yeah, we went on for almost two years after that. In fact, the last year, we had our own rodeo we picked up, a little outfit that had the ins and outs of all those indoor arenas back east. We partnered with him and used all of his stock and all his equipment and put on ten different rodeos, one every week at a different indoor arena. That went on for two or three years. Gene [Autry] broached the subject of us working together and I said, "No, I can't do what you do. I will not do one-nighters." He said, "Well, that's the easy way; you get in, you get out." And I said, "I'm not built that way." So we didn't do it; Jock and I went one way, and Gene and Gail Davis did it their way.

313

LM: How did *Buffalo Bill, Jr.* come about? You'd finished *The Range Rider*...

DJ: I had. I was under contract to Gene [Autry], and he had to figure out something to keep me working. I worked so many of his regular shows that somebody came up with the idea of Buffalo Bill, Jr. and a little girl and so he says, "Here, let's do this." It was good; it caught on very good. We were approached by Mars Candy to extend it another two years but their requisite to extend their sponsorship was we would have to have the same across-the-board station, same time, same slot with CBS. Then it came down to politics. CBS said, "We want 25 percent." And there wasn't 25 percent to give. So it just faded off into the sunset.

A collectible pinback button for the *Range Rider* TV series featuring Dick and Jock Mahoney.

LM: How did it feel having your own starring vehicle?

DJ: I didn't like it 'cause it put all the pressure on me. I just did my thing, tried to make it as wild and woolly as I possibly could. That's where [stuntman] Fred Krone and I just stayed up nights trying to figure out what hasn't been done and he'd do it. I think as far as the stuntmen's association is concerned, we did things that they had never even heard of. Never heard of doing a bulldog falling [a] horse into the camera. Never heard of doing a fight scene on top of a stagecoach, going down into the booth, into the wheels, up to the lead, under the horses and come back up, finish the fight off on top of the stage. That's the kind of stuff that we did, had fun with.

LM: Was it comfortable working with the same people you already knew from Gene's films and TV shows?

DJ: Yeah. He put together a crew that was like family. Everybody worked together with everybody. The other shows I worked on, it was just catch as catch can, run down to the U-Haul trailers and rent something. [For instance] *The Lone Ranger*'s main vehicle was a Ford station wagon with a platform out in front for the camera, and a rack on the top for the boom man. The recording was a reel-to-reel tape [recorder] on the tailgate. Well, Gene had a regular sound truck [from] Glen Glenn. Beautiful equipment. And a regular camera car. He had vehicles for all these different things to do. And he kept all the crew guys together. It worked out great. It was like working first-class compared to some schlock outfit.

LM: How and when did you realize that you weren't getting enough work to sustain yourself, that you had to make a change in your life?

DJ: Well, I never made a change in my life, I just filled in. I did a show down in Australia for Billy Graham [*Shadow of a Boomerang*—Ed.] and I made enough money on that thing to tide me over for six months. And I had been tinkering around with real estate, and I got tired of paying salesmen for doing stuff that I did, giving 'em commissions, so I said I'm going to get myself a license and I'll do it on my own. So when I got back from Australia, I had enough to tide me over until my first escrow would pay off. And I got into real estate. That lasted for about two years, and I didn't like sales but I was one heck of a lister. I could tell people within a percentage point of what the property was worth and what it would sell for. They didn't believe me, and I didn't get a lot of listings, but when they got tired of screwing around they'd call me back, and then I'd put it on the market and get it sold. So I would get enough listings and I'd get them sold without any problem on my part. I kept the people happy and then I'd go fishing. I liked appraising properties so I said, "Why don't I get out of sales completely and become an appraiser?" I found out that the Home Savings and Loan had a trainee's program and I hired onto Home Savings to learn how to appraise property. And 13 years later, after I became a vice president and senior loan officer, I said, "I think I'll hang out my shingle." And I got a little one-horse operation going up in Bakersfield just to keep my license working.

I never quit the business 'cause I keep going on interviews; they just don't hire me. So I didn't retire from the motion picture business. [chuckles] I'm just an actor without a job right now.

Conversations:

LESLIE H. MARTINSON

Long before I had any real awareness of directors and their careers, I knew the name Leslie H. Martinson. No one who watched television in the 1950s and '60s could have avoided seeing that name. It was emblazoned on countless television shows, ranging from *Topper* and *The Millionaire* to every Warner Bros. show imaginable, when that studio dominated the airwaves with *Maverick, Sugarfoot, Lawman, Hawaiian Eye, 77 Sunset Strip, The Roaring Twenties*, et al. He continued freelancing through the 1970s  and '80s (*Mannix, Mission: Impossible, CHiPs, Dallas*) and made a handful of feature films as well.

Learning that Les had started his career at MGM, where he worked as a script supervisor for John Huston, Vincente Minnelli, and other legendary directors, prompted me to request an interview from this genial gentleman. At the time of this interview, Les was 92, but you'd never have known it—he looked great. He apologized for a certain loss of long-term memory, but he still had much to share about his long and interesting life. He studied music at a conservatory, played baseball, sold classified ads for a newspaper, wrote nightclub reviews, fought in World War II, and became one of the busiest (and best liked) directors in television. His was quite a story. Les died in 2016 at 101. (Interview originally appeared in 2007.)

LM: Yours was the only Jewish family—

LH: The first Jewish family to move into Brighton, Massachusetts. These young men I grew up with [were] an illustrious group: Aloysius Sullivan was class valedictorian at Boston College in 1936. Hick Shea became a famous hockey coach and had a couple of men in the Olympics. That's just to show you my background. My father joined Temple Israel of Boston. New York has the first temple [in the United States] and the second oldest is Temple Israel. They had services on Sunday, which is hard to believe.

LM: Meshuggeh!

LH: Very meshuggeh. They had services on Sunday, and then a very famous man came and changed it back over to Friday, Dr. (Harry) Levi; he sponsored the child labor amendment. It's a very famous pulpit. And then [a] famous rabbi came in [Joshua Loth Liebman]. He wrote "Peace of Mind," which was a best nonfictional seller for two years.

LM: What did your father do?

LH: My father—a very unusual man. He graduated Northeastern University in 1922; I went to his graduation when I was seven years old. He graduated there cum laude.

LM: And what did he do with that education?

LH: He worked at the *Boston Evening Transcript*, up in the composition room most of his time, and [he] wrote many articles. I have wonderful stories about the *Boston Evening Transcript*. It was a financial newspaper, Beacon Hill-owned and run. There's a story about a butler [announcing], "Begging your pardon, Madam, there are three reporters and a gentleman from the *Transcript*." [It] was one of the three papers that were kept on file in France, England, and Germany: *The New York Times*, the *Chicago Tribune* and the *Boston Evening Transcript*.

LM: So, your father was paid to be a typesetter but he wrote articles on the side?

LH: Yes. The famous [critic] H.T. Parker—Hell to Pay Parker, they called him—went up to see how the type was set. He had never ever seen a movie and never would see a movie. When I graduated high school and then started to work at the *Transcript*, I would pick up his copy. And he gave me tickets to the first show [I saw], *Of Thee I Sing*.

LM: Why did you leave Boston for Hollywood?

LH: Al Marston, who lived across the street from me on Donnybrook Road, worked for RKO theaters and did all the advertising. But he was also a wonderful sketch artist. He came to me and he said, "You know, Leslie, I sold a deal to the *Boston Post*, to go to Hollywood and do [pen and ink sketches] for twelve weeks. If you could get leave, you come out [and] you would write the column." I went to the head of classified and I got the extension. And so we went. Do you remember a film called *Maid of Salem*?

LM: Mmm-hmm. Claudette Colbert.

LH: The *Boston Post*'s dramatic editor was out here, and she was the technical advisor on *Maid of Salem*. She found out that Al and I were there to do [the column and sketch]. She said [to the *Post*], "Absolutely not. You want them? I'm out of here." We didn't even have a signed contract. And that was it. Height of the Depression. So I said, "Well, we're back home again." And Al says, "Not for me." He said, "I'm not gonna go back. I think I've just decided I'm staying, Leslie." And I thought about it and I said, "You know—I'm staying. I'm getting into one studio, MGM."

LM: You wanted to get into MGM.

LH: Yeah. There was a young man here at this time, a young singer under contract to RKO, Phil McMahon his name was, and his manager was a Boston boy (and Phil was, too). Every once in a while we were over at his house, and we'd have a cup of coffee and so forth. A woman came out to visit the McMahons. We happened to be there that afternoon and told her our story. She took a liking to me and she said, "You know, my son is a Jesuit at Boston College, and he's very close with John Tobin, who is the plant manager for MGM." John Tobin, the most erudite Irishman I've ever met—and when they're erudite, they're erudite. He was a big man in Winchester, Massachusetts, and he suddenly gave it all up and became the plant manager of MGM because the number two man in the Mayer hierarchy, the Irishman—

LM: Eddie Mannix?

LH: Eddie Mannix had retired as plant manager. She said, "I'm going to call

Les (at left) rides on the back of a camera truck shooting Judy Garland—or possibly her stand-in—for a scene in *Summer Stock* (1950).

my son and see if he will call John Tobin." And he did that, and set up an appointment. He asked me [about] my background and so forth and finally he said, "What department are you applying for?" I said, "Well I majored at Boston University for two years in advertising. I'm highly qualified to work in that department." And he said, "You know, there's a Depression on. Frank Whitbeck is down to four people in that department." I said, "Well, I certainly qualify for publicity in Howard Strickling's department." He said, "It's even worse there; they're down to nothing. It's the height of the Depression." I said, "Well, I'll start in the front office as an office boy." He said, "That's the most difficult place to get in. Jerry Mayer—his two sons are there right now. There's a line waiting, Leslie, *this* long." I said, "I'll wait that long if I have to, if that's the only way, if you'll take my name." He said, "Of course, I'll do that." And I thanked him. Then he got on the phone and he called the chief of [studio] police, who was Whitey Hendry. He was the man who bailed out everybody and [he was] the pay-off man. Mr. Tobin, this very erudite, proper gentleman said, "I can in good conscience recommend a young man. I know you have a big waiting list." (Some things you just never forget.) "I can in good conscience recommend a young man who would really, I know, do excellent work for your department." He stopped for a minute and listened and said, "Well, I'll ask him." He said, "The chief wants to know, did you ever play baseball?" And I said

319

yes. He said, "Oh, did you play college ball?" I said, "No, but I was a letter man in high school." He told him, "Yes, he did play ball." And he turned to me and he said, "Which position did you play?" And I had a decision to make. I was a catcher. I had this nose broken and that's how I got my nickname, 'cause every Irishman has a nickname and I didn't. I had my nose broken, catching without a mask, a foul tip. My nose came out to here [and] I was called Bubs, Bubble Nose. That was my nickname with all the Irish; [that's when] I became full-fledged.

LM: So you weren't sure if you should admit you were a catcher?

A moment on the set of *Summer Stock*: (left to right) Garland, Gene Kelly, Les Martinson (partially obscured), and Gloria DeHaven.

LH: If I said I played first base or shortstop, I could be [placed] anywhere [on the team], but I was a catcher, and I just couldn't get the lie out. So I said, "I'm a catcher." And he says, "He was a catcher." And the chief said, "Send him over." Softball was the big, big thing in the day—MGM against Universal, Paramount, Fox—and they had just lost their catcher! Into the front office I went. About three months later, they sent me over [to] Jerry Mayer, L.B.'s brother, [who] was head of the purchasing department. They always took someone over there to arrange chronologically for the whole year; it was a job that took sometimes three weeks or a month. I was in there six o'clock every morning and I had it done in two weeks. Spencer, the second to Jerry Mayer, went to him and said, "This kid they sent over from the front office—just imagine what he did." [Jerry Mayer] said, "Send him over." He interviewed me and I gave my background, and I said, "Only one place I want to go to, the production office, [and] some day work my way up from there." He said fine and he picked up the phone. Charlie Chick was the head of production department. "Charlie? Very, very first opening you have," etc., etc. "And make sure and let me know when it happens." About three weeks [later] there was an opening, and there I was in the planning office.

LM: What were your responsibilities there?

LH: We copied all the production and unit managers who'd come in and dictate to us, and the orders went out. Sometimes [we had] 10, 11 companies shooting [at the same time]. Your next step from there [the planning office] was then you get out to the set. Then came an interruption: the war [was coming]. There was a draft and Jimmy Stewart and I were the first two to leave MGM in World War II. My father had a lot of juice in Boston, so instead of going to New York where everybody in the film business went, I sent my papers to Boston. They were forming the Yankee division, and I got into the Yankee division.

And then December 7. A couple of days before we'd come back from maneuvers in North Carolina; they called it the battle of the broomsticks because we didn't have rifles. Then Task Force 6814 was formed, which was seven ships. It left the Brooklyn Navy Yard in January, the first task force to leave in World War II from the Brooklyn Navy Yard is 6814. [That's] the Northern Star patch for the Americal Division, the only division in the Army with a name instead of a number. We were on the water 38 days, zig-zagging. Left the Brooklyn Navy Yard, [down past] Virginia, across through the canal, and then to Melbourne, Australia. The Americal division—our slogan was "The Golden Gate by '48." We fought the first ground action attached to the 1st Marines at Guadalcanal and fought from Guadalcanal to Tokyo, three years and four months.

LM: Wow.

LH: Tokyo Rose used to call us the lovely orphans of the Pacific, the Americal Division. And I had good fortune. I took the test for the OCS (Officers Candidate School) and the master sergeant had said, "You know, you passed at the top but you'll never [get it because] you lose about 20 or 25 points if your commander doesn't approve. Lt. Col. Newman, [said] it wasn't disapproval of [my] work. "I can't afford to lose him," [he said] and he jumped me from just a straight sergeant up into the big six, which is the equivalent of [Chief Petty Officer] in the Navy.

LM: So what was your position then?

LH: I was a master sergeant. There's only one, you know, in the company. And each year, I went up. But men who did get home and went back to [OCS] training went across the other way and didn't come home.

LM: And what were your duties?

LH: I'm a quartermaster. You know, we feed 'em and we clothe 'em and we get that ammo up to the lines. But, when you see a guy with cross guns, they do the work. Even the artillery and so forth [they're in the] back. So all those three years, that's why I was there. We fought from Guadalcanal to Tokyo. Then came a scene that they'd never done. They're taking us home for rotation, the first time and all the names went into a hat and what a scene: *a ticket home.* And my name came up. I left from Bougainville, and they left a week after I left for home—and that's where we really got clobbered. The kamikazes, they knew it was over, those last three and a half months and the division, including quartermaster, took as many hits as an infantryman did. Yeah, imagine going all that time. I came back and I was assigned to Taunton, Massachusetts, and I was the master sergeant there. And the war was over.

LM: Where were you mustered out?

LH: In Boston.

LM: And did you immediately come back to L.A.?

LH: Oh, yeah.

LM: Was your old job waiting for you at MGM?

LH: Yup. It was waiting for me. I was actually still in the planning office, you know. Then I got promoted out to become a script supervisor and that's where I worked with all the great directors.

LM: Let's talk about that job, because it's a really important job. Not just anybody could do that. And wasn't that job referred to as "script girl" at one time?

LH: MGM had a few women but mostly men. And you went from script girl to second assistant after years. My musical background didn't hurt; they put me with the Freed unit because I had that background.

LM: And you got to work with Judy Garland.

LH: I have a frustration; if the world only knew what a wonderful, wonderful, troubled girl she was. She had no opinion of herself. You know, as I look back, she never had the right man. Vincente Minnelli, who was a wonderful man, was not the right man for her. She's surrounded with this beauty, one after another, Hedy Lamarr and Virginia Bruce, each one more beautiful than the other, and the inferior [sense] gets worse and worse and—

LM: She had no self-confidence?

LH: No she didn't. She came to me one day, on this first film with her, and she said, "Do you know that your name works spelling backwards? You don't have to change a letter?" She says, "I was doodling that last night and believe it or not, yours worked. Martinson, a long name. And we will never call each other anything else as long as we know each other." She liked me at that point. Eilsel Nosnitram is Leslie Martinson backwards. I called her E-duj Dnalrag. I wish the world could have known Judy Garland as I know her.

With James Garner and Joanna Barnes on the *Maverick* set.

LM: Describe for someone who doesn't know what your job was as script supervisor.

LH: To sum it up, everything must match. You are a matching expert. In other words, you play a master scene, you move from here to there, you pick up something. Even in looks, the ship went that way and someone [looks this way]. You know that camera better than the man cranking as to which way they look when they cross what you call the center line. Not only that, these eating scenes were nightmares, you know, when you want to go into that close-up. I'll tell you one interesting quick story, about Sam Wood, may he rest in peace, with June Allyson; the film was *The Stratton Story*. Jimmy Stewart comes back from the

With Clint Walker in the Warner Bros. commissary.

ballpark, plays a big scene with her. She's holding a baby and the baby has a rattle in her hand and we play a big long master scene. Now, we're all lit for her close-ups, they roll the cameras. There's that silence and you wait for the word "speed," and the speed comes up and Sam says, "Cut! Cut!" They cut the cameras and he turns to me and says, "Leslie, wasn't the baby holding that rattle in the right hand?" Oh, Jesus. I didn't have that note. So I stall, I'm looking, I'm thinking, "Oh, God." The crew just waits; they love it when the script girl messes up. And then I turned, I looked up and I said, "Mr. Wood sir, was she holding a baby?" Broke up the whole crew, just fell apart and, of course, he fell apart and he says, "He's a big help, huh?"

LM: What about on a musical? That's got to be very complicated with the staging of a big production number.

LH: I graduated a conservatory of music and I'm sitting there and see it right from the very beginning. Fred Astaire did his own and Gene Kelly did his own—they were the dance directors as well. They do the choreography, but the man that comes out and just stands there and watches it, and then plays the one line. The one line is just what you call the music [the] rehearsal pianist has. Just the melody line and chords, that's it, and then the arranger comes out and watches everything and he goes back and writes for sometimes 36 instruments, including a harp and the timpani. This is the man that puts it all together, and to me, they were the heroes.

LM: You were going to tell me a story about Judy Garland.

LH: She started one picture weighing 136 pounds and finished it weighing about 98. This [was] *Summer Stock*. She sings "Better Luck Next Time" to a bartender, and when she was down to her low weight, there's such a vibrato.

LM: How bad was it?

LH: Well, she tried it and she finally said, "You'll have to settle with that." [The conductor] begged for one more, and she said, "Look, please don't worry about it. Go see the movie." What did she possibly mean? Dissolve—she is now singing to the bartender. [When] she gets to [that moment] she leans across, and [her] hand goes to his shoulder. She shakes him and that vibrato—

LM: She did it to cover up her problem.

LH: Well, of course. And I'm the only one who knows that.

LH: Years later, Mickey Rooney opened a hotel [The Riviera in Las Vegas, 1955—Ed.] [Mickey and Judy] had a relationship that was really like a brother-sister. And she had never been to Vegas. I'd now become a director and I hadn't seen Judy for six, seven years. Mickey says, "She said she'll come to my opening." So, I'm coming out of the men's room, right [near] where the big gaming is, and [there] with her hands on the door [is] Judy Garland pushing into the ladies room, 25 yards away. And I said, "E-duj Dnalrag!" And through the door went this big scream, and inside is coming back, "Eilsel Nosnitram!" Out the door [she comes] and the two of us just hugged. It's a moment you never forget.

LM: Getting back to your days as a script supervisor, tell me about working with John Huston.

LH: I'm working on *The Asphalt Jungle*. I had a great relationship with the leading man. That was Sterling Hayden, a beautiful human being. We were very close. I'll give him a triple-A rating, a man's man. We were doing pre-production work in Kentucky. The last scene of the picture was Hayden down on the grass. He had been wounded; they promised there would be no gunfire and there was; they betrayed him. He's struggling to get back, and [in] the last scene in the picture, he's lying [in] the green grass of Kentucky. All he wanted was some horses and little spot of green grass. These beautiful young horses were to go and surround him, and he expires as they're there around him. He got his dream but he was gone.

The wranglers just couldn't get those young little horses in. And John Huston got a clever idea. He said, "Call the prop man in and load that ring around with sugar. Get honey and oats and they'll get the scent then, won't they?" [The prop man] says "Good thinking, boss." And that was done.

Les shares a smile with James Garner, whom he directed in 18 episodes of *Maverick*.

Now, we're all waiting. It's a long shot where the camera moves in from [far] back and you see the horses all nudging [him]. We have the captain of a basketball team, a six foot five kid, who was [Hayden's] double for this long shot, [because] we already got his close-ups. I'm standing on the sideline just out of the camera line. Sure enough, [the horses] get the scent and they start coming in; they're all nudging, getting closer, and then it was just perfect. And I look up and [one of the horses is kicking his way] and the heel is missing [the kid's] temple by *this* much. I saw that foot going right against his temple and I jumped over that fence [yelling "hee-yah"] and I scattered the horses.

I was on the plane that night. [Huston] fired me and sent me home. I went to Joe Cook, the assistant manager of production who was very fond of me and he said, "Leslie, you got big problems. John wants you off this lot [and says you'll never] hold a script again anywhere." It got up to the main office, because apparently, they didn't get the shot; it got dark and they had to come back the next day. [But] I would have done it again. Joe Cook called me in and said, "Well, Leslie, I've got to go up to the iron lung. [MGM slang for the Thalberg Building, which looked like a hospital.—Ed.] What am I gonna tell 'em?" I said, "You're gonna tell 'em what I told you." I said, "That would look great, wouldn't it? Huh? His brains all over the green grass [of Kentucky?]" He said, "I'll go up and see what I can do, Leslie." He went up and talked to the top man, told him the story, and [that] Huston wanted me fired. And he came back and says, "Take my car to Speedy's for a wash." He tossed me his keys to his car, then he says, "You're okay." That's my John Huston story. Now, on the other hand, I have a letter here from his father.

LM: What was the occasion?

LH: He went to Boston to do a play. I worked on *Summer Holiday*, the musical. Walter Huston, of course, was in it, and he and I had a wonderful time together. So when he went back to do a play in Boston, I said, "Look up my folks." I told him about my dad who, as a young man, had worked at the Colonial Theatre. Walter called them and said, "Come as my guests." So [Walter] wrote a letter to me about how "it was a delight meeting your folks" and so forth, and I have the letter. That's the father. But [John] Huston was not a nice man.

LM: Let's talk about some of the directors you worked with, beginning with Sam Wood.

LH: I was part of his family. Brilliant—but not the best man to communicate to actors. He had a stub of a pencil and he could rewrite. [And he had] the luxury of take six, seven, eight, ten. In those days, you know, if you were the director you were the giant. A precious man and I was his script girl…

LM: Rouben Mamoulian directed *Summer Holiday.*

LH: And I was the script supervisor. I was Rouben's boy. And we were on it for a long time. He was brilliant and a nice man. No big flourish. It was work to be done and he did it in his own sweet way. You get to know a man [when] you're on it so long, because there were all those numbers to rehearse. He spent a lot of time on the [stage] although he didn't have anything to do with the choreography, but he was down there and we became very, very friendly. I was an honorary pallbearer at his funeral.

LM: How about Clarence Brown?

LH: I worked with Clarence two weeks only, on added scenes for *The Year-ling*. Two weeks.

LM: Here or on location?

LH: Backlot. He could be real tough, but I had no problem with him.

LM: Going back for a bit, how long did you play on the softball team at MGM?

LH: Just a very short while. It was getting [there] at the end of the season. It was just fate—

LM: Because Gene Kelly told me he was on that team.

LH: I have one Gene Kelly story. In *Summer Stock* there was a number, "You Wonderful You." And whenever I'd see Gene I would always sneak up behind him [and sing], "My arms around you, you wonderful Jew." One night years later, this is in the '60s in France, we were at the [Hotel] George V. It's a foggy night and walking across, coming the other way, [my wife] Connie stops me and says, "Look who's there, Leslie." A tired old director with his beret and a raincoat over his shoulder like

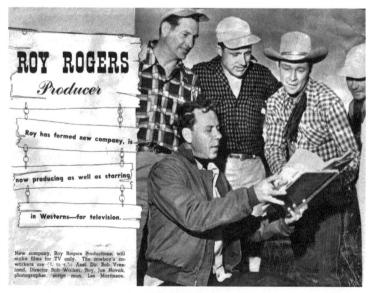

A trade ad with Les Martinson, lower left, script supervisor, assistant director Bob Vreeland, director Robert Walker, Roy Rogers, and cinematographer Joe Novak.

Jimmy Durante saying, "Goodnight, wherever you are." It's Gene Kelly and I come up behind him. (sings) "My arms around you..." I hit him with that and, oh, my goodness. "I don't believe it!" What a moment that was.

LM: Tell me about Fred Astaire.

LH: I have one distinction with Fred Astaire [in that] I was the only one he gave a gift to: my invitation [to play a round of golf with him] and Bing Crosby. He was a kind of a loner but he felt comfortable with me. I always remember a story that he told me about his marriage. He told me he only had just one argument in his entire marriage, and I can believe it with Fred. It was early in their marriage, and the [shooting] ran late. He neglected to call when he usually would, and then finally when he did call, she was very severe with him. "How could you do this?" He explained to her what it was like when you were involved on the set. He said, "And do you know, Leslie, in our entire marriage, that was the closest that we ever came to being severe with each other. Would you believe it? Never, never ever." That's Fred Astaire.

LM: You always hear the same stories about what a perfectionist he was.

LH: Oh, that number with the sand. [From *The Belle of New York*.—Ed.) Saw it, was unhappy. It was all a wrap, but he insisted that it be done over again. He said, "It's disgraceful." They called everybody back and with the dancers, we're talking bucks. Big bucks.

LM: Would there be a time when the director would be happy but he'd say, "No, I need to do it again?"

LH: Oh, yeah. Oh, yeah, invariably a director says, "Well, you know, to me, you can't do any better but go for another."

LM: How did you start working with Roy Rogers and Dale Evans, and why did you leave MGM?

LH: I listed the great directors with whom I've worked—quite a list—and I said I'm ready. Because what would happen? Maybe another two or three or four years, I might get to be a second assistant. They "made" three directors, in all those years I was at MGM; one was Freddy Zinnemann, one was a nephew, [and] one a film editor who won an Oscar.

329

LM: So you decided there was no future for you at MGM.

LH: I went in and I said, "I'm ready to direct." [I realized] I'll never get it here, and I just quit. Two weeks later, I went to a script supervisor's meeting and I sat down beside Robert J. Walker. Roy and Dale had made him a director. Over at Republic Studios, [he] was a script supervisor and now they're starting the TV series and they made him a director. So he sat down beside me and said, "What are you doing?" And I told him.

Martinson at work on the Warner Bros. backlot, where he spent seven busy years.

LM: You were at liberty, as the actors used to say.

LH: Even though we hadn't worked together, I was close with him and his family, and he said, "Great! Come be my script supervisor." I said, "No way. If we do ten setups a day [at MGM], that's a lot. I hear you guys at Republic on these Westerns do 35 and 40." He said, "Leslie, this is television. My first day—85 shots." He said, "Come with me. It could pay off for you. They made me a director. How long am I gonna be with 'em? It's the chance of a lifetime." And I said OK. He was [the] purest human you ever met. [Later he] sold the company and walked away from it. And went back to Boston and was head of publicity for the *Christian Science Monitor*.

LM: Tell me about working on *The Roy Rogers Show*.

LH: The pressure was incredible. Leave the studio at six in the morning, 13 of us [crew] in a bus. [Roy and Dale would] come with their house wagon, which serves as a dressing room. And that camera was turning at Iverson's Ranch and you work your way up the mountain up there to Panic Peak. [The highest point on location where you could still capture some daylight.—Ed.] That was it. I call it "the lost year." In the summer, you know, 8:30, when that sun goes down and you haven't made your day, you are in big trouble.

LM: What other kind of challenges did you face shooting that series?

LH: Now I'll tell you: the one thing a director doesn't do in Westerns is [check the ground before a chase scene]. Those wranglers go out there and they scout for potholes. You know, you're in an unseen territory. The light was getting yellow and it was Panic Peak time, and I needed one more run through with Dale on [her horse] Buttermilk. And I said to the wranglers: "I'm gonna have to kill this." They said, "We've run across the hill, Leslie. You need this one shot to finish it? Do it. Don't worry about it, it's clear." I said, "You're sure?" They said [yes]. I said OK. It went. The horse hit [something, and] down went Buttermilk, Dale over her head. And I looked at them and said, "I deserve [that]; I should have known better." The horse got up, Dale got up, and I'm waiting. She said to the cameraman, "Did you get enough of the shot?" He says, "Yeah, we got a good piece before the fall." And Dale says, "Thank you," and off she went. That's Dale Evans. No admonishment, no anything. And of course, I learned a big lesson. Shouldn't have listened to the wranglers.

LM: You have to be certain; you have to know it for yourself. But Roy and Dale handled the pressure?

LH: Never once [a problem], in the summer starting to shoot at seven and April when the fog was there. They'd bring their trailer [which we'd] use for lights. We didn't have lights, just shiny boards, and I'd shoot close-ups. Could you believe?

LM: I suppose once you've done 85 setups a day, everything else seems like velvet.

LH: Then, after one year, Bob Walker got an offer to go to MCA. They were just starting to go into television. He was among the first to shoot a half-hour film [in] two days, but [with] one rehearsal day. The only time in my career that I had rehearsal days was at the beginning of television. You shot two days, eight to five. And the plug [was pulled] wherever you were at five o'clock the first day, no matter where you were; that's making a half-hour teleplay. Carl Hickey was the production manager; he used to do those six-day motion picture things at Columbia. Killer Carl, they called him. I remember, I was rehearsing. I followed Bob Walker and I'm looking through my [view] finder. Suddenly a hand reaches in and snatches it out of my hand. It's Carl Hickey, and he said,

"Look, young man, I don't know long you're going to be with us but this will be in my top left drawer whenever you're on your way out. But I never want to see it again."

LM: So much for art. Incidentally, there's one director I forgot to ask you about whom you worked with at MGM, Anthony Mann, who made *The Tall Target*.

LH: I was the script clerk on that. I loved him. Excellent man. Triple A. For me, as a director, knew what he wanted. Very definitive. A delightful, delightful guy besides. Just all business.

LM: Was *The Tall Target* the first time you worked with Dick Powell?

LH: Yes. We weren't buddy-buddy [but] two years later, on his first movie [as a director, *Split Second*, 1953] a call comes in to the head of the production department and he [Powell] says, "Could I borrow Leslie Martinson? I'm directing my first film." And he [the production head] says, "Well, that's a strange request, but I suppose. He's not on a show right now but he would be ready for a show." I said [to myself], it's two years, I never knew he [knew I was] alive and he's calling? You don't put a script super on it, [when] a film editor is there who knows the directions and all the complications. I called him and I said, "No. You're too fine a person for me to do this. I'd be doing you a disservice; he can do twice what I can do." But that's my Dick Powell story—his first movie, which was a success.

LM: Did you wind up working for him later on?

LH: I did work at *Four Star Theatre*, holding script with Dick Powell. I was very close with him, and then I directed June [Allyson] in two movies of the week. Oh, Dick Powell, I could go on forever—a beautiful man. We had such a relationship with him. What a lovely human being he was. Absolutely. I wish everybody knew the Dick Powell I knew. And they had an excellent marriage.

LM: So many people credit him with giving them their first big break, like Aaron Spelling.

LH: I directed his first piece of writing. He was then a starving actor, and he wrote quite a good story. It was a pilot, and the man in the lead was Chuck Connors. And it was his first pilot. It was sold and unsold three times and Chuck Connors [did another pilot and then] had to make a choice of which one he wanted. He was the leading man, and he chose *The Rifleman* [instead of Spelling's show]. That was [Spelling's] first piece of material and it was just devastating to him at the time.

With Will Hutchins making the Western series *Sugarfoot*.

LM: But he stuck with it. He didn't give up.

LH: Obviously not.

LM: Les, you directed a show that I watched religiously when I was a kid, *Topper*.

LH: You're talking about a woman I still adore and [I'm]very close with her.

LM: Anne Jeffreys?

LH: Anne. One of a kind. I directed *Topper*, fell in love with her and still am.

LM: How quickly would you shoot an episode of *Topper*?

LH: *Topper* was three days.

LM: Wow. And you had to do practical effects on the set.

LH: Yeah. But we had a way [of doing it].

LM: And in the midst of all this television work, you got your first feature-film assignment?

LH: The first film that I directed was Mickey Rooney in *The Atomic Kid*.

333

Director Martinson tries to stay dry while giving directions to his *Cheyenne* star Clint Walker.

Twelve and a half days, at Republic Studios. All special effects, but I had the great whatchamacallit brothers—

LM: The Lydecker Brothers?

LH: Yeah, Lydecker. Only you could possibly know those two brothers.

LM: Yes, because their work was so extraordinary. Here they were at this low-budget studio, but they did the best special effects in town, didn't they?

LH: Incredible. They were just incredible. Imagine, twelve and a half days [to make] that film.

LM: I assume that working with Mickey Rooney on that film led to you directing his TV show, *Hey Mulligan*.

LH: But I [left] Mickey at one time. It was a Christmas Eve and [my wife] Connie was there. He had this wonderful wife, three kids, he had everything to be thankful for. And when Mickey took a drink, that's all he needed. He could not [handle it]. I called him aside and said, "I'm leaving, Mickey. You're my boy, but I'm outta here. You have all God's blessings here at this table and for you to act the way..." And I walked away; then he called me back and apologized. But, that's how I got to go with Jackie Gleason.

LM: How so?

LH: Jackie, when he had a "dark night," would call Mickey. Six o'clock back there, he'd call Mickey, it's three o'clock here. He'd call Mickey and say, "Hi, I want you to know that one loyal American saw your show; I had a dark night." It's 'cause we were on against Gleason. No one ever saw our show, except he saw it and he'd call and say, "One loyal American..." and so forth. That's when he sent Bullets Durgom [Gleason's manager] out to interview me because they were going to do 13 episodes of his show [*The Honeymooners*, on film] so they'd have something [that would last].

They didn't have the camera [set up] at that time. So Bullets came out, interviewed me. [This] was at a time where Mickey [would] call in and say he's hoarse. If he knew I had four or five in the cast, I would shoot all around [him]. Then he'd come in around noon and so about two o'clock or three I'd get one piece of a master [shot] and then go in and get his close-ups. I did 33 episodes. [Mickey] told Bullets, "You're with All State here, this kid; I don't know how he can do it." Anyway, that's how I went [to New York] and I began to prepare, set up the cutting room.

[Gleason] and Bullets were on holiday two weeks in Bermuda. [Jackie] came back, got off the ship, and went right to Dumont Studios and saw [the new "Electronicam" setup that the network had devised to film *The Honeymooners*—Ed.] I'm now in his office and he said, "Kid, I heard a lot about you from my writers, my executive producer," which he did. And he said, "I want to tell you, I'm sorry." I said, "Don't say another word." I had a contract for 13, but I didn't mention that. I said, "Look what I've got," and I held up a wire that Mickey had sent, asking if he could spring me for a week to do the opening of a show, *Kraft Playhouse*. And I said, "Don't feel bad; I have this." He said, "Well, you're right," and he hands to me, written out in longhand, the full payment for the 13 [weeks]. And he said, "You'll be seeing me when I come to Hollywood. Get into the big stuff."

LM: That's a rare story of generosity in this business.

LH: We had a contract, but I didn't ask. I didn't say anything. He volunteered it.

LM: When you made your first features, did you work on the scripts at all or did you shoot what they handed you?

LH: Never ever did I go on a set that I didn't prepare my script. I gambled with *PT 109* (1963) because I didn't prepare it and, you know, I took it over at the end of the second day.

LM: I didn't know that.

LH: Oh, yeah. And my idol was directing it, [who had done] *All Quiet on the Western Front*.

LM: Lewis Milestone?

LH: Lewis did the first two days. And he and Brynie (Bryan) Foy didn't get along. Brynie had done some quickies there; he was the producer of this film. Milestone prepared it but Brynie wasn't happy with him. I don't know what happened. He'd only shot two days. The film was in the can there; I saw it; it was fine. And Brynie went to Jack Warner, [and] said, "He's not going to cut it for us. We're in trouble. He is not what we know him to be." And would you believe it, I had already bailed out a picture seven days in, had to replace a director, went back to TV, [and] I was shooting a *77 Sunset Strip*. And next thing I know, I was called into his [Jack Warner's] office, and he said, "You're going to go down and take over." I'm taking over for my idol, Milestone, and I'm doing a picture about a president who's alive! Only Jack Warner...

LM: So, you started shooting with no notice and no preparation?

LH: Two famous men wrote the script. There was a bestseller—it was taken from that. And the boys who were all alive are all in it. [And remember] I'm a GI. I was there. Guadalcanal literally to Tokyo, three-and-a-half years.

LM: With all the work you did in the 1950s and '60s, you gave opportunities to a lot of young actors.

LH: Lynn Stalmaster was a young kid who became the number-one casting director. He was then at a little hole in the wall at Goldwyn Studios and came in with Frank Gorshin to read for the second lead in *Hot Rod Girl*. Thin as a rail, nice young man. I said, "Where are his credits?" And

Frank did his thing. He read. He says, "I also do impressions." Never been on a soundstage, nothing, but he apparently tied up with this young casting director. Eight-and-a-half days was the budget. Eight-and-a-half days. All hot rods going, racing up the straightaway stretch. Tremendous. The producer, a marvelous young man, was doing his first picture, very nice young man. I heard Frank and I knew I had a find. I said, "We've got our second lead," and he said, "Leslie, you can't do that. You're going to go with someone who has never been on a soundstage?" He said, "I've quit smoking for a month, don't do this to me, Leslie." And I said, "You have to trust me—you got a find. And if you smoke, then I'm not going to direct the picture and I don't know of anybody who's going to make this in eight-and-a-half days. But I know the cameraman and the crew I'm getting and I think it's going to be done. And no one will believe it anyway." *Hot Rod Girl* was so successful, [we did] the next one, *Hot Rod Rumble*.

LM: You gave other young actors important breaks, too.

LH: The thank-yous for the first breaks is where I get hugs and kisses. Angie Dickinson sees me, runs over. And Dr. Kildare.

LM: Richard Chamberlain?

LH: The right part in a *Bourbon Street Beat*, a second lead. [Bill Orr was producing.] I said, "You need a high-class guy, Bill, you know, who's done it all." And Bill Orr said, "But jeez, not a credit, Leslie." I said, "You don't think I put my neck out like that. You've got a find; he's perfect." We needed just the quality, a rich man's son. No credits. That was his start, and he never forgot it. Mary Tyler Moore? Her first part in a *Bourbon Street Beat*. It was the lead. Angie Dickinson had a bit part

Les enjoys a happy reunion with Dale Evans and Roy Rogers.

in a Mickey Rooney episode that I did and I walked her to her car. I thought it was going to fall apart; I thought, if you'd turn the key it's gonna just disintegrate. I told her, "You know, you did something. You only had three lines in this part, and that's the hardest thing to do 'cause you really don't have a character to work on," and I went through this with her. "You did it. Don't give up, You're in the right business." And just recently at the theater she saw us; we were waiting and it was a crowded room and I hadn't seen her for two, three, four years. Rushed over to me in front of everybody and threw her arms around me to give me a big kiss.

LM: You really were part of a special time in television. When Mike Connors gave you the Golden Boot Award, he quoted *TV Guide*, which said, "Martinson was to early television what the DC-3 was to aviation."

LH: [As I said in my speech that night], "There are three people to whom I shall always be grateful. Robert J. Walker, the director, who brought me as a script supervisor to Happy Trails. And to Dale Evans and Roy Rogers, who one year later, made me a director by asking those magic words, 'Les, are you ready?'

"And during the seven years I was under contract to Warner Bros., working with the brilliant Bill Orr—and he was. He took two losing shows when he became head of Warner Bros. Television and built a dynasty. Seven, eight hours of shows a week. He did it all. Those seven years working with Bill Orr, Hugh Benson, and Arthur Silver, and the incredible Roy Huggins, was the era of Westerns: *Maverick, Cheyenne, Bronco, Sugarfoot, Lawman.* I did all these pilots, and I'm proud to say with all humility that I directed the *Maverick,* 'A Shady Deal at Sunny Acres,' which won an Emmy. It's the only Western that ever won an Emmy.

"The career that Roy and Dale began has taken me around the world as a filmmaker and yet, the greatest impression that they made was the life they led. They were the finest example of my father's advice when I told him I was about to become a director: 'Son, though now you walk with kings, never lose the common touch.' "

That was [the gist of] my speech. And they applauded.

LM: I applauded too.

THE
FORGOTTEN STUDIO

RKO REVISITED

RKO is, in many respects, the forgotten studio. It wasn't created in the silent era, like Universal or Paramount. No one central figure was identified with it as Louis B. Mayer was with MGM or Harry Cohn with Columbia. What's more, it ceased making movies in the 1950s, although its corporate name lives on.

As to its output, any buff can rattle off virtually all of the studio's major movies during its heyday: *King Kong, The Informer, Stage Door, Gunga Din, Bringing Up Baby*, the Astaire-Rogers musicals, the Val Lewton horror cycle, *It's a Wonderful Life, Out of the Past*, the John Ford films, and some other goodies with Cary Grant, Katharine Hepburn, Carole Lombard, and Ginger Rogers, along with *Citizen Kane*. RKO's top-drawer product fills a short list while a similar roster for MGM, Paramount, or Fox would take pages. This means  that there are literally hundreds of RKO films unknown to film buffs and historians.

RKO's creation at the dawn of the sound era from components of Joseph Kennedy's FBO, David Sarnoff's RCA Corporation, Radio-Keith-Orpheum, Radio Pictures, and Pathé Studios, is a saga unmatched by other Hollywood corporate histories. Its financial ups and downs over the years, and revolving-door studio heads (William LeBaron, David O. Selznick, Merian C. Cooper, Pandro S. Berman, Dore Schary, and the notorious Howard Hughes, among others) pique one's curiosity as to how the company managed to survive at all. Thank goodness the entire story has been documented by the eminent historian Richard B. Jewell in his books *RKO Radio Pictures: A Titan is Born* and *Slow Fade to Black: The Decline of RKO Radio Pictures*, published by the University of California Press.

There is also the matter of the studio as a releasing outlet. No other major company had so many films pass through its hands without retaining ownership. For many years RKO released the works of Walt Disney and Samuel Goldwyn along with other independent producers, including Sol Lesser (the non-MGM Tarzan films), International Pictures (before that organization merged with Universal), and Boris Morros (*The Flying Deuces* with Laurel and Hardy). David O. Selznick acquired the rights to films like *Topaze, Little Women,* and *Notorious,* while Pioneer Pictures kept *Becky Sharp* and its other early color films. Series like *Dr. Christian, Lum 'n' Abner,* and *Scattergood Baines* did not stay with the company, and even their backlog of Pathé Newsreels left the company when Warner Bros. bought that library.

RKO lost still more properties by selling major films to other studios for remake purposes, or not renewing certain rights, resulting in tremendous legal snarls to clear the films for viewing in recent years. Among these titles are *Cimarron, The Animal Kingdom, Winterset, Hit the Deck, Little Orphan Annie, Of Human Bondage, Girl Crazy, My Favorite Wife, She, Roberta,* and *Bird of Paradise,* to name just a few. Fortunately, many of these have now come to light, but some remain in limbo.

It is no secret that the television package was once owned by the C&C Cola Corporation, because C&C refilmed the main and end titles of every RKO feature to herald "C&C MovieTime," obliterating the RKO tower trademark and any action or opticals that might have been on-screen at the head or tail of each film. Even worse, C&C altered the 16mm negatives and managed to cut off the end-title music on many features, leaving audiences hanging in the middle of an unresolved musical phrase. Fortunately, most significant titles have been restored in the years since Turner Entertainment acquired the catalog.

When RKO burst onto the scene during the first days of talking pictures, the company was looking to knock the competition for a loop with large-scale films like *Rio Rita*, based on the hit Broadway show produced by Florenz Ziegfeld and partially filmed in Technicolor. An announcement ad in the *1930 Film Daily Yearbook for Radio Pictures* showed the Radio Titan holding the company's lightning-bolt logo. The copy proclaimed, "Mightier shows...Mightier plans...Mightier progress. The Radio Titan

The Gower Street entrance to RKO Radio Pictures.

Opens the Curtains of the Clouds and a New and Greater Year Dawns for the Most Spectacular Show Machine of All Time! A New and Mightier Pageant of the Titans Is Forming...Titanic in Conception...Titanic in Development...Titanic in Reality! And Marching Irresistibly to Leadership of the Modern Show World!"

The Show World found a hollow ring to these statements as the studio, after initial blockbusters like *Rio Rita* and *Cimarron*, settled into the same mass-production groove as its competitors. The hiring of David O. Selznick gave a tremendous shot in the arm to the company's fortunes, and he paved the way for some of the studio's all-time best films. But after his departure RKO concentrated on a handful of major titles each year, filling in the release schedule with programmers and vehicles for its contract players.

This is the forgotten product of the forgotten studio, and it bears closer scrutiny.

Every studio produced its share of "filler" during these years, and every backlog has its share of overlooked gems. RKO's list is especially intriguing since so many films fit into this category. The studio had its own formulas. One was to take talent from the short-subject unit and turn them loose in the arena of feature films. This accounted for some unusual and rewarding work by Mark Sandrich and George Stevens, who blossomed around the same time and became RKO's leading contract directors in the mid-to-late 1930s.

Director John Cromwell told me that he enjoyed his period at RKO in the mid-1930s when he was able to make "little" pictures like *Jalna* and *Village Tale*, although he had difficulty getting major stars to work in such seemingly unremarkable properties. Consequently, RKO didn't feel it could successfully promote these star-less films. They were treated as Bs although they really weren't. Cromwell found them satisfying because they were "real and valid material, and not the usual concoction that you got from most studio writers."

Sixteen-year-old Dawn O'Day won the coveted title role in *Anne of Green Gables* and changed her legal name to Anne Shirley, her character in the film.

Another transplanted New York director, Elliott Nugent, rebelled at Paramount when they handed him B assignments but welcomed the opportunity to do a quiet character study at RKO like *Two Alone*. The studio's perennial problem was in marketing these pictures.

Other directors have said they enjoyed working at the studio because there was none of the stagnation that existed at companies like MGM. The reason was simple: no management regime was in power long enough to settle in that way, and men like Selznick, Cooper, and Berman gave directors a chance to try new ideas. Consequently, more modest but offbeat pictures came out of RKO than from any other studio. Like Columbia, RKO borrowed stars and directors, or signed them to short-term contracts, and the results were often felicitous.

The look of RKO pictures was largely determined by the art direction of Van Nest Polglase and Carroll Clark. Polglase's name has become synonymous with the lavish white-on-white moderne settings that we all remember from the Astaire-Rogers musicals. These sets and the photography of David Abel, Nick Musuraca, and Roy Hunt gave all the studio's films a certain veneer that set them apart from those of other mini-majors like Columbia.

In the early 1930s Max Steiner wrote virtually all the title and background music for RKO releases. This was primarily during the Selznick regime, and while the scores of *King Kong* and *The Informer* have become classics, Steiner did equally impressive music for such films as *She* and *Symphony of Six Million*. For many pictures title music was all that was needed, and the studio often reused cues from earlier films. (*Morning Glory's* main theme turns up under the credits for *Two Alone*, for instance) There was also "a song" at RKO. Whenever an incidental song was needed for someone to hum, to be played on a radio, or sung in a two-reeler, the answer was "Isn't This a Night for Love?" written by Val Burton and Will Jason and introduced by Phil Harris in *Melody Cruise*. Harris sang it again in a two-reeler called *Romancin' Along*, Ruth Etting crooned it in one of her starring short subjects, and it echoed through RKO soundtracks for the rest of the decade. No studio ever got more mileage out of a song, except perhaps Universal with "Swan Lake."

Here, then, is a random sampling of modern-day viewpoints on a group of RKO films: some obscure, some ignored, and some merely worthy of another look.

Street Girl (July 30, 1929) directed by Wesley Ruggles, with Betty Compson, John Harron, Jack Oakie, Ned Sparks, Guy Buccola, Joseph Cawthorn, Ivan Lebedeff. Songs by Oscar Levant and Sidney Clare. Predictable but charming little film with likable performances all around. Harron, Oakie, Sparks, and Buccola are a musical group called The Four Seasons, joined by a petite violin-playing refugee from Aregon named Frederika (Compson). Harron falls in love with her, becomes madly jealous when the Prince of Aregon (Lebedeff) arrives in New York, comes to see Freddi at their nightclub, and kisses her. Discord is patched up when Lebedeff explains that he was only being kind, and he doesn't love her. Says Harron, "Gee, you're a prince, Prince." The Four Seasons' theme, "Huggable and Sweet," is an infectious melody played frequently during the film, while "Broken Up Tune" is given a creditable production number. Remade in 1936 as *That Girl from Paris*, with Lily Pons in the lead and Jack Oakie in support.

Tanned Legs (November 10, 1929) directed by Marshall Neilan, with June Clyde, Arthur Lake, Sally Blane, Dorothy Revier, Albert Gran, Allen Kearns, Edmund Burns, Ann Pennington. Sex, intrigue, scandal, and an Orphans' Benefit at a summer resort; as silly as it sounds. The film opens with June and chorus singing "Come in the water, the water is fine," an Oscar Levant-Sidney Clare ditty. She then becomes Little Miss Fix-It to stop her bickering parents from flirting, save her father from being swindled, retrieve some letters her sister (Blane) wrote to slimy Burns, and try to ward off ambitious Arthur Lake, who wants to marry her. In a climactic melee, Sally tries to shoot Burns, but hits June instead. Lake immediately diagnoses it as a flesh wound.

Recuperating in bed, June explains all, patches up everyone's troubles, and Mother (Nella Walker) concludes, "And to think that she might have been killed because of us!"—which ends the film. The only salient feature of this limp early talkie is a rare screen appearance by Ann Pennington, who sings and dances "You're Responsible" with Allen Kearns, and appears in several other innocuous numbers.

Seven Keys to Baldpate (December 25, 1929) directed by Reginald Barker, with Richard Dix, Miriam Seeger, Crauford Kent, Margaret Livingston. Based on the George M. Cohan play derived from Earl Derr Biggers' story. This film, completed in 1929, was the third of five filmings of this engaging comedy-mystery about a novelist who tries to win a bet by writing an entire book in 24 hours while staying at a supposedly deserted mountain lodge. This is the kind of film that proves that talkies did not have to move at a snail's pace; while hardly cinematically inventive, it moves briskly through its delightfully serpentine plot. Dix was never more buoyant.

Alias French Gertie (April 11, 1930) directed by George Archainbaud, with Bebe Daniels, Ben Lyon, Robert Emmett O'Connor, John Ince, Daisy Belmore. There is simply no indication that this is an early talkie; one would never know it from the staging, direction, cutting, or from the vivid and completely natural performances by the two leads. Their characterizations are so fresh and full of verve that they put many a more distinguished stage-act to shame. Bebe plays a quick-witted sharpster known as Gertie the Gun, who poses as a French maid to gain entry to rich women's homes and access to their jewels; she meets her match in brash, happy-go-lucky Lyon, an equally nimble colleague, and they decide to team up, until Bebe gets notions about going straight. Perennial screen cop O'Connor has a good role as a flatfoot who takes a liking to the twosome and urges them to quit the racket, while frequent movie drunk Arthur Housman turns up as a burglar called Denver Dan. Handsome art deco settings in the homes they burgle enhance the enjoyability of watching *Alias French Gertie*, a thoroughly entertaining vehicle for a most ingratiating couple.

He Knew Women (April 18, 1930) directed by Hugh Herbert, with Lowell Sherman, Alice Joyce, David Manners, Frances Dade. As tiresome a photographed stage play as one could ever imagine, from S.N. Behrman's *The Second Man*. When dealing with a one-set, four-character film, you know you're in trouble if none of the four characters is particularly appealing; that's precisely the case with this tedious tale of lackadaisical poet Sherman, who's about to marry Joyce for her money, becoming entangled with the impending on-again, off-again engagement of Dade and Manners. It's all terribly sophisticated, and terribly dull. In 1935 *Variety* claimed that "Hix Nix Stix Pix," but one cannot imagine what so-called hayseed audiences thought of something like this, even in the early talkie era.

Midnight Mystery (May 30, 1930) directed by George B. Seitz, with Betty Compson, Hugh Trevor, Lowell Sherman, Rita LeRoy, Ivan Lebedeff, Raymond Hatton. A talky mystery whose plot is constructed in such a way as to virtually eliminate any vestige of suspense. Our nominal hero (Trevor) pretends to kill gigolo Lebedeff so as to throw a scare into his fiancée (Compson), who writes mystery books. But before he can let his other friends in on the joke, jealous-husband Sherman really kills the swain, letting Trevor take the rap. Since the audience is aware of the whole thing, the question is not "Who done it?" but "How can he get out of it?" and the answer to that question isn't particularly exciting. Director Seitz's attempt to make sophisticated use of sound in opening scenes doesn't work out either; in a party sequence the camera moves about, with many characters talking at

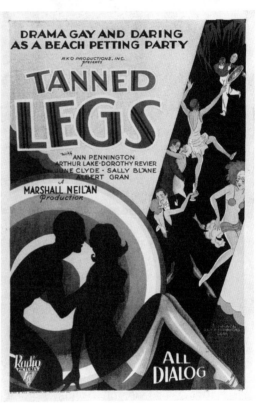

once, and a piano playing in the background. The mixing, however, destroys this ambitious idea, since the voices are not kept distinct, and the piano is playing so loudly that one can hardly hear the dialogue at all.

Her Man (September 21, 1930) directed by Tay Garnett, with Helen Twelvetrees, Phillips Holmes, Ricardo Cortez, James Gleason, Harry Sweet, Thelma Todd, Marjorie Rambeau. A Pathé Picture. Vivid atmosphere, fluid camera work (especially in some impressive tracking shots through the streets of backlot Havana) and some strong performances, particularly by Holmes

in an atypical role as a swaggering sailor, unfortunately don't add up as well as they should in this retelling of the "Frankie and Johnny" saga. Garnett often seems more interested in the contrived comedy relief of Gleason and Sweet than he is in the story (and indeed, this is what he recalled in his autobiography, and not the main plotline). Cortez makes a sleek heavy, but Thelma Todd's almost invisible role as Nelly Bly indicates some pre-release cutting. Twelvetrees and Holmes are excellent in the leading roles, and their love scenes come off beautifully, but the picture bogs down in the second half when the seams begin to show in bringing the story to its inevitable conclusion. Columbia Pictures purchased the remake rights, which kept the original out of circulation for many years.

The Silver Horde (October 24, 1930) directed by George Archainbaud, with Joel McCrea, Evelyn Brent, Louis Wolheim, Jean Arthur, Raymond Hatton, Gavin Gordon. Again a trite story situation is bolstered by several good performances and a strong location atmosphere. This Rex Beach tale has McCrea torn between his high-society fiancée (Arthur) and the tainted woman Cherry Malotte (Brent) who has fallen for him and given herself to a wealthy banker in order to finance McCrea's fledgling cannery. Film picks up in the second half when the complicated exposition is out of the way and action takes its place. There's an excellent documentary-like sequence showing the workings of the cannery, from catching the fish to packing the canned product; and an exciting fight scene between McCrea and burly fore-man Ivan Linow. Eternally hammy Gavin Gordon is strangled by Wolheim in the final minutes of the film, providing some measure of esthetic justice.

The Royal Bed (January 15, 1931) directed by and starring Lowell Sherman, with Nance O'Neil, Mary Astor, Anthony Bushnell, Robert Warwick. This rambling comedy-drama-romance adapted from Robert E. Sherwood's play *The Queen's Husband* tries to tackle romance, satire, high comedy, a serious statement on democracy and revolution, and a character portrait of a king (Sherman) seen as a lonely man who has had to sacrifice his enjoyment of life for the greater good of his country. Very little of this comes off, and the essential stageiness of the film only reinforces one's feeling of aloofness toward the main characters. Warwick stands out among the generally lifeless cast with an outrageously hammy performance, while "Carroll Naish" (so billed) has an interesting early role as a revolutionary leader. One senses that many of the faults in *The Royal Bed* are inherent in the Sherwood original, but this doesn't account for fluffed lines and cardboard acting.

Beyond Victory (April 12, 1931) directed by John S. Robertson, with William Boyd, Lew Cody, James Gleason, Marion Shilling, ZaSu Pitts, Lissi Arna, Theodore von Eltz, Mary Carr. World War I film goes to the battlefront, and tells in flashback how four comrades came to be involved in the war and the girls they left back home. Co-scripted by James Gleason and Horace Jackson, this incredibly noisy, smoke-clogged film has some good ideas in building an anti-war sentiment, but gets to be pretty tedious by the fourth episode. Best line of dialogue: man-about-town Cody tells Shilling that he's enlisting the next day in order to win her sympathy; she goes to bed with him, prompting his comment the next morning, "I always knew there must be a reason for people going away to war."

The Sin Ship (April 18, 1931) directed by Louis Wolheim, with Louis Wolheim, Mary Astor, Ian Keith, Hugh Herbert. Offbeat rehash of a familiar situation, with brutish sea captain Wolheim lusting for minister's wife Astor, who shames him into submission and makes him realize that he should clean up his mind (and his appearance). He becomes a New Man—only to discover that "minister" Keith is really a con artist on the lam, and wife Astor is in reality "Frisco Kitty"(!). Stock melodrama situations are given some life by the two excellent co-stars, while Herbert provides amiable comic relief as the Captain's mate, but the film moves too slowly to vindicate its story weaknesses. The most interesting aspect of *The Sin Ship* is that it was written by co-star Hugh Herbert, and directed by Wolheim himself, an example of the kind of possibilities RKO offered Hollywoodites in the 1930s, unlike some other more staid and tradition-bound studios. Wolheim's death in early 1931 made this his last film; whether or not he planned to pursue a directing career is not known.

The Common Law (July 17, 1931) directed by Paul Stein, with Constance Bennett, Joel McCrea, Lew Cody, Robert Williams, Hedda Hopper. This must have been considered quite risqué in 1931, with Bennett living with men to whom she is not married (!)—and even posing in the nude for artist McCrea (albeit in long shot) in his Parisian garret. But when Joel sends this devoted, affectionate woman away because she has "known" another man, the going gets thick and never lands back on target. Worse, there's Hedda Hopper as McCrea's excruciatingly obnoxious sister, determined to under-mine his reconciliation with Bennett; that she accomplishes her transparent goal is yet another tribute to the stupidity of McCrea's character in this film, scripted by young John Farrow. A highlight sequence in this otherwise pon-derous romance takes place at a huge Beaux Arts Ball in Paris—a dazzlingly elaborate scene that lasts but a few minutes on-screen.

The Public Defender (July 31, 1931) directed by J. Walter Ruben, with Richard Dix, Shirley Grey, Edmund Breese, Boris Karloff, Paul Hurst, Pur-nell Pratt. Dix plays a society gentleman posing as The Reckoner, an under-cover righter of wrongs who sets out to clear his girlfriend's father of charges of bank fraud. A lackluster film sorely in need of good atmospheric music. Dix's companions in "crime" are the erudite Karloff and thick-witted Hurst, but Karloff fans should not feel any strong obligation to seek out this film.

High Stakes (August 18, 1931) directed by and starring Lowell Sherman, Mae Murray, Edward Martindel, Leyland Hodgson, Karen Morley. This tur-gid drama was one of Sherman's two 1931 endeavors to resurrect the career of silent siren Mae Murray (she also appeared in *Bachelor Apartment* with him and Irene Dunne), cast this time as a baby-talking blonde who marries Sherman's older brother. Sherman doesn't like the Mae-December marriage in the first place, but when he discovers that she is really an experienced con artist out to get the old boy's money, he is forced to rouse himself from a perpetual half-drunk stupor and take positive action. Murray is insufferable as the coy child-bride, although how much was written into the role and how much was hers is impossible to know. As for Sherman, his standard witty-drunk characterization doesn't retain its charm forever, particularly in such leaden surroundings, although for once he provides himself with a hint of romance in the person of Karen Morley.

Friends and Lovers (October 3, 1931) directed by Victor Schertzinger, with Adolphe Menjou, Laurence Olivier, Lili Damita, Erich von Stroheim. An unexceptional film made interesting by its cast. Menjou and Olivier are Brit-ish officers stationed in India, both in love with Damita. When Menjou realizes the identity of Olivier's fiancée, he tries to describe his former relationship with her by saying intently, "I knew her very well." Von Stroheim is sheer delight in this film as Damita's conniving husband, who blackmails her lovers in order to support his expensive hobby, collecting porcelain. He handles his slyly humorous dialogue beautifully, and a showdown scene with Menjou is delicious.

The Tip Off (October 16, 1931) directed by Albert Rogell, with Eddie Quillan, Robert Armstrong, Ginger Rogers, Joan Peers, Ralf Harolde. A consistently clever, amusing little film with Quillan as a naive young man who inadvertently saves boxer Armstrong from a going-over by gangster Harolde, who has been the slow-witted fighter's manager. Eddie earns Armstrong's eternal gratitude, and his protection comes in handy when Quillan finds that the girl he's fallen in love with (Peers) is Harolde's moll. Fast-moving entertainment, with a solid comedy performance from Armstrong as the dumb prizefighter who's trying to better himself, always groping for big words, supplied by his girlfriend (a perky Ginger Rogers).

Mary Astor and Lowell Sherman in *The Royal Bed.*

Suicide Fleet (November 20, 1931) directed by Albert Rogell, with William Boyd, Robert Armstrong, James Gleason, Ginger Rogers, Harry Bannister, Frank Reicher. The opening and closing segments of this film are a delight; unfortunately, there is a middle portion to contend with that nearly sinks the entire picture. Shooting gallery barker Boyd, photographer Armstrong, and tour-guide Gleason compete for the affections of Ginger, who runs the candy-booth concession at Coney Island. When World War I breaks out, the three rivals enlist, and the film goes downhill, until an exciting finale with Chief Petty Officer Boyd and his two sailor pals risking their lives on a decoy ship, posing as a German officer and crew. Armstrong and Gleason's bickering in the opening scenes is a lot of fun, and Ginger is at her cutest; losing her when the film shifts to wartime action is a big letdown.

Girl of the Rio (January 15, 1932) directed by Herbert Brenon, with Dolores Del Rio, Norman Foster, Leo Carrillo, Ralph lnce, Lucile Gleason, Stanley Fields. Take one hoary stage play (*The Dove*, written by Willard Mack and presented by David Belasco), give Dolores Del Rio lines like, "My heart she is thump-thump-thump when I see you," add an asinine role for Leo Carrillo as the self-proclaimed "best caballero in all Mexico," and what have you got? *Girl of the Rio*. Needless to say, Del Rio is stunning—particularly in one scene where she wears a brief black negligée, but between her pigeon-English and Carrillo's, the viewer is ready to scream after 10 minutes. The final insult is the story's wrap-up, where after leching for this Latin lovely for more than an hour, letting no obstacle stand in his path, Carrillo suddenly turns Cupid and sends her off with her true love, Foster! Aaaarrrggghhh.

Prestige (January 22, 1932) directed by Tay Garnett, with Ann Harding, Melvyn Douglas, Adolphe Menjou, Clarence Muse, Ian Maclaren, Guy Bates Post. What could well be just another hackneyed melodrama about life at a remote British Army outpost is made surprisingly absorbing by Garnett's flamboyant direction, and good solid performances. The film opens with a long, long tracking shot through city streets which turn into miniatures via a fascinating optical link, and then continues on and on, past buildings, over rooftops, before settling on the Army headquarters where the first scene takes place. From there on, the camera does not stand still for a moment; there is constant movement, and if in one scene one can clearly see the shadow of a camera and mike boom with an operator sitting alongside, well, nobody 's perfect. As to the content of *Prestige*, the title refers to white man's supremacy over the black and yellow races, which stiff-upper-lip Douglas must maintain when transferred to a Far East hellhole called Lao Bao. While he inevitably cracks up during his first year, Harding then comes to join him and inspires him to uphold the dignity and authority that the white man represents in this colonial prison camp. Some of these plot elements have seen better days (probably so even in 1932), but they're carried out pretty well this time around, and *Prestige* boasts a selection of highlight scenes that more than compensate for some turgid moments in between.

Ladies of the Jury (February 5, 1932) directed by Lowell Sherman, starring Edna May Oliver, Jill Esmond, Kitty Kelly, Ken Murray, Roscoe Ates, Lita Chevret, Guinn Williams. A bright and amusing trifle with domineering socialite Edna May Oliver commandeering a jury that disagrees with her on the fate of a woman accused of murdering her husband. Through charm and cunning, she manages to win over her colleagues, one by one. Oliver is nothing short of sensational; her delightful performance glues the film together, and with the aid of a colorful supporting cast, makes it worthwhile, if no more plausible than the pallid 1937 remake, *We're on the Jury*. Engaging cameos by such disparate jurors as Irish mother Kate Price, Southern-accented Florence Lake, smooth-talking, wisecracking Ken Murray, and self-satisfied George Humbert add to the fun. It seems neither hasty nor unreasonable to conclude that Sherman's films as actor/director simply aren't as good as those on which he remained behind the camera. The former group tend to become showcases for his pleasant but one-note personality, and indicate a carelessness in his supervision of such directorial duties as pacing and control of other actors' performances. His success with such non-RKO films as *Broadway Thru a Keyhole* and the striking *Born to Be Bad* with Loretta Young and Cary Grant, bear out this theory and reaffirm Andrew Sarris' comment that "his civilized sensibility was ahead of its time, and the sophistication of his sexual humor singularly lacking in malice."

The Lost Squadron (March 10, 1932) directed by George Archainbaud, with Richard Dix, Mary Astor, Erich von Stroheim, Joel McCrea, Robert Armstrong, Hugh Herbert. Probably the silliest of many tales about ex-WWI aviators, devised by stunt pilot Dick Grace. This one pits Dix and his buddies against tyrannical movie director "Erich von Furst," played by guess-who with all the subtlety of a machine-gun ("This is a war picture," he shouts to his ensemble through a megaphone, "not a musical comedy!"). Herbert plays it straight as the pilots' ever-faithful flight mechanic, the kind of role that traditionally went to supporting comics in 1930s flying movies.

Carnival Boat (March 19, 1932) directed by Albert Rogell, with William Boyd, Ginger Rogers, Hobart Bosworth, Fred Kohler, Edgar Kennedy. Trifling but enjoyable story of North Woods logger Boyd whom father Bosworth expects to follow in his footsteps; but Boyd's attentions are divided between his job and Honey (Rogers), an entertainer on the carnival boat. Shot on location, this film's strongest assets are some hair-raising action scenes, one on a runaway locomotive, another as Boyd and Kohler try to plant TNT in the middle of a treacherous log-jam.

Girl Crazy (March 27, 1932) directed by William A. Seiter, with Wheeler and Woolsey, Eddie Quillan, Mitzi Green, Arline Judge, Kitty Kelly, Dorothy Lee. Unseen for many years because MGM bought the negative when it remade the film with Mickey Rooney and Judy Garland in 1942. As it turns out, this version of *Girl Crazy* is the most unmusical musical imaginable, with such great songs as "But Not for Me" getting the shortest shrift ever given a Gershwin score. Even a so-called production number on "I Got Rhythm" is weak, and hurt by the off-pitch vocalizing of Kitty Kelly. As a Wheeler and Woolsey vehicle, *Girl Crazy* is average, no better, with its fair share of wisecracks from Robert Woolsey and a good duet for Bert Wheeler and Dorothy Lee, "You've Got What Gets Me." Film music buffs should know that the opening credits feature a brief shot of Max Steiner conducting the RKO orchestra.

Symphony of Six Million (April 14, 1932) directed by Gregory LaCava, with Irene Dunne, Ricardo Cortez, Anna Appel, Gregory Ratoff, Lita Chevret, Noel Madison. This predictable Fannie Hurst soap opera has young doctor Cortez abandoning his Jewish-ghetto neighborhood, his family and friends, to join the Park Avenue set and make big money, leaving his crippled sweetheart (Dunne) behind. The film opens quite well, with a memorable musical montage by Max Steiner (not unlike Alfred Newman's city themes for *Street Scene* and *Dead End*), spurred on by Ratoff's delightful performance as Cortez's immigrant father. Only in the second half of the story does credibility evaporate, spoiling a clichéd but compelling movie.

Is My Face Red? (June 17, 1932) directed by William A. Seiter, with Ricardo Cortez, Helen Twelvetrees, Jill Esmond, Robert Armstrong, Sidney Toler, Arline Judge, ZaSu Pitts. Pleasant but unremarkable adaptation of a stage play based on the Walter Winchell phenomenon; this film pales alongside *Blessed Event* and lacks the punch of the more erratic *Okay America*. Cortez plays William Poster, a through-the-keyhole columnist who describes himself as "a mirror reflecting the spirit of the times." But Cortez's portrait of a grade-A heel lacks the inherent likability to make the film work, and our sympathies are not with him at several crucial moments, as when he two-times his faithful girlfriend Twelvetrees once too often. Add to this some outlandish plotting, and a sure-fire premise is seriously hampered.

Roar of the Dragon (July 8, 1932) directed by Wesley Ruggles, with Richard Dix, Gwili Andre, Edward Everett Horton, Arline Judge, ZaSu Pitts, Dudley Digges, C. Henry Gordon. Heavy-handed melodrama has a group of homeward-bound passengers and their skipper (Dix) stranded in a Shanghai hotel, which soon becomes an isolated fortress to protect them from a notorious bandit (Gordon). Gwili Andre is Gordon's mistress who falls in love with Dix. RKO's entry in the exotic-vamp sweepstakes of the early 1930s, Andre is neither attractive nor seductive, and wears enough eye makeup to choke a horse. The most interesting aspect of this film is Edward Everett Horton's characterization; starting as comedy relief, he turns serious halfway through the film and even gets to do a death scene. It's a shame that such a fine, unusual performance is buried within this unsuccessful, if not entirely uninteresting, drama.

Bird of Paradise (August 12, 1932) directed by King Vidor, with Dolores Del Rio, Joel McCrea, John Halliday, Skeets Gallagher, Lon Chaney, Jr. A film that unfortunately remains this side of paradise, despite lush photography, settings, and a tried-and-true story line of adventurer McCrea falling in love with native girl Del Rio. William K. Everson has called it "a property that belongs to the silent era, where lyricism and larger-than-life emotions can dominate, and where the dated dialogue (and trite comedy lines) of this version would not intrude." We feel no bond with the characters on-screen, and their problems remain steadfastly unmoving. Still, there is one unforgettably sensuous moment near the end where Del Rio treats a barely conscious

McCrea to some badly needed liquid, passing it from her mouth to his in an arresting ritual of loving devotion. Remade by 20th Century Fox in 1951.

Bring 'Em Back Alive (August 19, 1932) directed by Clyde Elliott, with Frank Buck. "A photographic record of the RKO Van Beuren Malaysian Jungle Expedition," this fascinating curio wavers from exciting documentary footage to utter phoniness, often posing the question that amounts to "Who was there to paint George Washington crossing the Delaware?" while pretending to be completely factual and spontaneous. Buck's claim to fame is that he never kills his prey, or uses a gun except in self-defense, but that doesn't stop him from adopting the Great White Hunter pose in his coy narration. Much of the footage is truly exciting: a black leopard battling a python, the same leopard attacked by a brutal tiger, etc. But the authenticity of many shots is dubious, with frequent cutaways to the same reaction shot of Buck, clever use of cutting to give the impression that one incident has triggered another, etc. The post-dubbing of music and sound effects is quite good, and believable, but these virtues are offset by lines like, "If ever a feller needed a friend, it was old Frank Buck, for I had failed," referring to a capture attempt that didn't work. Another segment follows the exploits of a baby bear cub who manages to escape from a deadly enemy. "How, we'll never know," says Buck, although we (the camera) just watched the whole episode unfold. *Bring 'Em Back Alive* is an important adjunct to any study of the documentary film, as one of the most popular films of its kind ever made, and as an indication of what filmmakers thought they could get away with in dealing with a Hollywood-oriented audience.

Strange Justice (October 7, 1932) directed by Victor Schertzinger, with Marian Marsh, Norman Foster, Reginald Denny, Richard Bennett, Irving Pichel, Nydia Westman. Despite its title, this predictable yarn is anything but "strange." Blackmailer Pichel pins the supposed murder of wealthy Denny on his chauffeur (Foster), necessitating a last-minute rescue of Our Hero from the electric chair. Marsh is a pallid heroine, while Foster is one of those stupid 1930s leading men who just doesn't seem worthy of her devotion. Bennett plays a super-Blarney lawyer, replete with tousled hair, in a film that boasts far too many cardboard characterizations. Offbeat subject matter for director Schertzinger, who was certainly more at home with musicals.

The Phantom of Crestwood (October 14, 1932) directed by J. Walter Ruben, with Ricardo Cortez, Karen Morley, Anita Louise, Pauline Frederick, H.B. Warner, Sam Hardy. A crackerjack whodunit with blackmail, jealousy, young love, disguises, thugs, secret panels—the works. Karen Morley is blackmailing all her respectable lovers in order to retire in luxury and calls them all together at Warner's home, where she is killed that night. Cortez, on the scene as a detective, knows he's a suspect, so he decides to find the murderer before the police arrive. A solid story is enhanced by an eye-riveting flashback technique involving a zoom-lens framework that literally sweeps the viewer to the scene being described.

The Sport Parade (November 11, 1932) directed by Dudley Murphy, with Joel McCrea, Marion Nixon, William Gargan, Walter Catlett, Robert Benchley. Basic plotline of college sports teammates and buddies McCrea and Gargan who eventually clash over the same woman (Nixon) is pretty lame, but director Murphy is full of camera tricks and unusual ideas—a wrestling match is vividly real, with natural lighting and low ringside angles, for example. His attraction for black entertainers is evidenced as well during a brief Harlem nightclub scene. Best of all, there's Robert Benchley in his feature-film debut as a befuddled sportscaster who never quite knows what it is he's covering; his hilarious non-sequitur remarks open and close the film.

Men of America (November 25, 1932) directed by Ralph lnce, with William Boyd, Dorothy Wilson, Chic Sale, Ralph lnce, Henry Armetta. Some clichés and half-baked plot ideas keep this from being more than an interesting curio, but *Men of America* does have some striking moments. A group of former Western trailblazers are now cracker-barrel tale-spinners in a small California town, suspicious of young newcomer Boyd, especially when a minor crime-wave breaks out in the community. The perpetrators of these incidents are a group of gangsters holed out nearby. One of them kills local farmer Armetta, who looks up at his murderer and murmurs, "One bad Italian like you give a bad name to all our people." The idea of these melting-pot pioneers (an Italian, an Indian, an Asian) now old friends living together is probably the most intriguing aspect of this film.

The Half-Naked Truth (December 16, 1932) directed by Gregory LaCava, with Lupe Velez, Lee Tracy, Eugene Pallette, Frank Morgan. Delightful comedy of wise-guy carny pitchman Tracy scheming to build up unknown Velez into an instant celebrity. Plenty of memorable wisecracks and funny ideas, with an unforgettable performance by Frank Morgan as a neurotic Ziegfeld-ish producer. A snappy score features the song "Oh, Mr. Carpenter," and an ingenious sequence has Tracy alone in his office, unable to stop thinking about Lupe because every noise or squeak seems to be producing strains of that song. Presumably these clever effects were devised by Max Steiner, although the idea itself sounds like LaCava's.

No Other Woman (January 6, 1933) directed by J. Walter Ruben, with Irene Dunne, Charles Bickford, Gwili Andre, Eric Linden. Mining-town couple Dunne and Bickford go from rags to riches with young Linden's great chemical discovery, but sacrifice their happiness in the process, with Bickford deserting his wife for the affections of sophisticated Andre. OK soap opera dignified by solid performances and highlighted by some typically impressive montages by Slavko Vorkapich.

The Great Jasper (February 17, 1933) directed by J. Walter Ruben, with Richard Dix, Florence Eldridge, Edna May Oliver, Wera Engels, Bruce Cabot. Turn-of-the-century tale of ne'er-do-well streetcar conductor Dix who goes to Atlantic City in search of success, finding it as a glib fortune teller who appeals to the feminine trade. Eldridge is his humorless wife who is left behind when Dix goes fortune-hunting, but the real treat in this mediocre film is Edna May Oliver as a veteran boardwalk palm reader who encourages Dix to set up shop on his own. Her scenes almost make the film worth watching, but tired soap opera plotting and dialogue weigh down a potentially colorful story.

Scarlet River (March 10, 1933) directed by Otto Brower, with Tom Keene, Dorothy Wilson, Betty Furness, Creighton Chaney (Lon Chaney Jr.), Roscoe Ates, Edgar Kennedy, Yakima Canutt. A delightful surprise amid the Tom Keene B Westerns of the early 1930s, this one opens with Keene and Furness as sole survivors of a wagon train, when suddenly it's revealed that they're actors on location filming a Western movie! The real plot gets going when the Tom Baxter (Keene) company hires Wilson's ranch for its next movie site, interfering with foreman Chaney's plans to steal the unsuspecting young lady blind. Numerous highlights dot this fast-moving outing: a scene in the RKO commissary with Joel McCrea, Myrna Loy, Julie Haydon, and Bruce Cabot as themselves, Edgar Kennedy as the movie director, Canutt predating his famous *Stagecoach* stunt almost exactly, dropping from a horse team to the ground, letting the wagon run over him, then grabbing the back of the cart. Both the actual story line of the film and the movie-making background are great fun, with the two elements combining in a slam-bang finale as the movie crew comes to the rescue of Keene and Wilson in real life! All of this is neatly dispatched in 57 minutes' time.

Melody Cruise (June 16, 1933) directed by Mark Sandrich, with Phil Harris, Greta Nissen, Charlie Ruggles, Helen Mack, Marjorie Gateson. Director Sandrich is the star of this entertaining opus, with an endless procession of flashy camera tricks and musical ideas: showing girls around the ship singing "He's Not the Marrying Kind," one line each before cutting to the next; having the stars form a musical staff during one moonlight song; showing the crew doing their chores in time to music; and best of all, producing a myriad of optical dissolves from one scene to the next—one a jigsaw puzzle, one a spilled-paint image, one a diagonal wipe step by step in time to a song, etc. Inspired by Sandrich's Oscar-winning short *So This Is Harris*, the feature is very much in the two-reeler milieu, with an appropriately stupid plot (by Sandrich and Ben Holmes) and many short-subject players, including Betty Grable as a girl who

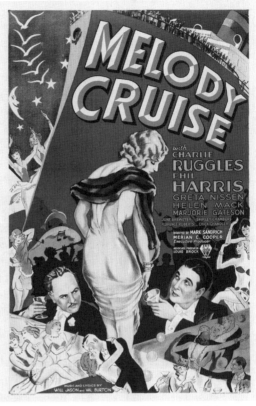

eavesdrops on Harris. Phil Harris is no Cary Grant, but luckily much of the footage is turned over to Ruggles. A completely winning film, and an auspicious feature debut for Sandrich, who must have had a ball with it.

Bed of Roses (June 29, 1933) directed by Gregory LaCava, with Constance Bennett, Joel McCrea, John Halliday, Pert Kelton. Fairly typical Depression soap, with ex-con Bennett falling in love with poor barge captain McCrea, but forsaking love for money, conniving a soft position by blackmailing wealthy publisher Halliday. Bennett's role as a totally unscrupulous gold digger is a pleasing change of pace, although the plot trappings are all too familiar. Still, smooth playing and a large quota of wisecracks make this quite entertaining. Kelton does one of her Mae West imitations as Bennett's chiseling pal.

Blind Adventure (August 18, 1933) directed by Ernest B. Schoedsack, with Robert Armstrong, Helen Mack, Ralph Bellamy, Roland Young, John Miljan, Laura Hope Crews. Here's a curiously overlooked comedy/mystery that's hardly ever mentioned in connection with *King Kong*'s co-creator, Ernest Schoedsack. This modest but entertaining yarn anticipates the lighthearted blending of romantic comedy characters and genuine mystery put to use in films like *The Thin Man* and *The 39 Steps* a few years later. Armstrong is an American in London who quite inadvertently stumbles into the midst of international intrigue, with a lovely young girl (Mack) as an innocent dupe. Together they try to unravel the mystery and enlist the help of a cat burglar named Holmes (Young), whose "experience" comes in handy in several tight situations. Armstrong makes a surprisingly adept tongue-in-cheek hero, with Helen Mack equally appealing as his partner in crime. No classic, *Blind Adventure* is nevertheless a thoroughly engaging film that doesn't deserve another 40 years of obscurity.

After Tonight (October 26, 1933) directed by George Archainbaud, with Constance Bennett, Gilbert Roland, Edward Ellis, Lucien Prival, Mischa Auer. With a title that has no bearing on the content of this film, *After Tonight* casts the ever-chic Constance Bennett as an intrepid Russian spy during WWI who falls in love with a European officer (Roland). There's nothing new here, except some rather incredible scenes of how spies pass information, but the stars' magnetic performances are backed by a strikingly good-looking production. Bennett gets to sing one song ("Buy a Kiss") in a cabaret sequence, accompanied by a brief dance with a feathery fan. The script tacks on a preposterous happy ending to allow Bennett and Roland a final clinch, which is probably what audiences wanted to see.

Chance at Heaven (October 27, 1933) directed by William A. Seiter, with Ginger Rogers, Joel McCrea, Marion Nixon, Andy Devine, Ann Shoemaker. An ordinary and implausible story given a certain degree of validity because this small-town yarn was actually filmed in a small town—an exercise in logic seldom followed by other studios, but quite often by RKO. The vivid atmosphere bolsters a triangle situation with honest, hard-working Joel leaving fiancée Ginger for Nixon, a society brat who sets her eyes on him. McCrea gets taken over the coals, returns home, and finds ever-faithful Ginger waiting for him with a hot dinner! The skillful Seiter gets sincere performances from his star trio, but is handicapped by the wearisome script.

The Meanest Gal in Town (January 12, 1934) directed by Russell Mack, with Pert Kelton, El Brendel, ZaSu Pitts, James Gleason, Skeets Gallagher. A sleepy little town is disrupted by the arrival of a hot-shot dame (Kelton) who's been stranded with a theatrical troupe; Pert decides to settle there, and when her fellow actors ask how she'll get along, she replies in her best Mae West tones, "I'll wiggle out of it somehow." When barber Brendel hires her as a manicurist, he incurs the wrath of longtime sweetheart Pitts, and therein lies the tale. A fine cast of pros milks every possibility from a clever script; a modest film, to be sure, but worth ranking alongside many more important comedies in terms of laugh content.

Two Alone (January 26, 1934) directed by Elliott Nugent, with Jean Parker, Tom Brown, ZaSu Pitts, Arthur Byron, Beulah Bondi, Nydia Westman, Willard Robertson. Orphan-girl Parker has been raised by hard-nosed farmer Byron, who raises the roof when she falls in love with young Brown, a fugitive from a state reformatory. A slice-of-life love story, with melodramatic overtones, this film never rises above the ordinary, despite good performances. A stronger and less predictable script would have helped.

Keep 'Em Rolling (March 2, 1934) directed by George Archainbaud, with Walter Huston, Frances Dee, Minna Gombell, Frank Conroy, Robert Shayne. Simple story of a soldier in the 16th U.S. Field Artillery who tames and trains a horse, goes into battle with him during WWI, and refuses to be separated from him for the rest of his Army days. Only an actor with the honesty and simplicity of Huston could get away with this kind of role and make it seem real. Actually shot at Fort Myer in Virginia, many soldiers were used for supporting roles, all too evident in their stiff reading of lines, while Gombell is most enjoyable as Huston's girlfriend, whom he sacrifices (along with everything else in his life and career) for his beloved horse.

Pert Kelton and James Gleason in *The Meanest Gal in Town.*

Sing and Like It (April 20, 1934) directed by William A. Seiter, with ZaSu Pitts, Nat Pendleton, Pert Kelton, Edward Everett Horton, Ned Sparks, John Qualen. Mobster Pendleton overhears bank teller Pitts singing a song about her mother in rehearsal for an amateur play, and goes to pieces. He decides that this is the greatest song and singer he's ever heard, and determines to get her into a Broadway show, by forcing himself into partnership with "the mad genius of the theater," played by Horton. Meanwhile, Pendleton's moll (Kelton) is burning, because her "daddy" has refused to let her return to the stage. All this sounds better than it plays, the belly laughs never really coming as they should. Still, there are moments (particularly the opening night of the show, "Silver Threads: A Fantasy in Music"), and on the whole, the film is modestly amusing, thanks to a gallery of fine players.

Bachelor Bait (July 28, 1934) directed by George Stevens, with Stuart Erwin, Rochelle Hudson, Skeets Gallagher, Pert Kelton. Amiable and often quite funny story of naive Erwin opening a matrimonial agency with sharpie Gallagher as his partner whose ex-wife (Kelton) shows up to make trouble. Pert Kelton is superb, as always, with constantly funny dialogue; after spending an evening out with oil tycoon Grady Sutton, she cracks, "No wonder he struck oil—he could bore anything." Smooth comedy playing by a large cast of reliables, including familiar faces in most of the bit parts. Stevens says the film came about because all four stars had one film to go on their studio contracts, and producer Louis Brock offered to use up all the contracts with one fell swoop. It was Stevens' second feature, his first at RKO where he'd been directing shorts.

The Fountain (August 23, 1934) directed by John Cromwell, with Ann Harding, Brian Aherne, Paul Lukas, Ralph Forbes, Violet Kemble-Cooper, Jean Hersholt, Sara Haden. Handsome but ponderous love triangle. While German husband Lukas is away at war in 1916, Harding rekindles romance with Aherne, a British prisoner of war interned at her family's estate in neutral Holland. Harding and Aherne go through endless pages of purple prose ("Lewis, do you think I'm a flippant, irresponsible, neurotic person?") before Lukas returns from war, and considerably enlivens the film with his fine, forceful performance. A major liability is Aherne's ineffectual characterization; the explanation given for his dreamy-eyed aloof manner is that "he reads, and writes books."

Lightning Strikes Twice (December 7, 1934) directed by Ben Holmes, with Ben Lyon, Thelma Todd, Skeets Gallagher, Pert Kelton, Walter Catlett. Engaging cast makes the most of an oddball script which opens as a whodunit, segues into comedy of errors, and only returns to the mystery element near the end of the film. Principal honors go to Kelton and Catlett as vaudevillians mistaken for Lyon's fiancée and future father-in-law by a visiting aunt. In one scene, Kelton has too much to drink and goes into her act, a tipsy fan-dance! Comedienne Thelma Todd has a secondary role, playing it straight as Lyon's bona fide fiancée, struggling to be nonchalant with lines like, "I wanted a husband with the virtues of a lover, not a lover with the vices of a husband." Meanwhile, sinister-looking John Davidson lurks around the house, for no apparent reason. Script by two-reeler experts Joseph Fields and John Gray.

Romance in Manhattan (January 11, 1935) directed by Stephen Roberts, with Ginger Rogers, Francis Lederer, J. Farrell MacDonald, Arthur Hohl, Sidney Toler. A seemingly predictable story that takes some unexpected turns, with delightful results. Lederer is an illegal alien who meets chorus-girl Rogers while hiding from the authorities in New York; romance blossoms and everything turns out OK with the help of some Capra-esque policemen (MacDonald, Toler), the friendly head of the marriage license bureau (Spencer Charters). and a befuddled justice of the peace (Donald Meek). Lederer has never been more ingratiating, nor has he had a better vehicle.

Captain Hurricane (March 1, 1935) directed by John S. Robertson, with James Barton, Helen Westley, Helen Mack, Gene Lockhart, Henry Travers, Douglas Walton. Pleasant bit of nothing with Barton as a salty New England seaman and Westley as the woman who's never consented to marry him but looks after him like a wife and mother combined. Elements of *Tugboat Annie* come into play, but the narrative is too leisurely and, at times, too choppy to create much impact. Some of this choppiness may be due to prerelease cutting, since Nydia Westman and Lon Chaney Jr. are listed in the *Film Daily* cast list, but not in the on-screen credits, and do not appear in the film. Some authentic Cape Cod exteriors would have helped too.

Village Tale (May 10, 1935) directed by John Cromwell, with Randolph Scott, Kay Johnson, Arthur Hohl, Robert Barrat, Janet Beecher, Edward Ellis, Donald Meek. William K. Everson has called this film a 1930s version of *Peyton Place*, and that's the best way to categorize such an unusual and offbeat picture. With no fireworks, and a deliberate pacing, this character study of a rural town where bigotry, pettiness, and just plain nosiness build to a crescendo of tragedy and hatred, really hits the bull's-eye. Scott and Johnson fall in love and try to ignore the whispers of the townspeople, only to find that they can't rise above it as they want to. A truly unpleasant story, and all the more striking for its effectiveness in a mid-1930s Hollywood film.

Hooray for Love (June 14, 1935) directed by Walter Lang, with Ann Sothern, Gene Raymond, Bill "Bojangles" Robinson, Maria Gambarelli, Pert Kelton, Fats Waller. A modest but very entertaining little backstage musical, with RKO's consistently pleasing light-romance duo of Sothern and Raymond. Many highlights include appearances by Bojangles and Fats Waller, a bright score by Dorothy Fields and Jimmy McHugh, and a hilarious bit by Kelton as the "protégée" of backer Etienne Girardot, who attempts to sing soprano arias in a voice reminiscent of Clara Cluck. Director Lang's light, sure-footed touch piloted many a more famous Fox musical in the 1940s.

She (July 12, 1935) directed by Irving Pichel and Lansing C. Holden, with Randolph Scott, Helen Gahagan, Helen Mack, Nigel Bruce, Gustav von Seyffertitz. The studio that made *King Kong* was obviously hoping for a film in the same vein that would capture the public's imagination, but the thrill of first seeing Helen Gahagan is a far cry from the excitement of Kong's initial entrance. Gahagan's lack of mystery and magnetism are a major handicap to the film, which otherwise has all the proper ingredients for great escapist-adventure. H. Rider Haggard's oft-filmed story has an expedition seeking the Flame of Eternal Life, which has given perpetual youth to an all-powerful woman, She-Who-Must-Be-Obeyed. Done on a grand scale, *She* is a good film, but not the great entertainment one would like it to be. Its most memorable asset is an outstanding Max Steiner score. Miss Gahagan, active in political life in later years, tried to bury this film; then the remake rights were sold, and the original film vanished for many years, supplanted by remakes in 1965 and 1984.

The Return of Peter Grimm (September 13, 1935) directed by George Nichols Jr., with Lionel Barrymore, Helen Mack, Edward Ellis, Donald Meek, Allen Vincent. Predating his performance in *On Borrowed Time*, Barrymore stars in this filmization of a hoary old David Belasco play about the patriarch of a close-knit family who tries to manage the lives of those around him, and in death, comes back to right his wrongs. If you're a sucker for this kind of thing, as I am, it's entertaining, but this creaky material needs all the help it can get, and flamboyant performances by Barrymore, Meek, Ethel Griffies, Lucien Littlefield, and other supporting players are quite in order.

Powdersmoke Range (September 27, 1935) directed by Wallace Fox, with Harry Carey, Hoot Gibson, Guinn "Big Boy" Williams, Tom Tyler, Bob Steele, Boots Mallory. Touted as "The Barnum and Bailey of Westerns," with the all-star leads supported by such Western names as Art Mix and Wally Wales, this quiet Western starts out slow and tapers off, thanks to lots of lumpy dialogue and an amazing sparsity of action. Partners Carey, Gibson, and Williams come to aid ex-con Steele from the plundering of a town boss, played by Sam Hardy with his usual heavy-handedness. The three likable stars are lost in this snail-like story, while Tom Tyler in a villainous role as a hired gun steals the show with a memorable performance. Noted not only

Francis Lederer and Ginger Rogers in *Romance in Manhattan*.

for its cast, but as the first story based on William Colt MacDonald's "Three Mesquiteers" characters.

Yellow Dust (February 22, 1936) directed by Wallace Fox, with Richard Dix, Leila Hyams, Moroni Olsen, Jessie Ralph, Andy Clyde, Onslow Stevens. It's difficult to imagine how RKO could cast its once-major star (and still a potent box-office draw) in such a third-rate Western as this. The title refers to gold-mining, which figures only marginally in this cliché-ridden yarn about Dix falling in love with ladylike saloon singer Hyams at first sight, vying for her affections with a slimy saloon owner. Dix tries to play some of the lines and situations tongue in cheek, but neither the script nor Wallace Fox's lumbering direction give him the kind of support that could have made this an enjoyable star vehicle.

The Witness Chair (April 24, 1936) directed by George Nichols, Jr., with Ann Harding, Walter Abel, Douglass Dumbrille, Frances Sage, Moroni Olsen, Margaret Hamilton. What can you say about a courtroom whodunit that gives away its punchline in the opening shot? *The Witness Chair* is polished but dull, with Harding as an ever-faithful secretary secretly in love with one of her employers (Abel), getting involved with murder in order to protect him from being framed for embezzlement. When the beans are finally spilled at the end of the film (for everyone but the audience, which has pretty much known what happened from the start) Ann says soulfully to Abel, "Oh, Jim, women are such awful fools." Although there isn't much to recommend this opus, there are two interesting bits of trivia: the RKO anthem, "Isn't This a Night for Love," is warbled by office boy Billy Benedict during one scene where he makes out like a crooner; and the trial takes place in a marble art deco courtroom that only could have existed in Van Nest Polglase's RKO world.

The Ex-Mrs. Bradford (May 15, 1936) directed by Stephen Roberts, with William Powell, Jean Arthur, James Gleason, Eric Blore, Robert Armstrong, Lila Lee. One of the best of many imitation "Thin Man" films during this period, this one casts Powell as an urbane doctor with a flair for detective work, and bubbly Arthur as his romantic ex-wife who gets in on the mystery of a string of racetrack murders. Film buffs will particularly appreciate a climactic scene where Powell gathers all the suspects in his living room to show them hidden-camera films he has taken at the track; Arthur makes apologies to the guests for her husband's passion for movies!

The Last Outlaw (June 12, 1936) directed by Christy Cabanne, with Harry Carey, Hoot Gibson, Henry B. Walthall, Tom Tyler, Margaret Callahan.

A delightful, unpretentious blend of comedy and Western formulas, with Carey as a once-notorious bandit released from prison after 25 years to find the Old West now gone, and himself an old man in most people's eyes, annoyingly referred to as "Pop." The veteran stars, aided and abetted by a fine supporting cast, make the most of a bright, original script which even gets in a hilarious dig at singing cowboys. John Ford co-authored the story and planned to direct this film, but was diverted to other projects. After World War II he had Fox purchase the rights for a remake, and while that film didn't materialize, RKO lost the original film through that transaction.

Without Orders (October 23, 1936) directed by Lew Landers, with Sally Eilers, Robert Armstrong, Frances Sage, Vinton Haworth, Charley Grapewin, Ward Bond. First-rate B entry spins an absorbing yarn that might be retitled "Airport 1936." Footloose stunt-pilot Haworth joins midwestern airline company run by his father (Grapewin), interrupting romance between veteran pilot Armstrong and stewardess Eilers and causing general havoc with his irresponsible escapades. RKO's outstanding special-effects chief Vernon L. Walker provides excellent rear-projection and matte work to make every shot believable, including a stunning sequence in which Sally must pilot the plane herself through a treacherous mountain pass to an impromptu landing field below. Her performance, especially in this climactic scene, is excellent, leading a strong cast in a typically plotty and entertaining B.

A Woman Rebels (November 6, 1936) directed by Mark Sandrich, with Katharine Hepburn, Herbert Marshall, Elizabeth Allan, Donald Crisp, Doris Dudley, Van Heflin, David Manners. One of Hepburn's least-revived films turns out to be a winner, with a women's liberation theme that makes it incredibly timely today. Hepburn rebels against her strict Victorian upbringing, and after personal tragedy becomes an outspoken feminist, publishing a magazine called "The New Woman." The soap opera plotting pulls out all the stops, but everything is done with such style and conviction that it works. Herbert Marshall gives one of his best performances as a diplomat who loves Hepburn, and unlike most of the men in the film, respects her independence. When he tells her that she hardly fits into the category of a helpless female, she replies, "Don't you think men invented the idea of the helpless woman for their own protection?" By no means a preachment, the film also avoids the pitfalls of painting its characters in blacks and whites only. A rare dramatic venture for director Mark Sandrich, *A Woman Rebels* is certainly due for wider exposure, as an example of first-rate storytelling, first-rate Hepburn, and further proof that not every Hollywood film of the 1930s had its head in the clouds.

William Powell and Jean Arthur in *The Ex-Mrs. Bradford.*

The Plough and the Stars (December 26, 1936) directed by John Ford, with Barbara Stanwyck, Preston Foster, Barry Fitzgerald, Denis O'Dea, Bonita Granville. Definitely a lesser Ford, although in many ways a typical one, with many favorite players on hand espousing Irish sentiments one finds throughout the director's work. But basically this adaptation of the Sean O'Casey play is tiresome and static, all too clearly shot inside a studio soundstage, with monotonously mournful women grieving for their men who stubbornly insist on confronting the British troops who have invaded their town. Unseen for many years due to rights issues.

We're on the Jury (February 11, 1937) directed by Ben Holmes, with Victor Moore, Helen Broderick, Philip Huston, Louise Latimer, Billy Gilbert, Charles Middleton. A time-filler that wastes the considerable talents of its two stars in a contrived and improbable jury story. There is a difference between being a lovable bumbler (as Moore was in *Swing Time*, for instance) and being stupid. One scene provides an interesting exercise in scene stealing as Billy Gilbert is seated behind the two stars in a jury box, commanding attention from the viewer with the slightest facial gestures.

Don't Tell the Wife (March 5, 1937) directed by Christy Cabanne, with Guy Kibbee, Lynne Overman, Una Merkel, William Demarest, Guinn Williams, Thurston Hall, Lucille Ball. An innocuous programmer with Overman unable to stay away from his old gang, veterans at bilking money from people via phony gold-mine stock. Merkel is warm and winning as Overman's wife, who desperately tries to keep him honest, but the film as a whole is pretty forgettable. Lucille Ball has a colorless role as a secretary.

New Faces of 1937 (July 2, 1937) directed by Leigh Jason, with Joe Penner, Milton Berle, Parkyakarkus, Harriet Hilliard, William Brady, Jerome Cowan. Using the same basic premise as Mel Brooks' *The Producers*, this forgettable outing has hotshot theatrical producer-director Cowan overselling interest in his shows, making sure they flop, and pocketing the extra money. Milton Berle is the patsy left holding the bag when Cowan skips town. There's a typical backstage romance plotline with Hilliard, Brady, and Berle as the improbable third corner of the triangle (giving him the opportunity to do a big scene near the end where he asks Harriet, "You really love that mug, don't you?"). Penner and Parkyakarkus have their moments, but the comic highlight is a long, beautifully played vaudeville set piece featuring Richard Lane as a fast-talking shyster stockbroker who takes Berle for a ride. Among the "new faces," very briefly featured, are Ann Miller and lovely Frances Gifford.

Super Sleuth (July 16, 1937) directed by Ben Stoloff, with Jack Oakie, Ann Sothern, Eduardo Ciannelli, Edgar Kennedy. Inconsequential, but very funny, outing with Oakie as a movie hero with a giant ego (his office has a self-portrait autographed, "From myself to me with sincere admiration") who tries to solve a real-life mystery. Edgar Kennedy has a plum role as the police detective on the case; at one point Oakie persuades the movie-struck cop to try wearing a toupee. Like all RKO comedies, filled with familiar comedy players (Fred Kelsey, Richard Lane, Bud Jamison, Dewey Robinson, etc.). Remade in 1946 as *Genius at Work*.

Music for Madame (October. 8, 1937) directed by John Blystone, with Nino Martini, Joan Fontaine, Alan Mowbray, Billy Gilbert, Lee Patrick, Grant Mitchell, Alan Hale, Erik Rhodes, Frank Conroy. Wholly enjoyable musical comedy. Martini is a naive Italian immigrant trying to make good as a singer in Hollywood, used as a patsy by jewel-robber Conroy and turned into a wanted man. The plot gets sillier as it goes along, but provides a fast, funny framework for Martini's charm, some not-bad songs (particularly "I Want the World to Know"), arias (an impressive "Vesti La Giubba") and a colorful array of character comedians. Mowbray is hilarious as egotistical conductor Rodowski, and Gilbert is in peak form as his bumbling aide Kraus. Young Joan Fontaine is also seen to good advantage, coming off quite nicely in a film brimming with domineering personalities.

Wise Girl (December 31, 1937) directed by Leigh Jason, with Miriam Hopkins, Ray Milland, Walter Abel, Guinn Williams, Henry Stephenson, Alec Craig. A friendly piece of fluff with screwball comedy elements that are most engaging. Rich-girl Hopkins pretends to be poor in order to track down her late sister's young children, who are living with unemployed artist Milland. Hollywood's conception of Greenwich Village and its free-thinking inhabitants is hilarious, with Hopkins, Milland, and Big Boy Williams able to earn $3 a night posing as Bohemians in a local café to add atmosphere! There are some memorable comic sequences, in a department store window and at a boxing match, with nice cameos by such old favorites as Margaret Dumont and James Finlayson.

Condemned Women (March 18, 1938) directed by Lew Landers, with Sally Eilers, Louis Hayward, Anne Shirley, Lee Patrick, Esther Dale. No surprises in this B-package, but smooth performance and direction make it passable fare. Prison psychologist Hayward falls in love with inmate Eilers, and in yet another variation on the old "Camille" routine, the father-figure warden tells Sally that she must make him forget her, for the good of his career. Shirley plays a meek little lamb who's serving a term so her guilty boyfriend can finish medical school. Of such hard-driving realism is *Condemned Women* fashioned, but one particularly bright spot has Lee Patrick atypically playing Eilers' hard-as-nails cellmate, who unofficially runs the joint and who plans their escape. Jack Carson is seen briefly as an attendant, Florence Lake as a cynical prisoner.

This Marriage Business (April 8, 1938) directed by Christy Cabanne, with Victor Moore, Allan Lane, Vicki Lester, Cecil Kellaway, Jack Carson, Richard Lane. Very mild B picture about a small-town justice of the peace who is used by a big-city reporter (Lane) to create a major story that has surprising repercussions. A murder subplot dragged into the proceedings in the final third is really off base, and the film's resolution of this story point is far from satisfying. But worse, the film doesn't do justice to top-billed Moore, who never seemed to work as well at RKO as he did in his tailor-made supporting role with Fred Astaire in *Swing Time*.

Border G-Man (June 24, 1938) directed by David Howard, with George O'Brien, Laraine Johnson (Day), John Miljan, Rita LaRoy, Ray Whitley, Edgar Dearing. ***Painted Desert*** (August 12, 1938) directed by David Howard, with George O'Brien, Laraine Johnson (Day), Fred Kohler, Max Wagner, Ray Whitley, Stanley Fields. George O'Brien's starring Westerns for RKO were far superior to the run-of-the-mill grade-B oaters being made at this time; like the occasional B+ Western series at other studios, these hour-long adventures boasted strong casts, good performances, striking locations, and solid filmmaking qualities (*G-Man* was photographed by Joseph August). In addition, they had O'Brien himself, one of the most likable Western heroes in screen history, whose strong personality and easy assurance lent authority to every film he did. Working with director Howard, who had piloted some of his big-budgeted early '30s Westerns at Fox, must have helped. *Painted Desert*, a remake of the 1931 film with William Boyd and Clark Gable, is not really an action film, relying instead on story situations and strong characterizations, which it has in spades, with slimy villain Kohler, hard-to-get heroine Johnson, Wallace Beery-ish sidekick Fields, and his Marjorie Main-ish partner Maude Allen. The climactic mine blast is stock footage from the earlier film, and a powerful scene, while a newly shot montage sequence of the mine operations adds a nice touch. *Border G-Man* has a lot more movement, with an impressive stampede sequence and a most unusual climax set

at villain Miljan's seacoast headquarters where horses and guns are floated out to a waiting boat and smuggled out of the country. In the cliffhanger finale, O'Brien lassoes Miljan and yanks him out of his escaping rowboat, pulling him ashore to see that justice is done! Laraine Johnson, one year away from stardom as Laraine Day, makes a pretty and spirited leading lady in both films, while Ray Whitley and his group provide some pleasing back-

Edgar Kennedy, Ann Sothern, and Jack Oakie in *Super-Sleuth*.

ground music, including a rendition of another cowboy's later theme, "Back in the Saddle Again," in *Border G-Man*, and a title tune for *Painted Desert*.

Mexican Spitfire (January 12, 1940) directed by Leslie Goodwins, with Lupe Velez, Leon Errol, Donald Woods, Linda Hayes, Elisabeth Risdon, Cecil Kellaway. After the success of *The Girl from Mexico*, RKO had the first "official" entry in its new "Mexican Spitfire" series on the screens within six months, at the end of 1939. Probably no other series in movie history confronts the viewer with so many films which are precisely the same. The original *Mexican Spitfire* is virtually interchangeable with any of the later entries: an extended two-reel comedy with awkward stretches filling in between bright moments of Lupe's fiery personality at work and Errol's all-knowing comic

expertise in a dual role as Uncle Matt and the perennially soused Lord Epping, whom Lupe's screen husband (in this case Woods) is always trying to impress. Here, the plot device is Matt's meddling wife (Risdon) conspiring with socialite Hayes to break up Woods' marriage to Lupe. The scheme works, and Hayes sets out to marry Woods immediately, but Lupe returns for a showdown, in the form of a largely ineffectual pie-throwing finale. One's enjoyment of this film, and of the series as a whole, depends entirely on how much one likes the two stars; these films are vehicles in the strictest sense of the word.

They Knew What They Wanted (October 25, 1940) directed by Garson Kanin, with Charles Laughton, Carole Lombard, William Gargan, Frank Fay, Harry Carey. Perhaps the greatest surprise of this film is how well Laughton manages to carry off his role as a Henry Armetta-ish Italian. It's his film, not Lombard's, although she is excellent as the hard-bitten waitress who desperately wants to find some route to a better life. Unfortunately, their relationship is developed too abruptly in Robert Ardrey's scenario from the Sidney Howard play, and Hays Office demands further constrain the story, in which Lombard becomes a mail-order bride but gets involved in a triangle situation with hired hand Gargan. Alfred Newman's score is stunning, but the editing (by future director John Sturges) is distractingly awkward, and overall, the film falls short of its mark. Another debit is Frank Fay's performance as a sanctimonious priest who hovers about dispensing words of wisdom, seconded by affable doctor Harry Carey. Despite its faults, it remains a worthwhile film, which like *Pygmalion* serves to illustrate how ideal the songs devised for its later musicalization (on Broadway as *The Most Happy Fella*) really were. Unavailable for many years due to rights issues.

INDEX

Leonard Maltin is one of the most recognized and respected film critics of our time. He appears regularly on Reelz Channel and spent 30 years on the hit television show, *Entertainment Tonight.*

An established author, he is best known for his annual paperback reference, *Leonard Maltin's Movie Guide.* In 2005, he introduced a companion volume, *Leonard Maltin's Classic Movie Guide* (now in its third edition), which focuses on movies made before 1965, going back to the silent era.

Leonard's other books include *The Best 151 Movies You've Never Seen, The Disney Films, Of Mice and Magic: A History of American Animated Cartoons, The Great American Broadcast: A Celebration of Radio's Golden Age, The Great Movie Comedians, The Art of the Cinematographer, Selected Short Subjects,* and (as co-author) *The Little Rascals: The Life and Times of Our Gang.*

Leonard has been teaching at the USC School of Cinematic Arts for the last 20 years. His popular class screens new films prior to their release, followed by a Q&A with the filmmakers. This direct access to top talent has proven to be invaluable in his students' own filmmaking endeavors.

As an expert and host, he is frequently seen on news programs and documentaries, and has enjoyed a long association with Turner Classic Movies, where he appears regularly. For three years, he co-hosted the weekly syndicated movie review program *Hot Ticket,* which was produced by *Entertainment Tonight.*

Leonard is a prolific freelance writer whose articles have appeared in *The New York Times, The Los Angeles Times, The London Times, Smithsonian, TV Guide, Esquire, The Village Voice* and *American Film.* He was the film critic for *Playboy* magazine for six years.

Additionally, Leonard frequently lectures on film and was a member of the faculty of New York City's New School for Social Research for nine years. He served as Guest Curator at The Museum of Modern Art film department in New York on two separate occasions.

Leonard created, hosted, and co-produced the popular *Walt Disney Treasures* DVD series and appeared on Warner Home Video's Night at the Movies features. He has written a number of television specials, including *Fantasia: The Creation of a Disney Classic* and has hosted, produced, and written such video documentaries and compilations as *The Making of The Quiet Man, The Making of High Noon, Cartoons for Big Kids, The Lost Stooges, Young Duke: The Making of a Movie Star, Cliffhangers: Adventures from the Thrill Factory,* and *Cartoon Madness: The Fantastic Max Fleischer Cartoons.*

In 2006 he was named by the Librarian of Congress to join the Board of Directors of the National Film Preservation Foundation. He also has received awards and citations from the American Society of Cinematographers, Anthology Film Archives, The Society of Cinephiles, San Diego Comic-Con International, and the Telluride Film Festival. In 1997 he was made a voting member of the National Film Registry, which selects 25 landmark American films every year. Perhaps the greatest indication of his fame was his appearance in a now-classic episode of the animated series *South Park.*

He holds court at *leonardmaltin.com.* Follow him on Twitter and Facebook; you can also listen to him on his weekly podcast: *Maltin on Movies.*